Hackberry House, Volume I

Two Years With North Korea

Bob Faulkner

DEDICATION:

TO OUR NORTH KOREAN
BROTHERS AND SISTERS IN JESUS,
TRUE HEROES OF THE FAITH

ISBN: 13:978-1477694237
ISBN: 10:1477694234

Hackberry House

What's Hackberry House?

Writing is a big part of where I "live". So is this house on Hackberry in the Chicago suburbs. It was only a matter of time before the two came together. When I write, I'm at "Hackberry House."

In case anyone was wondering.

And this volume?

Having finished my 19th book/booklet recently, Jesus' words to the apostles about gathering up the crumbs "so that nothing be wasted" became real to me.

That 19th book was the last full manuscript that had not been published. For awhile I thought the writing project was on hold. Then I saw this sizable pile of essays, blogs, articles that just cried out to be heard, too.

What could I do?

This first set is about the persecution of God's people centering in North Korea, a nation that captured my heart totally from 2007-2009.

Actually I was first touched by the persecuted church as a boy of 14 on a trip to the Kiamichi Mountains of Oklahoma with my home church. We had an annual men's meeting out there, and spent the week eating bean suppers, letting our beards grow - well, the men did - and listening to great speakers.

At the end of the week was the "mystery speaker." Some "big" personality who also had a relationship with Christ. It was usually someone whose name was a household term.

Not this year.

When *Richard Wurmbrand* was introduced, I settled back to be bored, for I had never heard of him. And besides, he was not from my evangelical background, or so it seemed from the backward collar.

Not until Wurmbrand, a Romanian Jew and Lutheran Pastor, stripped to the waist and showed us holes in his body, placed there by Communist torturers wielding red-hot pokers, was I suddenly involved in his talk.

This was the famous "Voice of the Martyrs," whose nickname was eventually given to the organization that is now headquartered in that same Oklahoma. As I write these words, I am a representative of that organization.

But from age 14 until somewhere in my early 40's, not much clicked along these lines. Then a trip to Wurmbrand's Communist Romania in 1985. Again in 1987. My heart burst for these heroic saints who gave all for Jesus.

It all re-opened while I was viewing a documentary about North Korea in the first decade of this century. I fairly shouted at the television as I viewed the atrocities of the Kims and their cronies.

I began to write, and to pass on stories of others who had written. You have here the essence of what I said in those two years. Over 300 articles documenting the persecution, the faith, and a whole lot more, of the people of North Korea.

I have long since stopped writing about NK, though there is certainly much more to be said. The evil continues, to be sure. But it is the same evil. And what I have written will easily serve to picture it.

And long after the Kim dynasty is only a bad memory to this world, long after liberty has once more claimed this tiny nation, and the tears have stopped flowing for the incessant pain, *these stories must be told*. For many, many years, these heroics will inspire believers to do and be all for Jesus, Who freely gave His life for them.

1. The Villagers of Goksan

North Korea. There is a constant price to pay for one's faith there. Voice Of the Martyrs, persecution.com, tells of 29 persons arrested there one morning in the remote village of Goksan. Among the group is a mother and her young daughter. They and the rest of this Christ-loving group, with their pastor, are bound and placed before a crowd of Communists.

They are told by a guard: "Deny Christ, or die." They all refuse to deny Him.

The guard addresses the adults: "Deny Christ, or we will hang your children." The young girl looks up at Mom and grips her hand. She knows she is loved. Her mother whispers to her, "Today, I will see you in Heaven."

For those who are looking for a happy ending to this story, you should stop reading now.

All of the children are hanged.

The adults, in agony already, are now forced to lie down on pavement in front of a large steamroller. "Deny this Jesus or you will be crushed." But they are already crushed. Their children are gone. And their life is hid in Christ anyway. they are ready to meet Him, and see their children again.

The driver starts the engine, and the villagers softly sing (in Korean). "More love, O Christ, to Thee, more love to Thee."

Please pray for North Korea tonight. Unimaginable horror continues...

2. North Korea strikes again.

Voice of the Martyrs is reporting the death of a North Korean evangelist. His crime reportedly was possessing and distributing a Korean New Testament. Though details are not yet available, prayers are being asked for family and friends.

North Korea is in the news often these days. But until Heaven we will not know all the evil that has been done in secret in this land. Underground nuclear explosions, the rise of radiation levels, the poverty, the madness of the rule, we hear about these things.

But how many know about those even in the Communist Party who try to get to freedom in China from that land and freeze to death on the way? How many know of the helium balloons sent over by the South Koreans to preach the Gospel?

Who knows about the woman who escaped to China and was sold to a Chinese man as a way to survive? She came to Christ, and now must run across the street to hide in a church when she is beaten by her new "husband." This same sister is regularly awakened at 2 a.m. to pray for all those who are now hurting her in some way.

Please pray for the North Koreans, perhaps the most repressed people on earth. I refer you to the Special Edition magazine put out yearly by Voice of the Martyrs to summarize the condition of the suffering church. North Korea is featured prominently. Go to persecution.com for free addition to a mailing list.

3. I wish I had not done my homework

(Based on a true story from North Korea, adapted from "Link Activity Book" of Voice of the Martyrs, published especially for young people.)

The homework game

"No written homework?" Mi Soon could hardly believe her ears. She looked around her third grade classroom. The boys were shouting, "Hooray!" The girls were smiling and whispering to each other. The teacher was quietly letting them enjoy the moment.

Every night, the children spent hours at home writing Korean words. They also worked many math problems. After they were done with all their homework, they were eager to tumble into bed. It was hard for Mi Soon to stay awake long enough to hear a story from the book her mother and father loved to read to her.

But tonight, they would have nothing to write! "How kind this teacher is!" thought Mi Soon. After the communists took over North Korea, many classrooms got new teachers. Mother and Father were worried about what this might mean. Mi Soon couldn't wait to tell them about the teacher's kindness! Maybe that would stop them from worrying.

"Children, children!" The teacher was rapping on her desk with a ruler. "Tonight, instead of writing your homework, I want you to play a game!" the teacher said. "It will be like a secret treasure hunt!"

The children got quiet and listened. They liked games.

"When you go home tonight," the teacher began, "I want you to look for a black book. Some of your mothers and fathers read this book to you before you go to sleep."

Mi Soon's eyes got wide. She was so surprised! How did the teacher know about the bedtime storybook? The teacher must be very smart as well as kind.

"Sometimes this book is hidden," the teacher was saying. "You may have to search for it. But don't tell your parents what you are looking for! It's a secret!"

Mi Soon had never kept secrets from her mother and father. For a minute, she wondered if it was a good idea to start now. But she was sure this nice teacher knew what was best. And besides - it was just a game.

"When you find the book, " the teacher went on, "bring it to school tomorrow. Whoever does a good job on this homework will get a wonderful prize!"

"A prize!" Mi Soon thought. "I've never gotten a prize for homework before!" Sometimes some of the other children got prizes for very neat handwriting or perfect math work. Mi Soon's work was always good, but never the best. She couldn't wait to get home and start on the homework game....

The Book

Mi Soon ran all the way home after school. Then she wished she hadn't gone so fast. There was nothing to do but wait until her parents went to bed so she could look for the book.

At supper, Mi Soon told her mother and father how much she liked the new teacher. "She is very wise!" Mi Soon told them. But she didn't tell them about the homework game.

Mi Soon got ready for bed early. Her parents were surprised. "We thought you wouldn't be tired tonight since you had no homework," said her mother. As Mother tucked Mi Soon warmly in her bed, Father went to the kitchen to get the book. Mi Soon listened carefully. She heard a strange scraping. It didn't sound like a drawer opening. It wasn't a cabinet door. Where could Father be keeping the book?

Father came back with the book and sat beside Mi Soon's bed. "Would you like to choose a story tonight?" he asked Mi Soon. Mi Soon thought and thought. She liked the story about the man in the big boat with the pairs of animals. The one about the man in the den with the hungry lions was exciting, too. What would she choose?

"I know!" she said. "Read me the one about the people who were in a little boat when a big storm came. They were scared, but the man called Jesus told the storm to be still!"

Mother smiled. "That's a good story, Mi Soon. I'd like to hear that one, too." Father read the story, then Mi Soon's parents kissed her and told her good night. She listened as Father put the book away. Again she heard the strange scraping sound. "If I can figure out what that sound is, " she thought, "it will help me find the book."

It seemed like such a long time until her mother and father went to bed! But Mi Soon had no trouble staying awake. She was too excited to sleep. She thought about how happy her parents would be when she brought her prize home.

At last her parents went to bed. Mi Soon waited a few more minutes. Then slowly she crawled out of bed and tiptoed to the kitchen. This would be the hard part of the game. Where would the book be hidden?

Suddenly, a stone in the kitchen wall caught her eye. It was not in line with the other stones. It stuck out too far. Mi Soon pushed the stone gently. It moved - with a scraping sound! Ever so slowly and quietly, Mi Soon pulled the stone out of the wall. As she had guessed by this time, the book was hidden behind the stone in the wall.

Mi Soon took the book out of the hole in the wall and carefully replaced the stone. She sneaked back to her room, trying very hard not to make any noise. Safely in her room, she put the book in her school bag. Happily, she snuggled under her covers and went to sleep. Tomorrow would be a wonderful day!

The prize

The next day, school was even better than Mi Soon had thought it would be. Only 14 of the 60 students in the third grade class had done a good job with the homework. At a big meeting in the school gym, each of the 14 was called up to the stage to be honored. All day, they were treated like princes and princesses. Best of all, they each received a big bright red flag and a red scarf to keep.

Many of the children at the school wore red scarves. They got the scarves when they joined the communist children's club that met after school. But Mi Soon didn't have one. Her parents had said they wanted her to come home after school. Mi Soon liked to please her mother and father, so she didn't join the club. But now she had a red scarf and a red flag!

Mi Soon ran home from school even faster than she had the day before. Her new scarf was around her neck and she carried her flag. "Mother, Mother!" she called when she reached her house. "LOOK WHAT I GOT!" But mother wasn't in the kitchen. "That's funny," thought Mi Soon. "Mother is always in the kitchen fixing supper when I get home."

Mi Soon ran from room to room in the small house calling for her mother, but the house was empty. "Of course, " thought Mi Soon. "Mother is in the barn doing the evening chores early." Mi Soon ran across the yard to the barn.

"Mother!" she called as she burst into the barn. "Come and see my wonderful prizes!"

But Mother wasn't in the barn, either. "How strange," Mi Soon said out loud to no one. She walked back to the house, planning how she would hang up her flag to surprise Mother and Father when they got home.

Mi Soon changed into after-school clothes and hung the flag on the wall by the front door. She washed her face and hands for supper. She even worked some of her math problems for school the next day. But still Mother and Father didn't come home. "I'm so hungry!" cried Mi Soon.

She lay on her bed. Tears fell on her pillow. Soon she was asleep. Staying up late the night before to find the book and all the excitement of the day had made her very tired.

A Sad Time

When Mi Soon woke up, the sun was coming up. "What a dream I had!" she said. "I dreamed I was all alone in the house." Sleepily, Mi Soon went to the kitchen to eat breakfast. No one was there! It wasn't a dream! She was all alone!Mi Soon ran fearfully to the front door. Three policemen were walking to the house. The policemen packed all of Mi Soon's clothes and books, and even her new flag. They took her to a government home to live.

Mi Soon cried and cried for many days. She missed Mother and Father. No one would tell her where they were. Worry and fear raced through her mind like a raging storm. Sometimes she dreamed that the man named Jesus came and told the storm to be quiet. In her dream, she felt very peaceful. Then she woke up and cried again. Jesus was just a man in a storybook. Even if He had really lived, He was surely dead by now.

Many years later

"I wish I had never done that homework!" Mi Soon said sadly. Mi Soon was visiting a house church with friends in China. It was 40 years since she had seen her mother and father. She was still very sad.

The Christians were kind to Mi Soon. She felt safe with them. She told them the whole story of her sad life. She even told them about the book, and about her dreams of the man named Jesus. The people in the house church explained to Mi Soon that her parents' black book was a Bible. They told her that her parents had probably gone to prison, because owning a Bible in North Korea was against the law there.Then one of the Christians said, "Mi Soon, I am very sorry for all the sadness you have been through. But I think I have some good news for you." "Good news?" said Mi Soon. "Yes," said the Christian. "It's about Jesus. He isn't just a story in a storybook. He really lived on earth!"

"That's nice," said Mi Soon. "He must have been a very nice man." Mi Soon still didn't sound too happy. "But Mi Soon," said one of the house church leaders. "There's more good news. Jesus is alive!"

"He is? He must be very old!"

"Jesus died, but He rose from the dead," explained one of the Christians. "We can't see Him now. But we can pray, and our sins will be forgiven, and Jesus will fill our hearts with His love." "You mean Jesus is like God?" asked Mi Soon. "Yes!" said another Christian.

"But I don't believe in any God," said Mi Soon. "Because if there was a God, He wouldn't have let me do my homework." "God loves you very much," said the house church leader. "He loves the whole world. That's why He sent His Son Jesus to save us. He didn't cause the bad people to take you away from your mother and father. But, Mi Soon, there's one more bit of good news. Your mother and father believed in Jesus. So they are with Him now in heaven. You can see them again someday if you go to heaven!"

Mi Soon's mouth fell open. "I can see my mother and father again?" she exclaimed. For the first time in 40 years, Mi Soon felt hopeful.

After Mi Soon heard the Gospel story, she gave her life to Him and forgave those who had done her such evil. She even began to pray for the other 13 students who had done their homework. She learned to know the peace of Jesus that had only been a dream before.

4. Name that nation

Who are they? They come over the border from their depressed land into a land of relative plenty. They come without permission. They get fake identities. They mingle with the population, trying to eke out an existence. They will work for almost any amount. Thus they take jobs from the nationals. They get benefits that some nationals cannot get. Some are desperate and begin to commit crimes. Technically they are illegal but many people tend to overlook that fact and allow them to stay to meet the needs of their adopted nation. In some cases they are rounded up and sent back.

Who am I talking about? Why, any number of people groups fit the preceding description. Do all of these groups fit into your thinking as equally worthy of help? Mexicans here in the US, Koreans in China? What do you think of illegal immigration? Where do you draw the line? Where should a nation draw the line? How desperate does one have to be to break another nation's rules? To steal? To kill? What would you do if you had little money and little prospects? No money and no prospects? And if you were single? Or married? Or a parent of 3? or 10?

Why, the answer seems to change with every new question. I suppose the bottom line is, we do not know how we will react when the bottom drops out. I personally cannot answer all the questions regarding myself, or my Mexican - unregistered - friends. I used to think I could...

But for one people group I have decided to answer. For one, I say, hang the rules and those who made them. For one I say, if at all possible get out of there and go wherever you can however you can. That nation is North Korea.

And may God help His people to respond to those who flee or those who stay. (Yes, some have even decided to stay to give the Gospel to their fellows). For one, many of His precious children (the born again variety) are in there. They fit the description of believers in prison whether they go to jail or not. Then, there are many who will love Jesus when Jesus in the person of His people comes in and ministers.

Have you prayed for a North Korean today?

5. Today Pyongyang, Tomorrow the World

I don't mean to imply that the present leader of North Korea will one day rule the world.

I do mean to say that if you want to know what tomorrow's world will look like, take a hard look at North Korea. The Bible describes a situation that mirrors the northern part of the hermit kingdom...

An all-powerful ruler who takes himself so seriously as to demand unquestioned allegiance, even worship... People unable to eat or do any business without the expressed permission of the dictator... A place where "rich" and "poor" is decided by the top man... A land where the Creator is not welcome, nor any of His children... Where worship of another god is a crime against the State, punishable by any number of horrible things. You can probably see other analogies.

The North Korean government has one other thing in common with the coming Man of Sin. Like it or not, their Christian subjects will receive help. God will always find a way to get his people into the pits of human hells to deliver comfort and aid.

That puts the whole Korean crisis in a different light, for me. It may sound crass to suggest it, but there is no better way to invest in one's future than to be a blessing to one who is suffering for Christ. The adage "what goes around comes around" is not in the Bible, but "Give and it shall be given to you" is.

What help, really, will a 401-K , a trust fund, a CD, an insurance policy be when the world is falling apart and a man rises to enslave the world? Let us give to the suffering while it is day. The night comes...

6. Prison break in prison nation

SEOUL, South Korea (AP) -- Some 120 inmates escaped from a political concentration camp in northeastern North Korea several months ago in an unprecedented prison break, news reports said Tuesday.The prisoners escaped from Hwasong camp in North Hamgyong, a province close to the Chinese and Russian borders, in December, the Dong-a Ilbo newspaper reported Wednesday.Daily NK, a Seoul-based Internet news site focusing on North Korea, also carried a similar report on Tuesday.

Both reports cited multiple unnamed sources in North Korea.An official at South Korea's Unification Ministry, which deals with North Korean affairs, said he was unable to confirm the reports but questioned their reliability. The official spoke on customary condition of anonymity.News leaked from the reclusive North, which shuns outside access, is usually hard to confirm.

The Daily NK report said the area was put in a "state of emergency" after the prison break, calling it unprecedented.North Korean authorities have since tightened inspections at Hwasong and adjacent cities to catch the fugitives, of whom 21 have so far been caught, the report said. So far, 21 prisoners have been caught, most of whom were found in China and sent back to the communist North after failed attempts to defect to South Korea, the report said.

The Hwasong prison camp -- located deep inside a mountain and encircled by high wire fences -- holds about 10,000 prisoners, Daily NK said. The escape seemed to have been carefully planned with outside help since the escapees drove off in a vehicle waiting outside the prison, according to the report.

Between 150,000 and 200,000 people are believed to be held in prison camps in the communist North for political reasons, according to U.S. government data.

Separately, Daily NK reported Sunday that 20 North Korean guards along the border with China had fled the country to avoid arrest for allegedly helping North Korean defectors cross the border.The guards had fled to China, where the North sent intelligence officials to capture them, the report said, citing a North Korean resident.

Hundreds of North Koreans leave the country every year to escape poverty and political repression, usually through

China. Defectors in South Korea say they usually bribe border guards to cross the border.

(copied from February 2007 story on NKmissions.com)

7. A woman's paradise: North Korea!

Any ladies want to move to North Korea? The following is from the "Korea Today" website, a propaganda piece in English put out by the NK government.

Here the "Dear Leader" praises and encourages the country's women, failing to tell of the women who do not "make it" by his standard, and are placed in his torture work camps for "re-education".

"As a chariot fails to move with only one wheel, so human society can hardly develop with the strength of the men alone. The women are obliged to turn one of the wheels of the 'revolutionary chariot'. This was what President Kim Il Sung used to say.

"The Korean women have now become a powerful force for revolution and construction, retaining their integrity as the flower of everyday life, flower of the nation and flower of the era."

(Unreported: Those who must get out of NK or die, and who are then often sold into a life of slavery in Big Brother China.)

"During the 'Arduous March' and the forced march the Korean women were compelled to bear a great burden for lack of food, power, and fuel. They were often seen spooning their own small portions of food out to their husbands and children, wearing a smile on their faces. Yet their devotion was not limited to their own families. They shared with their neighbours whatever they had—even a handful of grain—adopted orphaned children, married disabled soldiers and looked after helpless old people. The Korean women were scrupulous in keeping harmony in and out of their families."

(Here omitted is the story of the "arduous march" of thousands upon thousands of North Koreans who yearly take the trek out of his paradise , willing even to risk death to get away. They lose families and all that is precious to a woman because of Kim's desire to have a great military)

"The world 'marathon queen' Jong Song Ok demonstrated to the whole world how strong the Korean women were spiritually and physically. Hyon Yong Ra, Doctor of Science, spent all her youthful years working on a scientific research task, and Labour Heroine Pak Ok Hui from Jagang Province created a paradigm of the double- and three-crop farming.

"There are many such examples found among the Korean women: some raised scores of pigs year after year and sent them all to the workers at socialist construction sites; and others carried out steady production by supplying power on their own, maintaining clean environment in and out of their workplace and creating enjoyable life. In particular, the spirit and traits of military officers' wives, always putting the country before their families and dedicating themselves solely to the national defence, are models of the time for all the women to follow."

(Tell of the other heroines, Dear Leader. Tell of those who suffer in agony because they dare to follow another Leader who is more dear to them than even you, the Man Christ Jesus. Tell of the "tail-less" animals that one of your citizens wrote about after escaping from prison and from your prison nation.)

"Then, what made the women, the alleged name of sympathy for their frailty, strong enough to overcome untold difficulties and trials, optimistically?

"It is attributable to the leader Kim Jong Il's policy to hold the women in social respect true to the intention of President Kim Il Sung who empowered them to have equal political rights and freedom with the men by adopting the Law on Sex Equality..."

(Is it possible that one known the world over for depriving millions of their rights speaks of the equality of the sexes?)

We have heard all this before. Russia, Eastern Europe, China, Cuba... But the dear people of NK have been brainwashed so long that many of them truly believe this man.

Oh pray for this dark place. God truly is able to change things. And whatever He says to you to do, do!

8. How to bring down the Korean walls...

So they've told you that you can "only" pray, that you're not qualified to do anything else? Well, then let's pray! Here's a unique opportunity to be involved in the tearing down of a "wall" that is thicker than Jericho's or Berlin's. Let's join a worldwide movement asking God to take control of Pyongyang, capital city of North Korea, and once considered to be in the heart of Korea's "Bible belt". That's right, there was much of Jesus in what is now North Korea. I don't know what happened, but I do know what happens when God's people pray. Following is lifted from the nkmissions.com website. (I suggest you go there and find other ways to get involved with this work, if it strains at your heart as it does mine!)

Why Pray?The 21 Days of Breakthrough for North Korea is a 21 Day prayer campaign for spiritual breakthrough in NK. Within the last few months, with news of a prison breakout inside NK, 20 NK border guards defecting, and breakthrough with nuclear talks, we wonder what is God doing? The timing seems nearer and nearer and we believe that the time is critical for God's church to press in in prayer and worship. As one missionary said, "Now is the time to send in worshippers." This April 1-21, we will be sending teams to and around NK to worship. Let us join with them from all over the world and be the worshippers that God is sending in to bring breakthrough in the spirit for and around North Korea! Sign up to gather a group to pray for NK one day during the 21 Days of Breakthrough for North Korea.

9. You are what you eat...

We become what we ingest, whether the food of the body or the food of the mind. Read the following and be thankful that you live in a land of free press. Oh we have our prejudices and our perspectives, but what you are about to read is the solid diet of an average North Korean. These precious folk grow up hating everything Western, even to the point of "biting the hand" of those who would feed them. Jesus says, "You will know the truth and the truth will set you free." Join with me in praying that Jesus - the Truth- will be preached all over the towns and villages of the "Hermit Kingdom." What a day of rejoicing THAT will be!

Now, if you dare, from the Korea Central "News" Agency, March 25:

U.S. and S. Korean Warmongers' DPRK-Targeted War Exercises Assailed Pyongyang, March 25 (KCNA) -- A spokesman for the Korean National Peace Committee released a statement on Sunday to denounce the U.S. and south Korean warmongers for staging the DPRK-targeted RSOI and field mobile exercise in south Korea defying strong protest. The launch of the above-said war maneuvers is a product of deliberately planned and systematic moves of the U.S. and south Korean bellicose forces to prevent the desire for peace and reconciliation from growing stronger and escalate tension on the Korean Peninsula in a bid to frustrate the process of dialogue and peace and, furthermore, ignite a war, the statement said, and continued: The above-said RSOI and field mobile exercise is an extension of the moves to provoke a war against the DPRK and an extremely dangerous preliminary war, a test nuclear war before going over to an actual war. This saber-rattling just launched behind the curtain of "dialogue" and "peace" is a very rude act proving their utter lack of good faith and courtesy and an unpardonable perfidy to the dialogue partner. This clearly indicates that the U.S. and south Korean authorities' talk about "dialogue" and "improved relations" is nothing but hypocrisy and they are still persisting in their hostile policy toward the DPRK and confrontation with it. The army and people of the DPRK will bolster the self-defensive deterrence for defending the dignity and sovereignty of the Korean nation to cope with the provocative moves of the U.S. and south Korean warmongers for a war of aggression against it. If the aggressors ignite a war on this land, the army and people of the DPRK will resolutely retaliate against them with merciless deadly blows. The U.S. would be well advised to stop at once its reckless war exercises against the DPRK, which are harmful to the settlement of the nuclear issue and peace of the Korean Peninsula and driving the situation to a phase of confrontation and war. The south Korean authorities should immediately halt their criminal acts of participating in the war moves of the outside forces against the Korean nation and peace, well aware that their involvement in the outside forces-led saber-rattling against the fellow countrymen is a treacherous act of driving the inter-Korean relations to a collapse in violation of the June 15 joint declaration.

Oh my. Talk to you later.

10. Whaddaya know about North Korea?

Let's try a 10-question pop quiz.

1. What is the capital and largest city of North Korea?
2. What is the currency of North Korea? Is it a "hard" or "soft" currency?
3. About how many people live there in about how many square miles?
4. What is its official name?
5. Who is the "eternal" President?
6. What three nations border North Korea?
7. What is the total GDP? (How much money per year?) Per capita?
8. What nation had occupied all of Korea until its defeat in 1945?
9. Which parallel divides the two Koreas?
10. What is "Juche", NK's form of government?

Don't worry about it. Most people don't know a lot about this reclusive people. Let's see how you did:

1. Pyongyang, a major city whose population roughly matches Chicago's (without Chicago suburbs),around three million.
2. The North Korean "won", different from the won of South Korea by far. One dollar is today (2007) about 2 NK won, whereas that same dollar will fetch about 950 SK. It is a virtually worthless or "soft" currency on the world's markets.

3. 23 million people in 47,000 square miles. That's a density of nearly 500 persons per square mile. For comparisons Stateside, NK has about the same population as Texas in the area of Ohio.

4. Democratic People's Republic of Korea. Of course it is not a "democracy", for power is concentrated in a very few, some say one, at the top. It does not belong to the "people" as they have virtually no say in how things run. The definition of "republic" includes the right to choose leaders and representation by all the people in the government. NK is definitely not a republic. One must concede that it is "Korea", but a Korea that has been made over in the image of one family, abandoning much that has traditionally been Korean.

5. Not the present leader [Kim Jong Il, 2007], who continues the worship of his cult-inspiring father. Kim Il Sung is the "eternal" one. But he is dead. Here NK has once more been liberal with their definition of terms.

6. China, Russia, South Korea. The history of the peninsula is a fascinating one involving encroachments on the power structure of various peoples living there. China, Russia, and of course Japan, have been no end of trouble to this small but surviving people.

7. $40 billion. Sounds like a lot, but it is 85th in the list of GDP's worldwide. Each person receives about $1,800! And that is 149th on the list. For comparison, America has a GDP of 12 TRILLION, with an average per capita income between 25 and 30 thousand.

8. Japan. There is still much animosity between the average Korean, North or South, and the Japanese. It's a long story, and a painful one.

9. The 38th. There is a no-man's land there, complete with mine-fields, soldiers ready to start a war that never really ended, and a building that is half in North Korea and

half in the South. Some selected few are allowed to take tours of this area.

10. The biggest misnomer of all: self-reliance. Yet their government is totally dependent on China, South Korea, the United States, and tons of Christian ministries for its very existence. Without reliance on other powers around them, this tiny nation would literally be starved out of existence.

How'd you do?

11. Where have all the squirrels gone?

Dr. C. Kenneth Quinones and Joseph Tragert wrote a book a few years back that you should know about if you are going to get serious about North Korea. It's *The Complete Idiot's Guide to Understanding North Korea*. I'm not suggesting any of my readers are complete or even partial idiots. That's just the name of the book. Quinones narrates this tragic personal recollection on page 26:

I was in North Korea in August, September, and October 1995. Torrential rains in August caused devastating floods. The corn and rice harvests were destroyed. I saw women and children dressed in rags wandering in the fields looking for leaves, grass, anything theycould eat.

For months I never heard birds nor saw squirrels. They had all been eaten. One frigid day in January 1996, I saw thousands of people ice fishing on the Taedong River and nearby lakes. In July, 1996, I visited the zoo in Pyongyang. Most of the animals had starved to death. The few remaining animals like the elephants and monkeys were too feeble to stand.

Just as severe was the lack of fuel to cook food or heat homes and water for washing. The floods had filled the coal mines, making it impossible to continue mining for the nation's basic fuel for heating. Deforestation had already stripped the hills of wood. Rice straw, a common substitute for wood, had all been burned by mid-winter in 1995. By January 1966, smoke coming from chimneys of homes and factories was a rare sight. People appeared in the streets and in the offices in dirty clothes, and themselves unwashed. Only after I had become repeatedly ill did I learn to stop shaking hands because there was no warm water or soap for washing.

God, please have mercy on this land... things are better now, but oh so many go to bed hungry every night...God have mercy on us too if we hold back from our neighbor or our brother...

12. the 10 commandments replaced

Some months ago I read Helie Lee's book about her rescue of some family members out of North Korea *(In the Absence of Sun)*. I must hasten to add that although Helie has a healthy "respect" for Jesus because of *Halmoni* (grandma), my personal faith resembles that of Halmoni more than Helie. I do not condone the expressed lifestyle of this young Korean American, but I am captivated by the story and the very many details she shares of a land that I still wish to visit myself.

In telling the story, she mentions Kim Il Sung's "Ten Principles", a not-so-veiled replacement of God's Ten Commandments, created in an attempt to obliterate all things Biblical. All ten have to do with *Kim Il Sung himself*, his ideology, loyalty to him, his authority, his revolutionary thought, his centrality, confidence in him, the passing on of his thoughts to the next generation.

From page 101 & ff:

"The Ten Principles came with very specific guidelines. For example, Principle No. 3 went on to elaborate that 'Kim Il Sung's portraits, plaster figures, statues, badges containing his pictures, publications carrying his pictures, paintings portraying his image, monuments or public notices containing his instructions...must be carefully handled and protected from being spoiled.'

"In 1985, Burundi's ambassador to Beijing checked into the Botonggang Hotel in Pyongyang. When he unpacked his bags and saw that his shoes were flattened, he stuffed a sheet of newspaper into them. A bellboy reported the 'crime' to the police because the newspaper contained Kim Il Sung's picture. The ambassador was accused of damaging the dignity of the Great Leader, nearly causing a diplomatic incident."

Time and space fail me to record in detail Helie's reporting of the little 3-year old who caused her parents to be arrested by accidentally urinating on a Kim Il Sung booklet...

Let us allow the images of North Korea to disturb us, but only enough to pray. Depression and despair are not the goal of this blog. God will hear. God will rise up. He suffers long for His own purposes. But He is a jealous God and will not be mocked forever.

Remember Israel in Egypt 430 years! But He does arise. *Is this His time?*

13. *The power of education*

How serious is our desire for our children to know Jesus and His words? While we are not advocating brainwashing, certainly there is something a Christian can learn from the North Korea about child-rearing:

Speaking of the original Kim dictatorship, Bradley K. Martin says in his detailed treatise on the Kim dynasty, *Under the Loving Care of the Fatherly Leader:*

" 'As soon as you are born you are received by a nursery, then led through a flowery gate to an eleven-year education.'

"Indeed, officials told me, mothers were entitled to seventy-seven days of maternity leave before turning their babies over to public day nurseries, or in some cases full-time nurseries. 'Home education has an important meaning in a society where private ownership of the means of production is predominant,' Kim-Il-sung had said in a 1968 speech. 'But it has no important meaning in a different, socialist society.'

"The state, taking over much of the parental role, had been training youngsters to worship Kim. 'Our Great Leader is the Supreme Leader of revolution, its heart and the only center,' said one official policy statement. 'We have to inculcate in our future generations the absolute authority of the Leader, the indisputable thoughts and instructions of the Leader, so that they may accept them as faith and the law of the land.'

"Schoolbooks portrayed Kim in his heroic roles. Their illustrations were drawings in the style of children's Biblical literature... Some pictured Kim's exploits, whether real or imagined, as a child and as a young guerrilla commander. Others depicted a mature Kim, sometimes surrounded by children in tableaux reminiscent of the Sunday-school pictures that illustrate the words of Jesus, 'Suffer the little children to come unto Me.'

"The training and peer pressure that reinforced such images had intensified over the years. Thus, the young people I met struck me as more fanatical than North Koreans aged forty or older, whose indoctrination had not been as thoroughgoing."

So much to think about in that piece... The elder Kim truly was attempting to replace the Christ He heard about growing up in his parents' church... The power of education!... Are we not following the Communist model when we give our children over to state-run programs and schools just after birth?... Can we complain about the product of so many years of indoctrination?...What are American schools giving its children that has greater worth than what Kim gives?... Are Christian parents devoted to having the Life and Word and Way of our Dear Leader inculcated in their young ones?

14. Mr Kim church organist

For those who may not have time to trek through Bradley Martin's 700-page book about the history of the Kims in North Korea, *Under the Loving Care of the Fatherly Leader,* let me be a tour guide. It may take a little while ...

Here's one for you:

"Who would have imagined that the man whose rule wiped out nearly every trace of religion in North Korea - except worship of himself - had been until his late teens not only a churchgoer but, moreover, a church organist? The young Kim was both. Experience in church-related activities played a considerable role in training one of the most successful mass leaders and propagandists in the history of the world, not to mention providing a model for his own eventual elevation to divine status...

"One thing the families [of both his parents] had in common was that they were Christian churchgoers...

"The patriotism of Kim's family members, like that of many other Koreans, was linked with Christianity. Protestant and, to a lesser extent, Catholic churches flourished in Korean communities following the 1882 treaty with the United States. Pyongyang, in particular, was such fertile ground for American mission work that the city became known as Korea's Jerusalem."

What happened? The putting out of the light of the "candlesticks" in the Book of Revelation was always viewed as a judgment. Did the churches lose their focus, their first love, their zeal? Is antichrist-like destruction inevitable once it starts? Surely the endtime man of sin will defeat believers, sending them to Glory. Why have the two Kims been given this authority in our time? And is America about to enter a similar judgment?

No answers. Only questions. Being involved with North Koreans makes one think.

15. He couldn't see beyond his diploma

What promises keep us going from day to day? Christians want to believe that the promises of God are sufficient, that they are being guided along a pathway that will broaden into a glorious tomorrow with Christ Himself. May it be so.

For the world it is definitely *not* so. The world believes the lie. Nowhere is this more symbolically and actually true than in North Korea, land of lies. I quote from "In the Absence of Sun", 2002 narrative of Korean Helie Lee, who assisted in the liberating of several of her family members from NK. And once more I remind readers that the life-style of Christ is not promoted in this book, only alluded to.

Nine of Helie's family was in focus for release, but on the first attempt at freeing them, only four could be pried loose. Imagine it! A chance to leave, but empty promises were too real to ignore:

" 'Of all the children, Mun Churl could have convinced his mother to escape, but he couldn't see beyond his diploma and ran back to school... as angry as I [Helie's father] am with him, I know he doesn't know any better. Since birth he's been fed their propaganda. At twenty five a young man's the most passionate and idealistic...'

" I [Helie] tried to step back from who I was and look at it from Mun Churl's standpoint. He probably knew nothing about the world outside and what it could offer him. All he knew was what the party's propaganda pumped into him. The party controlled the newspapers and broadcasting stations. the Korean Central Television Station in Pyongyang offered only three channels. Other cities only received one channel. North Korea had just two AM radio networks and one FM network. Radio dials were fixed to receive only designated frequencies, preventing the reception of foreign broadcasts that might reveal the truth to its citizens...

" 'Fear cripples people [says Grandmother] and prevents them from making good decisions. The Reds control them with fear. Their brains are washed.' "

Eternally there is not much difference between the various lies that keep people from God and Heaven. But while we sit here on this side of the River, we gaze in horror at the extent to which our enemy will deceive those whom he desires to destroy.

Will you pray for the North Koreans today?

16. *My father should have been killed by a firing squad*

My thanks again to Hae Ri (Helie) Lee, who 5 years ago gave us "In the Absence of Sun". Though this is not a specifically Christian perspective of the North Korean situation, I find her narrative fascinating and most informative.

At this point in the story, the "long lost" uncle has been found and rescued from North Korea. He is asked, " 'Lee Yong Woon-ssi, what... would you like to do when you get to South Korea?' "Yong Woon Uncle paused to reflect. 'More than anything else, do something good for the church.' Inspired, he began singing a hymn he had memorized from his childhood.

'Without Jesus there is no hope Jesus, You are my life and my friend.

Without Your presence, I could not exist, Not even live for a moment;

May I awake each morning with You in my heart, May I sleep each night with You in my thoughts,

When I labor in the fields, may You be my overseer,

When I am alone at home, may I feel Your overwhelming love; Even if a fish can live outside of the water Our spirit apart from You cannot survive.'

"Yong Woon Uncle suddenly stopped singing, seeing [daughter] Ae Ran's eyes shoot warning sparks at him. " ' My father is a bad person. He could never be a true communist because he hid the hymns in his heart all those years. He should have been purged. He should have been killed by the firing squad.' Ae Ran laughed nervously, brushing back a wayward wisp of hair.

"Her response blew my mind. 'I didn't say Kim Il Sung is bad,' Yong Woon Uncle said almost in desperation, trying to explain himself.

" 'Believing in Jesus Christ means that you respect the United States. Father should have been singing worshipful hymns to our Great Leader instead.' Ae Ran suddenly brightened her expression and began to sing a song.

" 'At dawn in the morning I am thinking about our Great Leader; In the evening looking at the moon, I am thinking about our Comrade Leader.'" "Ae Ran sang with such sincerity and affection that I began to understand a little better why they did what they did. North Korea's system and ideology were so powerful, they could turn one family member against another. You couldn't trust your own spouse or children for fear they'd betray you if you said anything against the party. To them, this was normal."

Read this, and weep with me. Oh my God, how long, how long shall this cancer exist on the planet? Oh God, rise up! Living God, rise up and deliver us from this evil!

17. For the strong hearted only

In the Absence of Sun, by Helie Lee, is the source of today's quote. I quote from her today to point out to you a few more of the gruesome details of life in this suburb of Hades. My intention is to startle us all into more and more prayer   and   brokenness.

From pages 24-25: Asking her Chinese contact across the border how her relative has been eating in North Korea, she is told:

"They only earn about 20,000 won [about U.S. $22.00 in 1997] a month, which used to be enough to survive on with the help of government food rations. These days, rations don't come for months if they come at all.."When asked how they have managed to stay alive, their hosts reply: "They're living merely because they're not dead. It's the thought of their family in America that keeps them going. You're the source of their energy. People like them, who were sent to live in the harsh countryside, are the lowest class. The privileged get to live in Pyongyang, where they have modern houses, medical facilities, and special skills.

"We do as much as we can for them. We save food, package it in large bags, and send it over. Your two nieces and two nephews are wearing all our old clothing. There, people go without socks and underwear during the winters. I've seen so many homeless people, and children skinny as sticks. People are dropping dead in the streets, really. In some of the worst-stricken areas, I even heard rumors that when someone dies, the family will keep the body in the house until it begins to rot or else neighbors will dig it up and eat it. Being a Choson person myself, it's devastating to see our own people suffer like that."

Devastating indeed. How many of the suffering are our family, the noble clan called Christian? Is Christ being starved in the Hermit Kingdom's countryside? May God give us grace and means to go to Him.

18. NK: how it all began

We started through the 700-page book of Bradley Martin , *Under the Loving Care of the Fatherly Leader* some time ago. Time to continue on...

How does an evil so great as the NK saga get started? One place to start is the childhood of Kim Il Sung. He grew up surrounded by Christianity, even in his own home, but also under the oppression of the Japanese. He and his people had always longed to be free of foreign domination. So far so good. Coupled to his dream of Korean freedom was his military skill. Though nothing like the mythology he and his friends would write about himself, still the fact remains that he was somewhat successful in "guerilla" warfare.

Most people have trouble saying no to success, especially when it supports deep inner longings. His military work had been done in Russia, so the Russians noticed him, approved of him, and decided to use him in Korea after the peninsula was tragically divided into two parts. They of course taught him their communist ways.

He learned, for example, how to take control of the wealth of a nation and redistribute it. When he applied his new knowledge of redistribution to the northern portion of Korea, the poor loved him for it, and followed him slavishly. The rich who complained were eliminated. The others came on board and became the new ruling class, which Communism never has, but always has.

Young Kim soaked all this power in and longed for more. Power corrupts, they say. He began to need "absolute obedience" and lavish praise. Here was a man who never finished Middle School, suddenly the king of the mountain.

Poor Korea. They had never had a history of democracy. They were used to people coming in and taking them over. And that's what Kim did. And is still doing. Imagine two generations who have grown up thinking that Kim-il-sung-ism is normal.

That's how this nightmare all started. One man who turned his back on Christ and the church...

19. The never-ending war

I imagine most of my readers know that the Koreas are living out the world's longest cease-fire. Never have the terms of peace been worked out and settled upon. Some expect the war to continue at any time...

In 1949, an energized Kim Il Sung tried to convince Russia's Stalin that the "South" needed invading. The U.S. was dropping hints that it was too strapped to protect Taiwan, and the powers that were assumed that meant they wouldn't put out a helping hand to South Korea either. Bad assumption. But it was one of the reasons Stalin gave his nod to the plan. The great Russian ogre himself stayed in the background, maneuvering dependent China to the fore.

Kim actually believed that once the liberation army got south of the DMZ, down into Seoul and the rest of the country, hordes of disgruntled citizens would rise up and with him bring on the glorious day of Communism to the entire peninsula. Another bad assumption.

Only a few brainwashed pockets of SK residents "rose up" to join Kim's considerable army. Just before his invasion, in 1950, he made one last call for "re-unification" (a code word that to this day means, "Communism controls all"). He asked for diplomats to come to Pyongyang. He then attacked, but for a long time his ill-informed citizenry believed he was responding to an expected attack from the South. He made his people believe that they were being besieged and then called on their patriotism to defeat America and the wicked brothers below.

Before American forces, joined to the not-so-wonderful army of the South, could get their act fully together, Northern troops had pushed their way through most of the country. One last stand at Pusan in the far south kept Kim from taking the entire country for Communism.

We can say this miracle had something to do with American air power or we can give all glory to God who left a door of freedom open. I know my life would have been very different had Korea closed altogether: I am married to a former resident of Seoul...

More on the Korean War another time. I invite you to join me in prayer for a people who have been in pain for most of their existence. Look at her history, dating back to the days of Abraham. Then look at what Christ is doing in the last 50 years in South Korea. The contrast is so obvious.

Blessed is the nation whose God is the Lord!

20. misinformed by m.a.s.h.

Americans who know of the Korean war chiefly through the *MASH* series have been sorely misinformed. Hawkeye and company were programmed to make Americans hate the war and the government that sponsored it. Unfortunate.

But unless you are an underprivileged citizen of North Korea, you know that America and South Korea did not start the Korean War. You know that if America had not stepped in when it did and as powerfully as it did, the entire Korean peninsula would look like the huge slave camp of the North. Surely we hate war, but we love the liberty it can provide. Peacemongers consistently forget this.

Douglas Macarthur, today equally maligned and praised by the peoples of the earth, brings his forces behind the North Korean lines invading the South, to Inchon. The North is then wedged in between armies, as there are already forces in the South. Eventually he pushes the enemy back across the DMZ all the way to Pyongyang, and even to the Chinese border.

We hear bits and pieces about what Kim Il Sung is up to during this time. His busts of Stalin on whom he relies do not prosper him. But he vows to fight to the end. There is to be no armistice. Let all the people die, we will not give up. Unfortunately Stalin does.

And, to his chagrin, many North Koreans rise up to fight with the South when the reverse invasion takes place!

China, feeling threatened, pushes into North Korea, supported by Kim and his tired army, who are ready to resort to guerrilla warfare if need be. Seoul is retaken by the North.

McArthur wants to use "the bomb" again. That has certainly worked in Japan! End of hostilities. Peace immediately. Drop the bomb on China. But Truman fears Russia will enter. And that we will lose Japan or Europe. Too much blood has been shed. Let's make peace.

When it is all over, NK is in worse ruins than Japan. And all of this carnage is attributable to the father of the present ruler, both of whom desire reunification of the Korean peninsula at any price!

The South has not been angelic in its governmental systems through the years. But seeing Communism close up during these evil war years confirms for decades that, for sure, they will not follow Marx and Lenin south of the DMZ. Despite a few college-age rabble-rousing types that always know more than their elders in Korea (and throughout the world), that decision is holding .

But the threat of war continues to this day. I encourage you once more to pray.

Thanks to Bradley Martin again for history of this period.

21. North Korea martyrs

This post is from Mission Network News, January 10 , 2007. I have edited it a little...

North Korea (MNN) - We've heard the stories. Thousands of North Korean Christians have been killed for their faith. Many more are in work camps. Today another chilling story [A prominent Christian worker] says North Korean Christians are becoming increasingly uneasy about possessing a Bible. He brings sobering news from their worker there.

"A man that's known to be an "evangelist." He's probably not an evangelist to anyone other than his family members, but he was caught with two of our Korean New Testaments in his possession and he was executed for that."

This is just one of many stories coming out of North Korea.

"A North Korean Army General who became a believer and was trying to evangelize some of the people in his unit, was executed by a fellow officer." Another story included a woman who was washing clothes, "She bent over to rinse her clothes. A New Testament fell out. Somebody reported it and both she and her grandmother were quickly executed."

There seems to be no sign of the persecution easing any. "What you have is a leader who is proclaiming himself to be god. It's prescribed that they daily worship him. And, refusal to do that and being caught worshiping God just brings that kind of governmental response. And, as best we can tell the tempo of that is not lessening."

[The worker] says it's obvious what that increasing pressure on Christians is doing to Bible smuggling. "It becomes more and more difficult to get a person to risk their life to carry those in to North Korea." With rivers frozen, it's a perfect time to smuggle Bibles into the country. "Despite the oppression, there are positive signs," he says. God seems to be working. "In response to a very, very oppressive government (and) human injustices, people are looking for an answer other than their own government. And, I believe that's awakening the resilience of believers in North Korea to say, 'we have another answer. There is another way to believe.'"

22. reliant self-reliance

Still following Martin's *Under the loving care...* book, we enter into the years just past the Korean War, when most of us draw a blank trying to recall what happened next.

It is time to rebuild. There has been much destruction on both sides of the 38th parallel, and the contest is on to see which system will prosper: communism, backed by Russia and China, or capitalism/democracy, supported by the U.S.

Kim Il Sung's first actions are to remove persons upon whom any blame can be placed before they have a chance to blame him for something. Dictators have always been forced to remove opposition. It's not that people in these countries don't have common sense and great ideas. It's just that they are killed before their ideas can take root. Only through this method do Communist governments survive. Love there is forced. Minds are re-programmed. Bodies are intimidated.

At the beginning of the race for supremacy, the two Koreas are about even in per capita income. (That's the number you get when you take all the income of the nation and divide it by the number of people.) But by 1960 there is a marked difference. South Korea is... behind! Aid pouring into the North from China, Russia, and elsewhere creates a surge that Kim and company turn into early success. People begin talking about the "Korean miracle."

Though from the beginning and to the present day North Korea has been totally dependent on other nations for aid, she begins in the 50's to give the impression to the world and her own people that she needs no one's help. The famed "juche" policy which means "self-reliance" but actually is haughty pride, begins to bind the people of the North with a stranglehold that eventually chokes out its life.

Kim's own personal fame grows as he takes credit for the abundance. More and more opponents are silenced. The reform going on in Russia, as Khruschev dares to criticize (the dead) Stalin's policies, and gets away with it, is not to happen in North Korea. Russia is considered heretical, but the glorious North Korea will stay the course of communism until it blossoms into the perfect state. Some day. That seems to be the dream still. "Some day."

Slowly the history of North Korea is literally rewritten. Less and less credit to Russia for all they did to get this thing going. Then a cutback in praise to China. Eventually the books will read that Kim Il Sung alone is to be praised for creating and sustaining the (true) Korean nation! In saying this, Kim rules out not only his neighbors, but his God.

To be continued...

23. korea is my home

The following is a summary of one of many interviews conducted by Refugees International *staff with North Koreans in China , some time in '03 or '04. The interviews were conducted through an interpreter. For reasons of security RI did not attempt to obtain or record the real names of any individuals. You will note the absence of any "fancy" writing. For North Korea, all one has to do is tell the facts...*

INTERVIEW 1, MALE, Age 34 PLACE OF ORIGIN: Hoeryong FIRST ARRIVAL IN CHINA: June 2003 Three years ago, he was employed as a driver but then he got sick with a liver problem and was laid off. "Even when you go to the hospital, there are no medicines." His wife is good at needlework that they sell in North Korea. She can make about 15,000 North Korean won in 45 days of work. Because he doesn't work in a factory he doesn't get food, except on the Leader's [Kim Jong Il's] birthday or holidays. His daughter goes to kindergarten but must bring her own food to school.

It's his first time in China. The manager of the local church has known him for years because the manager often goes to North Korea. He came to China because his "house faced difficulties in surviving so I came to get help and to study the Bible." He came to China with another North Korean man on a secret route.

He will go back to North Korea tonight to bring back Bibles. He wants to stay in North Korea. His first impression of China is "freedom." [At this point he started crying.]

"Honestly speaking, I don't want to go back but North Korea is my home country." He might return to China alone or with his close friends but not with his family.

There is radio in North Korea but no international news. In some places the TV can receive Chinese stations. After the new economic reform, the situation got worse. It then worsened further when SARS started. Some people have committed suicide because the situation is so hard.

His relatives went for a trip and one of them, a woman, committed suicide. Before SARS, he could get one kilogram of rice for 150 Won. The price increased to 300 won per kilo and now it's down to 250 Won per kilo.

He has not had any problems with the Chinese authorities. "If you come to China for food the penalty in

North Korea is 1-6 months of prison. For meeting with foreigners a person could be sentenced to death." If someone gets caught with Bibles he or she will be sentenced to death. He knows many people who have been put in prison for getting food in China.

"I ask you to work for freedom of the North Korean people. I want political and religious freedom. In the law we have freedom, but that's not the reality."

That last paragraph is for us, the readers. Let us work indeed for their freedom, beginning on our knees.

24. north koreans starting over

...continued from http://refugeesinternational.org/ The story of the brave souls who dare to attempt escape from North Korea.

INTERVIEW 2 SIX GIRLS, Ages 17, 16, 16, 14, 13, 3 and a BOY, Age 17

PLACES OF ORIGIN IN NORTH KOREA: Not recorded for all; two sisters in the group were from Pyongyang

FIRST ARRIVAL IN CHINA: 2002

[This interview was conducted in a group setting, with the teenagers sitting on the floor in a circle.] They used to be tutored in China but the situation became tougher after the incidents at the embassies in Beijing. Now the teachers cannot come.

Girl (16): Her dad died in North Korea so she came here with her mother. She was arrested in October 2002 because she went with her mother to Beijing in hope of going to South Korea. They got out of the taxi and because they didn't speak Chinese, they were noticed. The man who arranged for them to go to Beijing turned them in.

She stayed in a Beijing jail with her mother for six days and then they were sent back to North Korea. Her mother was sent to a labor center and she was sent to an orphanage center (which is like a jail) in Undok.

She got three meals a day in the orphanage but it wasn't enough food. She told the orphanage that she was sick and said she'd like to go to the hospital. She ran away once she got to the hospital. She returned to China by herself in February. She has had no contact with her mother. When she came here she was very weak. Everyone could recognize that she was North Korean.

She's learning the Bible now. They go one by one to an elementary Chinese class because it's less noticeable.

When asked what they wanted to do in the future, one girl said that she wanted to be a pastor; another wants to be a hair stylist; another wants to be the manager of an orphanage. One girl (14) wants to be the President of North Korea and change things.

The boy said that he was sent to an orphanage in North Korea. There were rules there. One rule was that you had to kneel from 5:00 am until 10:00 pm before you get your sentence. Another rule is that you cannot move. If you disobey, you might be hung from your feet.

If you have not yet begun to pray for North Korea, perhaps today?

25. when the church is in place

No, we are not the social workers of the world, but when Christ's church is where it ought to be, what a blessing to the world! Here is our third look at refugees coming out of North Korea into what must seem like "heavenly" China.

Pray for a North Korean today, will you?

INTERVIEW 3
MALE, Age 40
PLACE OF ORIGIN: Ch'ongjin
FIRST ARRIVAL IN CHINA: March 2003

He came to China because he had a problem with his throat so he hadn't been able to work at his job of milling rice since 1996."It's difficult for me to survive. I was living like a beggar and almost died."

Two of his sons died of starvation in 1998.He had no connections in China but friends told him that he could find food in China. He came across the river by himself in the middle of the night and came to a church close to the border.

"My impression of China is that I can breathe. It was like there was no oxygen in North Korea." North Korea is closed and they have no way of knowing international policies. The North Korean government sends people to prison because when people leave they condemn the North Korean government because of what they have learned about the outside situation.

He's now waiting for an operation but it's expensive. He has no idea about the future. He's just waiting for his operation. "Life is quite okay here because NGOs are helping us."

"We don't want to go back to North Korea. We're definitely willing to go to South Korea. North Korea won't change."
(copied from http://refugeesinternational.org/)

26. meet another north korean

The subjects of these interviews are real people, possibly still alive. A face, even if not a name, to come before you in prayer. Let every detail sink in, and bring it all before the Father who watches after the souls of men and desperately wants to love them... through His people.

INTERVIEW 4 MALE, Age 25
PLACE OF ORIGIN: North Hamgyong
FIRST ARRIVAL IN CHINA: 2000

He first came to China in 2000 because his parents and siblings died of starvation between 1995 and 1997. In May 2002 he was arrested and deported, but he was sick with a kidney problem and his hand was injured during work. After being in prison for only two days, the North Korean government released him because they thought he couldn't work.

There were about 400 other North Koreans in prison (men, women and children). The law is that defectors will be punished in labor centers. But since January the law changed and people are sent to prison. The Chinese police do random checks to look for foreigners, Falun Gong adherents, and North Koreans.

One day the police came and asked for his ID; he said he had lost it. He's afraid to stay at home during the day because of the police checks so he wanders the streets and goes to his apartment just at night to sleep.

People who hire North Koreans get fined so they are afraid to hire them. [An NGO in China pays for his rent, food, and medicine.]

His health is improving but he's waiting for a cure from the doctors so he doesn't know his future. From http://refugeesinternational.org/

27. on giving away one's children

I am not one to endorse or praise the media. We all know the things of which they are capable. But one cannot ignore a good piece of journalism. This was back in 2002 and featured a serious and challenging Ted Koppel in the days when he presided over *Nightline*. I found the synopsis of the program at

http://www.familycare.org/news/nightline.htm and produce about half of it below. The actual videos can be ordered from ABC news. But I caution you. Your emotions could well lead you into serious issues having seen this story. I was emptied. It was unbearable. It still is. Yet it happened and to some extent still happens today.

Here is the summary:

June 10, 2002 - In the mountains of northeast China, an hour's walk into the forests, a family once hid underneath the earth.

Three years ago, Kim Kan-Su and Kim Young-Hee lived here with their 5-year-old son, Young-shin, in a hole in the ground, hiding from police. Their crime, in the eyes of China and their homeland, North Korea, was simply that they left their famine-stricken country to look for food.

Their underground hideout was only a couple of miles from the North Korean border, but it was one of many "homes" they had in the mountains since they fled North Korea.

Chinese police are paid a bounty to capture refugees like them and return them to North Korea. The Kims lived with the knowledge that if they were sent back, they would be labeled as traitors and possibly face execution.

"Though we don't have a house, living like this in hiding, at least we eat rice, which is rarely available in North Korea, even for well-off families. We just hope we don't get caught," Young-Hee, the mother, told Korean-American filmmaker Kim Jung-eun at the time.

"Everything else is fine, except for the fear and distress," said Kan-Su, the father.

In the forest, surrounded by caution and living in fear, the Kims tried to keep some sense of a normal family life for their young son. Kan-Su taught his son about the animals, and showed him how to set traps, to catch rabbits and birds. He used some of the game to trade for rice and vegetables at a local village.

Kan-Su worked at a tobacco farm an hours' walk from his hideout. His labor there was illegal and he received no pay, but he was compensated with a small amount of rice, which he brought back to his family every three days or so.

The family still bore the scars of their situation though. Malnourishment from the famine of North Korea stunted Young-shin's growth, and his parents mourned for their broken family.

When the Kim family first came to China, they had three children and Young-Hee was pregnant with a fourth. But they could not feed or educate them properly, hiding in the forest, and one by one, they had to give their children away.

The baby boy who was born in the hideout was first given to a childless Chinese family. Later, the Kims reluctantly handed their two girls to an orphanage. They considered it the girls' only chance of ever receiving a minimum standard of decent nutrition and education.

Soon, the Kims realized they could not provide enough for Young-shin either. So three years ago (1999), the Kims gave away the last of their children.

Is any sorrow like the sorrow of a bereaved parent or child? Can we not love God more as we see how He unselfishly, unflinchingly gave His only Son for us?

Where are the Kims now? Did the children return to anything like normalcy? Was the family united? And what of the thousands of other "Kims", scarred forever by the tyranny in Pyongyang?

[This update: So whatever happened to Kim Young-Shin, the little boy with the fugitive parents? I wanted to know, so I wrote the author of the story, the Korean lady who had done the original interview. Her response was not all that comforting...

Eight months after the painful tearing away, Young-shin is re-united with his parents. I'd like to think it is a gloriously happy event, this reunification. But the video shows the Kims visiting their girls, the ones they gave away, in the orphanage. And that reunion is definitely not a glad one. Children don't always know what it means when a parent abandons them.

So, happily ever after now? Not quite. While the family is hiding out in a small farming town in China, someone sees them and reports them to the police. They are sent back to North   Korea.

The email reads here: "Fortunately they are together (all?) today though they went through a lot to get to this point." I can only imagine what she means by that. She tells me that she simply cannot release all the details... But we've already discussed what happens when North Koreans are returned to their prison-land. What did they have to go through to be "re-educated"?

Last report is that they are living in a small town in North Korea, barely making a living, but somehow there is enough to keep the family together.]

Why don't we go to North Korea in the Spirit right now, and pray for this family.

28. praise unimaginable

Just when you think you've heard it all, along comes National Geographic. It's called *Inside North Korea*, it's from 2006. Visit http://nationalgeographic.com/channel For further details on how to obtain a copy of this devastating video.

Here are the bare facts from the jacket:

"Go undercover with National geographic correspondent Lisa Ling as she journeys into mysterious and reclusive North Korea. Posing as part of an international medical team, Lisa and her camera crew reveal the extraordinary, hidden face of this insular, little-known place, from the powerful control Kim Jong Il exerts over his people to the military powder keg of life along the heavily armed demilitarized zone.

Filmed against the politically charged backdrop of North Korea's nuclear ambitions, *Inside North Korea* is a fascinating search for the truth, and mutual understanding, inside one of the most isolated nations on earth."

Somehow, that doesn't say it all. You'll have to see it to believe it. Then you will still not believe it. Personally, I got ill from watching it. Imagine a medical team from another part of Asia doing 1000 (yes, one thousand) cataract surgeries in 10 (ten!) days, just because they enjoy bringing sight to the sightless. Imagine multitudes of Koreans seeing for the first time in their lives!

What's so bad about that? Keep imagining. Before the bandages are taken off, the patients are reminded that it is through the good graces of The Dear Leader that all this is taking place. As these horribly brainwashed folks see their first light of day, the first image upon which they are to focus is a picture of the "Dear Leader". According to script, they run and jump to the picture, bow down, raise their hands, scream, and thank Kim Jong Il for their healing.

What shall we do? How shall we pray? Oh God, how sick You must also be to see one robbing You of the glory that is Yours! Our hearts are heavy with You. Show us Your plan. How long oh Lord, for North Korea to see as You intended and see what You intended?

29. Bible balloons invade nk

It's been going on for many years. Bright orange balloons bearing Scriptures in the Korean language float over the northern border of South Korea into the southern section of North Korea. No DMZ mine field can stop them. NorthKorea's 1 million man army never shoots them down. Angry-faced soldiers can't stare them away. They glide for miles at a time filled with helium and punctured by an ever-so-small opening that guides them almost scientifically to designated portions of the Hermit Kingdom.

Delighted children find them in a field and run them home to aging grandmas and grandpas who weep over them, if they are of the remnant church still surviving in horror-land. Or they puzzle over them if they are of the great majority who have been brainwashed and totally uninformed about the outside world.

Hundreds of thousands of these plastic missionaries have been sent out by dedicated South Koreans and their missionary cohorts . No one knows the full effect of their flights, but reports confirm that at least some have found their mark. Lives have been touched forever! The government simply cannot keep the Word of God out. It is not bound. A little comes in on airwaves. A little on tapes. A few Bibles get where they were intended to go. Oh the precious life-giving Word of God! Let us pray for the success of this "foolish" balloon ministry which is confounding the "wise" regime of death.

[update 6-16-08... This project has recently been replaced by the sending of heavier balloons actually filled with tracts]

30. pitfalls of nk ministry

I'm told that when one enters the struggle for the lives of this isolated nation, he/she may be up against more than bargained for. North Korea is a Satanic stronghold on earth the likes of which does not come around every day. The fate of this nation will determine the fate of many nations, and the enemy is strategically and therefore firmly entrenched there, or so he thinks. One nod from the Father and a host of angels will be released to defeat him and change the course of history. For this we enter into spiritual warfare, never forgetting to address the day to day suffering of the people.

Many questions begin to form as the battle is waged as to the nature of the struggle, when one gets beyond prayer. Perhaps many will not get beyond prayer since the spiritual battle is the only one that counts ultimately. For those who feel called to give material aid or assist in escapes, what happens if:

-a person that you are helping tries to escape and is killed, or imprisoned for life?

-a person you are assisting does come out, but his family left behind is rounded up and imprisoned or executed?

-you are asked to "pay off" a lot of criminal mafia types and to bribe guards to get your person out?

-they succeed in getting to South Korea or even America, and become so engrossed in worldliness that they lose the precious faith that once saw them through every difficulty?

-you yourself get caught up in emaciated bodies and forget the higher calling of ministering to emaciated souls?

-you get so involved in people "over there" that you forget the hurting around you? (All of the above have happened, multiple times!) Then must come the question, of course, is the hurting around me to be compared with the pain of a North Korean? Will your wife or children be pleased with your answer to that question? What about the cross? you will eventually ask. Am I a soldier of the cross or are those only soldiers who must pay for their warfare in starvation, torture and death? Hard, hard questions for one who falls in love with North Korea. Do I love her because Christ loves her or because I "feel good" loving her? Is my love "romantic", unreal, unconnected, or do I have scars to show for it?

Thankfully for my readers, I stopped being an expert years ago. The questions I have asked must be tackled by those who hear them.

31. Is it God's open door?

To those who would touch a needy nation:

An available position does not always mean an open door. Men can open doors too. And shut them. The doors that God opens cannot be opened by men. Or shut.

Guys that are blessed with looks, charm, and all the rest, will have any number of "open doors" into a woman's heart. Although these are issues with which I have never had to deal, I can well imagine a line-up of females, each one telling my heart, "She is THE ONE." At least, in my dreams I can imagine such things!

A multi-talented person seeking employment will face the same dilemma.

But consider Paul (I Corinthians 16:9). "An open door has been set before me, and there are many adversaries." That is *true* vision. Paul was not "excited" about going through his open door. He was determined. He did not see all happy scenes. Paul's ministry was a series of incredible victories always coupled with incredible suffering. Those who go through open doors because they are "excited" about "helping Jesus" need to go somewhere and count the cost. If the cross is not a part of the call, it is probably a human door, not a Divine one.

Also, doors in the Scripture are entry-ways to the furtherance of the Gospel, not personal furtherance. When the "vision" sees a human elevated and Christ negotiable, it's not God's vision. When one sees a road of hardship but Christ lifted up, good things can follow.

There are, I have found, many doors open to North Korea. I have leaped for joy to know I can be of use in this dry and thirsty land. It would be the same for anyone reading who wants to go. There IS something for us to do! But which door is ours? I counsel myself and anyone who cares to listen: Walk carefully in the Spirit before the momentous decision is made. Listen carefully to what God is saying and to what various men are saying too. If the "call" does not "fit" and you find yourself volunteering to do *someone else's work* just to "be used", much damage can come your way, and to the ministry. The Lord of the harvest knows just where we belong. Some of us may well be asked to stay right here and pay the bills of those who go... but if Christ is glorified, so be it.

Bottom line, LORD save your people! Lord deliver the prisoners! Lord, whatever it takes, whomever it takes, however you want it done, oh just DO IT!

32. return to animal farm

1945. George Orwell. The days of Stalin. Orwell was not a believer in Christ and in fact thought that Marx and Engels really had something going. His issue was not with Communism but with the way this new Communist theory was being acted out by Lenin, Stalin, and the rest. It was obviously not working according to the original script. Some would argue that the original script came from Christ Himself. Equality. Peace. Brotherhood. You share with me, I share with you. But not at the point of a gun. That was added later.

Anyway, Orwell was an honest man who wanted to say something about the Stalinist regime of his day. He said it most effectively in his satirical novel, Animal Farm. There is a film version (1999) which I happened onto last evening. My wife and I sat in amazement as scene after scene reminded us, not of Stalin, but of the original and present dynastic regimes of North Korea... and actually this cycle is repeated in many places of the planet.

- the original corruption needing addressing
- the desire to end that corruption and bring justice in its place
- the bringing down of the corrupt society
- the hero worship, shifting empasis from the genuine needs of the people to the growing neurotic needs of the leader
- the slow replacement of the old corruption with a new and worse corruption It's all there, in North Korea, as we speak.

And Christians, myself for one, pray, "Lord, stop this man! Bring him down!" Praying believer, does your mind travel beyond his fall (and all leaders eventually do fall) to what shall be on the other side of a regime change? We know Jesus shall be King over all the earth.

"Jesus shall reign where'er the sun Doth his successive journeys run,

His kingdom stretch from shore to shore, Till moons shall wax and wane no more!"

What a glorious day is coming! All those who rejected His rule will themselves be rejected eternally. The world will be put right side up!

But what if Jesus' coming is not the next thing on God's calendar? What if the present ruler is to be replaced by another merely human leader? I believe we should pray earnestly for that man to be a righteous man, a man whose relationship to God is real and strong. Then when North Korea turns around, God Himself will receive all the glory!

33. the prisons of nk

It is what the Bible says: "Remember the prisoners..." I have to keep them before me on a regular basis or I forget. American life is brutal in its "pursuit of happiness." Pleasure and comfort are the gods we lift up here. Christians must be careful not to get caught up in it all and lose sight of the lowly Christ, still suffering in His people. Here is a picture painted by David Hawk in his latest book, Concentrations of Humanity. *Published by Freedom House, the work shows how Kim Jong Il is guilty of crimes against humanity and needs to be brought to   justice.*
Of course, our concern is the pain of our people, many of whom suffer in these prisons...

"The penal labor encampments are located in the mountains and mountain valleys in the remote interior of north and north central North Korea. They cover huge areas, miles long and wide. The outer perimeters are surrounded by barbed wire and guard towers, except where the mountain ranges are considered impassable. The encampments have multiple thousands of prisoners who are housed in scattered areas or discrete villages for different categories of prisoners in the valleys or at the foot of the mountains. Single prisoners live in dormitories and eat in cafeterias. The families live in tiny shacks, sometimes multiple families to a single dwelling...

"Prisoners come into the camps in one of two ways. Suspected wrong-doers or wrong thinkers are picked up by officers of the State Security Agency...detained in small cells and subjected to intense and prolonged interrogation, almost always accompanied by beatings and severe torture, after which they are dispatched to one of the prison labor camps. Initially, at the camp they express relief at being able to supplement their meager rations by eating grass and other edible plants and being able to stand up and walk around...

"...The new prisoners coming straight from North Korean society describe their shock at what they see: walking skeletons, covered in dirt with matted hair (from the inability to bathe or wash regularly), dressed in tatters and rags, many with hunched backs from bent over farm labor, and many hobbling about on stick crutches having lost arms and legs to mining or logging accidents, or minus fingers or toes lost to frostbite. It will be only a matter of months before all the food stores the new prisoners have brought from home are consumed, and all the clothing and household goods have been bartered away for food, until all they have left from their previous civilian life are the clothes on their back and the shoes on their feet. And these would shortly be dirt-covered, tattered and torn.

"These prisoners put considerable mental anguish into trying to figure out what precisely caused their family this dreadful turn of fate..."

God have mercy on Your people. And those who don't know you yet, save and rescue body soul and spirit. Bring great deliverance in North Korea! And help us not to forget, and to share some of this mental anguish with them...

34. roaring mice, naked kings, and the dane-geld

Once one is tuned in to the North Korea crisis, there is no end to the connections that begin to form, the reminders, the warnings, the obvious comparisons...

Take the 60's *The Mouse That Roared* . It was an awful movie, but the story line based on the original book sounds very much like someone we know. The head of a miniscule government decides to wage war on the United States, deliberately lose, and sit back and collect all the goodies that the great and forgiving U.S. government always doles out to its enemies (Japan, for example).

Or what about Hans Christian Andersen's classic, *The Emperor's New Clothes?* A proud king refuses to hear obvious truths from his advisors or people and makes an absolute fool of himself.

But in the light of current talk about yet another coming meeting of the great powers, where promises will be made and threats will be submitted and aid will be extorted from nations who fear North Korea's weapons, the following Kipling poem is the most appropriate piece for the day:

It is always a temptation to a rich and lazy nation, To puff and look important and to say:

"Though we know we should defeat you, we have not the time to meet you,

We will therefore pay you cash to go away."

And that is called paying the Dane-geld*;

But we've proved it again and again,

That if once you have paid him the Dane-geld

You never get rid of the Dane.

So when you are requested To pay up or be molested, You will find it better policy to say:

"We never pay anyone Dane-geld, No matter how trifling the cost;

For the end of that game is oppression and shame, And the nation that plays it is lost!"

English tax paid to Danish-led Vikings to keep them from raiding English lands.

35. the aquariums of pyongyang

Thirty or so years ago a 10-year-old boy entered a North Korean labor camp with his family. He lived to tell about it, the first story of its kind: *The Aquariums of Pyongyang,* by Kang Chol-Hwan.

The family was among the many that had, a generation earlier, relocated in Japan and become strong supporters there of Socialism, Communism, and North Korea . With the rise of Kim Il Sung, the family was enticed to come back to the fatherland and complete the reforms so badly needed there.

This very rich but very dedicated family moved back to a near hero's welcome. But growing suspicions about their wealth and their connection to the traditional foe of Korea slowly led the family from fame to ghastly impoverishment.

The entire family was arrested and a new life begun in one of Kim's infamous reeducation centers.

To get to a North Korean Camp, one must be either "a land-holder, a capitalist, a U.S. or South Korean agent, a Christian, or members of purged Party circles deemed noxious to the state." Division is made then between "redeemable" and "unredeemable" prisoners. Once classed unredeemable, life is over. Your only worth to the state is hard labor. You will be taken to work at secret sites since there is no hope of you taking those secrets anywhere but to the grave. You will work until you drop dead.

Redeemables, like Kang, have a chance. They are taught Kim propaganda. They are thoroughly redone in their thinking processes, and after a number of years, released to live their new life as a trusted member of society.

I present all these horrid but true stories on this site to encourage you to pray for North Koreans, that in their distress they will call upon the Name of the Lord, and that in calling they will unleash the Power that the Kim dynasty cannot withstand. Oh what a day of reckoning is coming to those who have abused humanity and the children of the living God!

More about Kang Chol-Hwan another time...

36. *you gotta be crazy to try to escape*

Yes, all of North Korea is a prison, if by prison one means a place from which escape is unlikely and conditions are difficult. But there are prisons within the prison, such as the Yodok camp in the northeastern section of the country. We continue our trek through *The Aquariums of Pyongyang* with a look at the escape possibilities:

When 10-year-old Kang Chol-Hwan arrived at the camp he was "educated" quickly about what to expect by another "kid.":(p. 56-57)

"The kid then returned to the subject of escape, which was clearly dear to his heart. Only once had he heard the sirens go off and seen the security agents form into search parties and head up into the mountains. It took a while, but they eventually came down with their prey. The escaping prisoner had been stopped midcourse, well short of the summits he had hoped might spell freedom. He was tortured for a week or two, then executed.

" ' The punishment for attempted escape is execution. No exceptions. The guards make the whole village come out to watch it... 'Yeah, you gotta be really crazy to try to escape. On the other hand, sometimes you gotta be even crazier to stay, especially if you're all alone, without family or friends. The work is hard, and there's hardly ever enough food to take the edge off your hunger... You'll have to stick together, help each other out- and remember, don't trust anyone.' "

And then from the "brigade leader" in charge of orientation: "You people don't deserve to live, but the Party and our Great Leader have given you a chance to redeem yourselves. Don't squander it and don't disappoint him."

What were you doing as a ten-year-old? Can the worst of our childhood memories compare to this?

Pray for North Korea

37. going to school in a forced labor camp

Facts gleaned from *The Aquariums of Pyongyang* by Kang Chol-Hwan, 2000.

Why go to school at all? Because the North Korean government believes you are worth saving if only you can be re-programmed. Here are some odds and ends about what it means to be a student in a concentration camp:

-teachers show total disregard for well-being of student

-address us in the harshest, crudest manner. ("Hey, you idiot in the third row.")

-"It was quite common for them to beat us."

-teachers wear revolvers. start with yelling, graduate to insults, then to beatings.

-asking questions of the teacher can earn you a slap across the face, to the delight of your fellow students.

-among school punishments is latrine duty. Tardy students can get a week of such.

-a boy who complained of such duty and insulted the instructor was beaten savagely until he fell into a septic tank. With much effort he got out. no one cared to help clean or heal him. A few days later he died.

-day begins before 7 with clean-up of room by students. 7 to noon, studies. one hour rest. minimal food. rest of the day, manual labor.

-quota system. groups (of 5) not released until quota reached.

North Korea needs some more good news, don't you think? We have it. How shall we get it to them?

38. how dare you die before we kill you

Still trekking through "The Aquariums of Pyongyang" (Kang Chol-Hwan), and what a ghastly journey our friend leads us through!

He writes on page 99 and ff: "Suicide was not uncommon in the camp. A number of our neighbors took that road out of Yodok. They usually left behind letters criticizing the regime, or at the very least its Security Force. They were heedless acts which virtually guaranteed that the letter writer's family would be sent to a place worse still than Yodok. Truth be told, some form of punishment would await the family regardless of whether or not a critical note were left behind. It was a rule that admitted no exceptions.

"The Party saw suicide as an attempt to escape its grasp, and if the individual who had tried the trick wasn't around to pay for it, someone else needed to be found. Some suicides tried to palliate the punishment their relatives faced by leaving notes in which they maintained their innocence but reiterated their faith in communism and in the regime of the much-beloved Great Leader. This sometimes induced the agents to treat the surviving family with relative leniency and merely add five extra years to the family's original sentence, whose length they, in any case, never knew."

These are the workings of sickness, my friends. There's a word for people who are so insecure that they feel compelled to punish someone else for the (supposed) crime of another person. How far has this sickness spread through the country? Christ, the Healer of men's minds, is the only answer for North Koreans.

39. how to eat salamander

Occasionally I have cautioned you of weak heart not to read . Today I must excuse those who are of weak stomach.

From "The Aquariums of Pyongyang" from which I have been quoting for a few days now, the following description of how some overcame starvation and its resultant health deterioration. Author Kang, in a concentration camp with his family, has been put on an outside detail. Normally outdoor work would be stimulating but this particular assignment has to do with burial of the many who die on a regular basis in this camp.

"The work did have one benefit, though it usually came too late to help the weakest among us. In the fields, it was sometimes possible for us to catch frogs, which were plentiful in this season. The amphibian could be skinned and cooked fresh or set out to dry in the sun and used later. Their eggs were also very much in demand.

"Besides the frogs, we also ate salamanders that we caught near a sweet-water spring. I never much liked the way they tasted, but they were said to be very nutritious. Eating three a day was supposed to keep you in great shape, like vitamin concentrates, though I have no idea whether this was science or faith.

"The way to eat a salamander is to grab it by the tail and swallow it in one quick gulp - before it can discharge a foul-tasting liquid. I often brought my grandmother salamanders so that she would stay healthy, but she never got the knack of swallowing them whole. We kids were the only ones who could do it easily.

"We ate anything that moved, making even the undiscriminating adults look picky by comparison. By the time a group of prisoners finished working a field, no animal was left alive. Even earthworms were fair game. When we were done with her, nature always needed a couple of seasons to recuperate before she could provide a fresh bounty of food. And yet our hunger remained, piercing, draining."

I won't have time or space to tell you of the rats that became a likewise prized meal. Besides that, it's just too awful. Yes, Yodok still stands, as far as we know. Maybe up to 200,000 prisoners still eat rats and worms, still bury countless dead, still prefer suicide to staying in this evil world any longer. Pray for Yodok, will you?

40. confessions in a communist camp

One more look at "The Aquariums of Pyongyang" and then I really need to get this book back to the library. Hope you can check it out yourself soon...

As one more example of how the North Korean government makes a mockery of, by trying to duplicate, the Christian faith, consider the biweekly "criticism and self-criticism" sessions.

"[the sessions] were nothing new to me. Such meetings took place in every North Korean school... But outside the camp, these ideological exercises tended to be peaceable and rather formal in nature. Nothing much happened if you didn't criticize well enough or happened to criticize too sharply. At Yodok, the stakes were much higher. Punishments consisted of hours of nighttime wood chopping, even for ten- and thirteen-year-old children...

"...At the far end of the room was a platform with a table where the prisoner sat to present his self-criticism. Next to the table stood two guards, along with a representative of the prisoners. There were no other chairs in the room. The other prisoners sat on the floor in groups of five, clustered with their fellow team members. The assembly hall was always overcrowded. Some prisoners dozed off, others became nauseous from the intensity of the body odor that hung in the air - there was no soap at Yodok...

"...The prelude to the ceremony varied somewhat, but the main action was always the same. The wrongdoer would step onto the platform, his head bowed, and launch into his self-criticism with a fool-proof formula such as 'Our Great

Leader commanded us...' followed by one of Kim's great 'Thoughts.' "

Then, says the author, the speaker would tell how he had broken faith with that thought. (In our confessions we would call that "sin". The parallel is so real as to be scary.) Then he would pledge some "penance", as we might say, some proof of reform or change. "I will wake up a half hour earlier and make myself equal to the task of fulfilling [Kim's] orders. I will renew myself," etc. etc.

If the prisoner succeeded in criticizing himself well enough he would then be allowed to criticize others. If not, members of the audience could criticize him further. And, "If the accused tried to defend himself, a third prisoner, and if necessary, a fourth, was selected to take up the assault.

"...it was hard to take [the sessions] seriously - despite the perfect silence imposed by the hard gaze of the guards. We were like bored kids in a class they find meaningless. The smallest distraction would set us off." He then relates how some member of the group might suddenly pass gas. The guards would become outraged, asking for the "guilty" party to identify himself.

When he did, he would be "pushed toward the self-criticism table to expiate his gas-passing with a mea culpa, at the end of which he usually received a week's worth of supplementary work detail."

Enough.If you want to know about public executions, postmortem stonings, forced abortions, and how the author finally escapes to China and then South Korea, you'll have to read it on your own.

Meanwhile know again that Yodok, and many other camps, still exist, still torture and kill your brothers and sisters in Jesus. Let's pray.

41. *you are what you eat*

We become what we ingest, whether the food of the body or the food of the mind. Read the following and be thankful that you live in a land of free press. Oh we have our prejudices and our perspectives, but what you are about to read is the solid diet of an average North Korean. These precious folk grow up hating everything Western, even to the point of "biting the hand" of those who would feed them. Jesus says, "You will know the truth and the truth will set you free." Join with me in praying that Jesus - the Truth- will be preached all over the towns and villages of the "Hermit Kingdom." What a day of rejoicing THAT will be!

Now, if you dare, from the Korea Central "News" Agency, March 25: *U.S. and S. Korean Warmongers' DPRK-Targeted War Exercises Assailed Pyongyang, March 25 (KCNA) - A spokesman for the Korean National Peace Committee released a statement on Sunday to denounce the U.S. and south Korean warmongers for staging the DPRK-targeted RSOI and field mobile exercise in south Korea defying strong protest. The launch of the above-said war maneuvers is a product of deliberately planned and systematic moves of the U.S. and south Korean bellicose forces to prevent the desire for peace and reconciliation from growing stronger and escalate tension on the Korean Peninsula in a bid to frustrate the process of dialogue and peace and, furthermore, ignite a war, the statement said, and continued:*

The above-said RSOI and field mobile exercise is an extension of the moves to provoke a war against the DPRK and an extremely dangerous preliminary war, a test nuclear war before going over to an actual war. This saber-rattling just launched behind the curtain of "dialogue" and "peace" is a very rude act proving their utter lack of good faith and courtesy and an unpardonable perfidy to the dialogue partner.

This clearly indicates that the U.S. and south Korean authorities' talk about "dialogue" and "improved relations" is nothing but hypocrisy and they are still persisting in their hostile policy toward the DPRK and confrontation with it. The army and people of the DPRK will bolster the self-defensive deterrence for defending the dignity and sovereignty of the Korean nation to cope with the provocative moves of the U.S. and south Korean warmongers for a war of aggression against it.

If the aggressors ignite a war on this land, the army and people of the DPRK will resolutely retaliate against them with merciless deadly blows. The U.S. would be well advised to stop at once its reckless war exercises against the DPRK, which are harmful to the settlement of the nuclear issue and peace of the Korean Peninsula and driving the situation to a phase of confrontation and war. The south Korean authorities should immediately halt their criminal acts of participating in the war moves of the outside forces against the Korean nation and peace, well aware that their involvement in the outside forces-led saber-rattling against the fellow countrymen is a treacherous act of driving the inter-Korean relations to a collapse in violation of the June 15 joint declaration.

Oh my. Talk to you later.

42. the song of general kim il sung

There was a time when North Koreans sang the praises of One Who is worthy. The good news is that although they sing the following to one who is unworthy, at least these are a people who will praise. Our job is to pray and work for the Name of the Lord Jesus Christ to once more be lifted up in old Choson. Kim Il Sung, you recall, is the father of the present leader of North Korea. Trained by Russia, and propped up by Russia and China, and set up unwittingly by our own government, this man stole the heart and soul of the Korean people living in the northern part of the peninsula. Yet, brainwashed and afraid, today they sing this "immortal revolutionary hymn" to him:

Starting with that three-word description, see how many words you can find in the following that are lifted directly from Christian thought.

Song of General Kim Il Sung

Bright traces of blood on the crags of Changback still gleam,
Still the Amnok carries along signs of blood in its stream,
Still do those hallowed traces shine resplendently,
Over Korea ever flourishing and free.
So dear to all our hearts is our General's glorious name,
Our own beloved Kim Il Sung of undying fame.
Tell, blizzards that rage in the wild Manchurian plains,
Tell, you nights in forests deep where the silence reigns,
Who is the partisan whose deeds are unsurpassed?
Who is the patriot whose fame shall ever last?
He severed the chains of the masses, brought them liberty,
The sun of korea today, democratic and free,
For the Twenty Points united we stand fast,
Over our fair homeland spring has come at last!
(words by Ri Chan)

Can you believe this? Flourishing? Free? Democratic? Spring? Read any news or commentary on North Korea. The truth is so obvious!

How does this message flourish? Easy. Close the doors and windows. Unplug computers and TV's. Hush the newspapers. Don't let anyone know what the world is really like outside our little paradise. Foster hate for all nations except ours. Even people of the same skin and language a few miles down the road, they are all evil! They all lie. Only I tell you the truth! Even when they come to help us, it is for hidden reasons. Actually we don't even need their help... Enough.

Please pray for North Korea's true liberation today.

43. *unimaginable poverty*

Today, take a look at the word "spiritual" in North Korean thought. Not only is the following piece a proof of the clear effort of Kim and company to rob God of his place in men's lives, it is also evidence of the unimaginable poverty of North Korea. When the only "spiritual" product of a nation is a mortal man and his equally mortal son, I say that nation is truly poor.

You may wonder about the wisdom of helping to spread this propaganda by printing it so fully and freely. I suppose there are some treatises of the enemy that are so subtle and crafty that I would not want to confuse the innocent by promoting them. Pieces like this one are so obvious that I feel the very poison is antidote against the disease. By the way, some of the following is probably true. It is how this man has interpreted the facts that brings us once more to the desire to keep praying for North Korea. From "Korea Today" website:

Spiritual mainstay is essential for a person all his life.

After my father died in battle in the Korean War (June 1950-July 1953) provoked by the US imperialists when I was four, I grew up under the care of my mother alone.

Now that I lost my father, I felt disappointed about my future though I was too young to know why. But the country saw to it that my desire came into fulfillment after learning at schools and university, and that I have lived a worthwhile life as an unassuming man of merit, the chief of an enterprise, and a representative to a power organ.

My children also studied free of charge under the benefit of the 11-year compulsory education system to become fine officials. The efforts I made to repay the great care of the country have filled my life.

I received three diplomas of invention and certificates of new-technology register and introduction, 38 certificates of innovations, three certificates of scientific and technological exploits, two gold medals and two silver medals, and the Master of Science degree. All of these are attributable to the care of the country, not my efforts.

I have a watch and a gold ring that bear the august names of President Kim Il Sung and the leader Kim Jong Il respectively. I still remember what my mother said in happy tears when I was elected to the municipal people's assembly-that our family and I were always having happy events as we were living up to the belief in Kim Jong Il alone.

It is not confined to my family alone. Today, we Korean people keenly feel that the country is just Kim Jong Il, and have a firm belief that their happiness of today and their destiny are guaranteed by his Songun politics.

Over the recent years our people suffered the greatest tragedy in the nation's history; we were faced with overlapping threats and blackmails and blockade enforced by the enemies. At that time, Kim Jong Il, turning the adversity into bliss by means of Songun politics, called upon the nation to rise for prosperity of the country.

I often say to my children, "I have worked with enthusiasm thanks to the leader Kim Jong Il who has defended and brought fame to my life. His is a wide and warm embrace that holds not only our family but all our people. He is our spiritual mainstay."

Written by: Ri Jae Han, manager of the Tongdaewon Daily Necessities Factory Honoured with Three-Revolution Red Flag

44. women for north korea

Any ladies want to move to North Korea?

The following is from the "Korea Today" website, a propaganda piece in English put out by the NK government. *Here the Leader of North Korea praises and encourages the country's women, failing to tell of the women who do not "make it" by his standard, and are placed in his torture work camps for "re-education".*

"As a chariot fails to move with only one wheel, so human society can hardly develop with the strength of the men alone. The women are obliged to turn one of the wheels of the 'revolutionary chariot'. This was what President Kim Il Sung used to say.

"The Korean women have now become a powerful force for revolution and construction, retaining their integrity as the flower of everyday life, flower of the nation and flower of the era."

(Unreported: Those who must get out of NK or die, and who are then often sold into a life of slavery in Big Brother China.)

"During the 'Arduous March' and the forced march the Korean women were compelled to bear a great burden for lack of food, power and fuel.

"They were often seen spooning their own small portions of food out to their husbands and children, wearing a smile on their faces. Yet their devotion was not limited to their own families. They shared with their neighbours whatever they had-even a handful of grain-adopted orphaned children, married disabled soldiers and looked after helpless old people. The Korean women were scrupulous in keeping harmony in and out of their families."

(Here omitted is the story of the "arduous march" of thousands upon thousands of North Koreans who yearly take the trek out of North Korea, willing even to risk death to get away. They lose families and all that is precious to a woman because of the government's desire to have a great military)

"The world 'marathon queen' Jong Song Ok demonstrated to the whole world how strong the Korean women were spiritually and physically. Hyon Yong Ra, Doctor of Science, spent all her youthful years working on a scientific research task, and Labour Heroine Pak Ok Hui from Jagang Province created a paradigm of the double- and three-crop farming.

"There are many such examples found among the Korean women: some raised scores of pigs year after year and sent them all to the workers at socialist construction sites; and others carried out steady production by supplying power on their own, maintaining clean environment in and out of their workplace and creating enjoyable life.

"In particular, the spirit and traits of military officers' wives, always putting the country before their families and dedicating themselves solely to the national defence, are models of the time for all the women to follow."

(Tell of the other heroines, Dear Leader. Tell of those who suffer in agony because they dare to follow another Leader who is more dear to them than even you, the Man

Christ Jesus. Tell of the "tail-less" animals that one of your citizens wrote about after escaping from prison and from your nation)

"Then, what made the women, the alleged name of sympathy for their frailty, strong enough to overcome untold difficulties and trials optimistically?

"It is attributable to the leader Kim Jong Il's policy to hold the women in social respect true to the intention of President Kim Il Sung who empowered them to have equal political rights and freedom with the men by adopting the Law on Sex Equality..."

Is it possible that one known the world over for depriving millions of their rights speaks of the equality of the sexes? We have heard all this before. Russia, Eastern Europe, China, Cuba... But the dear people of NK have been brainwashed so long that many of them truly believe this man.

Oh pray for this dark place. God truly is able to change things. And whatever He says to you to do, do!

45. *mirror, mirror*

In a late '97 Korean publication, you will find the following bit of information. Blanks to be filled in later. Grammatical errors will remain as published.

"The world people say that _____ Korea is the 'worst backward country in politics' at the end of the 20th century.

Above all, this is illustrated by the fact that _____ Korea is the last colony when the 20th century is coming to an end... its political backwardness finds its expression in... one-man and one-party dictatorships and clan government...Its political backwardness also finds its expression in ...fascist, murderous and repressive politics...

"In _____ Korea, barbaric tortures and murder, the worst human rights violations of medieval type, are institutionally inspired and tolerated by law... the bloodshed [names 2 incidents] of last year are anti-people crimes without an equal in the world, which concentrically reveal the anti-people, fascist and barbaric nature of the _____ Korean ruling system...

It is only too natural that the world people brand _____ Korea as a politically underdeveloped country without an equal in the world, a 'political infant' and a 'society below third class.' It is the historical truth that the government based on absolute power and corrupt politics... will never last long and its ruin is inevitable."

Now think carefully before you decide. Should we fill in all the blanks with the word "North" or the word "South"? While you are thinking, remember that there are persons in the world who manufacture their own truths. Truth is what they say it is. The people under them must simply "believe."

I've given you plenty of time. What do you say? You got it! The word is "SOUTH!" This mad raving, that perfectly describes NORTH KOREA was actually copied from a NORTH KOREAN propaganda publication called "Rodong Sinmun" (by way of Belke's *Juche*) and is meant to describe Kim Jong Il's neighbors to the south!

Can you imagine it? Until we can, there is no way we will understand what has happened to the precious enslaved people of the northern portion of the Korean peninsula.

Let's keep praying! God IS able!

46. of righteous nations

"Blessed is the nation whose God is Jehovah." Psalm 33:12.

That's not just poetry, that's revelation from Heaven. Is there a nation on earth totally sold out to God?If it is not prospering now, look for it to soon.

America truly holds the records for churches, missions, and most other Christian categories. God has spared her from the worst of judgments so far, and prospered her beyond her means to contain it. There are seeds of self-destruction here, (abortion, homosexuality, sexual perversion, and worst of all , a weakening church) but so far God has stayed His hand.

By contrast, North Korea has been forced into the worship of a man. What can be said about a nation whose God is anyone but Jehovah?

"Righteousness exalts a nation..." Proverbs 14:34 The opposite is true, too. Genesis 20 tells the story of a "righteous", that is, morally good man and nation that had fallen into disfavor with God because of its unsuspecting mistreatment of Abraham. Because Abimelech and Gerar were ignorant of what they were doing, God spared and continued to bless that nation when Abimelech cried out, "Will you slay a righteous nation?".

No. No curse . Until later. In II Chronicles the area around Gerar attacked the nation of Judah under King Asa, a righteous man. To attack the righteous knowingly is to incur the wrath of God and later Gerar was decimated.

North Korea needs to understand that if it attacks God's people knowingly, only problems will ensue. "Sin is a reproach to any people," says God. (Proverbs 14:34). On the other hand, a former Pyongyang prospered as the Gospel was allowed throughout the land.

Nations rise and fall under the clear direction of God. He is longsuffering, patient, but judgment always comes when men and their domains turn their backs on Him.

Let's ask God to raise up righteousness in North Korea. One thing for sure, any nation exalting itself above the excellency of Jesus Christ needs to take these words to heart:

"The kingdoms of this world [will] become the kingdoms of our Lord and of His Christ!" Handel did not make that up, it's from the book of Revelation, 11:15. Some day righteousness will be exalted all over this globe. I am looking forward with great joy to that day!

47. God's billion-man army

There are a lot of Psalms that I would like to read to a North Korean. The Book of Psalms was written largely under duress by suffering saints who trusted God for their deliverance. Take number 37 for example, by King David.

"Don't worry about evildoers... they will soon be cut down like the grass."

"Dwell in the land, and feed on His faithfulness."

"Rest in the Lord and wait patiently for Him."

"Evildoers shall be cut off... but those who wait on the Lord shall inherit the earth!"

Verse 25 may give some people pause. I admit I struggled awhile with it, knowing what I do about the situation in North Korea:

"I have been young and now am old; yet I have not seen the righteous forsaken, nor his descendants begging bread."

Have the righteous been forsaken in North Korea? Oh no! Not at all! We who know God know that in our worst moments He is there with encouragement, refreshment, hope and material aid as needed. We believe that such is the case with saints in this prison land. We see with the eyes of Elisha who refused to use mortal sight and could envision the hosts of angels surrounding him, giving him the majority in every battle.

With God's Spirit, God's angels, and the provision of God's people coming in from all over the planet as the need of North Korea is presented to the Body of Christ, how can these saints be considered forsaken?

We are not intimidated by a one-million man NK army. The very gates of hell cannot prevail against the church of Jesus Christ, wherever it is. We fear not those who kill the body but cannot touch the soul. Oppressors, without knowing it, are creating martyrs and heroes whose glory will shine forever. They are sending people out into eternity where they cannot touch them ever again but where they will be embraced by the Father Himself. They are rousing the worldwide church into action. In other words, they do the very opposite of what they want to do! They are building the church, not destroying it.

How marvelous are God's ways! He can take a hardened Pharaoh and get glory from him. A Christian-killing Saul of Tarsus is putty in his hands. We know not how the NK saga will end, but we know that God's glory will be gotten one way or another.

Psalm 37 again: "The salvation of the righteous is from the Lord; He is their strength in the time of trouble, and the Lord shall help them and deliver them; He shall deliver them from the wicked, and save them, because they trust in Him!"

48. lamentations, north korean style

Reading through the prophets recently I was struck with the plaintive wailing of Jeremiah for his people and the strange similarity to weeping going on around the world for North Korea. Israel had sinned and was being punished. Whether God's people in Korea have sinned or are being persecuted or both, for sure they are in similar pain, and they cry out to us to weep with them, and with the One Who has always wept for His hurting people. Let us join in... (Jeremiah 8:18-9:1)

I would comfort myself in sorrow. My heart is faint in me. Listen! The voice, the cry of the daughter of my people from a far country:... "The harvest is past, the summer is ended, and we are not saved!" For the hurt of the daughter of my people I am hurt. I am mourning; astonishment has taken hold of me. Is there no balm in Gilead, is there no physician there? Why then is there no recovery for the health of the daughter of my people? (Lamentations 1:9-12,16) ..."O Lord, behold my affliction, for the enemy has magnified himself!" The adversary has spread his hand over all her pleasant things..... All her people sigh, they seek bread; they have given their valuables for food to restore life. See, O Lord, and consider...

Is it nothing to you, all you who pass by? Behold and see if there is any sorrow like my sorrow, which has been brought on me, which the Lord has inflicted on me...

For these things I weep; my eye, my eye overflows with water because the comforter, who should restore my life, is far from me. My children are desolate because the enemy prevailed.

But there is good news, too. Hope! In the midst of the despair: (Lamentations 3:22-26)

Through the Lord's mercies we are not consumed, because His compassions fail not. They are new every morning; great is Your faithfulness. "The Lord is my portion," says my soul, "Therefore I hope in Him!." The Lord is good to those who wait for Him, to the soul who seeks Him. It is good that one should hope and wait quietly for the salvation of the Lord...

We wait, Lord. Show us if there is something we can do while we are waiting. Purge our hearts and make us all willing - on this side or that side of the world - to serve you with our whole body, mind, soul and strength. in Jesus' Name, Amen

49. we've waited 40 years for communion

[From day 92 of Extreme Devotion, a devotional put out by Voice of the Martyrs, about an incident that occurred several years back in North Korea]

"What is it?" the missionary asked his friend while preparing to go into North Korea.

"Just take it. You'll know when to open it."

Disguised as a businessman, the missionary journeyed into North Korea. He was assigned a Communist guide who had a habit of taking long naps! Seeing his opportunity, the missionary quietly left the hotel while his "guide" slept. He entered a nearby village and met up with a small group of believers. As soon as they realized the young missionary was an ordained minister, they said, "You must baptize us! We have waited for someone to baptize us!"

In a land where possessing a Bible can mean a fifteen-year sentence, a formal baptism could mean certain death. Without any lake or river nearby, the missionary simply prayed over the believers one by one as a symbol of their faith.

But to his amazement they were not satisfied. "We have waited forty years for Communion." One of the believers immediately brought out some rice cakes. The missionary thought, "They had a 'baptism' without water, maybe they could have Communion without drink."

Then he remembered the "gift" his friend handed him before going into North Korea. He quickly grabbed his travel bag and took out the package - a bottle of wine. Speechless, each villager wept openly, praising God for His timely gift.

[I've been an advocate for believer baptism (in water!) for 50 years plus. I still am. But I've never lived in North Korea. I still can't comprehend the price of being a Christian there. I am spoiled. And I'm not alone. Let us continue to weep and pray, not only for believers such as these, but for our own coldness of heart as we live in such abundance. In every nation, those, and only those, who draw near to God will find God drawing near to them.]

50. beaten to death for bringing in a Bible

"They begged and begged me, but I couldn't give it to them, " said the man. "I know Christians are supposed to share, but I just couldn't part with it." He sadly held out his hand so that his listener could see his prized possession.

"I really wanted to, but I couldn't. You see, people in North Korea told me that they have been praying for fifty years to get a Bible. But I didn't give them mine because I had been praying for twenty years, and I had just gotten it from a pastor in South Korea."

He sighed deeply as his mind went to the needy believers in North Korea desperately praying for one copy of the Bible. He hugged his Bible to his chest. He had escaped the Communist prison state and was now living freely in South Korea.

Bibles in North Korea are rare. Because of the opposition from the Communists, believers consider them more precious than gold. One man was beaten to death with an iron rod along the Chinese border when he was caught bringing Bibles into North Korea. Sadly, cases like this are reported over and over.

"I cannot forget those people, " he said with a sigh. "I cannot forget the look of envy on their faces when I showed them my Bible. I feel so bad for them."

I've been feeling bad for them lately too. It helps to pray, but I am regularly asking God how else I can help out. Will you join me? above article borrowed from "Extreme Devotion" published by Voice of the Martyrs, persecution.com

51. he was executed right in front of me

This story comes from "Extreme Devotion" put out by Voice of the Martyrs, http://persecution.com/

"What happened?" asked the North Korean mother as her son walked through the front door with a look of shock.

"I was with my friend today when two police officers stopped us. They knocked my friend down and accused him of being a Christian. My friend did not try to defend himself. Even with a gun pointed directly at him, his face remained peaceful.

"He looked straight into my eyes and without speaking a word, I knew what he was saying. He wanted me to believe the same thing he did. And then he just said, 'Bless them.' He was executed right in front of me because he was a Christian. I do not even know what a Christian is. I don't understand any of this."

After he shared his story, his mother held his head in her hands and simply said, "I understand." She then began to share with him the truth about Christ her Saviour. She taught her son about Jesus' miraculous birth and the opportunity for salvation that came through His death on a cross. Though it pained her that she had never dared to tell her son because she worried for his safety, she was thankful that God was giving them a second chance. "As those bullets hit your friend's heart, God planted a seed of hope in yours."

Today this young man is active smuggling Bibles into North Korea and planting house churches.

52. to live, just deny Christ

I do hope my stories are not depressing you. I say that because sometimes they make me feel a little low. In the natural, the news coming out of North Korea is horrible, a constant drip, drip of sadness. But then, these horrors are creating 21st century heroes too! Those Biblical giants of faith you have read about and thought existed no more, do exist! Since persecution did not end in the first century, heroic acts of courage did not end either. Saints of God, without these trials, how else can we shine? Check this one out for example: (from "Extreme Devotion" published by Voice of the Martyrs)

As he slowly came around, his eyes adjusted to the smoke. He cried out for his pastor, but no one answered. Horrified, he quickly began digging his way out of the pile of flesh and rubble.

That morning, he had been among a group of 190 North Korean believers when the police stormed in, rounded them up, and harshly marched them to the town center.

Their nation's leader, Kim Il Sung [father of the present leader] , stood before them. He walked to the center of the square and drew a line in the dirt, ordering those who wanted to live to deny Christ and cross the line.

Not one stepped forward. Infuriated, Kim Il Sung ordered the group thrown into a mining tunnel with sticks of dynamite.

The last thing the surviving believer remembered was his pastor, consoling and encouraging the group. realizing he was the lone survivor, he cried, "Why God? Why didn't you let me die with the others?"

God immediately filled his heart with peace, and he knew that someone must remain and be a witness to their faith. This was the first of many brutal attacks by Kim Il Sung's form of Communism and worship, called "Juche". News of the heroic event spread among the Christians and is still told today in North Korea...

...and in America, and through the internet, around the world. Everything Satan does to us backfires in his face. Eventually he will be the one dynamited into eternal punishment while the ones who were faithful and suffered with Jesus will "shine like the stars forever."

53. *just look for the cross*

From Day 341 in the VOM devotional, "Extreme devotion", learn of "Kik" from North Korea:

"Look for the cross," the young Korean man named "Kik" heard a villager say. Word spread to those who escaped from North Korea into China that they should look for a building with a cross. He finally found one, and with it, food and clothing. He also found a new relationship with Jesus Christ.

The church members discipled Kik for three months. But Kik knew he must return to North Korea to tell others about Jesus. Kim and another young believer were given five Bibles and food for their journey. However, border guards captured them just after they made it across the river back into North Korea.

The guards discovered the Bibles that Kik's friend was carrying. The guard then beat Kik's friend to death with an iron rod. Then they turned on Kik, but he managed to escape. After several months he began to share Christ with others and started an underground church in North Korea.

Before long, Kik realized he needed more Bibles for the rapidly growing number of believers. He remembered how his friend had given up his life trying to bring the Word of God back to their homeland. When Kik decided to return to

China for more Bibles, the believers were very anxious for his safety.

Kik remembered the advice given to him some time ago. He simply replied, "Just look to the cross."

54. *is dying for Jesus worth it?*

This is an eyewitness account borrowed from Thomas Belke's *Juche.*

Shortly after the Korean War broke out, communist soldiers overtook a small town outside Pyongyang. 190 Christians were apprehended, along with their Pastor, brother Kim. The soldiers asked, "Is it really worth dying for Jesus? We can save your life if you will just say you do not believe in Him. "

Pastor Kim would not deny the Lord, so he was hung on a cross amidst a slow-burning fire. The soldiers, thinking they had won the day, turned to the 190 and said, "Those who still believe in Jesus, come forth!" All 190 stepped forward.

The soldiers marched them all into an abandoned mine , threw sticks of dynamite inside, then left them for dead. Hours later, one man awoke. He was filled with remorse when he realized he had survived. "Why, Lord, did you not take me to Heaven?"

He found his way out of the mine after several days of digging. Then it was that he discovered that all of his fingers were missing, and his hands were swollen and bloody. Later he understood something else. God had spared his life so that he could tell the church and the family of Pastor Kim just what had happened. Had he not lived, no one would ever have heard this story.

God has his purposes for all of us too. Let us humbly seek Him and His perfect will.

55. adopted, kidnapped, returned

The following story is from some years back, and is adapted from "Extreme Devotion" put out by Voice of the Martyrs (persecution.com).

Communists tell North Korean children that they will suffer a horrific fate if they are ever caught in China. But the children also know that if they are fortunate enough to escape, they should look for a building with the shape of a cross on it to find help. Two North Korean children who managed to arrive at a Chinese church relayed their stories to the pastor.

"My name is Cheng Lee. My sister and I watched our parents starve to death. We managed to walk across the Yalu River while it was still frozen. Once on the other side, my older sister said, 'You stay here. I have to go on a little farther by myself.' She never returned."

Cheng is only six.

Hong Jun, an eleven-year-old boy, said, "I want to return to North Korea and tell others about Christ." Then he cried as he sang:

"Oh Lord, give us the voice of the Gospel, For our beloved brothers the Lord so loved before, Where are all these gone? The Lord is looking upon them.

"Oh Lord, send us to them, to our beloved Korean brothers,
Oh Lord, send us to them, to our beloved Korean brothers. Wherever they are, let them bloom as flowers."

A few months later, Hong Jun was kidnapped from the village and forcibly returned to North Korea. Perhaps he is witnessing to his captors even now.

56. what is it like being a nk Christian

I really don't know. But wait, since you asked, and since the Word tells me to remember prisoners as though I were bound with them, it's probably important to try to understand what they are experiencing.

Let's see, to be a North Korean Christian must mean to eat a lot less. Could I do that? Yes, fasting is a command and an opportunity to relate to the suffering church. I could skip a meal now and then. Or cut out a meal altogether. Who says I need three a day to survive?

North Korean Christians probably walk a lot. Hmmm. No wheels? Could I find ways to walk more? What if I were the one on the trail each day that the wheeled people were always saying "on your left" to? What if it were me that the cars were coming around and blasting away with their nasty horns? Yeah, I could do that. Could lose some weight in the process. Get back to nature. Live simply.

Believers over there don't go to church to "be" someone, or to watch videos, or to talk with their friends about the latest sports outcomes. They don't go to see a performance or to gossip about so-and-so. Their attendance is not casual. If they go, the meeting is in secret, and it is understood that it could end in jail or worse. They go to hear from God, regardless of the cost. Now how in the world can I relate to that? Well, I could take my church attendance more seriously. I could stop criticizing. I could lead a holy life that makes church necessary and not optional. I could develop a love for Jesus in my prayer life that would spill over to my church life.

Being a North Korean believer means no television to speak of. No constant distraction and temptation to look at what the world is doing , and try to be like it. Hmmm, not a bad idea. Could I get rid of my habit? My TV? At least one of the 5 hangin' around my house? Maybe I could trash all but one, and use it only for news? Or could I use my radio & computer for news, and pitch all the TV's? Am I too far advanced in my addiction to try any of this? Then how will I ever relate to a North Korean believer and have anything better to offer him?

In truth, some of the above things I have already done. I desire to do all of them and more. But even then it will not let me fully understand what it means to be a North Korean Christian. When the persecution comes here, then I will know.

I've said it before. We need North Korea more than they need us. As you read through the items above, doesn't it strike you that the life they are living is very close to the life prescribed in the Word? If I in my liberty have chosen not to live as they *must* live in their restriction, I must ask why? What's wrong with less food, no TV, lots of walking and vital church services? What's wrong with me and my culture?

Sorry. My answer to your question turns into another question.

57. religion in nk

Tom Belke's *Juche* is, I hope, on your reading list. VOM and others offer it on their websites. I quote today from the foreword by Bahn-Suk Lee of Fuller Theological Seminary:

Kim Il Sung's plan and the Juche ideology were initially presented as political... Soon after his taking control of North Korea, though, it became a manifest part of a plan for Satan to assume rights and authority over the North Korean people...

The veil continues to cover the eyes, minds, hearts, and spirits of the North Korean people... [who] believe that Juche (self-reliance) ideology will save the world. Hundreds die every day in total ignorance of God's love and mercy....

...The Juche mentality is Satan's fetter, shackling people's minds. Juche must be broken... [it] is the epitome of rebellion. God created us in His image to be fully dependent on Him. Juche holds the direct opposite...

...The small Kim Il Sung pin covering every North Korean's heart is in fact a symbol of worship, spiritually hindering them from giving their hearts to Jesus. Their slogans and songs deifying Kim Il Sung, Kim Jong Il, and Juche are used to keep them in spiritual darkness. As North Koreans are forced to worship the images of Kim Il Sung daily, they remain ignorant offenders, breaking God's commandment and falling under His curse.

For too long, North Korea has been a playground of principalities and powers. Millions of souls have entered eternity without having heard the name of Jesus. This must stop....

Amen and amen. Who will join forces against the enemy of our souls to bring about an end to this?

58. the amazing case of kim hyun hee

Her name is Kim Hyun Hee. Probably doesn't ring a bell. Today she lives somewhere in South Korea. Afraid for her life, they say. "Assassination" is the word they are using. Perhaps by North Koreans who manage to sneak in now and then. Perhaps by South. What a pained life this must be.

What could one 20-something lady have done (20 years ago) to warrant such hatred?

Born in North Korea in 1962 to a privileged family, Kim was soon discovered to be a talented child. She was bright and beautiful and eventually got the attention of the powers in Pyongyang. Normally for one to be praised by one's government is a happy thing, but in North Korea none of the rules apply.

Grabbed from her family against their will and better judgment, Kim was trained to be a spy. After the normal introductory assignments she was given one last mission: she was to help bomb a passenger jet coming in to Seoul, filled with South Koreans. This would convince the powers that be that the Olympic games should never be held in Seoul. Somehow this would lead to the reunification of the Koreas.

I know, it's a stretch. But that is what she was told. And raised to believe that the ruling powers were all-wise, she bought it. Her partner was a long-time professional, and the two of them posed as Japanese tourists. On their return to Korea, they planted a bomb on KAL flight 858.

Now you know who she is?

Mistakes were made. The two were caught. The old man killed himself. Kim tried, but to no avail. She was brought to trial in Seoul. Found guilty. Then pardoned by the government of Seoul!

We are told that the South Korean President was politically motivated in his decision to pardon Kim. His reasoning to the world was: The persons who ought to be on trial here are Kim Il Sung and Kim Jong Il. This child is as much a victim of this evil regime as the passengers aboard KAL 858.

And who can argue with his reasoning?

Kim truly repented of her actions both before the trial and after. She was led to see that she had been lied to all of her life. One look at Seoul told her most of what she needed.

She wrote a book I think you should read. All the proceeds from it went to families of victims. Though I write all of this today with a calm, almost cold, reporter's way, when I read her book I was -as I have often been over the last months - a basket case. Aptly named "The Tears of My Soul" the book will extract the tears from your soul, too.

Oh, did I mention? Kim Hyun Hee gave her life to Jesus Christ after these horrible events. Whether some will ever be able to forgive her is uncertain, but God has.

59. the 60's: decade of disaster in nk

Continuing our history lessons from North Korea...

When the new South Korean administration built an economy based on the successful strategies of Japan, North Korea began to lose the race for supremacy on the peninsula. Japan, modeling its structure on Western successes, with American assistance, was not the guide that the Kims of the North wished to follow. That's why the South from 1966 on outpaced the North every year, and by 1976, they had passed them in per capita income.

Kim Il Sung, himself leading a very un-communist lifestyle, nevertheless pushed his socialist/militarist ways on a people heading downhill. He also pushed them further into isolation.

Later in the decade, seeing the U.S. was involved and over-extended in Vietnam, it could be that Kim decided to take advantage of the situation. Much like NK is manipulating a similarly busy America today.

First, in 1968, there was the (aborted) assassination attempt on South Korean President Park Chung Hee.

In that same year a Uniteed States ship in international waters, the *Pueblo,* was fired upon, taken in, and its crew of 82 men was arrested. "Confessions" -in the way of the Communist- were forced, and the crew was released.

Amazingly, North Korea "got away with it."

So, they struck again. In 1969, an American reconnaisance plane was shot down.

Appeasing an enemy does not work. But I will leave political and military solutions to the governments involved. My job is to inform God's people of the situation in North Korea so that they will know how to pray and how to love this nation.

However, believers can learn about their spiritual lives from this lesson. When the enemy of our soul suggests compromise and offers rewards, we must remember that appeasement won't work. His purposes in us must be destroyed altogether.

History portions gleaned from Bradley Martin.

60. Jesus shall reign; no doubt about it.

Look at Heaven. Or if you cannot see that far today, look at the Earth that is promised in Scriptures in the age following this one. There, the Lord is King and is being honored and worshiped freely by all His subjects. The Father and the Son reign and are loved supremely.

Now take a look at North Korea. A nation given over to the worship of another Father and Son, pretenders to the Throne. Such vast differences between the two Kingdoms. In Heaven, the love for God is genuine, freely given, and motivated by the Truth Who He is. In North Korea, the "affection" is gained by thorough brainwashing and distortion of truth from cradle to grave. It is further enhanced by guns and imprisonment. Torture. Loss. Shame. Fear. In Heaven the One worshiped is worthy. The more He is known, the more He is worshiped. Eternity will not reveal all the depths of that worth.

But in North Korea, the subjects of lavish pomp and programs, kissing and bowing, buttons and banners, statues and signs... are not worthy. Oh every head of state is worthy of honor, mind you. This is God-ordained. But no head of state is worthy of worship. This is God-cursed and brings judgment on a nation. And the more North Koreans find out about the ways they have been deceived, the less they praise. Eventually the full truth, gained when exiting the country, causes them to loathe, not lavish praise.

May the North Korean government read the following and weep, as we read it and rejoice, the old Isaac Watts hymn:

Jesus shall reign where'er the sun doth his successive journeys run;

His kingdom stretch from shore to shore, Till moons shall wax and wane no more.

To Him shall endless prayer be made, and endless praises crown His head;

His name like sweet perfume shall rise with every morning sacrifice.

People and realms of every tongue dwell on his love with sweetest song,

And infant voices shall proclaim their early blessings on His name.

Blessings abound where'er he reigns; the prisoner leaps to loose his chains;

The weary find eternal rest, and all the sons of want are blest.

Let every creature rise and bring his grateful honors to our King;

Angels descend with songs again, and earth (including North Korea!) repeat the loud AMEN!

61. north korean official healed

In Thomas Belke's *Juche* the following story is quoted:

...years ago, a North Korean government official was dying of tuberculosis. "You only have a few months to live," his physician told him.

Mr. Park decided to pay his final respects to his relatives in Manchuria (Northeast China). One evening, while visiting a relative, Mr. Park overheard a Gospel radio broadcast, originating from South Korea. An American evangelist, aided by an interpreter, gave a message on healing.

"I cannot come to you," the evangelist concluded, "but if you believe God, He *will* heal you!" Mr. Park did not know what a Bible was, and asked his relatives for a Bible. He was handed a Bible, which he placed upon his chest. Echoing the broadcast's prayer, Mr. Park ended with a hearty "Amen," though ignorant of its meaning.

Weeks passed, and the incident was forgotten. Mr. Park returned to North Korea. Months later, Mr. Park realized that he was still alive. Puzzled, he visited his physician. "I don't understand," his doctor concluded, "but your health is normal!" Instantly, Mr. Park recalled the radio broadcast, the prayer and the Bible.

Requesting a leave of absence, Mr. Park hurried back to Manchuria to re-visit his relatives. He burst out that he had been dying, and that he had been healed. Word grew silently among the village believers, and they rejoiced. Laying their hands on him, they prayed, saying, "We are sending a missionary into North Korea!"

Upon his return, Mr. Park was bursting to share the Good News. Was it safe? Who could he tell? After much prayer, he told his mother. As Mr. Park shared his testimony, she broke out in tears, sobbing, "Son, please forgive me. before the War, I was a church deaconess... however I was afraid to tell you about Jesus. I feared you would report me to the Communists as others who had turned in their parents. Surely the Lord allowed this sickness that you might find Him and be saved."

Turning to the Lord, the elderly mother sank to her knees in gratitude: " Oh, Lord, forgive me," she wept, "thank you for saving my son, and returning the Gospel to our family."

Tearfully, mother and son earnestly prayed for guidance. Subsequently, an underground church was formed. Imagine, a North Korean Church! The fellowship numbers 80 members.

Story published by Cornerstone, 1993.

62. so what is juche really?

Thomas Belke has done us a great service by writing his descriptive work *Juche, A Christian Study of North Korea's State Religion.* On page 11 he quotes Kim Jong Il in defining Juche:

"The Juche idea is a new philosophical thought which centers on man. The Juche idea is based on the philosophical principle that man is the master of everything and decides everything. The Juche idea raised the fundamental question of philosophy by regarding man as the main factor, and elucidated the philosophical principle that man is the master of everything and decides everything. That man is the master of everything means that he is the master of the world and his own destiny; that man decides means that he plays the decisive role in transforming the world and in shaping his destiny. The philosophical principle of the Juche idea is the principle of man-centered philosophy which explains man's position and role in the world."

There you have it. Doesn't get more official than that.

Can a mere school counselor like myself dare to take issue with the learned scholar Kim Jong Il (most of whose work is ghost-written)? There are some glaring problems with the above description, beyond the NK tendency to be repetitive. I will narrow it to two words.

1. The word "new." The man-is-the-master-of-all concept has been around a LONG time! Self-centered God-defying humanism began in fact in the Garden of Eden and has never once slackened its pace.

2. The word "decide". If man is the master and decides everything, then *all men* should be in on the decision . The Chinese and the Americans and the Japanese are men. But Juche does not apply to them. The South Koreans are men, and they are making decisions too. But not Kim's decisions. So they don't count either. If the North Koreans were allowed to *decide* between what they have and what there is to have globally, they too would not determine their fate to be poverty, torture, and imprisonment. In fact the word "decide" in this definition only applies to one man, and at present it is the man Kim Jong Il.

But we declare that all other men *are* free to decide, and that Juche's decision is faulty. And if, as Juche demands, we must abide by the decisions of one man, many of us choose the Man Christ Jesus, whose concepts admittedly are also not "new" yet they make individual men and women and children all over the world to sing a new song, live a new life, participate in a new hope.

For the truth is that this *Jesus* is the "Master of everything" and ultimately decides everything. *He* is the "main factor." *He* is the "Master of the world" and its destiny.

93

He alone will transform this universe into a new heaven and a new earth. It is Christ-centered philosophy which "explains man's position and role in the world."

Let's get *that* message to North Korea, so that they know they have a choice after all!

63. maggots for the gov't

We need North Korea more than she needs us. We need those who live seriously difficult lives to remind us that our lives are not so difficult after all. To remind us of the cross. To remind us to pray. I quote today from North Korean Kim Hyun Hee as she describes what her days were like growing up in North Korea. And she was in the privileged class... (From *The Tears of My Soul* pp 17-18)

"We were told that to defeat the American imperialists, our country would need to buy weapons abroad, so we were sent out for hours each day gathering scrap iron, bottles, and other recyclable products that could be sold for foreign currency. We were assigned quotas to fulfill, and children who failed to do so were admonished publicly. Who could gather the most became a great source of competition among us.

"We were also instructed to search about and to collect the skins of rabbits and dogs, as well as (to this day I don't recall why) maggots. Maggots were most commonly found in the dungheaps at the public outhouses, where the toilets did not flush, and again we competed intensely. As for the dung itself, we were also required to collect that! When great heaps had accumulated, it was eventually shipped to farmers for use as fertilizer, and each person would be graded according to the quantity and quality of the dung collected. Later on, when rationing tickets were issued, these grades with which we had been rewarded were taken into account.

"And yet the most difficult thing of all was to collect flowers. These we were required to place in front of the many statues of Kim Il Sung around our neighborhood. Since there were no flower shops in North Korea, the only way we could fulfill our quotas was to bribe the local greenhouse custodian.

"These were the sort of activities that filled our days..."

Do you have fonder memories of your childhood? Do you fill your days a little bit more meaningfully than Hyun Hee? Probably.

64. the poor chongryon

Chongryon is an organization of North Koreans living in Japan, fiercely loyal to Kim Jong Il. In the past many have moved back to North Korea to go back to their "roots" only to find that their roots have been uprooted altogether and replaced with weeds. Given a hero's welcome at first, later they are viewed with suspicion and quite often incarcerated or executed. They don't exactly "fit", having been raised in free Japan. Eventually they say or think things that are not permissible in North Korea.

But while in Japan, at a safe distance from the dictator, they have a romantic love for their homeland and try to defend it against the "imperialists."

Following is yet another fascinating look inside the NK regime, an online article approved by the government, tearing down the Japanese leaders only days before big negotiations are to begin. This is the kind of thing NK can use as an "out" should they need one. First, though, the oil shipment and other promised aid must arrive...

(Grammar as found at website. Bracketed [ ] comments are mine.)

"Officials of Chongryon-lining [?] central organizations released statements in denunciation of Japanese Prime Minister Abe's reckless remarks branding Chongryon as a "criminal organization." [can't imagine why defenders of NK policies and government might be thought of as criminal]

Choe Song Yong, chairman of the Central Standing Committee of the Korean Youth League in Japan, lashed at the balderdash [NK English is decidedly British!] let loose by Abe branding Chongryon as a "criminal organization" for no reason. [note the redundancy of NK writers/speakers. Not much to say, so say it again.]

He demanded that Abe should immediately withdraw and apologize for the venomous outpourings, clearly realizing what a shameless [oh my!]crime it was that he stringed out [?] anachronistic remarks against dignified Chongryon. [poor victimized Kim Jong Il]

Kang Chu Ryon, chairwoman of the Central Standing Committee of the Korean Democratic Women's Union in Japan, representing the wrath of all the officials of the union and the Korean women in Japan, bitterly denounced Japanese Prime Minister Abe and the right-wing reactionaries knee deep in building up public opinion against Chongryon and Koreans. [and we'll see you all in a few days with smiles on our faces.]

She stated that all the Korean women would never [that's a big word] pardon the Japanese authorities and right-wing reactionaries for smearing the image of Chongryon and spreading the climate of "hunting Koreans." [isn't this also a smear tactic?]

Kim Tong Hak, secretary general of the Korean Human Rights Association in Japan, said Abe made the outburst abusing the rights of Koreans in Japan [specifically which rights?] when the innocent Koreans in Japan were subjected to discrimination with chauvinistic sentiments running high in Japan.

[and just what were the exact words and context? Yes, there is a history of Japanese abuse of Korea, North or South, but its correction is not served well by bombastic articles like this. "Someone" may be trying to pick a fight...]

It's so obvious that the grace of God is needed in all of this. We continue to pray.

65. nk history: the 70's

We continue with our modern history of North Korea, following Bradley Martin. We've come to the 70's.

Park Chung Hee of the South and Kim Il Sung decide that a series of meetings might boost their poll numbers. Both are in trouble with "the people." By July 4, 1972 (interesting date) they agree on a joint communique, wherein a telephone hotline between the two nations is proposed amidst the normal pledges of reunification, "someday".

By 1973 all bets are off. There is disagreement as to how to proceed, and the silence resumes. Kim Il Sung goes off in another direction, joining in with the so-called "non-aligned" nations, peoples who have not yet chosen a side in the huge global game. While his people begin their decline into abject poverty, Kim offers some of these poor nations, especially in Africa, aid. And arms. All of Madagascar, for example, is armed by the Hermit Kingdom.

Everyone's best friend, Jimmy Carter, is elected President in 1976, and to the liking of everyone, especially Kim Il Sung, he promises to bring home all troops from Korea! Later he has second thoughts. August 18, 1976, to be specific. Some American soldiers at the DMZ are trimming some trees so their view of the enemy is not blocked. North Korea soldiers wave them off, but the Americans stand their ground... and are axed to death.

Carter waters down his plan a bit. In that same decade, Kim Il Sung digs tunnels under the DMZ and builds his army to an incredible 600,000. That is the 5th largest in the world at the time. Proportionate to his population (only 17,000,000) it is probably number one. You'd think that one soldier for every 28 citizens is a bit excessive.

Following China's lead, in 1979 Kim opens up to American visitors in the form of ping-pong diplomats, and attempts to open talks again. Carter bounces over immediately to Seoul encouraging the dialogue to begin but challenging the human rights issues. Kim is angered that Seoul is even to be a part of the new talks. He wants a bilateral discussion with the attached recognition of his regime, with the United States. Not to happen.

So one can say perhaps that some progress is being made as we look around today. North Korea is talking again. North Korea is willing to sit down with old rivals... which includes most of the human race. But North Korea still has its hand out and a gun pointed to those who will not get with the program. It will be fascinating, if not tragic, to see what the next days and weeks produce.

Pray.

66. *weeds in the garden*

Brother Luke tells us (Luke 8:14) that a life can be choked with riches and pleasure just as easily as with the more serious cares of life. A North Korean or an American are equally vulnerable to the devil's tactics.

Weeds, the kind Jesus talked about in his parable of the 4 soils (Matthew 13) , are stubborn things. You find them everywhere. But they remain because most people don't want to pull them out. It's simpler just to go with the flow of life. In the end they will overcome the field and starve the fruit.

To those who are allowing weeds to grow mercilessly in God's garden, Amos cries out (chapter 6):

"Woe to you who are at ease in Zion...woe to you who put far off the day of doom... who lie on beds of ivory, stretch out on your couches... invent for yourselves musical instruments... and drink wine... but are not grieved for the affliction of Joseph [the people of God]... "

Haggai adds (chapter 1), "Is it time for you yourselves to dwell in your paneled houses, and this temple [God's House] to lie in ruins?... you have sown much, and bring in little. You eat, but do not have enough; you drink, but are not filled with drink; you clothe yourselves, but no one is warm; and he who earns wages, earns wages to put into a bag with holes..."

Granted, the prophets spoke to particular situations. In the days of Amos, the enemies of God threatened, but so many of God's people didn't seem to care. In Haggai's day, the doors were wide open to build up the house of God, but God's people cared only about their own things.

Like I said, weeds grow everywhere and at all times. The same weeds threaten us. Here's North Korea, not only a starving pitiful nation of prisoners, but a place where God's own special people have been entrapped and are crying out for help. Can we hear their crying? Have the weeds of materialism so smothered us that we are deaf to their cries?

What shall we do, Lord? How can we reach your people with comfort, and the other North Koreans with the Gospel? Destroy everything in our life that is not as important as your Kingdom! Give us grace to help You pull those weeds out today!

67. ji hae's prison experience

The story is long. I will condense this page from David Hawk's *Hidden Gulag*. Hawk's idea in writing his book is to expose to the light of day what is going on in North Korea. That's one of my goals too, so that people like you will pray.

- Ji Hae born in 1949, South Hangyong Province, North Korea.
- Active part of propaganda ministry. eg, patriotic work songs at factories.
- By 1989, age 40, her faith in the Party begins to waiver.
- Ji Hae sees a NK TV show mocking South Korea's President.
- A song on the show intrigues her. She memorizes it.
- December 25, 1992, she teaches the SK song to 4 women at a party.
- She is reported and arrested. She is beaten and sexually abused.

- Tries to commit suicide by swallowing cement.
- For teaching song and trying to get extra food illegally, sentenced to 3 years.
- Released 1995, but as ex-convict hard to make money.
- Tries peddling food etc, then selling her blood at transfusion centers.
- 1998, escapes to China, caught by trafficker, sold to Chinese man.
- Locked up by new "husband" as a "sex toy," 7 months.
- Escapes to Weihai (China), works in restaurant.
- With 6 other NK's, steals boat, engine breaks down on way to South Korea.
- Later steals another boat, but intercepted, turned over to Chinese border guards.
- Repatriated to North Korea!
- Beaten with broom sticks, forced to kneel hours at a time, and more...
- Once more released, December 25, 1999.
- Once more escapes, crossing the frozen Tumen River by Musan into China.
- Meets SK pastor who assists her and others in escape.
- Escape route: Weihai to Beijing to Kunming in China. (A lot of miles!)
- Caught by Chinese police near Vietnam.
- Released. Walk over mountains into Vietnam. Through SE Asia. To Seoul.

And when asked if she still sings the song that got her into all this trouble, she immediately replies, "Yes! And now without fear."

I don't know if she ever came to the Lord, but I know she had the opportunity. Millions in the North Korea "Paradise" do not.

Right after you cry today, will you pray? God, what can we do?!

68. how communist is nk?

From Belke's *Juche* regarding the "religion" of North Korea:

" In the Juche ["self-reliance"] ideological view, the Chinese and Soviets did not go far enough to implement Communism..."

Even from the point of view of classic Communists: "You Korean comrades are *not* Communists at all; you are nationalists. All you are after is our ruble." [Vladimir Lenin!]

Belke: "Of course, Lenin was right about the Oriental Communists. Mao Zedong was expelled from Commintern, Deng Xiaping was more capitalist than Bill Clinton, Ho Chi Minh was a 'Sunday' Communist, and Kim Il Sung went so far as to rename the Communist Party of Korea to 'Workers' Part of Korea'.

"They all professed Marxism-Leninism adapted to 'local and today's' conditions... [but] Marx and Lenin would be shocked to see China's 'revised' Communism..."

"...Kim Il Sung ordered his scholars to come out with a new political philosophy germane to Korea..."

And so we have Juche. But one who studies the tyrants of earth and their systems will see a common strain. These men hate God, and live like kings. They oppress their people and bring them to ruin. Naziism, Communism, Kim-Il-

Sungism, they're all the same. Their origin is Satan. Their doom is sure.

And their people are unhappy. What an opportunity for the Gospel to show itself and do what It does best: set the captives free! proclaim deliverance to the oppressed! give good news to the poor!

Please stop and pray now for the re-entrance of the Old Old story to the Sad Sad people of Chosun.

69. lies countered by light

I quote today from a book by David Hawk and the U.S. Committee for Human Rights in North Korea. I strongly recommend that you download and read their entire work on the Hidden Gulag. This particular quote is from Anne Applebaum, who wrote the preface:

In the fullest possible sense, the contemporary leaders of North Korea are the intellectual and moral descendants of [the] Stalinists... North Korean camps were built according to a Stalinist model, and ... they continue to be run that way...

...As in Stalin's time, North Koreans are arrested for trumped-up political "crimes", such as reading a foreign newspaper, singing a South Korean pop song, or "insulting the authority" of the North Korean leadership. As in Stalin's time, North Korean prisoners - even children - are given ludicrous and impossible work "quotas" to fulfill and are subjected to brutal, irrational punishments. And, as in Stalin's time, North Korea's leadership doesn't want anyone to know any of these details, since such revelations not only will damage their foreign reputation but also put their own regime at risk.

[That's why reading Hawk's book is so important! It comes complete with aerial photographs of camps whose existence is still denied by NK's leaders. Also Stalinesque.]

...Certainly after absorbing [the details of this book] it will be more difficult for Americans or Europeans to ... negotiate coldly with their Korean counterparts and not mention human rights violations. South Koreans... will find it more difficult to argue in favor of appeasing the Northern regime... North Korean police and admministrators... will find it more difficult to justify their own behavior, or to claim that they don't know what is really happening in the camps.

And if the full truth about the camps becomes known to the wider population, then whatever support remains for the state constructed by Kim Il Sung and Kim JOng Il will begin... to ebb away. This is not to say that words can make a dictatorship collapse overnight. But words certainly can make a dictatorship collapse over time... Totalitarian regimes are built on lies and can be damaged, even destroyed, when lies are exposed.

Well said. And we who believe in the Eternal Word will keep praying that North Korea will be exposed to Its life-changing power ASAP!

70. Christ in nk

Using James and Marti Hefley's By Their Blood we now begin a series of articles on the history of the church in Korea. As is true of much of Korean history, the pathway is a bloody one.

In 1122 B.C. 5,000 subjects of Chinese rule rebelled and fled to the peninsula we now associate with Korea, organizing a new state, "Chosun", land of morning calm. For the next 3,000 years this "hermit kingdom" suffered the abuses of Mongolians, Chinese, and Japanese until in 1876 a trade treaty was forced upon it by Japan. Korea was brought out of its shell, and over the next quarter of a century all of its ports were opened to the West.

Japan pushed even farther, however.From 1910 to 1945 it occupied Korea totally. What Christian witness had spread was slowly extinguished, not by the Koreans, but by their foreign "hosts." At the end of World War II, the country was divided. More intruders came in, and in the North they still are there. Christians have been murdered en masse during the long occupation of Russian/Chinese style totalitarian Communism. 500 pastors were killed during the Korean War period alone.

Thousands to this day languish in a prison gulag, trusting Christ daily for their perseverance and deliverance. That is the rough outline. We go back now to fill in details.

It was in the early 1800's that Korean diplomats in Peking, China, met members of the Catholic world system. Contacts were made, and secret entrances were attempted into Korea. Catholicism spread rapidly, but was countered by Buddhist priests as Rome, a foreign power, was a political threat to their authority over the lives of the Korean people.

This anti-foreign fear in Korea -well founded, unfortunately - climaxed in 1846 by the all-out slaughter of the entire Romanist hierarchy along with 10,000 members. The name of Jesus was dealt a heavy blow. But the Protestants were not far behind in their own advance into Korea. More when this church history cycle continues.

71. nk history: assassination, massacre, ronald reagan

...continuing our history of North Korea via Martin' s *Under the loving care...*

In the South Korea of 1979 there is discontent. Traffic jams, pollution, inflation, no middle-class. In October President Park is assassinated by a South Korean. One can only imagine the delight being experienced by the North's reigning leader, Kim Il Sung.

It isn't over yet. As the new President of the South begins a "crackdown" to regain order in his country, citizen movements rise creating havoc. 200 such "rebels" are killed in a massacre at Kwangju, May, 1980. North Korea once more is on full alert. Is this their opportunity?

Eventually stability returns, and to strengthen things further, in 1981 Ronald Reagan comes to power in the United States. Though the South's new leader can be called a dictator, Reagan gives him his unqualified support. Kim Il Sung's "window" is being shut in his face.

Meanwhile, throughout the 70's the North tries to speed ahead of the South on borrowed money. Lacking the moral conscience and the ability to repay, Kim soon gains a bad reputation, one that has stuck until this day.

A visitor to North Korea in 1979 is made to feel that the country is prospering. But not everything is shown. That too remains a policy to the present time. There are still portions of the country that cause websites like my own to come under question. Seeing children marching to well-organized picture-perfect schools every morning, one would never know that just "up the road" is suburban Hades, AKA the "hidden gulag" where multiplied thousands suffer as slaves and help keep the economy afloat.

One thing that Martin does see on his 1979 visit is a great majority of women in the workforce. That makes sense, because the men are serving the country in the military. Women are not needed at home, because the State takes care of their children almost from birth. Seems that America is heading that same general direction. May the Church rise up here and tell the people of God that in His order of things, women are liberated to stay home and raise a family! We've had enough of the pseudo-liberation of women.

History of North Korea to be continued...

Please pray for this land today!

72. of korean heroes

Korean history is chock full of heroes. Christian martyrs. Nation builders. Kings and presidents and ordinary folk who suffered much. That's why I have cringed recently to see the ongoing saga of Dae Joyoung. In Chicago you can see it twice a week on the "Korean" channel. Frankly I was sucked into it for awhile, and we don't watch a lot of TV.

I had just gotten into the study of North Korea, and Korean history in general, when my wife told me I should watch this ongoing "historical" serial about a legendary national hero, Dae Joyoung. When I began to watch, I held a history book in one hand and the remote in the other. I could see the connection, but I had to marvel about how much extra there was on TV. Then I discovered that the saga of Dae is not meant to be taken as "true" in every respect.

It's obvious that there is some heavy "Hollywood" connection to Korean broadcasting. Though the programming is done well, well enough tro make me (then) want to watch every episode, the rationale for its existence seems faulty.

I began to compare the product I was watching from "free" Korea to the real-live pack of lies that comes out of the North every day. School children throughout that land are literally taught to sing the praises of the Kim conquerors, they are made to memorize their words, and facts about their history. But alas, that history is not real either! Facts and fiction have been masterfully blended into a legend that causes thinking persons to blush. It's ridiculous. I'll share some pieces of it in future posts.

My point now is, the real Korea has real heroes. Why does the South have to stoop to northern tactics of legend-weaving when it can tell the exciting truth about so many men and women? Yes, I know, why do Americans practice this too?

By the way, there was a Dae Joyoung. He was a leader in the old "Gorguryo", a nation that preceded the modern one. That land was defeated by the Chinese, but Dae rose up to re-conquer, re-name (Parhae) and establish the northern regions forever for its descendants. That's history. It's great history all by itself. There was no need to add that Dae basically dies and is resurrected. That he could fight 15 men at one time. That he was such a holy man that he would suck the blood and the poison out of a wounded soldier so that the soldier could live. That he could be arrested, escape, and re-arrested and, well, you get the picture. A perfect human being.

I've chosen my heroes. Many of them are Korean. They are the ones who faithfully and daily live for Jesus Christ in a nightmarish land that I cannot comprehend. May God give us all grace to follow them as they follow Christ.

73. the reincarnation of kim il sung

The following ideas were gleaned from Tom Belke's Juche which I recommend for your reading, and from my own thoughts:

One of the ways that the North Korean political philosophy ("Juche") looks like a religion is in the realm of the "incarnation theory". It is strongly believed that the present leader, Kim Jong Il, must carry out "the will of the father" and previous leader, Kim Il Sung. They call Dad the "Eternal" Suryong (leader). If he is eternal he must still be with us somehow, and not just in our memories. Maybe "in the person of his son," using Christian terminology.

Presently Kim Jong Il is being referred to as the "Great" Leader, a phrase that originally was only to be applied to the father. Do the North Koreans believe that the father lives on in the son, directing their every move still as he did until his death in 1994? Yes, it seems that the idea being promoted is that Kim Jong Il (present) IS Kim Il Sung (past), that is, the one is an incarnation of the other.

This could well be a deliberate swipe at the Christian faith, either by the NK government or by Satan himself who has for aeons been looking for a way to supplant the original Father and Son. Reincarnation itself is not a new concept but to see it taking place in this Father-Son way brings about a twinge of jealousy in us in whom the Spirit of the one true God strives.

One more reason to pray for North Korea, as though you did not have enough already.

74. calling the kettle black

The latest news out of the Korean Peninsula, from KBS news. NK is now saying, "Hey, we can shut down the nuclear facilities, if you bullies will stop being so hostile to us!" (My paraphrase)

I am curious as to which "hostilities" are being referenced.

Perhaps Bush's "axis of evil" statement, made in reference to the fact that North Korea is a known seller of weapons to nations that desire to wipe Israel and the U.S. off the face of the earth?

Certainly not our policy of feeding hundreds of thousands of North Koreans and keeping that nation afloat while it threatens us and the free world daily?

And not the fact that we have a military contingent in South Korea prepared for a possible attack from the North, like the one that started the Korean War?

Hostility? Has there ever been a nation that has blessed its sworn enemies so much? The world hides a grin as it hears Kim and sees who the truly hostile player is in this game.

Well, at least the 6-party talks are on the way! Believers can pray that God will use this meeting of minds to bring about a solution, even though the NK government may already be planning an escape route. Surely someone there will be asking for God's Mind on the situation? And if these politicians don't think to ask God, we must. Someday we shall rule the world in fact, with Christ our King. For now we can help pull strings behind the scenes. Through prayer.

75. *from nk to God*

It is interesting, in reading the stories of those who one way or another get out of North Korea, to see just how many come face to face with their need for God. Whether they find the Truth that is in Christ, or just a momentary crying out before their emptiness attempts to fill up with western decadence, still the chance is there, the chance that everyone on this planet needs to have at least one time.

Kim Hyun Hee's time came after her heinous destroying of scores of innocent South Korean airplane passengers under the direction of Kim Il Sung. (See her book, *The tears of my soul.)* She is arrested, her partner commits suicide. She tries but is unsuccessful.

""And then I did something for the first time in my life, something very strange : I prayed."

I do hope that was not her last prayer, because it has still gone un-answered: *Please God, wherever you are, help me to die, right now. PLEASE.*

For the first time in her life she had called out to someone other than Kim Il Sung, "who was the closest thing to a deity that I had ever known."

Later she comes to hate Kim Il Sung even as she learns more and more appreciation for the One Who would not lie to her. She comes to Christ and begins speaking in South Korean churches, experiencing God's greatest gift:

"The Lord has shown me his great works and miracles" she says to one church. After her speech are many "amens," and members of the congregation are in tears.

"It was overwhelming to me that I should be shown such forgiveness, and I was thankful that I had found this sanctuary of God to help me in my new life."

As I have documented elsewhere, her new life includes hiding from North and South Koreans alike who want to finish what they would call the real justice that Hyun deserves.

They don't understand Christ. But this North Korean does. Pray that many more will.

76. the presbyterians come to pyongyang

Still following the Hefleys' By Their Blood *I glean and paraphrase the following facts of the history of the church in North Korea.*

In 1882, the United States and Korea (there was only one Korea then) signed a trade treaty. Protestants now found their way into this little kingdom on the other side of the world. Medical doctors led the way, followed by evangelists and educators.

The general pattern of church formation at the beginning was laid out by China missionary John Nevius. Churches were to start in the homes of nationals, and as quickly as possible they were to be under the complete control of the national church. This was not to be an "American" thing, nor a Roman one. Christ would prove Himself a sufficient leader of men through His Spirit and His Word. Missionaries would serve as advisors and specialists, then move on.

By 1907, Hefley says that over 1,000 self-supporting churches served 120,000 evangelicals. And that was just in the Presbyterian part of the church. A major revival swept across Korea in that year. Mass prayer meetings. Confessions of backsliders. Conversions of hardened sinners. God was preparing His Church for a trial by fire.

Those of us who pray for such revival in our own day must remember that God's Spirit is poured out for a reason. Pentecost was followed by persecution, and probably ever shall be.

Next time in the church history cycle: The 1907 revival in Pyongyang itself.

77. so this is paradise

Hyok Kang is still a young man. 21 or 22 years old. But as a much younger man, in 1998, he escaped from Kim's Korea. Later he told his story to those who could publish it, and what is becoming a "classic" of the genre was born: *This Is Paradise.*

I want to say I recommend it with all my heart. But I must add serious warnings. This book goes deeper than any I have read so far into the disgusting and nauseating. If you are not prepared to have discussed before you the details of people eating people, for example, I suggest you read something a little lighter.

Philippe Grangereau was Hyok's assistant in writing this story. His preface serves as a preview of the book. I quote in part:

"The young man (Hyok) told me how he had survived famine in North Korea: tree-bark soups, rat hunts with his friends, hours spent digging coal in the galleries of the mine, night-time raids on state farms; the weakening, then death of several of his schoolfriends... Hyok related these episodes casually, as though he were talking to me about just another ordinary day. What he had seen with his child's eyes some years previously, millions of North Koreans had also experienced every day of their lives- and continue to do so today. Because even now, in 2005, famine still rages in North Korea..."

I feel especially weak this morning. So frustrated. So helpless. The "old" man wants to rise up and punch someone, and say, "You can't do that! Let these people eat! Lay your weapons down and buy food! No one is trying to hurt you! The whole civilized world is trying to help you!"

But all my shouting and finger-pointing at the well-fed government in the middle of the famine will be to no avail. God will repay. Vengeance is His. And when something significant is done for Korea, no man will be able to take credit. For it is "not by might, not by power, but BY MY SPIRIT, says the Lord!"

But I still want to shout. Will you join me, and lift your shouts to the only One Who can hear and do something about them?

78. ignorance: not bliss after all

I keep finding resources that I must pass on to you. Here's NK Freedom Watch, a series of "newsletters", though not on any particular schedule, that form a project of Freedom House, based in Washington D.C.

In Issue 3, May of '06, in an article entitled "The Power of Information", some random quotes & paraphrasing:

"None are so hopelessly enslaved as those who falsely believe they are free." - Goethe

"North Korea is the world's most closed society. The North Korean people do not exactly realize how harsh their current situation is since the North Korean government prohibits any information from outside their country. They only know what the government tells them." - Tae San Kim, North Korean defector.

"All citizens are entitled to the freedom of speech, publication, gathering, demonstration, and freedom of association." - Article 27, North Korean Constitution. (Well, *most* citizens? A majority? A good portion? People in and around Pyongyang? The military, the government.... would you believe, the Leader ?! Article 27 definitely needs some re-working)

The media in North Korea does not function as the eyes and ears of the citizens. Its single purpose is to deliver the propaganda of the regime... the Party defines the press as a "tool for advertising and propagandizing the party's policies and revolutions." It is the "blood vessels of the Worker's Party."

Not only is the media useless to the people, the NK penal code actually includes listening to foreign broadcasts and possessing dissident publications as crimes against the state, punishable by IMPRISONMENT and/or DEATH!

I really must stop here before I get emotional again. More about this subject another time. For now, something more to bring before the Heavenly Father, Whose Word we pray will soon be published THROUGHOUT THE LAND!

79. *my favorite government*

My western friends may be disappointed to know that I do not believe democracy to be the purest form of government. In its misunderstood form, the "rule of the people" does not exist. All the people cannot rule. They merely designate who will rule. If you think you are in charge, try a late payment to the IRS or parking in a spot designated "no parking."

But even representative rule, true democracy as we know it, which we have experienced so beneficially for these 200 plus years in America, is not the preferred way. Corruption enters into systems like these, precisely *because* they are run *by the people*, not in spite of that fact.

No, give me an iron-fisted ruler.

One will will speedily punish wickedness. But let the definition of wickedness be properly spelled out.

One who will reward righteousness. But let righteousness also have its proper definition.

One who cannot be toppled by some greater power. One who is unquestioned in his right and capacity to rule.

Give me a perfect monarch, who can settle all disputes with justice. One from whose lips will drop perfect wisdom, from whose hands will flow perfect compassion.

You say, There is no such one. I say, There is. King Jesus , Messiah of Israel and of all believing gentiles too, meets the requirements I have listed. His reign of 1000 years will be the very prelude to eternity. The earth awaits Him. His people elect Him, but He was elected by the Father for this very position before the worlds began. He shall rule, even though the "people" of earth attempt to strike Him down .

So in speaking so often against the rule of oppressive tyrants on earth, we must remember to oppose them on the right grounds. It is not because they are "all powerful" or "unopposed" or a "totalitarian" leader. Jesus Himself will be all of that and more.

We are against them because they take from the hearts of men their right to choose King Jesus as their Lord. They supplant Jesus with their own ways and principles and songs. Rather than allowing their people to experience the fact that a nation is blessed whose God is Jehovah, they show the world that a nation without this God of Gods is cursed. In this they have been a mighty revealer of the truth of God but their end shall come, all rulers and nations that despise the Holy One.

All hail, KING JESUS! Lord over all the lords of Earth!

80. the children of nk: carefully taught

Time for our next history lesson.

We're in the late 70's. North Korea is still trying to expand, but is finding it difficult in a divided land. The peninsula's northern minerals and southern grains had at one time been a perfect complement insuring wealth throughout the nation. But the powers that be have decided there shall be two independent Koreas. No grains in the North. No metals in the South.

Towns begin to grow up throughout the nation that are merely miniature Pyongyangs, forced into conformity. Men are in suits. Children are marched to and from school in uniforms. A true police state.

The education system that begins to form is the key to future years, as in every country. Out of 1979's 17 million persons, nearly 8 million are in some level of education: a nursery, a regular school, a post-secondary school. At merely a few weeks old, a child is compelled to begin his government training. Though children tend to be "normal" in many ways, the academic food they are force-fed all their lives is meant to produce little Kims in thinking process.

Only 1-2 hours per day are spent with Mom. Preschoolers learn, instead of nursery rhymes and family values and morals, the strange stories of Kim Il Sung's childhood and how to bow to his picture. According to Kim, the "primary aim of education lies in training people to faithfully serve the existing social system." Most nations grudgingly admit that that is what education does. But when your nation is a slave state whose mindless pedagogy creates robots and not humans, the tragedy is even worse.

It was Engels who said that we must "prevent the old ideas of their parents from exerting influence on children's minds." Surely in Kim's thinking one of those "old ideas" is Pyongyang's Christian past. His attempt to stamp out Christ by replacing Him with himself has brought on the untold suffering of the Korean people.

Thus we pray, Lord, change the history of this place! Lord, let the people of God rotting in Kim's gulag rise up and do mighty exploits! Christ, anointed and coming King over all the earth, let your reign in the hearts of many North Koreans be established!

General outline of history following B. Martin's Under

the Loving Care of the Fatherly Leader.

81. *i can only imagine*

I can only imagine how there could be such smart people in the world, and such powerful people, and such talented people, and yet no one can find a solution for North Korea.

Men are so arrogant and love to point to their technology and colleges and monuments. But a Stalinist government still reigns in this "advanced" world. North Koreans starve. Torture and desperation have become a way of life there. Can some smart someone imagine what needs to be done?

Smart men, call on Jesus!

Some days I imagine that the persecution has come to the West. Churches are closed. Radios and TV's are confiscated. The government controls all. Wages are what Washington says they will be. No free market... and so on, add what ever other perversions come to your mind, because you cannot imagine something more horrible than what the Word says is coming to this entire world.

In the midst of all this, you offer a prayer: Father, bless me in the same way I blessed your people when they called out during their suffering! Exactly what would that mean in your life if God answered you literally?

It could mean that some well-off saint somewhere will think about you when a special speaker comes to church. Or that a hidden sister will call your name out to God. Some banker brother may try to get you some money. Others may visit you.

Christian, call on Jesus on behalf of the suffering church! Today is your day to invest.

Other days I am one of those Zinzendorf Moravians, you know, the ones who deliberately sold themselves into slavery, so as to win fellow slaves for Jesus. Yeah, that's me! I'll defect to North Korea, become a Korean somehow, and suffer alongside my brothers.

So now they have one more suffering saint, but one less person sending in offerings. Maybe that's not so good. Or so I tell myself, knowing that my imaginings are the pure fantasies of a wannabe saint. I loathe, in my flesh, the idea of physical pain and deprivation.

May God give us all the desire to call on Jesus Who is the only One who makes saints. What if God wants to make me holy by sending me to that same old job that seems to be so grievous and worthless? What if I find I can touch North Korea more here than there?

I continue to imagine but I anchor my imagination to the written Word of God so it does not soar out of control.

What do you imagine?

82. the agreed framework

Whenever I use this particular reference, I have to begin by apologizing to my audience. The name of the book really is: *The Complete Idiot's Guide to Understanding North Korea* by Quinones and Tragert. I highly recommend it to those who are beginners in studying NK, but wish the title were a little more endearing.

One of the complicated matters the book breaks down for novices like myself is political statements like "The Agreed Framework." You may have heard that phrase lately in connection with the current round of talks. What is it?

- The first formal agreement signed by diplomatic representatives of the USA and North Korea.

- It has no binding force, it is only an understanding.
- It helped "freeze" NK's nuclear activities for awhile.
- It was signed October 21, 1994. (Clinton years)
- In 2001 the new Bush administration ignored the agreement.
- In 2003 NK withdrew from the Treaty on the Non-proliferation of Nuclear weapons, and in essence nullified the agreement.
- It is believed that this accord will have to be revived if the present crisis is to be resolved.

Some of the main features of the accord:

- The U.S. will help NK build a light water reactor.
- The U.S. will offset some of the energy withheld by a freeze.
- Oil will be delivered at a rate culminating in 500,000 tons annually.
- Therefore, North Korea will dismantle certain nuclear facilities.
- The Atomic Energy Agency will be free to monitor.
- U.S. and N.K. will hold more talks.
- Talks will move toward full political and economic relations.
- U.S. will assure N.K. it is not going to use nuclear weapons against them.
- NK will meet often with South Korea.

- NK will remain a party to Treaty on Non-
Proliferation (already broken)

So, do this for us, give this to us, promise us you'll be nice, and we will not threaten you with extinction. Sure, whatever you say. That was the Agreed Framework. Let's pray, and listen to what is coming soon. More of the same or a distinct attitude shift in Pyongyang?

83. Food for 5 days a month

www.refugeesinternational.org will get you the full interview report done by Refugees International with refugees coming out of North Korea, 2003-2004. Here are a couple of interviews that show once more that the food crisis is far from over.

Interview 5, a 17-year-old girl from Musan, North Korea, first arrived in China, 2003.

She misses her parents, two sisters and brother. Her father works in a mine and her mother is a homemaker. Her father received food distributions but only enough for 4-5 days each month. Before the economic reform he earned 100 won/month (in 2003, about U.S. $45.00). Now he gets 2000 won/month (in 2003, about U.S. $900.00). She has a big family so it's difficult to survive.

She came because she lost the $120.00 that was supposed to be for her older sister's marriage. She couldn't go home after losing that money because she was ashamed, so she came to China. This is her first time in China but she had some Chinese money. After she came she was dining alone in a restaurant, met a man, and they married.

She finished high school. Her sister is at the university.

She came to China because she wanted to have a stable life and give money back to her family. She married a 27-

year-old Chinese man. She can't work because she has no identification. She lives in a village and her husband is a peasant. She likes living here but hasn't betrayed her country. If she doesn't get caught then she'll be fine going home. She sends messages to her family saying that she's safe here but she's heard no reply.

Interview 8, 51-year-old woman, first arrived in China 2000.

Her husband died six years ago. Her 23-year-old son lives in North Korea and is a beggar. She got married to a Korean-Chinese man here and is doing farm work.

"China's good for living because the more you work, the more you get... In North Korea it's difficult to get rice. North Korea was better when Kim Il-Sung was alive."

Food distribution was good until 1994. After 1995 the distribution slowed down until it stopped.

She's nervous because of the police checks. She's heard that they'll beat you if you get caught. She wants to stay here with her husband.

More real people with more real burdens for which we can pray. Poverty. Malnutrition. Split families. Lost home-land. Daily fear. The facts of life for North Korea.

84. do not fold the great leader's face

Anne Penketh, in the UK's *Independent*, September 17, 2004, tells some of the legend of Kim Il Sung, North Korea's dictator before the present one. I paraphrase and add a little to her article.

She relates the story of a passenger on the Air Koryo flight out of Pyongyang. He had finished for the present with the reading of a North Korean magazine, and had folded it in two so as to stuff it in his bag. A watchful and stern stewardess reminded him that he must not fold the Great Leader's face, which of course filled the entire cover.

A British diplomat on the same flight asked another stewardess to leave his drink on the magazine while he read a newspaper. No go. He first had to take the magazine off the tray so that the precious face would not get wet-marks on it.

The present dictator has likewise been elevated to god status. Murals in Pyongyang and elsewhere depict a log cabin surrounded by a high (and holy) Korean mountain, and fir trees. A star appeared over those mountains, says the legend, when Kim Jong Il was born.

In fact, Kim Jong Il was born in a prison camp near the far eastern Russian city of Khabarovsk. But North Koreans, brainwashed from birth, believe the myths.

Like the one that says that NK is a Paradise, whose problems are nothing compared to the horrible situation in South Korea and the United States.

And the one that points to the 150-story hotel on the other side of the Taedong River that was never completed. Why? Financial problems caused by the United States (the country that has given North Korea multiplied TONS of food and oil and more).

And the other one that explains "juche", self-reliance: "I am master of my destiny, without relying on anyone else." No foreign contribution to the economy can ever be recognized. This may be the greatest myth of all.

North Korea is shrouded in darkness. The North KOrean government has thrown a giant virtual tarp over the land and no one is permitted to see through it. But cracks have been noticed. Light is filtering in. It's only a matter of time now before all will be exposed, Jesus will be preached, and those called to salvation will rise up to give glory to their God.

Come, Lord Jesus!

85. the most famous mountain in the world

Source: Thomas Belke, *Juche*

One of the fascinating aspects of the North Korean government is its attempt to replace -not merely copy or even wipe out - the Christian faith. Belke, p. 49:

"The most recent development in Juche theology is the elevation in late 1997 of Kim Jong Il's mother, Kim Jong Suk, to the status of a Juche goddess. Possibly because of the historical strength of Christianity in the North, Christian influence on Juche theology is reflected in the Trinity-like image of the Juche godhead and the surrogate gospel of Juche. However, unlike the co-equal three-Persons-in-One God of Christianity, Juche propaganda presents three separate gods with Kim Jong Suk in a non-Su-ryong [leader] supporting role to Kim Il Sung (the father) and Kim Jong Il (the son). The following 1998 sample of North Korean propaganda provides an example of how these three personages are now glorified as 'the three generals of Mt. Paektu':

"Cards carrying pictures of the three great persons of Mt. Paektu were recently distributed to houses in... South Korea... Printed on the front side of each card are letters *Let us boast of and uphold the three generals from Mt. Paektu, the most famous mountain in the world* ... Carried on its back are pictures of the three generals in army uniform, with letters *ever-victorious brilliant commander Kim Il Sung, peerlessly brilliant commander Kim Jong Il, and heroine of Paektu General Kim Jong Suk.*"

So out with Calvary and Sinai. And the world can forget 20,000 foot McKinley and 30,000 foot Everest . Because Kim says so, a 9,000 foot elevation in North Korea's hill country is now the most famous mountain in the world. And by edict of the same dictatorial family, father son and lady Kim are to be North Korea's only choice for a worship-worthy trinity.

It may be a bigger world than Mr. Kim thinks. Why not tell his people the whole truth about all the choices they have, and see which way they go? It is the "people's" republic isn't it?

86. associated with Christ? Guilty!

Time to revisit David Hawk's *Hidden Gulag* (2003), available online.

Hawk describes "two distinct systems of repression" in North Korea. First there is the network of "forced-labor colonies, camps, and prisons where scores of thousands of prisoners - some political (which includes followers of Christ), some convicted felons - are worked, many to their deaths, in mining, logging, farming, and industrial enterprises..." Second, there are some shorter-term detention facilities used to punish (often severely) North Koreans who flee to China (e.g.: those who search for food during a famine!) but are arrested by Chinese police and forcibly returned "home."

Hawk says that in his studies he found "extreme phenomena of repression" that to his knowledge are unique to the Kim regime of the last couple of generations. This is the legacy that the Kims will pass on. These are the things by which they will be remembered when all the dust settles...

- Guilt by asscoiation. That is, if you are found guilty, three generations of your family and anyone else who is close to you, are all locked up in a labor camp. But the truly "guilty" person is separated from the rest of his family members, who are viewed as "redeemable."

- No judicial process. Once it is decided you are guilty, you are guilty. There is no one to defend you in these cases. And your sentence is usually life in the gulag.

- Forced abortions or murder of newborns. To keep Korea pure. Many women, you recall, head north to China looking for food and a secure life. Often they become a victim of the human trafficking that goes on up there. They become pregnant by Chinese men. When they are captured, they must be relieved of the burden they bear. Got to get rid of that non-Korean contamination!

Kim Jong Il denies the existence of forced-labor camps. In these days of "let's get along" we'd all like to believe that. So, help us, Mr. Kim. Help us to believe you. Open the doors of your Kingdom and let us look around until we are content we have been mistaken.

Until then, brothers and sisters in Christ, we believe the many witnesses who have come out and told the horrors of the slave labor institutions. Let us pray earnestly for our family members, *guilty by association with Jesus Christ*, who suffer demonic torment day after day. Let us "remember the prisoners as though bound with them!" (Hebrews 13:3)

87. the glorious pyongyang church

As we continue our study of the Body of Christ in North Korea, we simply must stop and talk about the 1907 Pyongyang Revival. The Christian Koreans have a glorious history and a glorious future. Though we cannot understand some of the goings-on in the North today, we are confident that the situation is only temporary. God HEARS and ANSWERS the cries of his people! I quote below from Young-Hoon Lee's Korean Pentecost: The Great Revival of 1907.

The origin of the 1907 Pyongyang revival could be traced to a prayer meeting of Methodist missionaries at Wonsan in 1903, and attributable to Dr. R.A. Hardie, a medical missionary working in the Kangwon province. Although Dr. Hardie worked arduously in his ministry, he was able to achieve very little. Frustrated, he entered into a period of self-reflection. He was strongly convicted as his prejudices, sins and efforts of self-reliance were revealed to him.

Deeply moved, Hardie began to share his testimony of the work of the Holy Spirit and publicly repent before other fellow missionaries. Subsequently, he shared his confessions and repented before Korean congregations, which ignited a flame of revival and a receiving of the Holy Spirit as never experienced before. As the revivals grew in number and intensity throughout Wonsan, the following year witnessed the outbreak of an enormous blessing and revival that swept the area through Pyongyang, Seoul and beyond.

The height of the revivals that took place between 1900-1910 came on January 14, 1907 when over 1,500 gathered for a meeting and were invited to pray. The entire congregation burst into prayer and public confession lasting throughout the night until the next day. The Spirit that came through this Pentecost spread to the children and youth sparking revivals of a similar scale among high school students. It is said that the repentance and forgiveness was to the degree that the jails in all of Pyongyang were empty!

Men and women became walking testimonies of the power of the Holy Spirit as their daily lives were completely transformed to the amazement of friends and family. Korean Christians gained a new strength and boldness as they took leadership in the independence movement and endured terrible persecution during a dark period of Korean history. The face of Korea was changed forever and the spirit of the 1907 Revival has endured throughout the history of the Korean church.

100 years ago God's Spirit poured out on Pyongyang. Then persecution. 2000 years ago God's Spirit poured out on Jerusalem. Then persecution. But persecution leads to deliverances and miracles and church growth. Let us join in praying that the present darkness hovering over the North will soon erupt into glorious light as the Enemy is again defeated.

The true Korean War, the one for the souls of men, is in the Spirit as in the natural: no final peace has ever been declared. So let us fight on!

88. nk: near total eclipse

This is Paradise is the personal story of Hyok Kang who at age 13 managed to escape from North Korea. Here is one anecdote from his tale: (p. 5)

"When I was very small, Kim Il Sung came to Onsong in person. My father told me that the whole city was cleaned from top to bottom in anticipation of the event. A massive parade had welcomed the Great Leader, with all the inhabitants mobilised to sing in chorus, salute in unison and wave bouquets of flowers as he passed. Subsequently, a hymn was composed to commemorate his visit. The guest house where he had stayed near Onsong became a sort of little sanctuary with a plaque: no one could use the bed he had slept in, or even enter the room. In fact, all the bedrooms throughout the country where the 'perfect brain' had slept on his many travels have become prohibited places. No one else can sleep there- how could you occupy the same room as the 'sun', the name by which Kim Il Sung is referred to in North Korea?..."

I have a simple announcement to make today. How I wish and pray that even one North Korean will read it:

Kim Il Sung was not and is not today, the sun of Chosun.

Nor is his son Kim Jong Il the sun.

Only to one person in all Eath's history has that title been affixed. Jesus Christ is the "Sun of righteousness" that arises in the hearts of His followers all over the world. One day that Sun will arise in North Korea and every nation when the "kingdoms of this world become the Kingdoms of our Lord and of His Christ! And He shall reign forever and ever!"

Because the Kims have attempted to eclipse the true sun, a reign of darkness has descended on North Korea. But eclipses never last forever. These pretenders will move on, and the Korean people will once more know and rejoice in their true Suryong, their GREAT and DEAR leader, JESUS.

Even so come, Lord Jesus!

89. where has the korean culture gone?

Today we continue our (secular) history of North Korea, following the work of Bradley Martin, *Under the Loving Care of the Fatherly Leader.* We're still in the late '70's.

We were talking about the education system last time. Throughout this system and the whole Communist life-way, individualism is rejected. Indeed one of the staples of discipline is peer criticism. Peers are not only encouraged but often *forced* to put a fellow student in place by a criticism session following a confession of some weakness.

In terms of subject matter, of course everything is Kim centered. Writings of and about the Kims are the main diet. Korean classics are taught only at University level. Strange. The Japanese are blamed (rightfully) for trying to stamp out Korean culture. But a Korean seems to have succeeded in this task to a much greater extent. No pottery classes. The songs have new words. No modern music.

At least in 1979, the schedule is 8 hours work, 8 hours study, 8 hours rest. And while "the people" are saddled with this heavy burden, the Kims themselves live a rather extravagant lifestyle, according to Martin. Many mansions. Many women. Jobs for all his many relatives. The Kims live like the old "nobles" (*yongban* in Korean) that ruled for centuries and are despised by Communists, as is the old Yi dynasty. But that dynasty has now been replicated by the new dynasty, about to enter its 3rd cycle.

Excessive funds are spent on buying royal villas, and entire neighborhoods are given over to the new royal class, all of whom eat very well while those less favored by the government starve and die.

Which is where we come in, and beg God for favor on this nation.

90. don't feed the foxes

I couldn't believe it. I've been out in Nature all my life, but I'd never seen a fox out in the open, in full knowledge of my presence, just enjoying a sun bath while I gawked. A man passing by remarked how sad it was that the foxes of this area are so cozy with humans. The reason of course is that humans are feeding them. Within months, as the humans move on to more indoor pursuits, some of these foxes will be dead, never having learned how to care for themselves.

Everything that happens to me these days is translated into the North Korean situation. I could not help but connect this fox thing to the feeding frenzy that the kinder nations of the world have been on as they keep propping up the fox of Pyongyang.

Is it loving to feed the poor? Always? Or does it just make the giver feel good? And when one gives money to a poor Korean, is he sure it is not going to line the government's pockets?

Did you know that the North Korean leadership has so much money that it has financed tyrants all over this planet? That they live as royalty? That some have called the President of that nation the wealthiest man on the planet?

We've got to quit feeding . He has learned to depend on us and eventually will bite the hand that meant him well. Let's be sure our gift can find its way into the mouth of a deserving citizen. Those avenues are few and narrow, but they do exist.

The "Idiot's Guide" about North Korea says things have improved since the horrible famine years of the 90's . The U.N. Nation's World Food Program reported in '02 that the proportion of underweight children had dropped from 61% in 1998 to 21% in 2002. The rate of acute malnutrition (wasting) had fallen from 16% to 9%.

"Food production has improved considerably since 1998, but still North Korea depends on several hundred thousand tons of imported food annually." South Korea and China are the main donators. U.S. and Japanese aid has declined.

The true famine is caused by lack of the Bread made in Heaven. We know that when people are filled in this way, everything else they need will be provided. (Matthew 6:33)

Meanwhile, no food for the foxes.

91. what's next in nk?

Jesus said that when the evil spirit goes out of a man, it goes around looking for another body in which to live. If it has difficulty in this enterprise it will often return to the man from whence it came. If that "house" has not been occupied since his departure, he will move back in, and bring some friends along.

Is it too much of a stretch to apply this same principle to nations? Is not Satan the "prince of this world" ? Is there not a hierarchy of demon powers with which angelic powers struggle for the lives of nations? (The apostle Paul and the prophet Daniel agree.)

If one day North Korea is delivered from its present oppression, what shall follow? Shall Satan be allowed to re-enter in another form?

One scenario I have heard more than once is an invasion by the Moonies! Quoting a brother in North Korea ministry (who shall go unnamed on this site):

"The Unification Church is an aberrant cult that was founded in 1954 by [Korean] Sun Myung Moon. Moon claims to be the messiah of the Second Coming and that his wife is the Holy Spirit. He and his wife, called the "True Parents" claim to be the first couple to be able to bring forth children with no original sin. The Unification Church claims to have 4.5 million 'full-time' followers...

"Moon is also head of a huge empire worth billions of

dollars...

"...Moon was born in North Korea and thus has great interest in seeing his homeland 'evangelized' under his cult. He has been actively pursuing inroads into North Korea since 1991 as described by *The Los Angeles Times*:

"The unlikely relationship between the Unification Church and North Korea dates back to 1991, when Moon visited North Korea's founder and chief ideologue, Kim Il Sung. That paved the way for Moon, an archconservative who nonetheless supports dialogue with the North, to buy two hotels in Pyongyang, the North Korean capital, including the 161-room Potonggang, which boasts of being the only hotel in the isolated country with satellite television. The North Koreans also allowed Moon's followers to develop Jongju, the northwestern town where Moon was born, into a pilgrimage site- another coup for the Unification Church because the communist nation bans all practice of religion."

Difficult to read, isn't it? More about Moon when this cycle continues.

92. don't complain about NK

While I am tempted to comment on the news coming out of North Korea today (extreme flooding that has caused Kim Jong Il to request a postponement of the upcoming talks with Roh of South Korea) I will only say for now that we must pray and believe that this modern-day Pharaoh-like government will one day consider that these constant plagues may well be God's judgment on the regime, before they loses an entire nation. North Korea must let God's people go! Meanwhile I continue in the cycle of reporting which I have begun, and today is "interview" day. Interview 6 of the '03-'04 interviews by Refugees International

WOMAN, age 37, and her son, age 15
PLACE OF ORIGIN: unknown
FIRST ARRIVAL IN CHINA: Woman in 1999, her son June 2003

She is sad that she left her children in North Korea. Her other son, who is 13, is still there. Her plan was to come to China to find work and then go back to North Korea to help her family. When she came to China she came with a neighbor and he got arrested. She lived along the border for a year and found work in the quarry. She worked very hard cutting stones for three months but was paid nothing except room and board. She worked like a man, using dynamite to break up the rock formations. Then she went to another place to work in a quarry but again found no pay. She worked very hard there also.

In February 2003 she met a Korean-Chinese man who told her she'd have a good job in the northeast province of Heilongjiang, which is about 1,000 kilometers away. She agreed to go with him, but felt something was strange about this man. She heard him whispering about her to another man about how they might sell her. She pretended to go to the washroom and then fled to the railway station even though she didn't know any Chinese. She met another Korean-Chinese who helped her and wrote down how to get a ticket and travel. She had stayed in that province for one month and then returned in March 2003 by train.

Her son is happy that he has enough food, but he doesn't like his mother to complain about North Korea. He's patriotic. He wants to return to North Korea.

The people of North Korea are fed lies from cradle to grave. It is hard to overcome what you have been taught by people you trust. But God is able. Let us not cease praying for a breakthrough of TRUTH into this land of darkness.

93. even bullets avoid him!

Back to fantasyland awhile. From the "Korea Today monthly journal" I extract one of the many legends of Kim Il Sung. To be a North Korean means to be fed this strangeness from infancy.

You say, do the Koreans really believe all this? I imagine it is with him as with our Lord, Who is the Truth Incarnate. There are some who really do believe everything that is written, and pass it on to those around them. Others are guarded and questioning in their beliefs. Some disbelieve and yet keep quiet from fear. But the legends persist and must be known if one is to understand the North Korean mind-set.

It happened at the battle at Luoziguo during the early days of the armed struggle against the Japanese imperialists. It was a joint operation with the Chinese anti-Japanese forces.

The greatest obstacle in the battle was the fort on a western hill. The battle went on for three days because of the enemy's desperate resistance from the fort.

Some soldiers of the Chinese units, dispirited by the wounds suffered by their commanders, began taking to flight in a disorderly manner.

Shots from the fort pinned everybody down on the ground so that nobody dared to approach the fort. At that moment Kim Il Sung, Commander of the Korean People's Revolutionary Army, shouted, "We must seize the fort at any cost!" and charged forward with a Mauser in his hand.

The shower of machine gun bullets from the fort grazed his ears, and a bullet even pierced through his cap. Mortar shells fell all around him.

But he dashed forward without pause. The KPRA men sprang to their feet and followed him. The "impregnable" fort fell into the hands of the KPRA in 30 minutes after a few days' resistance. A red flag was hoisted on top of the fort. After the battle, commanders and soldiers rushed up to see Kim Il Sung, and he was smiling as if nothing had happened.

In the days when the KPRA was commencing the record of victory, there was already a legendary saying that even bullets avoided him.

For students of history, there is more than one "red flag" hoisted in the preceding story! More of that in another post. For now, enjoy the picture of a smiling fighter that bullets cannot touch. And keep praying for people in bondage to such as he.

94. Kim and Graham. who used whom?

Why did Billy Graham go to North Korea twice in the 90's? I quote from Juche by Thomas Belke.

During the last three years of Kim Il Sung's life, he was visited twice by Billy Graham... Despite claims in Graham's autobiography that his 1992 and 1994 trips to North Korea were solely for preaching the gospel, his translator, Steven Linton... stated:

"The Graham policy has not been to go there and make converts, but to be constructive in a way that raises the prestige of the Christian community generally."

Belke goes on to say that while Billy was there he "lectured" on Christianity. Graham's autobiography adds: "I had just been to Pyongyang and had spent several hours with President Kim Il Sung. President Kim had been very warm to me personally, despite our differences in background, and I felt that he sincerely wanted to move forward in establishing better relations. I told Mr. [ex-President Jimmy] Carter this and urged him to go.

Belke: However, upon being asked about Billy Graham's interactions with Pyongyang, John Akers, a Graham advisor, stated, "I'm not sure who's using whom."

When Dr. Graham presented the gospel to Kim Il Sung on January 29, 1994- less than six months before the dictator's death- Kim remained non-responsive.

From "Just As I Am" by Graham: "When reminded about Kim's mother's faith, Kim acknowledged that she had taken him to church sometimes as a boy, although he admitted with a smile that he always wanted to go fishing instead. He listened respectfully to what I said but made little comment."

Who was the winner in that whole 2-year episode? The Democrats Clinton and Carter in Washington, who could now be branded "peacemaker" ? Kim Il Sung for being visited by such a prominent American, and a Christian at that? Surely such a man would not be allowing his Christian citizens to be tortured and killed! What a PR bonus for Kim Il Sung!

We can look at the politics of it all and wince a little for Billy. We can even get concerned with what looks like a man of God cozying up to a dictator. Did he discuss Kim's prisoner situation? The concentration camps? Did he attempt to get prisoners released?

Or we can take just one step backward and look at the bigger picture. We can say that 6 months before he died Kim Il Sung was given the chance of a lifetime. The chance to inherit eternal life through Jesus Christ, offered by the man who has preached a straight Gospel message to more people than anyone in history.

Yes, we can talk about the strange doors Billy has gone through to preach that message, and get a bit annoyed at his seeming naivete and lack of concern about his reputation. But it won't be long - if we know Christ at all - before a still small voice will arise and remind us of the Christ Billy serves and how that Christ gained the very same reputation for doing the very same thing. And if we dare listen any longer we will be reminded of our own cringing compromising avoidance of almost any Gospel-sharing opportunities that come our way.

No, thank God that someone told Mr. Kim.

95. Hidden gulag

The title is not my own. It belongs to David Hawk of the U.S. Commiteee for Human Rights in North Korea. To download his entire work free visit the HRNK website .

Mr. Hawk describes the entire hierarchy of prisons to be found in North Korea's captive nation. It is difficult for me to talk of these things since in my later years I have become mildly claustrophobic. The thought of going to an enclosure where I will be locked in for an unknown period of time is pure torment. Add to it that I go there because I am hungry, or a Christian, or because I accidentally crumple a newspaper with Kim's face on it... unspeakable horror.

First there are the *Kwan-li-so* , to which a prisoner is banished for life with his entire family. It is run by the federal government. It is huge, covering as much as four or five hundred square miles! Tens of thousands of prisoners can be in such a place. The prisoners are "politicals" , that is, persons who said or thought something against Emperor Kim.

The *Kyo-hwa-so* is smaller. There is much hard labor. It is for those who commit "normal" crimes, if anything in North Korea can be called normal. Some political prisoners are mixed in. Sentences are set. But many persons die due to the hard work expected of them before their sentence is up. The true "penitentiary."

Then there is the *Ka-mok* or *Ku-ryu-jang*. These are along the northern border, where escapees can get to China. When it is their misfortune to be returned to their home country, it is here that they are interrogated and punished. We'd call this a "jail."

The *jip-kyul-so* is for low-level crimes and for repatriated refugees. They can stay here for up to six months of hard labor. Here there is a high death rate because of the nature of the work and the serious lack of food.

And then there is the *ro-dong-dan-ryeon-dae* , where sentences are even shorter, created by locals to deal with the over-flow of famine-related cases.

Odd. Here we say that misfortune is worthy of compassion, aid, support. There, he says it is worthy of prison, punishment, pain. And maybe death.

96. I'm gonna tell on you

When we last spoke of the history of the Korean church (using the outline in Hefley's "By Their Blood") we were talking of the Pyongyang Revival of the early years of the 20th century. It could well be that the spiritual fortifying that went on there strengthened the church for what was to come. Others have opined that what came was a judgment on compromising believers as well as a test for the faithful.

What came was Japan. For many years a threat and a power to deal with, Japan now makes its move on Korea. The entire country is to be a Japanese colony, with the accompanying Shinto religion. Koreans, for cultural reasons, and also because Christ now means so much to so many of them, reject the Shinto "missionaries" . The Japanese then begin to arrest Christian leaders, and the persecution begins.

As an excuse for their actions, and all persecutors have deemed it necessary to have such an excuse, they claim that believers are planning to kill the newly imposed governor. For "political" reasons, therefore, three Christians are immediately tortured to death. Nine are exiled with no trial. 123 others are brought to "trial" in June of 1911. Some have already signed confessions under torture, though they repudiate these "confessions" later. No one is permitted to produce witnesses. Nearly all of the 123 are given prison sentences of up to ten years.

But believers stand up. The missionaries get the news of these horrible happenings to western nations, many of which already are forming a low opinion of Japanese ways. To "save face", an action critical to eastern peoples, the Japanese release all but six of the prisoners!

Then they announce to the Presbyterians of America that all they will have to do for the release of the six is to confess to the Japanese government their sorrow and their guilt for having sent these missionaries and caused all this trouble. The Presbyterians refuse. But by 1915, pretending to be magnanimous before a watching world, all prisoners are freed.

The method of "telling on" bad governments has worked many times through the years. It is why Kim Jong Il keeps his prisons a secret today. And it is why believers like myself and a host of others, continue to expose him before what we hope will be a watching world.

And why we continue to pray.

97. *childhood memories: darkness in paradise*

The unusual thing about Hyok Kang (*This is Paradise, 2004*) is that he was only 13 when he escaped from North Korea. The childhood he recalls is probably not like yours or mine:(p. 7 ff)

"The power station always switched off electricity at night, plunging the city into darkness. As far as I can remember, when I was small, electricity cuts during the day lasted several minutes. Then they gradually became more frequent, and, in around 1995, they started lasting all day, then weeks. This meant that water wasn't being pumped, so we had to turn on the taps and hoard supplies as soon as the electricity came back on. But when the intervals were too long, we had to go and collect water from a village not far from the city...

"...Even when everyone's resources were exhausted, the statue of Kim Il-Sung continued to light up the night, even more brightly than before in some people's opinion. But no one ever kicked up a fuss on the subject..."

Hyok quotes Alexander Solzhenitsyn, chronicler of the Russian gulag in a most appropriate way:

"Someone that you have deprived of everything is no longer in your power. He is once again entirely free."

One can manipulate others by threatening loss, but when all is lost, who cares? North Koreans who get to the bottom eventually try to get out of the darkness into the marvelous light of freedom. Many even come to the dazzling Light of the Gospel and discover not only Truth, but real Liberty.

For this we continue our prayer vigil.

98. *placing God under arrest*

If in the passages referring to the trials of Jesus one substitutes the title "God" in place of His name, the result is striking. John 18:12 ff becomes:

"Then the detachment of troops and the captain and the officers of the Jews arrested *God* and bound *God.* And they led *God* away to Annas..."

You get the idea. The thought of puny man being given the opportunity to control his Creator is at once startling and sickening. But, yes, God is still being arrested and tormented in our own day.

The North Korean leadership has unknowingly placed the Deity in custody countless times. For Jesus promised to come to His disciples in the form of His Spirit. The church is truly the very body in which the Lord of Creation lives in our day. The house of God. To arrest church members is to arrest God Almighty.

Today's equally despicable men continue the assault, and God allows it, in the main. All of our prayers cannot be directed to "GET THEM OUT OF THERE, " for Jesus suffers willingly for the people of earth.

But we also say, "Lord give them grace while they are there. May they faithfully bear their cross without complaining. May they in fact be faithful until death, for we know You have said we will never be tested above what we are able to bear."

And after we finish such prayers, we look in a mirror and see if there is a cross on our own back.

99. strange regime

Jasper Becker is the author of the latest book to hit the "cycle". Every couple of weeks, Lord willing, I will share a selection from this powerful book to give you more of the startling realities about North Korea. Copyright date of the book is 2005.

For today, let me introduce the book, *Rogue Regime* and its author. You may want to read it immediately!

"What happens when a dictator has absolute power and isolates a nation from the outside world? In a nightmare of political theory stretched to madness and come to life, North Korea's Kim Jong Il made himself into a living god, surrounded by lies and flattery and beyond criticism. As over two million of his subjects starved to death, Kim Jong Il roamed between palaces staffed by beautiful girls and stocked with expensive international delicacies..."

That's from the jacket, which also describes author Jasper Becker as a man who has "worked as a foreign correspondent for twenty years, including eleven years based in Beijing. He has written four books on the region..."

Reading his book, the *New York Times* says Becker's work is "not for the faint-hearted... The facts almost defy belief." The *Times Book Review*: North Korea is "...the worst man-made catastrophe in modern history." Nicholas Eberstadt of the American Enterprise Institute: "... this dynastic dictatorship genuinely empowers evil... only regime change is likely to bring a better life to the millions of ordinary North Koreans suffering..." Suzanne Scholte, Defense Forum

Foundation, "Kim Jong Il is in a category of tyranny all on his own... encouragement and appeasement only strengthen him... [we must care about] the slow certain genocide of the North Korean people..."

As we continue learning about the rogue regime, let us never fail to pray about what we have learned.

100. the mandate of Heaven

I don't subscribe to Confucius, but it is built into North Korean thinking that, in order to found a dynasty a certain amount of clout must be gained from "heaven." By the same token, a king who may have earned the right and then "backslides", so to speak, can hear in some untoward ways from the "ancestors".

Now, a "bad" king might be one who is arbitrary, exploitative, greedy. One who pockets the wealth of his subjects... Sound like anyone you've heard of?

If the forefathers -heaven- get angry, the forces of nature can be unleashed upon the domain. Flood. Famine. Trouble of all sorts. Eventually the people will rebel and rise up to overthrow the tyrant. Sounds familiar also, minus the nation-wide rebellion.

This "Divine Right" of kings (as in Europe) is also known as the "Mandate of Heaven". For some it is an easy way to blame a person they do not like or to exonerate themselves. However, the idea is not without precedent in Scripture. "Blessed is the nation whose God is Jehovah", is not just poetry. It is fact. The good kings of Israel and Judah were a blessing to their nation. The evil were a curse.

And look at Egypt. Babylon. Moab. The roll call actually gets pretty lengthy after awhile. Some say America is also being warned.

And North Korea? Oh my! Pray for revival in that land before all is lost!

Today's ideas from "Idiot's Guide to Understanding North Korea"

101. sun or moon?

Renewal. That's the word we need to bring before God. They are saying things must change, etc. But do believers feel comfortable with the alternatives? Is Sun Myung Moon in North Korea's future? Everyone who knows of Jesus in North Korea today knows of the Biblical Jesus. But a false Christ will be made manifest if Moon replaces the present "Sun."

According to one ministry,

"In April 2002, the Unification Church(aka "moonies")- owned Pyonghwa Motors finished construction of a $55 million automobile assembly plant in Nampo, North Korea, with plans to spend up to $300 million in expansion. Who would have thought the Unification Church would be able to open up an automobile plant in North Korea? But they did it, to the amazement of all... the only non-governmental billboards in North Korea are billboards for Pyonghwa Motors.

" In addition... Pyonghwa plans to expand its presence in North Korea by opening a department store, gas stations, automobile showrooms and what the company describes as a 'World Peace Center' in Pyongyang to promote cultural and educational exchanges."

The Moonies to replace the Communists? You say that maybe this is better? A false Christ for no Christ at all? Why must North Korea choose between such evils throughout her history? Let us pray for a viable alternative, wherein the true Gospel message is able to permeate all of Korean society.

How will God do this? I have no idea, but if He can permeate the world dominion of the Roman Empire (and He did!), he can cover a nation the size of Indiana.

102. in nk, it's death

INTERVIEW 6

(from refugeesinternational.org) Another story of a nameless desperate North Korean refugee who has found a reason to go on living in China.

WOMAN, Age 30. First arrived China 2001.

She was arrested and deported in 2001, but returned to China immediately. In November 2002, she was arrested again and returned in December 2002.

She originally crossed into China with an unknown North Korean man that she met at the border. "There are North Korean men who look for women along the border to sell them. The Chinese client pays. In the back of my mind I was going to be sold."

She was taken to a Korean-Chinese man's house and thought she might be sold so she escaped by going to the washroom and fleeing at night. She wandered around because she didn't know where to go. She tried to go back to the house because she didn't know where else to go, but she couldn't find the house, so finally came to the village where she currently lives.

The family she stayed with had two sons and wanted her to live with one of their sons. She married the 30-year-old. After four months of living with him she was arrested when the police came to the house one night.

She was so sick in North Korea that they released her. She found that it was still difficult to survive there so she left immediately and took a taxi to the house she's in now. Her husband paid for the taxi ride because he's happy to see her.

Her parents-in-law said she could go to South Korea if she wanted to and they found a businessman to help her. She was trying to go to Beijing in November 2002 with the intention of getting fake documents and going to the embassy. But she was arrested on the train because she had no ID.

"If you go to South Korea it's freedom and in North Korea it's death." She was sent to a labor-training center in North Korea. After one month she got stomach problems and almost died. They let her go and she returned to China in December 2002.

Her mother (age 69), younger brother, and younger sisters are still in North Korea. Her father died. Her younger brother is handicapped.

She saw some people in North Korea die of hunger. "The word 'dying' is easy to say but when you face death it's much harder to deal with."

Those who downplay or forget what is happening in North Korea need to come face to face with people like this one, look into their eyes, and cry their hearts out before God.

Please ask God for this lady's salvation.

103. kim's mom: i go to church to relax

I've shown you elsewhere how Kim Il Sung was brought up in an active Christian home, and how he even became the church organist. Slowly he tired of Christianity and was overcome by Communist philosophy. But Kim himself tells it this way in Reminiscences With the Century, vol. 1:

Only when my mother went to church in Songsan did I go. She went to church, but she did not believe in Jesus Christ.

One day, I asked her quietly, "Mother, do you go to church because you believe in God?"

She smiled, shaking her head.

"I do not go to church out of some belief. What is the use of going to 'Heaven' after death? Frankly, I go to church to relax."

I felt pity for her and loved her all the more. She often dozed off during prayers. When everyone else stood up to say amen at the end of the minister's prayer, she would wake up with a start. When she did not wake even after the amen, I would shake her to tell her that the prayer was over.

What do you think? Does it ring true to you? First you have the ever-self-aggrandizing Kim looking down at the church. Then you've got an overworked mom who goes to church to rest, instead of crawling into her own bed. Then you have Kim's own atheistic beliefs being communicated via an [imaginary?] conversation with Mom: "What is the use of going to 'Heaven'...?"

The above is an example of "revisionist" history. It seems to be the staple diet of the poor North Koreans. It is the reason they are in bondage and impoverished. Oh God, arise!

104. whom do you trust?

In your research for North Korea, as you grow deeper and deeper in love with this nightmarish land, you will inevitably begin to hear conflicting reports and wonder which is true. For example, per David Hawk in *The Hidden Gulag* ,

"In 1988, the North Korean Ambassador to the United Nations wrote to the Minnesota Lawyers International Human Rights Committee that violations of human rights do not take place and are 'unthinkable' in North Korea. In 1994, an official publication, *The People's Korea*, proclaimed, '...there is no human rights problem in our Republic either from the institutional or from the legal point of view.' North Korean diplomats at the United Nations in Geneva continue to deny that there are any -*any* - violations of human rights in Korea."

Hawk goes on to list sources that say the opposite, including his own detailed research. He documents the "wholesale denial of fundamental rights and freedoms," and points readers to:

- the 1988 Minnesota Lawyers/Human Rights Watch Report
- the annual human rights reports by the U.S. Department of State..
- various reports by Amnesty International and
  Human Rights Watch Chosun Journal, http://chosunjournal.com/
- the Network for North Korean Democracy and Human Rights, http://nknet.org/
- Citizens' Alliance for North Korean Human Rights (http://nkhumanrights.or.kr/)
- the annual *White Paper on Human Rights in North Korea* published by Korea Institute for National Unification.

Believers will want to add to that list the findings of Christian organizations like Voice of the Martyrs and Open

Doors, that continue to list North Korea as the place where, in all the world, Christians are most oppressed.

Seems like that's enough evidence that we're on the right track.

105. japanese-occupied korea turns against the church

We've been following the Hefleys' By Their Blood history of the church in Korea.

Before Kim Il Sung and Kim Jong Il, came the Japanese stranglehold of Korea. Failing in some of its more brutal attempts to smother the church, Japan in Korea, saving face before the world, tried more subtle approaches. Ordinances forbade any religious instruction in mission schools. Classes in these schools had to be conducted in Japanese. No more Christian schools could open without a permit, and preachers had to be "licensed." But licenses were hard to obtain. So many regulations caused some institutions to shut down altogether.

In March 1919, Koreans rose up against the heavy-handed oppression. They took to the streets in several major cities, announcing their desire to be free. The Japanese resurrected their brutality at this time. They burned mission schools and churches to the ground. Those admitting their faith in Christ were killed on the spot. Pastors and other church leaders were rounded up by the thousands and put into jails that reeked and froze thier occupants. Torture abounded.

The great Pyongyang revival at the turn of the century had prepared the flock for decades, now a century, of difficulty. Yet the church lives in North Korea to this day. Only in eternity will the entire story be told. More details about the Japanese cruelty when this cycle continues.

106. my first execution

This is Paradise, Hyok Kang, 2004

"At the age of nine I saw my first execution, in the grounds of the brick factory. The man had been condemned to death for stealing copper wire from electric pylons to sell in China, crossing the border under the cover of darkness. He was dragged to a recess dug at the foot of the mountain, near a railway track. A train that happened to pass just at that moment, by a barely believable coincidence, stopped to let the passengers watch the scene.

"Executions were a frequent occurrence in our small city. Five or six a year. But the inhabitants never tired of them. As soon as an execution was announced, they hurried to the place where it was to be performed. The locations often changed, but I don't know why.

"The children went and stood in the first row, ready to leap forward to pick up the rifle cartridges or the bullets that were left stuck in the execution post after passing through the victim's body. People flocked in huge numbers. Primary and secondary school pupils even skipped school to join the audience, which always consisted of hundreds, or even thousands, of people.

"Small posters went up in the city several days before each event. When the time came, the condemned man was displayed in the streets before being led to the place of execution, where he was made to sit on the ground, head bowed, so that everyone could get a good look at him..."

Yes, there is much more. I commend the book to you. And as always I ask you to weep and pray with me. Imagine a land where public execution is sport.

And, think of it. Condemned to death is bad enough. Death is death. Guilt is guilt. People must "pay their debt" to society. But infinitely, eternally worse: no chance of eternal pardon from the debt that cannot be paid by men. No Bible. No chaplain. No advice as to how to call on the Name whose blood cleanses away all sins, before entering that place from which there is no recall.

North Korea is tragedy upon tragedy. But not without hope. Let us call on the Name in their behalf.

107. for nk lovers: 3 thoughts from scripture

1. Remember the coin Jesus found in a fish? Jesus could have blasted the government because of its excessive taxes. He chose instead to look to His Father for provision of His needs. When life is unfair, we trust God. I need to remind myself regularly that, although we make people aware of the conditions of North Korea so they can pray, we are not political activists who believe that the government, Kim's or Bush's , is our source of all good and evil.

2. When Jesus healed, He demanded nothing in return, although He was pleased to accept glory for Himself and for His Father. When the NK government brought in a vision expert to remove cataracts from 1000 blind North Koreans, it demanded that all worship the leader before they do anything. Even the doctor who performed the seeming miracles was ignored. Showing of course who the really blind are. It is proper to be grateful and respectful to our government. It is not proper to worship it and ignore ther true Giver of all.

3. We owe it to ourselves, our families, and in my case and perhaps yours, to North Korea, to abide in Jesus. The

Scriptures say that those who abide in Him can ask whatever they want and it will be done. If I want North Korea to be blessed, how much more does Jesus. And He knows the way to do it best.Let us cling to Jesus and allow His own requests for Chosun to flow through us in prayer.

108. nk: the blame-it-on-bush approach

The first problem I have with Bruce Cumings' 2004 *North Korea* is its title. Probably should have been called *The United States,* or better yet, *George Bush.* Mr Cumings is a respected historian and even teaches not far from where I am sitting, so I will try to be respectful. But his book shifts the blame for most of the evils of North Korea to the West, and to the man who in many people's minds caused the Islamic worldwide crisis, invited 911, drowned New Orleans, and a whole lot more. Cumings' book is more a review of the Bush administration than the exposing of what most thinking men consider to be a threat to world peace.

It's convenient to blame. But great leaders all over the world cannot find a solution for North Korea. The fact that North Korea is still a problem needs a response other than blame. Is the renowned historian *sure* that what is happening is Bush's fault? Will not a dictator be a dictator regardless of the international pressures he faces? Will he not spurn the strong of earth and despise the weak panderers? Since he certainly will, is not Bush's truthful approach ("axis of evil") a better option for men of conscience?

I'm sure the book went over well in Pyongyang, and even sounds in places like those propagandistic diatribes one can find on *Rodong Sinmun.* In trying a little too hard to "understand" our enemy, and one can do that, has Cumings become a partner *with* the enemy?

From the jacket: "North Korea is a country Americans love to hate." But hatred of evil is a good thing. Many good men and eyewitnesses have documented the evil. Let us continue to call it what it is and to hate it.

He goes on, " [North Korea is usually] depicted as a secretive police state led by an 'insane" dictator...' Depicted? Does he question the word "secretive"? Probably not. Is there a nation about which we know less?

Or is it "Police state" to which he objects? Do not the military and the police control the moves and even the thoughts of the Korean people? Has anyone found evidence to the contrary? Certainly not Cumings.

As for the term "insane," it is more than a truism that "power corrupts and absolute power corrupts absolutely." Those in North Korea who have absolute power, seem to have had their thinking processes changed into something other than rational. Sane Koreans do not behave in this way. Sane Koreans do not allow people to starve if it is within their power to save them. Sane Koreans do not sponsor public executions that even children must attend. Sane Koreans do not punish people for being hungry and wanting to go somewhere to find food. You be the judge as to whether or not this behavior of Kim is "insanity". In my judgment it is.

Mr. Cumings has adopted the "denial" method of argument, whereby one states a fact , then simply denies it. When he cannot outrightly deny, he blames others for it, especially his President.

Needless to say, the book was a disappointment, and reminded me to stay as far as I can from politics in searching for answers for this nation. God's people must pray, then do what is in their power and God's strength to do. Getting caught up in merely human opinion and the strife that politicians engender because of their limited views, is fruitless.

As to what our view is: "Blessed is the nation whose God is Jehovah." When NK gets God, NK gets blessed. And even Bush can't stop that.

109. communism, kimilsungism, and Christ

The "Idiot's Guide" we have been following devotes some space in chapter 10 to a comparison/contrast of Kim Il Sung with Karl Marx. He says,

"Juche [Kim's self-reliance philosophy] is a faint echo of Marxism." While rejecting parts of Communism, Kim did buy into the whole "class struggle" idea. People fight. Groups of people fight other groups of people. While Marx singled out the clash between "capitalists", people who have money, and "urban workers", who don't, Kim saw things, like neighbor Mao, in terms of landlords vs. peasants. But rather than lift these peasants into the revolutionary class, Kim believed that role should be assigned to soldiers and teachers (mostly soldiers, it turns out!).

Juche is human-centered and nationalistic, as opposed to Communism's universal emphasis. And while Marx and Engels saw mechanical forces governing the world, Kim focused on human conduct.

The goals of the two systems are likewise different. Communism seeks to overthrow the entire world order, replacing all vestiges of capitalism with socialism. The state must "wither away", and all classes with it. A truly equal society. (The dream has never been even closely realized in Communist nations, as there are always some who are "more equal" than others.)

Kim's view was state-centered. It is hierarchical, with clear divisions based on favor. Though he also believed in "collectivism" it was of a different flavor. In the original pattern, collectivism refers to equal sharing of goods. In North Korea, it is a shared effort to unite behind one leader. In essence, Korean collectivism becomes nothing more than the old dynasty mentality, a true monarchy. Titles have changed, but no one questions that Kim was and is king.

I cannot help coming back to a central theme in these blogs: The Kingship of Jesus Christ. I keep hearing it said that "Jesus is in control of North Korea, so don't worry." I think we all understand that ultimately the strings are pulled by a living God. He raises up whom he wills, and whom he wills to abase, he abases. God is in control only in that sense for now.

But when Jesus is truly the Lord of North Korea, every knee will bow to Him. Every tongue will confess that Christ is Lord on that day. When Jesus comes and sets up His Kingdom there will be no more concentration camps, though the Lord will govern with a strict justice. All will be free to worship the King Who will reign in Jerusalem. Godliness will flourish. There will be no more hunger, no need to leave the beauteous mountains for China or any other place.

Those who have already made Jesus Lord of their lives experience how wonderful it is to be ruled by a perfect King. Our ongoing prayer is that soon Kim Jong Il will be set aside so that the Gospel of the Kingdom can be preached throughout the land, and many will come to know what a Heavenly King is like.

110. for nk, a return to the dark ages?

Again we ask, What happens after the present phase of North Korean history? We talked about the "Moonies" and the threat they pose to a post-Kim Korea. But there are other religious forces. Consider the Mormons, who have such power in our own nation now, and whose structure is such that they could send multitudes of proselyting "missionaries" overseas in a heartbeat. The Mormons are even more threatening in our day as they begin to look more and more like traditional Christians. The fact that a leading Presidential candidate is of that persuasion cannot be harmful either.

I imagine the Jehovah's Witnesses are equally prepared, and a host of others. But there is one religious threat that may go unnoticed unless someone brings it out. No, I don't speak of the Muslims, though who can count them out of the race? Or the Buddhists? And the whole Confucian philosophy that looks very much like a religion at times?

No, I'm speaking of something that poses the greatest threat of all: a re-united Christendom.

Whoa! put that rock down! Hear me out. Even Stephen was allowed a major address before he was stoned!

It has stressed many Bible-believing, born-again Christians (and I take my place among them) to see the rising among us of a "World Church." It is a church that in one breath can invite the purest of evangelical adherents and those who claim no Christ at all, to unite under the banner of the Pope in Rome. The Reformation, during which some of the godliest men of all time were massacred because of doctrinal difference with Rome, is all but forgotten, and with no regret great leaders of the Christian faith turn to Rome, scorning "the rest of us." The rest of us, they say, are divisive, old-fashioned, afraid to come of age. They say we don't understand the Scriptures, especially John 17, Jesus' prayer for unity. I have much to say about this chapter over the next weeks, but first these introductory comments.

It may seem strange for me to be suddenly shifting to doctrine and church history when this column has been so directed to North Korea. But it is precisely the subject of North Korea that brings all this to the surface. Rome calls for unity of the believers on many bases, but the basis upon which the Korean invitation comes is the most subtle of all. It is argued that North Koreans will be confused if Christians of so many stripes approach them, all of them claiming to be the true Body. Unite! they say, so that when we finally go in, we go in as One. For Korea's sake. (Won't hurt Rome, either.)

My short response is that the last time the "church" was united in this way it caused far more damage to the image of Christ than the fact that we have a lot of different types of Christian groups. Believers were killed. Jews were killed. Ungodly potentates claimed to be Christ on earth. Salvation was sold. Power was grabbed by the sword, not the Word. Physical unity creates a huge political force, but not a strong spiritual one. I will elaborate on this later.

I hope to show you that God is not calling us to sacrifice the simple faith of the Word of God, the simple grace by which we were saved, the simple forms His Church was given, the simple structures of government, for the monolithic monster called Rome, so as supposedly to help the poor Koreans. Unity to any system that sells the grace of God and causes men to trust their own works will not profit Chosun or any people. God is calling us to be one *in the Spirit* with the true Church that exists -united!- even now all over the planet, to be obedient to the Spirit that calls this one and that one to do mighty works for Him, to believe that in simple, weak, small, and foolish things, is the salvation of North Korea.

111. it's a bird, it's a star, it's not what you think...

At 6 a.m. on top of old Baekdu Mountain in North Korea, a bright double rainbow rises in the sky, along with a brand new star. This mysterious event has been foretold by a swallow, and includes flashes of lightning and thunder, and the breaking of the ice on a mountain pond. What is happening here? What great event is being announced to the wondering world? Why, none other than the birth of Kim Jong Il!

Believe that? A lot of North Koreans do. That is the official story one is taught from a child growing up in North Korea. By the time one gets to the University level, he is admitted to the "Kim Jong Il Department" of the school where what he was taught as a child is not finally re-worked for an adult mind, but is in fact reenforced!

Mt. Baekdu, long considered a holy mountain by ancient Koreans lost in their paganism, has been designated in our enlightened age as a "milyong," a secret camp, the holy birthplace of the son of North Korea's god Kim Il Sung. People are encouraged to visit this site as though it were sacred, though anti-religion is still the standard fare in textbooks too.

The truth is not quite so exciting. One can easily read the Russian records that show he was born in the Russian village of Vyatskoye. His father Kim Il Sung commanded the First Batallion of the Soviet 88th Brigade, a mix of Chinese and Korean exiles. Dad was there under extreme pressure from firepower of the Japanese forces. He was in fact retreating from Korea into the Soviet Union.

What do you do when those whom you trust tell you strange stories? Like, when son Kim was 4, he smeared a Japanese map with black ink, causing a huge rain to fall on Japan! Or how he could, by the touch of his hand, turn the sea into not only land but a paradise, kinda like North Korea is today.

Well it is greatly true that the Kims have made NK what it is today, but Son is not quite ready to admit to what it really is today...

Jesus said, "You shall know the TRUTH, and the TRUTH will set you free!" Long live the TRUTH in North Korea!

112. clearing fog, blooming trees

The "positive confession" movement may have had its start in North Korea. The people there are taught to revere their leadership by giving them fanciful titles. It is assumed that the saying of the name makes it so, I guess. Kim Jong Il, for example, is called the "Center of the Party," the "Dear Leader," the "Guiding Leader," the "Unprecedented Great Man," the "Outstanding leader."

But is it actually worship, you say? *Rodong Sinmun* , North Korea's propaganda mill, says:

"The Korean people absolutely worship, trust and follow the General as god... The General is the mental pillar and the eternal sun to the Korean people... They are upholding him as their great father and teacher, united around him in ideology, morality and obligation. So, their life is a true, fruitful and precious life without an equal in history."

Korea Today News talks about mysterious phenomena in connection with Mr. Unprecedented. Supposedly on a certain day the Secretary's arrival at his office brought a clearing of the fog, and the blooming of two apricot trees!

Conclusion: "Kim Jong Il is the famous general produced by heaven."

Whether it is the Pope calling himself "Lord God" and "Holy Father", or a Muslim exalting his Son-less god five times a day, or a modern North Korean head of state, fostering praises to a false god will only bring down curses on a people eventually. When the cup is full, the world will see how smart it is to go after anyone but Jehovah. We must pray and work for the Koreans to hear of the true God who loves them for their own sakes, and wants to live with them forever, the God and Man Christ Jesus.

Thoughts and quotes from *Juche* by Thomas Belke.

113. nk's Christian warriors: be strong

May the following 19th century exhortation from Dr. Maltbie Babcock, Presbyterian pastor, ring true in your heart as it does in mine. We live in a society that plays too much, that runs from fights, that executes well the blame game, that moves on to other ventures when the present one is too demanding. In the context of this website I say that North Korea needs strong unflinching warriors as never before, to speak, to pray, to go, to give. And for those within the nation itself, to stay. May we all be strong.

Be strong!
We are not here to play, to dream, to drift;
We have hard work to do, and loads to lift;
Shun not the struggle- face it; 'tis God's gift.
Be strong!
Say not, "The days are evil. Who's to blame?"
And fold the hands and acquiesce- oh shame!
Stand up, speak out, and bravely, in God's name.
Be strong!
It matters not how deep intrenched the wrong,

How hard the battle goes, the day how long;
Faint not- fight on! Tomorrow comes the song.

114. All i did was spill some ink

An Hyuk was arrested for crossing over into China, out of curiosity. All his life he had belonged to a loyal party family. He had received a government scholarship to a physical education school at age 12. But one day he was out ice skating and China called. He was caught just over the border and of course sent back. But "sent back" to North Korea isn't the same as "sent back" to Mexico. He was detained in solitary confinement *underground* for 20 months! Then sent for a second dose of punishment,18 months, at another site.

While at the first location, guards kept him awake constantly and forced him to sit motionless for days. All for ice skating into China. Down the hall from him was a man who had spilled ink on a picture of North Korea's last leader. Another who had not adequately dusted a photograph of the "Great Leader."

At the second site, it was time to get to work. His first job was to break the ice, jump in the water, and wade waist-deep looking for stones and laying boards to re-channel the water. Many died at this same job from exposure, or lost body parts to frostbite. Second job: go to the top of the mountain, cut down huge and heavy hardwood trees, and carry them down by hand. Many died in this project too.

Thank God he was able to escape, tell his story, and be a part of the gradual unfolding of the evil that is North Korea. Too bad for most of us, the book he published in Seoul *(Yodok List)* was written in Korean.

Now, my brother-sister in the Lord. If spilling ink, not dusting photographs well, and ice-skating into China brings on periods of misery such as this, imagine the pain of a believer in Jesus who will not give up his faith in our Lord Jesus. What can we do for a North Korean prisoner today?

Information for this article gained from David Hawk's The Hidden Gulag, *available free online.*

115. the long night of the Korean peninsula

Some of my readers/hearers may be feeling down today. It happens to me on a regular basis in the school system where I work. Some may be facing sickness or financial loss. But chances are none of us are experiencing anything like the constant stream of evil perpetrated on the Christian inhabitants of the Korean peninsula. We're back in the early part of the 20th century there, during the Japanese occupation. The new masters became so oppressive that native Koreans, led in large part by believers, took to the street. Japan reacted. The torture began. A reporter of the day wrote:

"Men and boys were trussed and suspended from the ceilings so that their weight hung on the shoulders. Thus they were raised and lowered til unconscious. They had their fingers pressed over red hot wires. Their naked flesh was lacerated with sharp hooks and seared with hot irons. Toenails were torn from the flesh with pincers. Men were placed in a tight box and then screwed up. They were tied up, their heads forced back, and hot water or a solution of water and red pepper poured down their nostrils. Slivers of wood were shoved far under their fingernails. They were flogged until they had to be taken to hospitals, where big slabs of gangrenous skin had to be cut off. In many cases they were flogged to death. [These tortures] were not done once or twice, but repeatedly for days and nights, hours at a time, until the victim confessed, whether he had anything to confess or not..."

A 21-year-old Christian female from Pyongyang gave Presbyterian missionaries a signed statement of how women were treated. I will not be able to share all of what she said. But the most dedicated followers of Jesus were humiliated, beaten into unconsciousness, burned with lighted cigarettes, compelled to "baby-sit" the bodies of dead men, bound hand and foot in stocks, exposed to vile indecent remarks, and on and on. "Some of the girls were so changed that they did not look like human beings."

Oh how the enemy of our soul hates us! Though it is promised that if we resist his temptations he will flee from us, there is no fleeing from the vicious hatred he is at times allowed to pour out on those willing to bear the cross of Christ.

How foolish our little grievances, yes? In the midst of the ups and downs of life, may Jesus keep His cross before us, and the joy of meeting Him, having borne it faithfully.

Quotes above also used by the Heflins, authors of By Their Blood.

116. born to lose

Let's go back to "paradise" again. Specifically, Hyok Kang's *This Is Paradise* . It's the 1990's, during Hyok's childhood. Things we suspect about the government turn out to be true. For example, when the U.N. delivers food, the cadres in the country who are in charge of distribution take most of what is sent and funnel it to the ones who need it least, while "ordinary" people never even get a glimpse of it.

Then there's the ideal "class-less" society. In fact there are three major categories of citizens, based on loyalty to the government, and 54 variations or gradations of those three. One of the most "stigmatised" groups, as in all Communist countries, is the descendants of land-owners, the ones who had any holdings before the take-over. Another step down is members of families of South Korean soldiers taken prisoner during the Korean War. Among the worst groups also are families of traitors sentenced during that same war. And persons who have family in South Korea or Japan. Or families of criminals. Or families of those condemned for listening to South Korean radio broadcasts, reading South Korean books. The list goes on.

Guilt by birth. Condemned to an evil life by genetics. It's called *caste* in India.

Yet by the grace of God there is a remnant of believers sprinkled throughout the land. And these atrocities are whetting the appetite of the North for more calling upon the Lord of Heaven. When the truth is known of what has been done, the people will be free to leave their "class" and join the family of Heaven, where one is *innocent* by association with Christ.

Lord haste the day!

117. certainly not

"This man dealt treacherously with our people, and oppressed our forefathers, making them expose their babies, so that they might not live..."

The tyrant spoken of here in Acts 7 by the soon to be martyred Stephen is Pharaoh but he lives on in the persons of tyrants today. One that I know of kills all that oppose him, including their children. If he could he would wage war with the world and bring all under his dominion. One day a man will do just that.

In the parable of the vinedresser, Luke 20, Jesus says that the Judge of all will one day consume those who have dared to oppose His work. His audience, smug Jews who felt God could never oppose them, gasp, "Certainly not!"

Today equally smug Christians of the West hear of the tribulation that is coming to the entire planet, and fantasize, some through a carefully worked-out theology, that it can "never happen here." That the "poor believers over there" could become the one they see in the mirror every day is incredibly unbelievable to them. "Certainly not!" they would cry.

But it will come on all flesh, including believers'. The persecution, the suffering, homelessness, joblessness, pain, torture and death. It will come. Will this Western church survive it?

I hear of churches having "teaching" sessions built around a book written by some rock-and-rollers. I think, what if the church of my childhood would have had a small group meeting based on the life of Frank Sinatra? He claimed to have some religion after all. And Elvis! Why, he had whole albums of Christian music. Why was he not held up to us as a model? Will this sort of methodology change our world and prepare it for the test?

I see a parade in a town near here this summer. Three Christian floats. The first one, a band is playing rock music. No words. No message. Only rock. The hint: Come to our church, it's cool! Another one , more rock music. People singing words this time. But as is the norm with this kind of music, one couldn't make out what was being said. A third display was some simple children's tunes. All 3 had a chance to share the love of Jesus. They could have even had a short testimony of the saving power of the Lord. The people lining the street only saw the music wars, and the churches promoting themselves.

That sort of religion won't make it when antichrist rises. In the first round of terror, those groups will shut down and never be heard of again.

What about your church? What about you? What about me? Do we have the sort of community and personal walk with God that will walk us through the fire that is coming, unscathed?

They say that North Korean believers pray for us. It does seem that we are in the greater danger, doesn't it?

118. tragedy in the regime

Jasper Becker. *Rogue Regime.* Ten years ago.

The author of this powerful book interviewed Kim Ae-Sang at a town that borders North Korea. This withered 32-year-old had been knocking on doors when she finally came to a Korean family that would talk with her. Her story was so typical but still so hard to grasp.

She had left her five- and seven-year-old with the grandfather in Hamhung, NK. She was desperate for food because since the factory where she worked shut down, no food rations were being given out. Her husband went to the countryside hoping to work for food. For some reason he never returned. So she stripped some copper from machinery at her old factory and headed for the border, hoping to sell the metal for food there.

It's 300 miles to the crossing point into China from Hamhung. People have to wait long hours for a train to take them there. Starving and cold, at least 20 of the prospective passengers die every night. When the old train finally took its heavy load of passengers slowly towards China, it took so long that eight of Ae-Sang's fellow travellers died.

She had no ticket. Not even a permit to travel. So the railway guards had beaten her. She got to the border, still hoping to sell her metal. But border guards caught her and confiscated the copper. Still she planned to cross the river, with nothing to take into China but herself and the clothes on her back. Her new plan was simply to beg for food.

After teaming up with a younger woman, she found a guide who offered to help cross the river. His plan was to sell both women upon arrival in China. Then the guide found out that Kim Ae-Sang was married. He took the other girl, and Ae-Sang ran away.

Now what to do? Stay in China where she might find work and survive, or go back and save her children somehow?

We who know Christ believe that humans ought not to be having to make choices like that. Dads should not have to leave homes because there is no food or money or work. Moms should not have to leave children. Men should not be preying on others' misfortunes. And governments should not create conditions whereby only a few have the right to "normalcy."

There are more tragic things, to be sure, like eternal damnation, souls without Christ. Put all those tragedies together and one has North Korea. If ever there has been a nation that collectively said, "Help us!Pray for us!" it is this one.

119. meeting of the Presidents. what did it all mean?

Historic events are taking place in Chosun today [October, 2007]. For only the second time since the Korean War, Presidents of North and South Korea are talking. And for the first time, the South Korean President is going by car. To dramatize the trip even more, President Roh stopped at the border, got out, and walked across the line that divides the two countries, vowing that many more will be crossing this line someday, and that eventually the line will be no more.

Almost sounds like the landing on the Moon, "one small step for man..." Or is it more like Reagan telling Gorbacev to tear "that wall" down?

While one wants to be positive at times like these, other images come to mind also. Both Presidents are in dire need of support. The North has always seemed on the verge of collapse. And though Kim showed precious little in the way of emotion compared to his excitement in 2000, it is almost assured that his condescending into the world of men for a few days will have a huge price tag attached.

For his part, Roh has a serious election coming up. Need I say more?

So what will they talk about, this "King of the North" and "King of the South," to use Biblical imagery. We hope the Biblical picture portrayed of these two kings is not true of Kim and Roh: "speaking lies at one table." We hope and earnestly desire that they are sincere and honest and... well, it is possible, you know.

They say they will discuss the ending of the Korean War. Always sound strange to Western ears, but, yes, the War is still on. Trouble is, the United States and China will need to get in on this discussion before it can be officially over. Maybe Russia and Japan, too?

Then there's the economy. The North's economy. Oh how we pray that whatever support is pledged will be connected to freeing slaves in Hoeryong and the other Gulag communities. And that if food goes over it goes into the mouths of the truly hungry.

And they will talk of lasting peace. Everyone wants it. Everyone defines it differently. For Kim of the North, it means the peninsula is Communist. For Roh of the South, it means the peninsula is free. Unfortunately, historically the surrounding countries have considered a peaceful Korea to be a Korea to which they can all lay claim for their own purposes.

That's why Korea is ripe and ready for true peace. Only available from Heaven's Prince of Peace, Jesus. Will you join me in praying that that Peace will come to Korea?

120. Plowshares to swords

Kenneth Quinones of the *Idiot's Guide to Understanding North Korea* reports that North Korea had 70,000 tractors in 1979, but only enough fuel for 20,000. In 1998 NK was begging the UN for thousands more agricultural vehicles and tires for them. But it was in that same year that it was estimated that motorized farming had declined 60% over the past few years. Oxen had become the mainstay of the field.

Why less farm machines used in farming when they were available? A visit to North Korea's largest *tractor* plant by the UN revealed that production had been shifted to *tracked military vehicles, armored personnel carriers, four-*

wheel drive military vehicles, like scouts. Tractor tires production had shifted to *military use tires*.

Abandoning its effort to become self-sufficient *(juche) in farm implements,* NK decided it would express its independence in the military. From '84 to '92, says Quinones, 1,000 new tanks showed up, along with 2,500 armored personnel carriers, 6,000 mobile artillery pieces and rocket launchers, and a whole lot more.

Not all of this build-up of weaponry was used for the North Korean army. Much was used to pay African and Middle Eastern nations for oil and raw materials. The cash value was something like $700 million in 1998.

So the NK regime takes free food and farm machinery from the West, so that it can invest what capital it has into military products to fortify its own army and the armies of some of the West's enemies. Then it complains about how evil the West, especially America, is, literally biting the hand that feeds it and keeps it alive. What a scheme.

Strangely enough, America keeps its bitten and scarred hand held out within reach of this torment. Many are asking why.

I cannot deal with the answer to that question now, but we know that the Christ in His people is similarly reaching out His wounded hand to this torn nation, begging its leaders to repent, and encouraging His true church to hold on a little while, as He purifies His people and readies them to reign with Him on that glorious day of His return.

Soon after He comes, they will beat their tanks into plowshares once more.

121. john 17: only God can do this

In what state will the church have to be, in order for North Korea to be blessed when things there change? (Of course they will change!) The church will only need to be in the *state of grace*. For God's church is united by God to His purposes, not by men to theirs.

The subject today is church unity.

Most people point to John 17 when speaking of church unity, and so will I.

Point one. This prayer of Jesus is addressed *to God*, not the church. There is nothing in this chapter that any man should try to do. Jesus asked His Father for grace on the church of all ages, and we believe the Father granted that grace.

Point two. Specifically, the *prayers for unity* offered in John 17 were given to God. Unity of the type that Jesus prayed for MUST be created by God. When man attempts it, it starts looking like the old "Holy" Roman Empire, with its political correctness, its lack of toleration for dissension, its hierarchy, its made-to-order meetings, its uniforms, and its armies standing by to enforce the rules in the flesh. This is not God's unity.

Point three. There's a clue given to us in verse 21 of John 17 as to what kind of unity Jesus prayed for. Jesus said that He wants us one "so that the world may believe You sent Me."

Now I ask you, when Christendom was assembled under one roof with the Pope on top, did the world want to come to Jesus and examine His claims? I think not! In fact, the world hurried away from that to our shores and others' so as to be able to seek God without Papa's help!

But when through the Spirit of God, a Christian prisoner of the Nazis lives her life to such an extent that a brutal guard working for those same Nazis wants to come to Christ, and is even forgiven totally by that same prisoner who bore his abuses, and those two are united in Jesus' love, I say the world looks at that unity, and says "I want this Christ." (The true story of Corrie Ten Boom)

Men, get your hands off of John 17. Let God do the work of saving and thus unifying His people in His Spirit, and using THAT kind of unity to reach into North Korea.

More, much more, as the Lord leads...

122. *stand by your man*

It didn't end in the mid 90's. The North Korean refugee tragedies came on into the new millennium. We continue our series of interviews from refugeesinternational.com .

Interview 9

Woman, Age 28

First arrival in China: 1999

This unnamed refugee came into China with two friends and her cousin. Some Chinese "businessmen" at the border captured the women and sold them into the section of China that is south of Beijing. All the women were "assigned" to a man. This lady stood by "her man" for all of two hours! When he went off to work, she climbed over the fence and ran from the area. She had to walk all night to reach the nearest major city.

She had to keep quiet so that her Korean tongue did not betray her. But somewhere along the line she had learned to write Kim Il Sung's name in Chinese. A lot of blank stares this brought her until finally a Chinese man figured it out and arranged for her trasportation back to the border area of North Korea and China. Nothing was required of her in return.

Meanwhile her cousin escaped her "assignment" which had been much closer to home, in Yangi. But, soon she was discovered and sent back to her home land.

The lady whose story we are following then stayed in "Yanbian", the Chinese side of the border with NK, for three years with a Korean-Chinese man. In 2000, however, there was a random check of the area by the government, and she was arrested. Upon arrival in North Korea she was sent to a labor-training center for 2 months. Here, fed corn porridge, she was forced into digging and construction jobs by day and singing and memorizing Kim propaganda by night.

Her parents became aware of her imprisonment and signed a contract swearing her loyalty to the regime, for her release. Then she escaped again. She's hoping her parents only received a warning.

Brings up a lot of questions. How many women are still on the run? How many have died on the run and their parents still do not know? Did her parents receive "just a warning?" How do these Chinese "businessmen" get away with their very obvious trafficking? How can the Chinese be so brutal to those wanting freedom of speech (Tiananmen Square, eg) and so lenient to human traffickers? How many women just give in and lead lives of bondage?

And, "How long, O Lord, how long?" Such huge evil in our world. How long before He comes and makes all things new?

123. What could be worse than 1984?

Christopher Hitchens, "Slate" internet magazine, May, 2005, gets the credit for today's comments, and I've given you a link to his entire article below. He points out that, although George Orwell in 1948 came up with what might have been considered a "horror story" in that day, the novel *1984* , North Korea has topped Orwell's imaginings by far. In fact, the original Kim and Orwell started their work at roughly the same time. Hitchens says it's like Kim got hold of "an early copy of the novel and used it as a blueprint."

Then embellished it. And Kim's finished product was far worse than Orwell's description of a future society the world might be heading towards. Here are some other points of Hitchens' article:

- Far from criticizing Bush's mention of the fact that today's leader runs concentration camps, Hitchens avers that the "Democratic People's Republic" of Korea IS a concentration camp, aka a slave state.
- There's something about the working of the American conscience that is called into play when it sees horror-filled situations as exist in North Korea.
- Never in Nazi Germany or in the Russian gulag, or in Mao's China were ALL the subjects of the system actually enslaved! But in North Korea, they are.
- In NK, every person is mere property, owned by one family. Every minute of every day is spent in absolute subjection.
- In Orwell's novel, one could get alone on a walk, rent property, etc. Not in NK. NK has a curfew for all.
- Everything is broken in NK, except the police and armed forces.
- At least in slavery, the master fed his servants. Not so in NK. Millions have died from starvation.
- Survivors of the famine have grown up stunted and malformed.
- Whole towns have been ruined and abandoned. Mines flooded beyond repair. Factories idle.

- People run away but at the risk of their lives.
- It's time to move these people to South Korea, America, China. The more and the sooner, the better. Involved nations need to get together and work out a plan that makes it feasible to get Koreans OUT and FED.

Until then, thank God for His church that PRAYS, meets and ministers to refugees, gets Bibles in, supports ministry inside NK. May their tribe increase.

Weep and pray for North Korea! Let it touch your heart until you are filled with Christ's pain! I know the two Korean presidents have signed an agreement. I know 6 nations are talking as I speak to you. But so far I have not heard of one concentration camp dismantled, one prisoner released, one refugee sent back without consequences. Until there is fruit produced, we must pray for the tree to be cut down!

The Christopher Hitchens article is at
http://www.slate.com/id/2117846

124. nk's unique education system

From *The Hidden Gulag* available online free: Another witness of the reality of the North Korean regime.

He is Kim Tae Jin, and comes to us by way of China, North Korea, China again , North Korea again (this time through the prison system including well-known Yodok), again China, Mongolia, Seoul. And that's just the outline of his story. If you dare, read on.

His father was Chinese military, so he started out there. But he and his Korean mother returned in 1961 to North Korea when he was five. Went through the "educational" system, got a job, all in South Pyong-an Province. At age 30, a full grown adult, he decided to visit family in China. There he was arrested and forced back "home."

Then he was passed through North Korea's other education system, where one learns even more. The lessons are about fearing and then hating the Nortth Korean government, though that is not what is intended. First, torture in the "People's Safety Agency" (great names, yes?) near Chongjin. Four months later, more torture at the "National Security Agency" (right!). He was eventually accused of treason because of his family visit.

The torture? Beatings. Sleep deprivation. Forced to kneel or sit motionless for hours. Not permitted to wash, thus fleas, lice. Freezing temperatures in the jail cells.

Then on to "university." The "Revolutionizing Process Zone" at Yodok. Four years six months. A slave labor camp. Helps the body. Helps the mind. Keeps North Korea's economy barely afloat. Farming corn. Cutting trees into firewood. Making furniture. Serving the neurotic whims of Master Educator Kim Jong Il.

So what's so bad about farm work for a prisoner? Hey, after 8 months in confinement as described above, that's what the prisoners think at first. I can move around! But the food is meager, even before famine rations. To survive, he has to eat plants, grasses, rats, snakes, frogs. People around him dying from starvation every week. Personally witnessing public executions of those trying to escape. Still enduring beatings. Sit-down-stand-up exercises until he can barely sit up.

Four and one half long years. But at least, now free at last. Happy? No. His wife has to denounce him. It's the Communist way. Denounce and divorce anyone suspected of treason or you are supporting him and may be punished yourself.

Five more years. Finally he must leave this cruel land. Off to China. Off to Mongolia. Seoul in 2001.

I tried to warn you. It's not pleasant . Let us bear Kim Tae Jin's name to the Father tonight, along with all the other Tae's who are still at Yodok, Hoeryong, Chonjin, and all the others. How helpless we feel. But let us keep believing that God is working in all of this, having His perfect will. And as Mary said to the servants at Cana, "Whatever He says to you, do..."

Say the word, Lord.

125. ot banned in NK

Early 20th century Korea, end of World War I. Japan has taken over. Christians are being severely persecuted. Church papers in the U.S. are telling the truth about the atrocities as they hear them from the missionaries. So the Japanese have to get rid of the reporters. Two hundred "thugs" are brought over from Japan to terrorize the representatives of Christ's kingdom. Homes must be guarded every night. People are beaten. Others sentenced to prison terms. Then the world press picks up the story. Japan relents and produces reforms, which last about ten years.

In the thirties there is a fresh crop of Japanese hardliners that rises to repress Christians. More arrests. More rules. In 1937 students at Christian schools are told they must worship the Sun Goddess. Surely all Christians said NO! Wrong. The Methodists go along with the idea, saying that this is merely a cultural patriotic thing, not a religious one. Presbyterians do not comply but they decide to close their schools. The witness of Christ is snuffed out.

Some churches are given similar regulations. Christians who fail to worship at a Shinto shrine are to be imprisoned.

Then in '39 all foreign missionaries are forced to leave the country altogether. The believers who are left behind continue to be pressured into compromise. No more Old Testaments allowed in worship. No New Testament passages that claim Christ to be Lord and King can be proclaimed! Families are forced to "baptize" their children into the Shinto religion. Church buildings confiscated. Clergy drafted for work for the war effort (World War II).

All of this before Communism. And all of this after Pyongyang is known as the "Jerusalem" of the East. What a history this peninsula has known! How God's people have paid a price over the years! Gets you to wondering afresh, would I have stood firm? Would I have mentally sought escape from the cross by saying Sun worship is merely "patriotic"? Would I have hid an Old Testament and taught it faithfully to my children, as I did in the free world? Would I have found ways to preach Jesus IS Lord and King, and will one day rule the world when He comes in glory? I have now. Would I have then? Would I have let them force me into infant baptism and a false religion. I fought all of that here. What about there?

Easy to say, Lord we are able to bear the cross, to drink the cup. It all sounds so poetic and romantic and wonderful. But Peter found out that all the talk in the world doesn't prepare one for an arrest in the middle of the night. May Jesus' Spirit make us ready. For now let us keep praying for those who gladly give their lives away to Jesus.

Above facts following outline of By Their Blood *by James and Marti Hefley.*

126. nk's untouchables

"Special education" in America is getting a bad rap. And rightfully so. There are parents who are trying to cash in on their "slow" children, demanding that they be tested at school, and hoping the child's "disability" will turn into dollars. Then there's the zoo that is created by dumping students with bad behaviors, autism, academic challenges, and more all into one room and hoping they will all eventually turn out "normal." Won't work. Then you've got the shortage of special ed teachers which means that what was meant to be a help for a child, in the hands of a rookie becomes a disaster area. And we can't leave out the psychologist-dominated team that is coldly recommending that children be drugged up to curtail their behavior, rather than suggesting good God-ordained discipline in the home.

I say all of that because I am a school counselor and case manager in the inner city, and deal with some of this craziness in my line of work. It's very sad. But let's all go on record as admitting that there really *are* slow children. Emotionally disturbed children. Children deformed in mind and body and attitude. They really *do exist* and it takes a very "special" adult to deal with them. I've known only a few of these people, but they're out there too.

So why is this North Korea blog going off on all this? You surely must have guessed it by now: With all our mess-ups here, let us be thankful we do not have to deal with special needs children in North Korea. Hyok Kang, who grew up in that strange Kim-ruled society, tells of the fate of the handicapped there. It all has to do with "usefulness", he says in his book, *This Is Paradise,* which we return to every couple of weeks.

Children with deformities in NK are deported from the main cities, often at birth. They must be cared for by their families because there are no specialists trained to do so. Many see them as sub-human, he says, useless to society. They are not spoken to in the street. They are the "untouchables" at the very bottom of the social strata, the scum.

That is not to say that every parent feels this way about his hurting child. There is often a mixture of feelings within the family. Kang tells the story of one of his neighbors who looked after their mentally handicapped son very lovingly. But one of the boy's uncles took it upon himself to encourage the family to euthanize the child! He lost his argument. But what is it that brings such things into people's minds? Kang suggests that perhaps having a handicapped relative would compromise his career, and bring "dishonor" on the family.

North Korea's unique combination of Communism, Naziism (nationalism), Juche, Confucianism, and what they call Kimilsungism has brought about some very undesirable outcomes. We who have power with God to pull down strongholds and whole nations, when we pray in His will, are asking that the ideas and the very Person of Jesus Christ will be so introduced into the thinking processes of Koreans of the north, that it will be demonstrated in time who the truly handicapped have been.

Oh God, heal this land!

127. God without borders, we thank you

Would you pray with me ?

Thank You, God, for North Koreans. They teach me how to recognize the difference between want and need. They show me what is pain and what is merely inconvenience. They demonstrate "cross", while I experience a little "trouble". Thank you for giving me heroes over there when so many of my countrymen have become lukewarm, and I with them. They let me know the church is alive and passionate and of God, not cold and culture-dominated and irrelevant. They tell me You are alive and worth living and dying for.

Thank You that North Korean Christians are not sports-obsessed. If they have any obsession, it is hunger. Yet in the face of their hunger and difficulty, many of them choose to stay and bring the Gospel to their countrymen. Thank You, God. Thank You that I can go to what I called my "prison" of a job with its dead end and sorry work and I can be thankful and rejoicing in having a place to earn money for Your people. Thank You for working on my complaining spirit, for lifting up my head far enough to see around the world.

Thank You that You are a God without borders. Thanks that I can be in touch with my Korean brothers in the Spirit any time I choose. Thank You that You created one holy church, and that denominations and nations are only fiction that will dissolve in a little while, when all the divisions of earth become the Kingdom of our Lord. Thank You that, even though we are so far apart, I can feel their pain a little, they can feel my liberty a little, and together we can know You a little more every day. Thank You.

Thank You that even though our sin and theirs has abounded, Your grace has abounded more. We know there is no greater sin than resisting Your Spirit's call to Jesus, so we share the world's load of guilt for we have resisted that call often. But we thank You for the forgiveness that abounds at Calvary still.

We know You have saved great sinners. Like us. Would You touch Mr. Kim's heart? Would You change him? Would You protect Your people from his misguided ways from this day on?

Oh have mercy on Your people. Like You already did. And thank You.

128. confession to NK: we left our Bibles at home

As I was reading the words to an old familiar hymn in church this morning, from the overhead of course, I began thinking about what we will tell the North Koreans when they ask us why we don't use songbooks any longer. The Koreans as a rule use many of the traditional songs of the church, a great deal of which have been around since the Reformation. The songbook to a Korean is a precious thing.I imagine that songbooks as well as Bibles have been smuggled in to the North Korean churches by now. But overhead projectors may have not. Here, besides giving up the content of those old hymns on which we were raised, we've stopped bothering with the containers, the books, too. So what should we tell them?

And Bibles, that will be an even greater challenge of explanation. In America not as many people carry their Bibles to church these days. Many pastors have given up trying to get their people to buy one standard version, like the new King James or some such solid translation. So they put Scriptures on the same overheads as the songs. People can leave their Bibles at home, so they do. How do we tell North Koreans they won't need to bring these precious Books into the House of God any longer when "freedom" comes? How will we break it to them that those who risked their lives to get them the Bible did it only for their home reading, that the church is taking another step away from its rich tradition? What will we tell them?

I know. The first Christians had neither Bible nor songbook. But between their age and ours has come the

Roman usurpation of the Church and the Word. The Reformers tried to restore the Message to all the people. They wrote it, translated it, published it, distributed it. Because of that heritage, from a child, most of us have learned to cherish it, knowing it was given to us at the price of much blood.

But the times they are changin'.

Britain and America led the way for the longest time in getting the Word to the world. But Britain's influence waned long ago. America now follows, and seems to be leading the charge into apostasy, spreading its doctrines and strange ways into the universal church.

One thing American workers in Korea, whether they be of the South Korean variety or the standard European stock, need to remember if they are to be effective servants to the emerging (and it will emerge!) North Korean population: we do not sell the new Americanism to the Korean church. We don't go to Westernize but to Christianize. Liberty has its limits and the North Koreans must be carefully taught what those limits are. It is easy to imagine a starving population eating everything in sight once they're free, of physical food as well as all the other thingsthat can be ingested in a man's mind and soul.

Oh for the gift of discernment for North Koreans! Oh that Americans had it too. Who will stand up and ask for the hymnals and Bibles to be restored to the American church? Not for show, but for use. To get people turning pages and finding chapters and listening and reading as the preacher preaches, and growing thereby. To reverse the trend of the electronic age lest we all get swept away into something we will regret as much as did true believers in the Medieval church: the loss of God's Word.

It is coming, you know. One big happy religion with no Bibles, no songbooks, no preached Word, no real praise. No strong message. One huge political power that will speak for moral correctness but will not know what sin is about. 'Cause they left their Bible at home. And no one encouraged them to read it, at church or at home.

129. the war effort

I've got to stay out of politics. Really. Every time I start listening to the current talk about North Korea in political circles I am led to the conclusion that George Bush is the tyrant and the governors of North Korea are the poor victims. PLEASE! Or that it's not really that bad. Or that Juche has a point. Or that Korea really needed the current governments. (But South Korea did all right without it!)

A certain Mr. Pritchard spoke recently at the "Korea Society" and unabashedly bashed the President of these United States, putting the blame for nuclear weapons in North Korea squarely on his broad Texan shoulders. Then in the next breath or so he admitted that in the 1990's, when he, Pritchard, was helping make policy under [some unnamed] President, they too had made some mistakes...

Even people who know they are to blame love to join in the hate-Bush chorus that is sung in North Korea with glee.

But there I go again. Dabbling in stuff I know nothing about. Except that men will be men. They do some great things and they make some great mistakes, on both sides of the aisle and on both sides of the ocean. Mere men is not what this ongoing struggle is about. It's about the war for Korea in the heavenlies.

I cringe when I hear of the great plans people have for "going in to North Korea" when "the door opens." There's never been a door or wall that has kept the Gospel out totally. Never. Word gets in and the Word we send is a powerful Word that gets things done.

The cruel war is waging as we speak. The question is, what part of the "war effort" will you join? Very few of us (actually I must say "you", because I just missed it) remember the horrific days of World War II. We've seen the footage though, and we know that everyone in this country realized what was at stake, and got involved however they could. Women showed up at the factories. Churches prayed and gave. Clubs were formed. Oh so much more. The war effort was not just about the front lines, but total immersion.

Are you in the war effort for North Korea? There are many ways to get involved. Don't wait until the visible doors open. It may be too late then, because those who walk by sight will be entering then and could ruin things. Go now!

There's a song making the rounds these days that would be appropriate to close out today's comments.

"Watch and Pray."

Christian, do not seek repose.
Cast your dreams of ease away.
You are in the midst of foes,
Watch and pray, watch and pray.
Wicked forces, evil powers
Gathered in unseen array:
they wait for your unguarded hour,
Watch and pray, watch and pray.
Put your heavenly armor on.
Wear it always, night and day;

To defeat the Evil one,
Watch and pray, watch and pray.
Hear, above all, hear your Lord,
Love Him, serve Him, and obey:
Treasure in your heart His Word,
Watch and pray, watch and pray.
Watch as if on that alone
Hung the issue of the day.
Pray that victory shall be won,
Watch and pray, watch and pray.

AMEN!

130. witnesses must see before they can say

"Oh, you can't believe refugees, they will tell you anything you want to hear." This quote is from *Rogue Regime* by Jasper Becker and is not his feeling but the attitude of UN officials back in the days before the rest of the world believed North Korea was in serious trouble. Other Western minds figured that all the horror stories coming from real eyewitnesses were some kind of South Korean plot to make the North look bad. The South Koreans on their part thought the North Koreans were making all this up to squeeze more aid and sympathy from their neighbors. Smart people who work at the Pentagon looked for mass graves with their satellite photography, as one normally sees such mounds during famines as in Africa. No mounds. Must be no graves. Must be no famine. Others knew the truth but downplayed it so as not to insult the NK government and harm nuclear negotiations.

And today it would seem that history is repeating itself. Though organizations have painstakingly sent interviewers to listen to independent stories from individual refugees... Though these eyewitnesses without corroboration continue to tell the same story of the horrors of North Korea... Though escapees and defectors join in the chorus, write books, create websites... there is still a group of politically elite folks in Eastern U.S. cities who think just like the no-holocaust crowd. They are in denial of the real North Korea. They tell us it's not really that bad. They say the NK government is being victimized. They say it's all political. They say Bush is the problem.

We Christians know about this phenomenon. In the first century Jesus told His people they would be witnesses. That was a promise, not a command. Witnesses see things. If you don't see anything, you don't say anything. Makes sense to me. We've got believers running around today like the seven sons of Sceva in Acts 19. They know the name of Jesus and try to use it to promote thier own interests, but they've never seen Jesus or known Him. They are false witnesses.

And yes, there are a lot of people who have been to North Korea. Ambassadors. Politicians. But when they are there they see what they are supposed to see and that's it. They come back, blind witnesses, telling us to hold our peace and not believe everything we're hearing. They're afraid to ignite more conflict.

Well, on this site, I will continue to see through the eyes of those who have lived there, grown up under Kim's strange and awful ways, and been forever damaged by his government. I choose to believe those who know the prisons from the inside, not satellite photography guesswork. I choose to believe those who have starved in North Korea over the soft Washingtonians who may have never missed a meal in their lives. I choose to believe ex-guards from North Korean prisons over reporters bound by a party line and a salary.

Truth is more important now than all the nuclear bombs put together. We have seen what lies will do. Rip the cover off North Korea though the stench is overwhelming, and let the healing light of Truth make it anew.

That's my prayer anyway. And my God can do all this and more. Let's keep praying.

131. unity. it's already here

When we last visited the idea of renewal in NK, we were talking about how men are trying to organize the church and unify it on human principles rather than accepting the fact that God's church is one even now, and through the Spirit in unity with His Body the work of entering North Korea has already begun and will continue without political force.

It is the Father's intention to continue answering the prayer of His Son in John 17, making people one in Him as He is in the Son. This is true spiritual unity. An externally "United Church" with no opposition was experienced by the planet from the days of Constantine until the Reformation was in full swing. About 1000 years. Not a pretty sight.

Never has Jesus been ignored by the Father in prayer. Jesus prayed the perfect will of the Father and therefore all His prayers were answered, including the phrase, "that they may be ONE." Yes, that prayer was heard and we humans can stop trying to put the church together. There IS one church. It defies description. But it exists in unity with the Father, as the Father and Son have unity. Theirs is not a physical unity because the Father is not physical.

John 17:20-21. How will the later disciples, like us, ever hear of and believe in Christ? Through the Word of the apostles. How will that Word go out? Through unity of Christ with them and in them. He does not say that [external] unity brings people to Christ. He is talking about the Spirit bringing people to Christ. When God and His people are of the right Spirit, the Holy Spirit, that Spirit will reach to a fallen world, calling out His own through men. He prays for our communion with the Godhead, the same communion He had, so that we, Spirit-filled believers, will touch our world.

Collectively, that which the Spirit fills *is Christ* on the earth today. We start from a position of unity and are perfected from there. We are not *striving* for unity with God and therefore with each other. The unity already exists. Churches may split. The Church cannot. Denominations may form. The unity continues. Rome, pagan or papal, may rise and control the masses (in more ways than one). But Christ knows His own and His church remains defined *by the Spirit*, not the Emperor, not the Pope.

Oh we long for the day when the current North Korean regime moves aside and makes way for new things in Chosun. We long for Christ to have His rightful place, for people to breathe free and drink in Christ. But we must step aside and allow the Spirit of God to call whom He will to get this task done, not assume that human organizing will do it.

Oh, God, breathe Your Spirit on Your true Church and raise them up from within North Korea and from without, even now, as You choose. May we not be in the way, but following Your Way. May we not assume You need us but may we not be disobedient when we hear Your call.

Amen

132. a lesson out of pyongyang

Shaped like a rocket, nose like a needle, largest structure in all of North Korea. It's the Ryugyong Hotel. Meant to be the largest hotel in the world, it met a few obstacles in its construction. The concrete was of poor quality. The elevators could not operate in its crooked shafts. Power failures nation-wide plus the famine of the 90's finally shut it down. The only real sign of ongoing "life" is a construction crane perched forever at the summit of the building. I say "real" because postcards show the building all lit up and wonderful. This is an unfortunate manipulation of facts, using trick photography.

One feels sorry for the builders of the colossus, the Baekdu Mountain Architects and Engineers. Hmmm. From "Baekdu" has come the Korean gods (so they say), the present leader(so he says), and the world's tallest pile of useless concrete (for real).

Ryugyong, old name for Pyongyang, "capital of [weeping] willows" is aptly named. It was to have 3000 rooms, seven revolving restaurants, and a worldwide reputation, all by 1989. Well, it got the latter, not as expected, and costing the country 2% of its gross domestic product that year! It is a deserted place of sorrow and shame now.

We can't help but smirk a little until we realize that this aborted dream is not only typical of the whole North Korean project under Communism, but very reminiscent of some of our own personal plans. Christians, we've been warned, and comrade Kim has now given a modern day illustration for us, to sink forever into our awareness: *Finish what you start* when Jesus leads you into His work. Above all, finish carrying the cross until it becomes the crown. I close with the words of the Master Builder Himself in Luke 14:27-30:

Whoever does not bear his cross and come after Me cannot be my disciple. For, which of you, intending to build a tower, does not sit down first and count the cost, whether he has enough to finish it, lest, after he has laid the foundation, and is not able to finish, all who see it begin to mock him, saying,

"This man began to build and was not able to finish."

133. the refugee way of life

Not that many years ago, this story emerged from Northeast China. It is the next in our series of interviews borrowed from http://www.refugeesinternational.org/

Woman, age 37. Her daughter, age 15. Her son, age 13.
Place of origin: Onsong, North Korea.
First arrival in China: 1997

An entire family, mother, father and children, come to China in 1997. Five years later husband, wife, and son are arrested. Daughter happens to be out and is not caught.

Of course they are deported to North Korea and sent to a county "labor-training center." The bigger prison is full. In the camp they do construction, and work on paving roads. Their food is some bad-quality corn porridge.

After a 2 month sentence, all three go back to China. Son goes one way and Mom and Dad another. To be sure they will have money they swallow some cash and "retrieve" it three days later. (You heard right.) All this time Daughter is in China.

The family now enters into the life of farming. But only for three months. In September, 2002, the police get wind of the situation, come and arrest the family, and once more they are deported! Four days in a general "training center" then 20 days in a "local" training center in time to help harvest. Here they meet the same guard they had had before, and life is not too sweet.

Released by October, this time only Mother and Daughter try to get to China, believing they will be less detectable if they do not travel as a family. Back to the same house in the same rural area. Now the police know they are there, because they keep coming to the same place. But the police won't bother them unless they get an order to do so.

February, '03. Husband and Son attempt to join them. They are caught. Son is sent to an orphanage, husband to another "local training center." A neighbor tells Mom that her husband gets sick and dies only three days after being released from the center.

Son is arrested four times trying to get back into China. Back to the orphanage each time. Not until March is he successful in his bid to flee his home land.

April, 2003, Mom and daughter arrested again. Son is free and lives alone in China. Taken care of by the Church! Mom and daughter have only a short stay at the LTC. Why? A new guard. He is sypathetic to the fact that Mom has lost her husband so when she begs to be able to go see his grave, the guard lets them go. They go directly to China!

At the time of this interview, she is wanting to get to South Korea and stop this tortured nomadic living. Will she be able to handle more arrests?

America used to say, "Give me your tired, your poor, your huddled masses yearning to breathe free, the wretched refuse of your teeming shore, send these, the homeless, tempest-tossed to me..."

Unfortunately, you won't find too many tired, poor, bound, homeless North Koreans in our prosperous land. The politicians can tell you why. I haven't figured it out. We can pray, though. Will you lift up these nameless but real refugees and the multiplied thousands like them?

134. human bombs

No, I haven't suddenly switched to talking about Islam. North Koreans too have pledged to defend their land and their Emperor with their own bodies, their own lives. Christians have long known the principle of self-sacrifice and have produced true martyrs through the ages. The Muslims picked up on this much later. And of course we remember the Japanese who came against the American military in World War II in this same selfless way. According to Tom Belke's *Juche* it's also a North Korean thing.

In March 12 of 1998, the present leader declared to some of his troops:

"The soldiers of your unit have turned your naval port into an impregnable fortress and become brave sailors ready to defend your leader with your lives as human bombs and make suicidal attacks."

Belke goes on, "New Year's editorials of 1996 and 1997 featured 'Red Flag' terminology. Red Flag ideology calls on the people to embrace the spirit of self-reliance (Juche), the revolutionary struggle and spirit, and to become 'bullets' and 'human bombs' to protect the Leader. ...the 1998 Joint New Years editorial declared, 'We should firmly defend General Secretary Kim Jong Il and guarantee his absolute authority in every way in the spirit of defending the leader at the risk of life and the spirit of human bombs.' "

Typical NK wordiness and redundancy, but you get the point. People, just like you and me, willing to give all for their lord. People who have had very little in this life anyway, willing to lay their lives down before any more of their dreams are met. To serve as a living weapon for a man who has lied to them, hurt them, intimidated them, they pay the ultimate price.

Our Lord has told us the truth about ourselves, our world, and Himself. He has never hurt us, only brought good things to us. But He asks us to give our lives in the very same way. How many excuses we throw up at him only your heart and mine know. But it's time to stop that. That beautiful thing that is on your heart to do for Christ, and perhaps for North Korea.... just do it. Rebuke the fear, the distractions, and give your life away.

Again the North Koreans are being used by God to serve as an example to His people. The challenge is there. How about it?

135. 25 kernels of corn today

Hidden Gulag , David Hawk's serious study of the prison system of North Korea is must reading for NK lovers. I summarize one of his testimonies but refer you to his whole (free online) book, which even contains aerial photographs of concentration camps which Mr. Kim says do not exist.

It is not hard to imagine that many believers, "political prisoners", are locked up inside Kwan-li-so No. 14, Kaechon-kun, in South Pyong-an Province. Read and weep with your brothers and sisters as they experience horrors few have had to even imagine.

This camp, according to eyewitness Kim Yong, is in the mountains. Its area is about 600 square miles (20 x 30). There are maybe 15,000 prisoners there (Kim was there in 1995-96).

Mining, farming, livestock are the occupations of the slave laborers. Many want to farm so that they can steal animal food and pick through their droppings for undigested grain. Otherwise meal times mean 20-30 kernels of corn and watery cabbage soup.

Unfortunately Kim is assigned to the coal mines, where he meets skinny discolored prisoners who seem to be nothing but soot-covered cartoon stickmen. Two years of this, seeing nothing but the insides of mine shafts, and at night barracks containing 50 persons per room. His supervisor is a man who dares to believe that Kim Jong Il should not be the ruler of North Korea. How many more will be in this camp when they are honest?

Many prisoners die of malnutrition and disease during his stay there. None of the common public executions occur, but up to 25 are executed by guards privately. Like for example pitiful Kim Chul Min, shot for collecting ripe chestnuts without authorization. And Kal Li Yong, who "died after having his mouth smashed by a feces-covered stick" for stealing a leather whip, soaking it in water, and then eating the softened leather."

Even more deaths are attributable to mining accidents than to executions.

How wimpy and foolish I feel after I share these tragic stories with you. What shall Americans offer to God of value on the Day when He through Jesus judges the House of God? Beautiful stains on church windows? A comfortable pew? Sink-in carpet? Huge collections of instruments? An awesome sound system? A cathedral?

Who will be able finally to lay down the cross he has borne, at the feet of an understanding Jesus? Or are

America's church aisles already strewn with abandoned crosses ?

What can we offer, Lord?

136. the true weightwatchers

Are things getting any better in North Korea? Yes, in some ways. But we're not ready for a "Weight Watchers" program there yet. The crisis is far from past.

The Amnesty International Report of 2005 cites the following human rights situation in North Korea. *Always remember that what is happening to the population at large is happening to your Christ-filled brothers and sisters too.* You'll soon see it is no time to stop praying for them.

A condensation of the report:

- Public executions continue. Those who proselyte or practice in the underground church are some of the victims of these executions.
- Anyone seen to be in disagreement with the government faces severe punishments.
- Access to international media denied to most citizens. TV and radio receivers are set to government channels.
- Reporters who so much as misspell a senior executive's name can be punished.
- Christians, just because they are Christians, can be put in labor camps.
- In the prison camps, torture is common.
- Prisoners found communicating can be beaten with iron bars.
- Cold water, even in freezing weather, can be poured on a prisoner or he can be subject to forced intake of water.

- Repatriated refugees (sent back from China when caught) have been imprisonerd, tortured, and/or executed.
- Even children who are caught and returned are considered criminals, not victims.
- 10-11 million still do not have enough to eat.
- 6.5 million are chronically malnourished.
- Food rations actually declined from 2003 to 2005. There was enough being given out in '03 to give every person 319 grams of food per day. That shrunk to 250 grams in '05.
- Food can be bought at privatized markets, but the cost is many times higher than the government issue. Many urban families spend up to 85% of their income on food.
- The number of children whose growth has been stunted from malnutrition lessened from 42% in 2002 to 37% in 2005.
- Acute malnutrition is down from 9 to 7 percent.
- Underweight children aged 1-6 has risen by 2% .
- One third of NK's moms are malnourished.
- There have been alarming reports about increases of maternal mortality rates. No numbers given.
- Lack of access to clean drinking water and poor sanitation continue.

The question always comes back to the richest and most prosperous believers on the planet at present: What shall we do? My answers are still forming for me and my house. Present activities combined with some future plans respond to this huge need. Perhaps God will speak a plan into your life? What if *tens of thousands* of God's people responded, and showed the world what Christ does when people hurt?

137. a dollar and ten seconds

I've been saying a lot about the regime on the northern part of the Korean peninsula. Slowly but surely I am seeing the evils of my own nation, as we creep into a godlessness that can only mean death and destruction to the American civilization. And then there's me...

Two e-mails awaited me this morning. You've probably seen one of them circulating. It's a picture of the new dollar coins. The sender of the e-mail is urging that all of us refuse to accept these new dollars as change. Why? The words "In God we trust" are curiously missing. Well, we can be angry about that. But is America a land that trusts in God? Or does it trust more in its military might? And its strong economy? I sorrow not for the words on the coin as much as I do for the fact that most Americans cannot say truthfully that they do trust Him. And you? And me? Subtract the comfort and ease and great food and prosperity? Trust still there?

The 2nd e-mail was from the school system for which I work. It too was stating only a symptom of the disease. It too was a scary reminder of how far America has backslidden. Its freefall seems irreversible now. The memorandum from headquarters, which was really our own way of enacting a bill that came out of the Illinois legislature, demanded that every student be asked to give *10 seconds* to "silent reflection and prayer."

Yuk. America's public schools were founded on the Scriptures. Ever heard of the *McGuffey Reader*? Reading the Bible and studying spiritual truths were the in thing. Slowly that Christian base eroded, to the point where now any official mention of our beginnings is *verboden.* But as a nod to someone or some political pressure, we *shall* be allowed to stop what we are doing first thing in the school day and have a full 10 seconds worth of reflection. (But no religious content is to be mentioned by the teacher.)

All sad enough. Then I heard the sermon that came up on my ipod. It was about "enemies of the cross." Right away you think I'm talking about the government agencies and public schools, or the Communists, or the Muslims. Of course they are our enemies. But they are not the worst.

When the Bible uses that phrase, "enemies of the cross of Christ" it is talking about believers, that is, church members, who are *only concerned about earthly things*. One who knows about the things of God and still cares more about the things of this world is the worst enemy Christ has. For he is a daily advertisement of what it means to be a Christian.

Since I have entered the struggle for my brothers in Korea, I have been made aware of my own need to be liberated from this world and to take up the cross of Jesus where I am. To stop crying and fussing and complaining and be a true soldier of Jesus. Without such an attitude how can we be a blessing to the suffering?

138. short-lived joy

Christian history of Korea continues, following outline of *By Their Blood* , James and Marti Hefley.

The ultimate surrender of Japan finally came. The Empire was crushed and humiliated. Koreans were ecstatic, and rushed into the streets to celebrate. What glory! What joy! Their longtime enemy defeated! One could hear Christians raising up praises to God, singing hymns loudly that they had been forbidden to sing at all. Worship, witness, all restored after 35 long years of oppression.

But from the North, not the East, came the next blow. Due to a decision made far from Korea by persons definitely not Korean, the land of Chosun was to be divided into two parts, "temporarily." The Soviets would be asked to supervise activities in the northern part of the country, and America would restore order to the southern section.

Naive American policy placed a division line roughly half way down the peninsula that has remained to this day. The Soviets decided they would not leave, not at least until they had a government established that resembled Moscow. In 1948, two separate Korean governments were formed, and the persecution began in the North, where Christ had made the largest inroads.

Five million people, many of them believers, got out of the "paradise" before it could turn into the chaos that would evolve over the decades. At least in the South the President seemed to be a Christian, and there they would worship freely. Then, nearly 60 years ago, the curtain closed. Christian blood began to flow freely. The persecution has continued until now.

Many thousands of Christ's followers were killed and/or placed in forced labor camps. And unlike in the Japanese occupation, the goings-on became very private. Even now, not too many people know what is happening in North Korea. A few have escaped and reported to us. In weeks to come we will share more of their stories, Lord willing.

What a tragic history is the Korean one. What a lot to pray about.

139. when God abandons

It is a sad and scary truth but one we must face. God does abandon people and nations.

- Samson was abandoned when he persisted in his disobedience.
- Israel was abandoned when she would not stop going after other gods.
- Jesus Himself was temporarily abandoned on the cross. For our sin, the Father turned His ear from the cryings of His only begotten Son.
- North Korea was abandoned when its leadership turned its people away from worship of the one true God and caused them to worship human idols that took over the country.
- The United States is in the process of losing its protection as it allows more and more of the things that God hates. December 7 and September 11 are only two of the tragedies that have befallen our country. One thing that is playing itself out as I write today is the inability of God-fearing moral men to find a candidate to run for the Presidency. Some of us may have had trouble with Billy Graham's ecumenical ways, but where now is the "prophet" who whispers in the ears of our leaders the things of God? Where is a national voice of righteousness being raised up that people are hearing? Unless America repents there will be many more tragedies.

So how does the abandonment of God get reversed? We use the same cast of characters:

- Samson repented. For the rest of his life he wanted to be God's man and win God's victories. God gave him that chance and came back to him.

- Israel followed hard after God in Babylon and God heard her cries for restoration. Another chance, another temple, revival! God's people prayed.

- When our sins were paid for, Jesus was released from the old beaten bloody body, and was glorified and resurrected. Perfect obedience.

- Consider also the persecution of the Roman Empire. As God's people preached the Gospel "underground" the entire Empire was salted down and made worth saving.

- Ex-Communist countries of our day have the same testimony. Freedom came to them as the underground church became such a factor as not to be ignored any longer. Life erupted out of the death in persecution.

- Today there are believers inside of North Korea spreading the Word of God, praying, believing God for a great national miracle. They are repenting that they ever followed and believed the government. It seems to me that our job now is to keep feeding that surge of life until it too erupts. Keep the Bibles flowing into North Korea. Keep sending men and women in. The refugees who come out must be reached for Christ. Many will go back in and lay their necks down for Jesus. And North Korea will be abandoned no longer.

- As for America. May she only look at Chosun and see her future if she does not straighten up her act. Mercy! Mercy! Today pray for America, perhaps so very ripe for judgment. Could it be that a time will come when the prosperity of this nation will be swallowed up and totally forgotten in unimaginable poverty? Why not?

But for today, let us remember the prisoners, as though bound with them, in beloved Chosun.

140. meet a privileged american

There's no way to get around it. I am a man of privilege unequaled on the Planet. Consider how I lived my life just yesterday.

When I arose, I turned on a switch and voila! there was light. Incredible! No fumbling in the darkness. No lighting a candle or even a match. Light just streamed through my room automatically.

I shuffled sleepily over to the bathroom, moved a faucet lever and behold again! response! water came surging through a labyrinth of clean sturdy piping to do me service. If I had wanted to, I could drink the water. When I was ready, I made the water hot without boiling it over a stove or fire. The chair located in this room contains its own miracles but I will spare you those details.

I dried my face on a towel that had been cleaned in a machine, not down at the river. In just minutes of human work, this towel and a whole basket of other clothes were placed in a huge bucket. More switches. More pipes. More faucets. Less than an hour later, clean and on the way to being dried. From there to another machine, clothes were lifted out and lifted in. Switches. Heat. Finished. Ready to iron or put away.

Did i say iron? Do all civilizations have an electricrified piece of metal that flattens clothing into smooth surfaces? Mixers to put foods together? Toasters for that crunchy feel on the bread? Blankets that get warmer when plugged in?

The furnace had been running all night at my house. Did not have to add coal or logs. Was warm as toast in every room. One setting of the thermostat works all winter. Is this privilege or not?

My wife gave me a great breakfast. I ate to my heart's content, then stopped when I was full.

Being the weekend, we decided to get out of the house. We climbed into our little machine (we have two of them actually), turned on yet another switch, and the machine took us many miles away with no effort on my part except turning a wheel and pumping a pedal.

Being in a different part of the state we could view fresh scenes and fill our minds with good memories. We stopped at a restaurant and once more ate to our satisfaction. And then some. We stopped for ice cream...

OK, stop, stop! Point made. But why bring it up at all?
Well, it's this thing I have for North Korea.
What! Another guilt trip for American believers?
Bear with me. If you look at the list above, and think North Korea, you see there is this great gulf between us. Electricity irregular if present at all. Water defiled. Sewage

system sadly lacking if existent. Machines unimaginably expensive - again, if available at all. Heating. Food. Automobiles. Are you kidding? Restricted travel. Bondage. Oppression. Hunger. Almost nothing that I did yesterday has ever been done by a North Korean.

So the point? How can I stop being an American? Stop being affluent, privileged, satisfied, fat? It's not my fault I was born here!

The cross of Jesus held before your eyes long enough will help you to focus on the answer God has for you. For me it has been a succession of things. Give them money. Send them material blessings. Realize that our materialism goes too far and cut back on my own lifestyle. Pray for them regularly. It may mean for some, even for me, sell all you have and give to them your very life. Transplant.

So everything's "on the table".

Yep. Only we say in church, "on the altar." Being born into privilege is great but it's a great responsiblity too. Maturing believers finally realize that all this "stuff" around them is for someone else, not just themselves. "To whom much is given, much is required." That's when life becomes really fun, when we discover the *privilege* God has given to His own to share.

141. how bad was it?

North Korea is not out of the woods yet, though somewhat improved. Just how many died during the famine? One organization says 3.5 million. A north Korean document traced monthly death rates in one mining town. 19% of the town died between 1995 and 1998. That's not counting 20% who fled, and many others who died of a cholera epidemic.

Another group interviewd 440 refugees from North Hamgyong and concluded that the death rate was around 13%. If that statistic was true of the whole country this famine was the worst in human history.

Even a North Korean official admitted in 1999 that 220,000 had died from 1995-1998.

The misery of those years and to some extent these years is indescribable. Many despaired and took poison. Many took their children to railway stations so that perhaps someone else could feed them. Others sold their children.

Cannibalism was widespread. A man was caught and shot after they found the head of a corpse in his house. A couple was executed for murdering 50 children and salting and storing their flesh, mixing it with pork and selling it in the market. A family of five was shot for luring small children into their house, drugging them, chopping up their bodies...

Enough for today. Enough to bring us to a place of prayer for a nation and a government. Enough to ask God to raise up His Word and our Lord to rule over North Korea. Where Christ rules, little children are not eaten. Oh that North Korea will hear about Jesus and proclaim His Lordship!

Today's facts gleaned from Becker's 'Rogue Regime.'

142. falling star

If you were to travel back in time and see the Korean peninsula of 1980, you might be shocked. Consider:

> Pyongyang's grain production reached record highs. Seoul was dependent on U.S. food aid. "South Korea's export and light industry-oriented economy was depressed by mounting competition

from Taiwan, Hong Kong..." (This and other facts & quotes from Quinones' *Idiot's Guide to Understanding North Korea.*)

North Korea's army was getting better and better, fully supported by Soviet-designed tanks, armored vehicles , and ballistic missiles. South Korea was not progressing militarily.

Pyong was a "picture perfect city of two million well-fed and clothed people. Seoul was a chaotic city of narrow streets." Students demonstrated there against the government. Labor disputes were suppressed. Journalists were jailed. Politicians were corrupt.

Today everything is reversed.

Seoul made persistent progress toward democracy. And the Church was allowed to grow. Pyongyang went the other way.

Seoul was asked to host the Olympics. Pyongyang was enraged and hosted its own rather than admit inferiority.

Seoul became a power in the world market. Pyongyang shriveled and nearly died economically and in most every other way.

Seoul has diplomatic or commercial ties with nearly every nation on earth. Obviously North Korea's range is a bit more narrow.

In Seoul there are parks (not just the opposite of Kims, but green places where people relax), a middle class that is growing still,cultural diversity. In Pyongyang there is little of beauty, little of the non-Korean, and only two major classes: The haves and the near-destitute.

Today's ROK army is modernized, focused on national defense.

Aid from Russia and Beijing has nearly stopped for North Korea. The South has emerged as independent and survives on trade.

Agricultural and industrial production have gone "south", literally, in North Korea. The South continues to grow.

North Korea cannot compete with the high quality goods coming out of the South, and has lost its markets in Eastern Europe and central Asia. It has had to resort to selling weapons to the enemies of mankind, and just plain begging, to stay alive.

Am I naive and politically daft in suggesting that South Korea is being "blessed" because so many of its citizens love and serve Jesus Christ? And that North Korea is being cursed because it has been turned away from Christ and turned in on itself? Can any nation prosper where Christ's kingdom is not allowed to prosper? Egypt came down. Rome came down. Moscow came down. Eastern Europe came down. Enemies of Christ, every one.

North Korea then... Will Christ work a powerful work of grace from the inside, or finally say to those in charge: That's as far as you go! Now I will rule North Korea!

One way or another, what a day is coming!

143. no more power plays

Suppose, when the door to North Korea opens wide, we could bring in the Rome-based ecumenical church in all its glory. Hundreds of opposing teachings. Man-made catechisms and formulas. An array of cultures bringing along their religious biases and somehow incorporating them into the Roman system. A true Babylon that spans from "fundamentalists" to Buddhists. And we would then say to North Korea, Here is Christ, partake!

OR suppose we could send only one man, full of the Holy Ghost, totally given over to the written Word of God, to preach from village to village, Paul-like, the unsearchable riches of Christ.

I'll take the one man over the system any day. Rome has proved what it will do when given the chance. Christ has proved what He can do through one man. Let us follow Christ alone into North Korea.

What produces spiritual, true, unity? John 17:22 says that it is the glory of God, evident in a Spirit-filled believer. Man's glory fades and grows dim and dies out altogether. That which seems right and good and powerful among men is a waste of time in Heaven.

Our goal is not church unity, according to Jesus, John 17:23. Our goal is oneness with Christ. Our goal is Christ in us and us in Christ. There follows spiritual perfection, holiness. This holiness and glory of God is broadcast to those around us and they want to know Christ too. The wording of the verse calls for one cause and two effects: The cause is Christ in His people and God in Christ. The first effect is perfection of the church. The second effect is that the message of God's truth and love will be given to the world.

Hey, read it for yourself: "I in them, and You in Me; that (1) they may be made perfect in one, and that (2) the world may know that You have sent Me, and have loved them as You have loved Me."

Where did we get the idea that if the church all gets together, everyone will get saved? It's not in the prayer of Jesus!

I sound again the warning to those members of the Body who will read this: Beware false "official" unity that has as its end a political power with which the church will "overwhelm" the world, and in our case, the newly-opened North Korea. Seek to know Him intimately and personally and the Koreans will come to you asking for what you have.

No more power plays! Let Christ enter North Korea by the people of His choosing!

144. memberships available

What is the cross? And how can I relate to my North Korean brothers and sisters who love Jesus to the death? Two parts of the question that travels with me day after day since I met this land. I can never be the same having been challenged by their faith.

I live in a land of comfort and pleasure. Should I concentrate on being uncomfortable? Is that the cross? Why not a Daniel fast? I tried that for a week not long ago. Vegetables and water. Seemed feasible. I meant to go for two weeks, though. After a few days i realized what I was in for. And I headed for familiar land. Better to fast altogether than to keep eating like that.

"But in North Korea," the Voice comes...

I read in a northwest Alabama newspaper online about the 21st century Underground Railroad in NK. The author "met groups of people who live every moment with sickening fear," not knowing when the sound of footsteps outside the door might mean the Chinese police are there to force them back to North Korea and misery. He speaks of "wretched" people who come from a "national torture chamber."

How can I relate? My wife purchased a tour package out West so I could get back up in the air, and eventually visit or even work in Chosun. Because of an unfortunate flying incident, I have been "sickened with fear" at the thought of flight and claustrophobia. I struggled for weeks with the thought of even going on this pleasure trip, and at the last minute called it off. Such a hero.

But in North Korea believers can't "call it off." It's not about pleasure packages and making up one's mind what one will do. It's the cross, the cross, the cross...

I am truly the wretched one, flinching from imaginary pain while they suffer the real thing.

What is the cross? Denying myself more and laying my life down for my wife, my children, my church, my workplace? Or presenting myself before Kim Jong Il and others of Christ's enemies and saying "Here I am, do with me what you will, but I will preach Christ until I die." Or both? Or more?

There are some no-doubt statements about which all of us need to meditate, I think:

"If we suffer with Him, we shall reign with Him." That means if we don't, we won't.

"All who live godly in Christ Jesus will suffer persecution." Again, those who don't won't.

"Anyone who wants to save his life will lose it." And vice versa.

And then there's Paul's classic description of enemies of the cross of Christ: those who do not mind heavenly things, and whose god is their belly.

There is only one church. It is the suffering church. Let us all apply for membership, being willing to die to our own plans effective immediately.

145. far from home

Interview #12 from Refugees International. For the uninitiated, this organization traveled to northeastern China to document the plight of the hungry people leaving NK's "utopia." Here is my latest offering in the series.

A woman, age 28

Her daughter, age 4

First arrival in China, 1998.

She came into China with a 45-year-old brother. The brother had already made contacts and had acquaintances in China. He is involved in the smuggling business and so could not stay with his sister.

She came to China because, for one thing, her family is listed as part of North Korea's "hostile" class. This is among the lowest of the already low groups of people it has pleased the North Korean government to create. Those most loyal all the way to those most hostile all have a group of their own, scores of different classes in all.

She was faced with three choices. 1) go to South Korea. 2) Marry a (Korean-)Chinese man. 3) Take care of an old person. She was afraid of endangering her North Korea family by a move south. She opted for marriage.

As a younger woman she was doing all right, but as she matured she desired more freedom than she was being offered. She was especially interested in becoming a teacher in China, but this door would be hard to crack open. She had actually done some teaching in her homeland and had learned some about the outside world.

At the time of the interview she expressed a certain amount of satisfaction about her life, especially in comparison to how it could have been in North Korea. She often wishes she had gone to South Korea. The last thing she did before the interview was have her mother brought to China with her. This was in 2003.

But her mother was arrested. And deported. And life goes on.

Another object of prayer. This is a real person, but she is symbolic of many more in the same shape. Alienated from their homeland, separated from family members, barely making a living, suppressing dreams of careers and normal home life...

May our merciful God meet the North Koreans soon!

146. think not of death

Not too many years ago, and perhaps yet today, North Korea was training up to 140 suicide bomber pilots "to plunge into key South Korean targets if war breaks out on the divided peninsula...the new unit appears to be fashioned after the Japanese kamikaze pilots of World war II." The quote is out of Belke's *Juche*.

Anyone reading who remembers the kamikaze? These suicide warriors patterned their lives after the old samurai spirit, embodied in these oders to 1940's Japanese military men:

A sublime sense of self-sacrifice must guide you throughout life and death. Think not of death as you push through with every ounce of your effort, fulfilling your duties. Make it your joy to do everything with all your spiritual and physical strength. Fear not to die for the cause of everlasting justice. Do not stay alive in dishonor. Do not die in such a way as to leave a bad name behind you.

Must be hard to defeat an enemy like that. What if we, soldiers of Christ, were that kind of enemy? What if an army of believers would simply rise up and preach Christ in North Korea, as the apostles did in the dangerous terrain of their time? They died. They were beaten. Imprisoned. Made to suffer loss. But somehow they considered that the norm.

What do we consider the norm? The cross? Or the western way of life?

147. *unhappy medium*

Should you decide to take up residence in the Democratic People's Republic of Korea you would most likely be given three choices for television viewing: North Korea Chosun TV, Mansu Hill TV (Pyongyang only) and Chosun Education and Culture TV. All three of these are used to spread propaganda throughout the land.

Now don't get me wrong. I know that our hundreds of channels are used for propaganda too. American TV propagates carnal knowledge, violence, various political opinions, entertainment, and even a small percentage of decent information. But in North Korea all the messages center on the cult .

Radio has only one station for local consumption. Radios are all fixed to receive this one channel. Correcting your radio to receive intake from surrounding nations is punishable. And the monotone message is the same. About 34% of the programming praises the dynasty. 28% encourages workers to work even harder than they do. 17% preaches the Juche (sel-reliance) theme. 12% is about the poor South Koreans and their suffering, or denigration of the Seoul government.

Other North Korean radio is sent elsewhere, mainly to South Korea. One airs beautiful music with generous helpings of criticism of South Korean ways. Another, with more criticism, actually claims to be broadcasting from South Korea using South Korean dissidents. To sound genuine, the broadcasters are a combination of defectors and the abducted.

No system is fool-proof. Up to a fourth of the citizenry has "fixed" their radios. AM and shortwave signals are getting through in spite of the hokey radios and NK's attempt to jam signals. The people hear. At first they have trouble believing it, but eventually, even at this human level, truth gets through and sets people free. The knowledgable often leave.

If true on the human level, how much greater it will be when Koreans hear the Truth known as Jesus and are set free body soul and spirit. Let us not grow discouraged in our prayers and efforts and gifts. Whom the Son sets free is really free!

information gleaned from HRNK newsletter of 5-18-06

148. the chosun people

That's what it's called in North Hamgyong: "Chosun People's Security Unit 2209." Or "Pueksan-ku Ministry of State Security." Or Kwan-li-so No. 22. Sometimes just "Hoeryong", after the town where the headquarters is located. It's a concentration camp. Some say the worst in the world. Some say the worst ever. You can read all about Hoeryong on another page on this site. My own pet name for the place is "The worst place in the world."

But what do I know? Take it from an eyewitness, a former guard. His name is Ahn Myong Chol, and he and his story are described by David hawk in *The Hidden Gulag* available free to all online.

Ahn, born in 1969 to a "good" (Party Member) family in Hangwon, did his compulsory military service in four consecutive prisons from 1978-1994. His last assignment was Hoeryong, the only one of the four that is still operational.

Ahn's father was a "good" man in other ways. He actually was caught doing something good. He gave food to one of his neighbors without authorization. This is reactionary and subversive in North Korea. Knowing that his father was facing trouble, and that the whole family would therefore be dragged into it, Ahn took his wife across the Tumen into China. Eventually he reached Seoul, where he began telling his story. This developed into a book, and even testimony before the U.S. Congress.

In 2002, when technology allowed us to see certain truths about North Korea by satellite, Ahn was there to identify what we were seeing. We now know the location and purpose of every building in the Hoeryong camp. Ahn was able to be so conversant about these things because of his position as truck driver.

Ahn confirms the shock one experiences upon the first arrival at camp. Walking skeletons. Dwarfs. Cripples in rags. It doesn't get better with time. He was aware that as many as 2,000 people died in the camp of malnutrition every year. Most of these were children. Perhaps ten executions per year, of people who had been caught eating from the harvest food. More deaths, by beating, of prisoners who had not been meeting production quotas.

The only meat people ate was from rats, snakes, and frogs caught. Marriage nearly totally forbidden. One pregnant woman executed because of her pregnancy.

Where is the outrage at a Hitler-Stalin-like operation in existence in our day? Who will rise up and say to the North Korean government, ENOUGH!?

What is our role? What is yours, believer? Mine? Praying? Yes, of course, but let us listen for part two of the plan that He whispers in our ear if we allow Him to get close enough.

149. this too shall pass

In about 1400 B.C. one of the Pharaohs of Egypt got it into his head that the Israelites living in his land were becoming a threat and needed to be destroyed. He knew or cared not that these were a uniquely privileged people called by the very God of Heaven to be a treasure to Himself. He threw their babies into the river and became guilty of mass murder.

A few hundred years later another servant of Satan determined that all who did not worship his statue would likewise be slaughtered, this time by fire. He had already seen Jerusalem fall and could not comprehend that the people he held captive meant anything to anyone. But they did. Nebuchadnezzar too threatened and attempted to kill the worship of the one true God.

Then came Darius with his promise to throw into a den of lions anyone who would worship Jehovah. And the Persian king who teamed with Haman to destroy the Jews altogether.

There's a family resemblance here. And it doesn't end in the Old Testament. Herod likewise was slaughter-happy as the unfortunate babies of Roman Jerusalem discovered too late.

The Caesars, the Popes, the Nazis, the Communists. Hitler, Stalin, Mao. All have set their sites on the People of the living God. But the "People" remains while all these tyrants are in their graves, and worse.

Tyrants remain in our day. The Tyranny family has been permitted a place on earth for the purpose of purifying the people of God in every generation. Whence comes the martyr? From the tyrant. Whence come the robes of white? From the slaughterer of God's people.

Even the final horrendous torture of the faithful will be permitted . Antichrist will rule and reign, wearing out the saints. (And these are not a special class of "tribulation-only" saints. These too are the very people of God, your brothers and sisters) But only for awhile. They will get their new address and he will be consigned to the flames.

One name I have omitted from my narrating. I have mentioned him often enough. But his fate is as sealed as all the rest. Unless he repents of his treatment of the people of God, and receives God's gracious forgiveness, he shall be tormented with all of the lost forever and ever.

What horrors we speak of today. Yet realities. The fires of hell are licking up all around, yet how often do we see them?So many that we converse with so casually every day have missed Christ and will miss the joys of eternity. Not only the Hitlers and Stalins, but all who have turned Christ away.

A solemn reminder to pray. The God who rejoiced at a Cana wedding calls His people to more serious moods too.

150. the birds of yanji

In 1997 the North Korean government decided there were just too many people roaming around the country. A royal decree came forth in September demanding that all street children were to be arrested and placed in institutions. Some have opined that the real reason behind the action was cover-up. These beggars made the country look suspect in the eyes of UN officials that were still there in '97. Got to save face before a watching world.

Jasper Becker, author of the book where I found this information *(Rogue Regime)*, decided to visit one of the so-called "9-27" camps, so named from the date of the edict. He was shocked at the effects of malnutrition on the children that had been nicknamed "flower-swallows". They are compared to birds because they flit from eating place to eating place like their tiny winged counterparts. Here he met...

Chi Gang. 15 years old. Four feet tall.

A 13-year-old. Three feet six inches.

Kang Minghwa. 16 years old. Looked barely 9 years old. Kang's testimony is chilling. Her impression is that the children were being brought into custody to die out of sight. A mixture of bean powder and unknown "food substitutes" was fed the children day after day. And day after day, children died. Kang crawled through a camp window, then under a railway bridge that crosses the Tumen River into China. Making her way into Yanji she begged for food on the street.

Because of the love of Christ manifested by many believers in the area, some children in this condition were cared for. But oh so many were and are not. To this day an average North Korean is 20 centimeters shorter and weighs half as much as his South Korean counterpart. In the late 90's a survey indicated that 2/3 of North Korea's children were stunted, living proof that the famine had been going on for some time, that it was not some temporary problem brought on by merely natural causes.

Many nations have natural disasters, including our own. But through modern communications and transportation, the peoples of Earth rally together and have, even from the world's viewpoint, a remarkable recovery in a relatively short period of time. Add the love of Christ in many of Earth's people, and "miraculous" can be added to the description. But Mr. Kim and company are trying to save their land from the evil influences of a world that hates them. And in so doing he is slowly permitting the genocide of the Korean people.

Who will heed the call? Who will rise up and save this land? Oh God arise! Only You have the key that will unlock this tragedy! Be not silent in this horrible time, Lord God Jehovah, Lord of the armies of the earth! Mercy, Lord! Mercy on North Korea!

151. getting out

I do hope you are availing yourself of my home page with its updated-daily North Korea news. Like for example this great MSNBC story that gives a very recent picture of how things in North Korea are changing while staying the same. "The same" piece is the constant desire of people who discover the truth to get out of North Korea. What's developing into a news story is the organized business that is evolving to get them out.

"Planned escapes" are making not a few brokers financially comfortable, even if the business is a bit risky. Any there's a whole range of prices, from a budget plan $2000.00 to a super deluxe escape that runs about 5 times that much. Now, the low-cost exit involves some difficult river-crossings, pedestrian travel, and even several weeks in a Thai immigration jail. But at least you're out. Free from Kim. The high-end plan will get you a forged Chinese passport, and an airplane ride from Beijing to Seoul. The whole ordeal can be over in three weeks!

Though one hears regularly of crack-downs and tighter security, this article explains that the bigger change is the conduct of bribe-hungry guards. The word has got 'round that looking the other way is a great method of having a little extra spending money, and that's surely hard to come by, by any legal means in Chosun.

It was the Christians who led the way out of North Korea, thanks be to God. They did it out of love and serious compassion, risking their lives only because of the workings of the Spirit within them. But others caught the idea and decided it would be a great way to make a living. Now there are more paid than unpaid "rescuers."

The description of the refugees has changed over the years too. A trickle of mostly 30-40 year old males with "important" jobs was the original flow. For them it was not such a difficult thing to get out. A total of 41 such people made the journey from North to South Korea in 1995. But the numbers have grown exponentially since then. With agents galore willing to help, the count rose to over 2,000 in 2006 alone. And there are more women and children now than men.

Not everyone uses an agent. There may be 100,000 self-led North Koreans hiding in China waiting for their breakthrough to the South, or somewhere safe.

For those who do buy their way out, there is always someone willing to take their money. There are scams. But generally the men come through on their promises. And no one is claiming this is easy money. Some get caught. A former NK military officer who defected in '99 says the "policy is for 100 percent execution of those caught helping people to defect. I personally saw several such executions." Of course, citizens trying to escape are accused of treason. 5 years in prison with all the accompanying horrors, is possible for them .

Even those who reach the South have a serious issue to deal with: guilt over those left behind. In fact, families of escapees are quite often imprisoned. One such lady heard that "her mother, father, and sister were forced from their homes by the authorities and relocated to a farming area in the interior." She then hired brokers to find them, but they too were arrested. She says, "You cannot know how heartbreaking it is to leave your family in this way."

We will not judge them. We simply cannot comprehend... We will pray that the reason for all this sorrow and grief will soon be taken away. And that North Koreans will continue to be pointed Upward as they are directed outward.

152. beware the unity of men

It is God's glory that produces the unity for which Jesus prayed, not outward politics. Not Military might. Not strong leadership. John 17:22. *The glory which You gave Me I have given them that they may be one just as We are one.*

That unity with Christ produces perfection and the winning of souls. It does not produce a super-church. Nor a watering down of truth. John 17:23. *I in them, You in Me. That they may be made perfect in one, and that the world may know that You have sent Me...*

Jesus kept His group together based on His Name. Not based on strong-arm power-plays. He asks the Father to do the same. John 17:11-12. *Keep through Your name those You gave Me... While I was with them, I kept them in Your name.*

When the prayer is answered, we will be united, as Christ is united with the Father. If *we* try to answer a prayer prayed to the Father, we will be united *as men unite with men*. Very imperfectly. Only God can make us one. The early disciples were already together physically, in one group. He prays that when the Spirit comes they will be made one. *One* is a totally different idea from *together*.

John must give way to Paul to show us how the prayer was answered historically. I Corinthians 12:12. *As the (human) body is one... so is Christ. By one Spirit we were all baptized into one Body...* Paul is not looking to a future time when all the Corinthian factions will be united into one big humongous group of people that can take over the Empire. He asserts that already the Body is one. Jesus' prayer is already answered! And continues to be whenever the Spirit falls on one new member of Christ.

There is a huge difference between *striving* for unity and recognizing the unity that already exists. The striving, when taken to the wrong extremes, becomes fleshly activity and creates men of renown ruling over "forces" to be reckoned with, challenges to the world's systems... but on the world's level. The *recognizing*, when viewed through the Spirit, leads to men and women submerged in a deluge of true Power that confounds God's enemies in God's time.

North Korea may be won to Christianity, Medieval style, by a show of "Christian unity," when the floodgates swing open and let the Light in. But North Koreans will be won to *Christ* only when the Spirit-filled Church hears from God and does His bidding.

There is absolutely no reason to lay down the precious truths of God's Word in order to unite with those who wear Christ's name but do not know Christ. Beware, Christian ministries! Read afresh the story of Jehoshaphat and be wise.

153. a man and a woman

Yes, they have names. But more important is their story. It will help to reinforce the images of the reality of North Korea. So you and I will pray. The stories are borrowed from http://www.refugeesinternational.com/ .

The man was in the North Korean army, and was discharged in 1997. When he went home he found there were no jobs. He moved to Musan, heard of the flow of refugees into China, and joined it. In 3 months he was caught and sent back. Ten days in a Chongjin prison. Escape. Back to China. 'Tis a familiar tale, though not as often considered to be a part of the "protected" military's existence.

1998. Chinese crackdown on North Korean refugees forces him to move to isolation in the mountains.

The woman, also North Korean, comes to China in 2001 with an uncle who promises to find her a husband. The man and the woman are introduced one day. Married the next. She joins him in his mountain hideaways.

August, 2002. Husband is lin a nearby village obtaining food when he is arrested by Chinese police and once more sent back to North Korea, without his wife. The wife is afraid and asks permission to live in the house of the manager of the shelter where they have been staying. Permission granted, but someone reports her, she is arrested and likewise deported. It is October.

In prison she gives birth. Her hometown people hear of her ordeal and bribe officers to release her.

One positive note. There are so many prisoners this second time around for the man, that he reports things have lightened up. There simply are not enough enforcers to make life miserable for everyone. The "light" version is a cell 5 square meters. Containing 40 people. They kneel and cannot move. They must sleep in that position.

His wife even gave birth in that position.

We cannot imagine what the more difficult version was like.

The man wants to go to South Korea, he tells the interviewer. But he knows it will be very hard. He says that people who try to go to South Korea are sent somewhere else and they are killed. He says that the first question they ask you when you are deported to North Korea is, "Have you been to church?" Those that say "Yes" will be killed right away or sent to a prison camp for life.

What is his plan now? He says, "Surviving day by day."

I am speechless. I cannot even comment on this horror today. All we can do is keep listening to what the Spirit is saying to the church. God has a plan too. He WILL be glorified somehow.

154. a thanksgiving prayer

On this Thanksgiving day, a prayer.

Thank You God, for Jesus. His life. His teaching. His death. His resurrection. His Spirit.

Thank You, God, for the church, His Body, scattered all over the earth.

This year I must thank You especially for that part of the Body I have discovered in North Korea.

Thank You that there are still people in whom You enter and make them willing to carry Your cross to the death. Thank You for still setting heroes before our eyes.

Thank You for getting my attention and helping me see how pitifully little I have cared about the cross. Thank You for showing me my weaknesses in the light of the strengths of true believers.

Thank You for worldwide communications that allow us to be aware of Your Body's plight. TV's. Radios. Computers. Men have abused their usage, but You have found a reason for them to be.

Thank You that I will eat and sleep and drive and give to others this day out of Your abundance. Thank You for showing me what abundance is for.

Thank you for airplanes that fly back and forth to and from North Korea, to transport willing believers into a battle front.

Thank You for Calebs who only want another mountain to conquer.

Thank You for the rising tide of prayer and gifts surrounding Your people in North Korea. Thank You for those whom You will call soon.

Thank You that evil men and evil kingdoms do not last forever. Thank You that Your Kingdom-in-waiting is here and slated for eternal glory and that the meek really do inherit the earth.

Thank You for Your Word, our antidote for fear excited by bullies. Thank You that Your perfect love casts out all fear now and forever.

Thank You that from the foundation of the world You have had a plan, and that today is no exception. Thank You that You have not been surprised or defeated or taken off course. Thank You for Victory.

155. for ex-prisoners of nk: healing needed

Lee Soon Ok is the author of *Eyes of the Tailless Animals: Prison Memoirs of a North Korean Woman*. I really think you should get a copy. This is the story of a member of the privileged class falsely charged with theft and bribery. She was imprisoned and tortured until finally after 8 years she signed a "confession" to be released. She was not a Christian believer in prison, but saw the Christians being punished even more unjustly than herself. Their witness turned her to Christ after her escape to South Korea.

She details 80's and 90's NK prison life for us, and I tell her story and all the other stories, lest there be some carried away with the idea that things haven't really been "that bad" under the Kims. May I simply list some of the details?

- High wall with electrified-wire fence.
- Prison population included Koreans who voluntarily left Japan to support their homeland.
- Prison population included housewives who stole food so their families would not starve.
- The 25-ounce-per-day food allocation for prisoners was almost totally eaten by guards.
- Prisoners were forced to fight one another for scraps of food.
- Prisoners were used to make garments and shoes for domestic and export use.
- Prisoners formed into work groups which had to do everything together. Even toilet breaks not allowed until group's scheduled time.
- An entire group was punished for the imperfection of one of its members. Punishment: even less food.
- Prisoners learned to work through pain so as to meet quotas, as rations became less and less.
- Continued lack of progress or rule infraction meant solitary confinement in a cell too small for standing or lying down, leading to loss of circulation and severe pain.
- Dormitories: cells 16 x 20 feet. 80-90 prisoners in each.
- Those whose bodies finally gave out were dumped in the mountains like dead animals.
- Men who broke under pressure and cursed a guard were executed publicly.

- Prisoners watching the execution were required to file by the corpse. Those who screamed or acted out in any way were sent to solitary.

Think of those, not who died, but who eventually were released. Ruined lives. Tormenting memories. Who shall help these dear precious souls, many of whom survive to this day? What therapy could possibly heal these wounds? We lift up Christ Jesus to the people of North Korea and we pray God to send His Gospel now. What other hope is there for this beaten down population?

Facts gleaned from Hawk's Hidden Gulag *available free online.*

156. report. korean slain for using phone

I'll be honest. There are times I wish it would all go away. This North Korea thing. I wish I had never discovered it some days. The famine. The growth-stunted children. Separated families. Nightmare concentration camps. People eating rats. People eating people.

I hear rumors that things are getting better. Things are opening up. The government is changing. Korea is changing. Then I open up to my own website, and read the news. And it's back to praying, OH GOD! WHAT CAN YOUR PEOPLE DO?!

Like this article yesterday from the Associated Press, Kwang-Tae Kim. Says that frequent public executions have returned. The Communists are shooting people for sport again. Like this guy who was the head of a factory in South Pyongan Province. He had the gall to install 13 phones in the basement. He even USED the phones for international calls. Oh my, what a crime! Executed by a firing squad in a stadium with 150,000 people watching.

And while they exited the edifice, six more were killed in an apparent stampede. Sounds like one of our rock concerts. But in Korea the event that draws the crowd is a shooting.

This report comes from the "Good Friends" Aid Agency.

But certainly the North Koreans are not a violent people. Certainly their government would not be guilty of such atrocities. Their media stoutly denies reports like those of "Good Friends." But the same media, on the same day as the above story, published a vicious attack on one Ri Hoe Chang of South Korea. Now this guy isn't all that popular in the South, but he is running for President on a platform that threatens NK in some way. Understood. But is this how to address all those with whom we disagree?

You be the judge as to what the government of NK would do with this South Korean if they met him in a dark alley. Or kidnapped him and took him to that dark alley, which is more in line with their method. I quote highlights from this KCNA article which offers the words of a spokesman for the "Committee for the PEACEFUL Reunification of the Fatherland" (!):

"The south Koreans should decisively eliminate [whoa!] such traitor to the nation and war maniac Ri Hoe Chang so that he may not raise his head again." [in lay terms that means KILL HIM]

"[Chang is a] wicked anti-reunification traitor and anti-DPRK confrontational maniac [you already used that word] ..."

"He is so wicked a traitor and charlatan...[who wants] to gratify his dirty political ambition."

[and the unkindest cut of all: he is a]"pro-U.S. ultra-right conservative... and a vicious advocate of showdown..."

If he becomes President, "the divided Korean nation will suffer a disaster of another war."

So kill him, South Korea. Eliminate him. That's how we solve our problems up here. Give it a try.

So whether Kim and company are killing telephone users or verbally slaying politicians, it seems clear to me that our enemy remains basically the same and should not be taken seriously at any bargaining table.

It seems equally clear that Christians will have to "pray the price" if this saga is going to have a turn for the better.

Any good news in old Chosun? Yes! Day by day, the prayers of God's people surround this nation. Day by day, the Gospel goes in via believers, Bibles, tracts, and miracles. God is alive. Time will show what great things he has done.

157. no, shoot me

Is it hatred that motivates us to tell the whole truth about North Korea? No. Love demands that you know so you will pray. Do we call curses from Heaven in judgment of those who have ruined the lives of so many millions of people? No. God is able to forgive. And it is God who will judge the unforgiven. We must "judge" ourselves and those given to our care, and even this, in love.

We call for His mercy. We desperately plead for His intervention.

Consider again today the sad history of the Korean Christians: (Per Hefley's *By Their Blood*) We are in the late 40's, when the triumph of the World War soon led into the disaster of the Korean War. But just before that conflict, while the sides were still being chosen, multiplied thousands of Koreans from the north rushed south to escape the Communist threat of horror, a threat they have made good on for 60 years.

Escapee Chulho Awe gave us a book in 1965 (*Decision at Dawn*) that relates how he gave up wealth and position in

North Korea to become a fugitive. That is, he refused to become a part of the Communist Party, and was forced to run. At one point in his journeys he was able to get back to Pyongyang to see how his church was doing. Wasn't doing well. At least the building. Furniture smashed. Pews toppled. Files scattered. And outside the city in a stack of corpses, a choir member helped him pick out his pastor and one of the elders.

Before the lines were clearly drawn and Communism was clearly evicted from the South, chaos reigned in some areas. Communist infiltrators agitated local rebellions and brought about the demise of more saints. Consider Tong-In and Tong-Sin, sons of one Pastor Son.

"Number one son" Tong-In refused Japanese pressure to worship at a Shinto shrine and was thrown out of school. But after the War he went back, and was even elected president of the Campus YMCA. When the Communists instigated their uprising, he was once more in danger. Eventually a pistol was in his face with the order to renounce Christ. Tong-In's reponse was to preach to his enemy and plead for him to accept Christ.

At this moment the second son, Tong-Sin, rushed up and demanded to be shot in his stead. The brothers quarreled awhile over who should be martyred, when finally the Communist shot them both.

Not end of story. The pastor-father was of course sad but proud of his boys. And soon he had a chance to avenge them, for the uprising was quelled and their murderer was on trial. Response: Since nothing can bring my sons back, what good is it to kill this man? Let me have him. Maybe he can finish for Christ what my sons left undone.

Further response: The murderer's parents are overcome with gratitude and offer to feed and clothe the pastor's 16-year-old daughter in return.

Who knows how many "further responses" there have been to this courageous series of events? Perhaps you are responding even now. It is for such responses that we pray. When Christ is truly seen in North Korea, when the cross is truly lifted up, when love's message is told and understood, the present message of fear and hatred and deceit and tragedy will go. Perfect love casts all this out and more.

May our God send His perfect love to North Korea.

158. growing up with the great leaders

From Hyok Kang's *This Is Paradise* I offer the following tidbits about what it means to be a student growing up in North Korea. I will try to present the facts without comment and respectfullty. This is exactly what the author saw...

- In every classroom hangs a photograph of Kim Il-Sung and Kim Jong-Il. They are placed above the blackboard so as not to escape anyone's notice.

- Children are taught patriotic slogans: "We will fight the puppet party of South Korea," "For the Great Leader, let us become human bullets and bombs..." "Every Korean is worth one hundred enemies."

- Children are taught songs of the same sort: "The bayonet gleams, and our footsteps echo... who could withstand us? ...we are the army of the comrade leader."

- A chart... lists children who are considered to be good or bad examples. The latter are warned to change their behavior.
- No kind of artistic work can be produced without either the Dear Leader or the Great Leader being mentioned in it. It is actually forbidden to sing a song or write a poem that does not mention the two Kims.
- Children do not grow up with the idea of going to college. The military defence of the country is praised as the highest ideal. In the second year of primary school children begin preparation for soldiering by taking Tae-Kwon Do.
- Every four years Kim Jong Il makes available to every student two new uniforms, one for the summer and one for the winter. Part of that mandatory dress is the wearing of a Kim badge over the heart.
- Classes are divided into units of 4 children each, two boys and two girls. A girl usually becomes the "head" of the unit because the chief job of the leader is to clean the classroom, a job boys tend to avoid.
- School starts at 7:30. There are 5 45-minute classes in the morning, lunch at home, then 3-4 more classes in the afternoon starting at 2:00.
- Two of the mandatory classes are "Era of Childhood (I)" and "Era of Childhood (II)" during which children are taught, and made to memorize, every possible detail available about the young life of, well, who else?

Next time we visit this book, I will share with you some of the things children actually learn about the Kims, including the fact that "one plus one equals one" the origination of "fuzzy math." Maybe you will want to buy the book between now and then. I strongly recommend it!

Meanwhile, consider and bemoan a generation thoroughly stripped of its senses. *Who can save the utterly deceived?* I know one Who can. Oh pray for North Korea.

159. nk history: the plunge downward

Our history of modern North Korea continues:

I mean no disrespect of another human being in relating the things I have discovered in my research. My motive is informative and meant to have people praying.

In 1980, Kim Il-Sung announces his successor. By the mid-80's Jong-Il is placed in day-to-day charge of the Party, the government, and the military.

It is difficult at first for the people to promote the son. Dad has been a warrior, an obvious descendant of the "mighty" men who formed the backbone of Korean history. He has been a hero in a time when Korea needs one. Pushed around by the world's monster-powers he has been the dragon-killer.

But the son? Martin says that since they cannot cast him in a military mold, they create a genius. The be-all know-all head of state who will appear god-like in his infinite wisdom. Dad even gets behind this promotion, a stretch if there ever was one. Inventiveness even creates a *new birthplace* for the younger Kim, atop Korea's Mt. Baektu, a location already holy to the legend-minded nationals.

During this period, all the old Communist alliances with NK are being broken. Old friends form relationships with rising star South Korea. In response, the North begins to resort to terror. In 1983 the infamous Rangoon assassination attempt on the South's President, a bomb that kills 21, including Korean officials in Burma. In 1987 the destroying of a domestic Korean Airlines flight, killing 115 people. The government is once again getting attention.

In 1988 the Seoul Olympics galls North Korea's leadership, so they have their own version, paid for by allowing the nation to stay in its billions of dollars in debt. Unfortunately for the leaders, this episode occurs shortly after the Tienemen Square massacre when Asian Communist countries are having trouble "saving face".

1989. In yet more desperate attempts for world attention, the government builds the first Protestant and Catholic churches in Pyongyang in decades. Of course they are just show, but they are intended to signal a new era of freedom in North Korea. Right. Closer to the Leader's heart is the introducing of Rock and other Western music.

As the young successor year after year spends many of the nation's resources, disaster strikes, and the nation is not able to fight back. When our history continues, we discuss one of the worst famines in earth's history.

So that Korea's future is not as bleak as its history, let us continue to pray that Jesus Christ will be offered a chance to show what He is able to do when people call on His Name.

General outline of my history follows that of Bradley Martin's book, Under the Loving Care of the Fatherly Leader.

160. could the famine have been averted?

...or even minimized? I speak of course of the horrendous episode of the '90's in North Korea, headed up by its Stalinist government. My source for information today is *Rogue Regime* by Jasper Becker.

Consider:

The ruling dynasty rejected the use of private gardens. 70% of the population was moved to rural areas but strictly forbidden from growing private food.

The military had always survived by taking a share of the country's crops. But just before the famine hit hard, the government extended the length of military service from 7 to 13 years, and added females to the ranks, creating a monstrously large army with an equally monstrous tenure. Soldiers were sent to the fields to -forcibly - grab the harvest. Rural households were starved out.

The government did everything to prevent people from finding other ways to feed themselves. It said in 1996, at the height of the starvation: " Telling people to solve the food problem on their own only increases the number of farmers' markets and peddlers..."

Party officials were told to crack down hard on any kind of commercial activity. Those who reacted and rebelled, as in Musan, were arrested. In that unfortunate city, 200 men and women who saw the light of truth about the government went to jail, and a dozen were executed in public. Because NK's leaders refused to hear their cries for common sense, half of the town's 130,000 people died or ran, according to refugees' later stories.

One thing that was allowed, and even promoted, was the use of so-called "alternative foods". The poor and dying people of Chosun were told to collect roots, bark, seaweed, husks, and cobs to make food. Problem. These "food substitutes" were not food. They had no caloric value. People died of blocked digestive tracts when this dense matter, never meant to be eaten, clogged their system. One of the worst features of this whole period is the way the NK media bragged about what it was doing to save its people from the American ogre. But in fact, the Korean people have known what and how to eat for millennia. How tragic that government misinformation was allowed to suck them in and destroy them.

Forgiveness is built into our blood as believers in Jesus. We must be ready to forgive even the grossest of sins committed against us or our Korean family members. But at this point, no one in leadership seems to be asking for such forgiveness. No one is admitting to the watching millions of Earth that anything incorrect has been done.

Gives us a lot to pray about. Remember the prisoners of this sad nation.

161. invasion of nk

How will Christ change North Korea, when He goes in with His people? If this happens before His powerful second coming, He will go in with the power of His own unity, not with the organizations of men.

Clues from Paul, Ephesians. 1:2,3: The true Church is the very Body of Jesus. Not just a body of believers that happens to belong to Him. The Church IS Him! 4:3. What do we do? Keep the unity (that already exists) in the bond of peace. Recognize what is already there and flow in it. 4:13. Unity of belief may not exist until later, but essential unity is now. In

God's eyes there is unity. Always has been. Men are divided, growing, imperfect, but unity is here. I Corinthians 1:10 ff. The Corinthians were divided. But Christ was not divided. Denominations formed. A sectarian spirit developed. Personality cults sprang up. But Christ was one. And is still.

Why the "division" today? *People* divide for a number of reasons.

1. Some separate because they never belonged to Christ. "They went out from us, but they were not of us."
2. Some believe they are called out to better things. *Dangerous idea*. But sometimes true.
3. Simple differences of opinion. Paul and Barnabas, for example. But Christ was not divided during that incident. The ecumenists of our day would have begged Paul and Barnabas to stay together at all costs. "Together" is not unity in the Spirit. God had other plans for both of them. We can't figure out everyone's motive and don't need to. Unity continues on regardless. There is One Body filled with One Spirit, just as at the beginning!

Our options today as we consider moving into North Korea when things change there (soon we pray!):

1. announce to all denominations, "Come together!" and let's go in to conquer. But in the large group there is much that is false. Always has been since the days when Roman Emperors forced people into the "Church." One cannot force someone into the Body. Most pagans who came in did so to save their lives. They brought their pagan ways with them and the external church has lived with them ever since. No, a

thousand times NO, don't bring this mess into North Korea!

2. seek God as to who is born again in the crowd that will try to press in. Let God call His true people together. He will then give discernment to those inside who are waiting for the Gospel. God's sheep will hear His voice. There will always be false Christians and cultists offering competition to the truth. The answer is not to join with those who grieve the Spirit, but to preach the truth and let God call His own to Him.

The boundaries of the true Church of Jesus remain invisible to human eyes but very visible to Christ and those who know Him. And consider:

If Christ does not go into North Korea until His second coming, how "nice" will that be? Will Jesus gingerly gather all those who wear the name "Christian" and set them up as little kings all over the land? Is that the picture you see? The Bible says He will come with wrath and judgment, utterly destroying all His enemies. Only the true Body of Christ will remain to judge the earth with Jesus.

So why not join with those true ones now? Making alliances with "Christians" that have not the Spirit of God is always a deadly unproductive road. And it gives the wrong message to the North Korean people who have been deceived these many decades.

Christ, lead on, show us how to win back the hearts of the Korean people for You, Who so deserve this offering.

162. the nk famine: broken lives

From http://refugeesinternational.org/, another refugee story.

A woman, age 43. Her son, age 11. First arrival in China, 1997.

In 1997 her husband went to China and hooked up with a family who hired him. With the money he bought some oil to bring back to NK. But even though he was in North Korea, all he could think of was China and its wonders.

A second man, with family connections in China, also went there, and upon his return he joined the first man. But the second man was caught (such travel is illegal) and when in jail he revealed that the first man had been to China also.

The first man, husband of the lady being interviewed, escaped immediately with his entire family, into China. Eventually the husband died, but her three daughters all found husbands in China. She has since remarried also. Someone actually received money for giving her to an old poor man.

Enough trauma for one lifetime? Not nearly, not for a North Korean.

Her first daughter disappeared in 1997. Kidnapped and sold, they found out later. At the time of the interview Mom was in contact with someone who found her.

Meanwhile she was unhappy with the new marriage. She did not speak Chinese. The new husband did not like her son. She saved up money from her grocery allowance, and eventually left him and came to Yanji (where the interview took place).

In North Korea she had been well known for her farming skills. She never wanted to leave her homeland. And in 1999 she was caught and sent back. She was not arrested because she was so well known. She lived in North Korea for over a month and then was forced to go back to China to be able to eat.

Her recollection of North Korean government is that Kim Il Sung was "a really good man" who tried his best but failed. She feels that Kim Jong Il grew up spoiled, not ever having had to go to war, incapable of relating to commoners. And because his subordinates were always feeding him false reports, "this sucked the blood of the normal people."

Her sister's whole family died of starvation.

She does not believe anything is going to change anytime soon. Her hope is "unification."

Unification. It seems to be the hope held before all Koreans. But what if unification is under the present leader or his descendant? Our prayer for these precious souls is that a return to Christ will be the next event on the peninsula. And that if there is to be unification it will be under a free people.

When God's people pray, all things are possible. Is that not what He taught us?

163. of bribes, nukes, and ransoms

How many times would someone have to trick you before you would stop trusting that person? How many times would you allow that person to threaten you and force you into compromise and demand bribes before you would walk on down the road and find another friend? Consider the strange tale of North Korea vs. the world*:

1985, North Korea signs the nuclear nonproliferation treaty. "Read my lips," says North Korea's government, "NO

MESSING WITH NUCLEAR WEAPONS." They promptly ignore their own signatures and begin their nuclear program.

1991, promise by North Korea to South Korea, "We'll not SEEK or MAKE nuclear weapons. In fact, you can send inspectors in to check me out!" But the weapons machine rolls on and inspectors are rolled out.

1992, promise by NK to the International Atomic Energy Agency (IAEA), "If those Americans will stop their military exercises in our backyard, you can come in and look." Guess who keeps their end of the bargain, and who does not?

1992, North Korea promises the U.S., "You take your tactical nuclear weapons away, and we'll stop dabbling in the nuclear." U.S. agrees, Korea renaeges.

October 21, 1994. To gain "regional stability" (to bribe the NK government into not starting a nuclear war), the United States flat out gives two entire nuclear reactors (the good kind) to Chosun. Ballpark assessment of cost: MULTI BILLIONS OF DOLLARS. (And you know where the U.S. government gets its money!) Doesn't seem to work. While the work is being done as we promised, North Korea is in their nuclear weapons kitchen, stirring up trouble. And inspectors are denied access.

1995-1999, a famine-paralyzed but still hard-hearted (Pharaoh-like) government demands that the U.S. give it food. Merciful Americans cannot resist. The spin in NK government circles: "You see how the United States repentantly pays us for the grief it has caused?" More than that, many of the neediest Koreans never see the relief. Only those who support the regime, and especially the military, prosper during that time, if staying barely alive through one of the worst famines of history can be called prospering.

1998, NK says to Bush," Hey, we're keeping our nose clean. We haven't sold missiles to your enemies (lately). You should pay us for the lack of revenue that has created!" Sure enough, the good old U.S. of A. dishes out the dollars.

1998, North Korea does the unthinkable. It launches a multi-stage missile over Japan. Harsh rhetoric follows from world leaders, including the Americans. But soon the yearly shipment of 500,000 tons of fuel oil is sent as scheduled and as promised in the 1994 Geneva settlement. What a strange nation, this America, that props up its enemies so they can hit again. And what a strange nation, this North Korea, that can make such outrageous demands of a nation that could demolish it in a few days. Some argue that our monthly gifts are nothing but a ransom.

1999, NK says, "Okay, you can inspect our facilities. Just give us a $300 million inspection fee!" Done.

Where does your hard-earned (tax) dollar go? For one place, into the nuclear pockets of a Stalinist regime on the other side of the world. So we are involved in this thing after all. So it is hard to ask people like you to dig deeper, and voluntarily, but I ask anyway: There are some truly empty pockets in North Korea, many of them belonging to our brothers and sisters in Christ. Let's find a way to fill those, also.

*today's facts derived from *Juche* by Thomas Belke

164. blessed holy birth

A lot of believers have nothing to do with December five and twenty. I understand. I've actually been in that crowd a good portion of my life. I can take it or leave it even to this day. But, I enter into the thinking of the season by asking my readers and listeners, "What can we get for North Korea?"

We all have folks and family members who are hard to shop for. But what do you get for someone whom you have never met, who lives on the other side of the planet, whose culture is totally different, and who may never have heard of the Christ Whose birthday you proclaim to be celebrating? The One Who was born into our world from Heaven has answers to this question. Of course these gifts I suggest are year-'round for believers, but again, I speak as a Christmas-celebrator today.

Let's look around. What does my brother need? He looks so hungry. His growth is even stunted from his hunger. Food would be nice. Who will assure me that the food will get where I send it. Here I am unable to assist you, as Christian organizations are not too keen about being on a website list, and therefore serving as a target for evil men. So do a Google search, make some phone calls, it won't be long before you'll find a group that is getting food to the hungry of North Korea. Yes, a great gift.

North Korea starves for God's Word too. Those same groups that feed the body often feed the soul and spirit of man. Why not help send the Word in?

> 1.   How about planning a trip to Northeast China, where multiplied thousands of Koreans live outside their homeland, looking for someone to help them? God will guide you to those here who are planning trips in. Or plan your own. One of my own dreams - I hope it is not a fantasy - is to pack up a blanket or two, and visit the Northeast in the dead of winter. I find a hurting North Korean and whip out my blanket and present it to him as though he were Jesus Christ. Now there's a happy Christmas! Is there anything State-side to compare with the joy of giving one's life away for someone in need? Isn't that what Jesus did for us all?

2.   So not much money? No time to travel? Great ideas but not for you? How about "remembering" the prisoner? Some day I hope to do a study on that word. It's the same thing as remembering Jesus in the Communion. Not just looking back at past events, but somehow communicating with present realities, too. Try some identifying. Offer it up to the Lord and perhaps in His mercy He will see your heart and touch a North Korean for you, as you pray. Here are some identification presents:

3.   Next time you do your exercise, skip the treadmill. How many treadmills in North Korea? No sighing and crying for those poor people. Get out in the cold yourself. You'll not match their 20 below temps, but you'll get a little piece of it, and God will warm your heart. Yeah, bundle up, walk 2-3 miles in the coldest messiest weather you can stand, and all the while be lifting up your friends in NK.

4.   Fasting is always a way to relate to poverty. Deliberate hunger offered up for the real hunger there. It makes you weak. And weak in Christ makes you strong. And strong Christians pray more. And when they pray they pray for North Koreans, among others. That's right soldier, push that plate away. How far can you go? Until you think you'll not make it? Jesus went farther. And many Koreans through the years have paid the last full measure of devotion. They responded to Jesus' challenge, "Greater love has no man than this than to lay down his life for his friends."

5.   Got too much stuff? Give it away. Find where a container of goods is being sent into Korea

and get rid of those excesses. Be ready to travel. Be ready for those marching orders. Travel light. None of that stuff is really yours anyway! Time for judgment to begin at the house of God. If we judge ourselves, He won't have to. That stuff you're hangin' onto could be such a blessing to someone. C'mon, let go!

So much to do. So much need. Lord give us wisdom to know the first step to take and courage to take it! Merry Christmas, North Korea! Better yet, *Chuk Song Tan,* "Blessed Holy Birth!"

165. of people who live in glass houses

Rodung Sinman is a mouthpiece of the government in North Korea. Here's one of their latest concoctions.

Pyongyang, December 9 (KCNA) - The imperialists and the paid bourgeois trumpeters are forcing other countries to introduce Western-style "freedom and democracy" ... But this is an insult to genuine freedom and democracy.

"Freedom and democracy" much touted by the imperialists are sham ones and they are nothing but camouflage to hoodwink working masses and cover up the reactionary nature of bourgeois dictatorship and the unpopular nature of the capitalist system. Bourgeois freedom allows a handful of the privileged to exploit and dominate popular masses, absolute majority of population, and lead carnal life. The Western-style "democracy" is the most reactionary and unpopular policy as it ruthlessly defies the desire and demand of the popular masses for freedom and democracy...

The article goes on in the same vein for several paragraphs. Strange stuff, don't you think? Joseph Stalin and

Comrades Lenin and Marx could not have said it better. We can say the NK government is consistent anyway.

Do we need to answer the charges? We are "forcing" other nations into democracy? Referring to Iraq? Where a dictator was taken out? And replaced by free elections? Is this what NK fears?

"Genuine" democracy? Surely this article is not suggesting that North Korea is a model of true democracy? The rule of the people? And genuine freedom? Has anything ever been more ludicrous to consider? Can you imagine a shopping mall in Pyongyang that has music about Jesus running through it? Yet that's what you'll experience during this Christmas season, sandwiched in between music about our other heroes. Oh, my people don't serve Jesus, in the main, but His message is here, freely announced and by some happily received. Where is the freedom to do that in North Korea? Freedom? Are you kidding?

A handful of the privileged exploit America? Surely some have gotten rich here. It's the nature of freedom that some will rise to the top. It is the nature of NK's prison that most will sink to the bottom with never a chance even for normalcy, let alone prosperity.

"Lead a carnal life." Well we must agree with that. All who live outside the Spirit of God are carnal whether the rich American or the poor Korean. No governmental system has a monopoly on the flesh. And for a study of fleshly living at its max, a close scrutiny of the private life of the government leaders in NK would be in order. All the carnal pleasures government leaders there deny to the American masses have been enjoyed by them.

The last statement I quoted is pure Communist double-talk. Western *democracy* defies the desire of the masses for *democracy*. Can you figure it out? Has he even defined

Western democracy? Has he defined *pure* democracy? What evil is it that America is supposed to have committed? Oh, we're plenty guilty, but does that government have any clue why?

These childish ravings don't bother us so much as the fact that there are still quite a lot of people under his lordship who believe every word that proceeds from his mouth. Time for new things, new ideas, fresh starts. Time for Jesus in North Korea.

166. where hard-hats wear hard shirts

"Remembering the prisoners" of North Korea is one thing this website is about. One way to remember them is to see before us on a regular basis their prisons. David Hawk has given us a tool to do that. It is online, it is *called The Hidden* Gulag and it is free. I quote bits and pieces from it every couple of weeks. Today, an unnamed prisoner's recollection of "Kyo-hwa-so No. 4" a prison in South Pyongan Province.

First the prisoner: While he was incarcerated he contracted a lung disease after 3 months' work. He lost 65 pounds. He noticed that extremely sick people were sent home to recuperate, so that the statistics showing prison deaths would not expose Kim's intentions. So he deliberately drank some dirty water, developed chronic diarrhea and was given a release. Sent home, his lungs recovered. But instead of going back to prison he escaped to China.

The prison: His recollection of the horrors he saw there, point by point,

- 7,000 prisoners mining limestone and making cement
- Housed in a factory built by the Japanese during their occupation of Chosun, a difficult time for

Koreans, but still not as wretched as their current situation

- Nearly one mile square
- All men
- Most sentenced to 5 - 20 years
- Most did not expect to live long enough to finish their sentence
- 10-15 hours work per day
- hard labor
- dangerous conditions
- chest ailments/lung disease common
- nightly group meetings of up to 500 men for self-criticism and lectures about the Kims
- infractions punishable by reduced rations, extended sentences, punishment cells
- eight public executions in eight months
- executions came from 1)trying to escape 2) failed attempt to escape 3)crimes during "sick leave" 4) committing capital ofenses elsewhere and brought here for execution
- 2 ounces food per meal. mixed corn and wheat. cabbage-leaf soup.
- most prisoners around 100 pounds
- no bathing, changing of clothes; face-wash possible 3 times a month
- clothes hardened as dirt and sweat combined; skin abrasions-infections resulted
- high death rates. in this prisoner's unit, over one third died in eight months

Not all prisoners in this camp are believers. Some are. Not all have to stay very long. Some do. Aren't they worth our attention tonight?

And soon some of them will be with the Lord. Most won't. Lord, we need to know how to pray.

167. they killed him twice

Credit to Hefley's *By Their Blood* for the following account.

We're studying Korean Church History and have gotten to the war years, II and Korean. It was during this time that young Christian teacher Sung Du died twice.

When the Japanese ruled Korea in the early part of the 20th century, this novice yielded to pressure and began to worship at the shrines set up by the invaders. What a disappointment he became to himself and his peers. Not unlike our own falling away under the pressures of materialism... but that's another story.

Sung Du repented. "I will die before denying the faith again!" he promised. He was given that very opportunity. Twice. He accepted it both times. One canceled out his denial, and the other... We will allow God to offer His own praises on that day, but isn't it wonderful that a man like Peter, who denied 3 times, was permitted to accept 3 times (John 21)?

Sung Du went to seminary to prepare for the ministry. Ordination followed. His first assignment was a church near Suyang-Ch'on. The Japanese were gone. But the Koreans, under Communism, turned out to be worse. He was arrested and sent to a mine as a slave laborer, a practice which continues to this "enlightened" age of our own in dark Chosun.

Brother Sung believed that the first day of the week is the Lord's Day and that work should not be done then. He refused! He was therefore beaten. This is the Communist response to any number of ills. They beat him so badly that it seemed he was dead. Since he was "dead", they threw the "corpse" into the river. Watching church members dived in when the Communists went away, and pulled his body out of the river.

They took him back to the village to prepare him for burial. But - and I know you are way ahead of me- he was not dead! (Sounds like a Dae Joyoung episode, only this one is true!).

Months later he was again preaching, almost as strong a testimony as raised Lazarus. But the Communists arrested him again. This time they shot him. They wanted to be sure.

Of course we know the rest of the story. Sung Du woke up once more, in the arms of His Saviour, and he waits there for the rest of us to die for Jesus and join him there. Are we willing to die, even once?

Thank God for the Koreans!

168. decision at dawn

He was there. World War II Korea. Japan-dominated Korea. Korean War Korea. The early Kim Il Sung Years. The Christian persecution. The underground. The flight south. He was there, and saw it all. His name is Chulho Awe. His escape to South Korea and subsequently to the United States gave him the liberty to pass his story on to us in 1965. And personally, I'm so glad he did.

It's an old book and not exactly in circulation now, but "Googling" Amazon.com will turn up a way to purchase it for only a few dollars. At least it worked for me.

Not sold yet? I quote from the book's jacket:

Decision at Dawn is the personal story of young Chulho Awe, who lived through the Communist brutalities in North Korea. The son of aristocrats, he had been thrown into prison because he refused to give up his Christian faith for

Communism. His mysterious release and the terrible months that followed read like the story of a young Christian in the days of Nero. There are the same tensions, the same terrors and self-sacrifice, that existed for Christians in those long-ago days.

This is also the saga of the Korean agony- the blood and tears, the hunger and cold, and the shining beauty of abiding faith. All of the things the people in this little-known [in 1965] , far-off land endured and survived are here.

When Korea was liberated from the Japanese following World War II, its people were naively convinced that now their troubles were over. Now, they thought, there would be no more tyranny, no more poverty, no more hunger. They soon learned how terribly wrong they were. Under Communist rule in North Korea they live cat-and-mouse existences in mortal fear even of lifelong friends and neighbors in spy-ridden communities.

Not all of *Decision at Dawn* is a tale of hardship. The author gives a warm and vivid picture of family life in Korea- the filial ties, the ancient customs, even the kinds of food they eat. There is a delightful chapter describing Christmas festivities in a Korean Christian home which will enchant the American reader with its glimpse into another world.

Yet another look at a people in need of our prayers. Happy reading.

169. nk's believe it or not

Are you ready for this? Ten birds on a branch. Hunter shoots one. How many left? Nine, you say. But future North Korean dictator Kim Il-Sung says, None. The others fly away.

Hyok Kang in *This Is Paradise* tells that and several other anecdotes that tend to glorify the dynastic duo that have held sway over Chosun lo these many years. Here's more:

War against Japan. Jong-Il throws a rock from the top of a mountain with deadly aim. Literally deadly. The rock strikes a Japanese soldier in a boat below. Kills him. Don't believe it? Hmmm, try this:

Daddy Kim is sleeping between battles. Boy Kim is worried that a bunch of noisy birds will awaken him. He starts to chase them away, but of course he can't make noise either. So he gestures to the birds in signals that somehow they understand, and away they go. Really smart guy.

Then there was this competition at school to see who could advance a feather through the air the farthest distance. All his fool friends tried to throw their feather like a rock. Little Kim won by just blowing the feather through the air. Wow.

Did you know that Jong-Il was such an idealist that he literally chased rainbows? He actually succeeded. He caught one! Really. Why don't you believe me?

In fact most North Korean youth grow up hearing such tales and swallowing them whole. How disappointing and even crushing it must be to discover the truth . What if NK could be introduced to a Hero Who called Himself and truly was, the Truth?

One final story, for those who never have dared to challenge the religion of modern mathematics. Dear Leader is observing a class of very small children. The teacher is illustrating via apples that one (apple) plus one (apple) equals two apples. $1 + 1 = 2$. Pretty basic stuff. But the star of our show rises to his feet and reminds the class that one portion of water added to another portion of water equals one portion of water still. Hence, $1 + 1 = 1$. Not so basic anymore.

Christians have had this notion since Genesis, when the ONE true God said, Let US make man in OUR image... But to the sheltered Koreans who are not permitted to hear such things, or any outside information, Kim himself suffices for Divine utterances.

I ask again, How long, how long? The lies, the false worship, the bondage, the darkness. Oh God, shed Your light!

170. self-criticism: nk's confessional

It's easy to find fault. And the greater the fault in the "faultee" the easier it becomes. I sit at my computer almost every day and find fault with the government and governors of North Korea. It's SO easy. It's become second nature. But a Christian who practices this activity for very long will sooner or later be asked to deal with his own faults. His wretched condition minus Christ.

Who was the greatest sinner who ever lived? Nero, Hitler, Kim Jong Il? The Bible's answer is *the apostle Paul.* Paul said he himself was the chief of sinners. The worst. He killed and had killed a multitude of God's people. Not like the ignorant head of state who knew no better, but as a "good Jew" whose God was the same as the Christians' God. Paul never forgot who he was before Christ changed him.

Today I must answer a bit differently of course. Paul may have been the worst of his day, but I have moved into contention for the prize in our day. I who have known the Light streaming from the Word of God for over 50 years. I who have understood great portions of the Great Book. The same I who is still disobedient. Proud. Lazy. Fearful. And more. Kim doesn't know any better. He's not had an encounter with Christ, to our knowledge. Christians are a threat to him. So he tries to hurt them. He was raised to believe what he believes about life. Just as I was.

But I have no excuses. I have had everything life can offer. This life *and* the next. I am well aware of my culpability and cry out to God often for change, for renewal, for His fire.

Just so you know.

The North Korean government has adopted the "self-criticism" tactic, and used it, like the Roman Catholic "confessional" system of the Dark Ages (and oh they were dark!), to control its people. A man or woman or even child who is forced to stand in a public meeting or sit in a private box and confess faults of all kinds is controlled by that audience. Beaten down inwardly. Kept from advancement.

How different is confession of the Christians , from whom Rome and Pyongyang and all the others copied. For example, the confession I gave in the paragraphs above was not in any way coerced, yet from the inside I knew it was time to even the score, to place myself, but for the grace of God, in the same boat with Kim Jong Il. We Christ-followers don't look down at evil men. We recognize evil in us instinctively when the Spirit is in our lives. We confess it freely, and it is forgiven by Christ just as freely. We are well aware that evil is not just something "out there" but that it is lurking within each of us at any moment, ready to attack our new life in Him.

May all of our fault-finding start with the chief of sinners. Me. But may we never be afraid to speak the truth about evil in our world either.

171. of bread, bribes, and bullets

Under the Loving Care of the Fatherly Leader, by Bradley Martin, has been our guidebook through modern Korean history. We are not directly quoting but following his basic outline. We're in the mid to late 80's now.

Shortages in food are starting to be noticed. If the government is concerned about it, it doesn't show it by any major policy changes. It may be a cultural thing that causes some folks to stay set in their ways. It may be pride. "Face-saving" they call it in Korea. How can one admit he's made such a serious blunder with an entire nation's provision?

Communism itself is pretty unchanging. But Kim tries to toe the line even more when it comes to the "old" ways of the Party. He is mildly disgusted at the failure of Communist nations around him to be "truly" Communist, whatever that means. To Kim it means we don't work for money in this nation! Period. The capitalists are pigs in every sense of the word. We will not follow them.

That's all surface talk. In fact, money rules North Korea in a much more sinister way in the 80's and at present. It's called the bribe. There's just a lot of things that need doing and obtaining, and bribery is king.

America continues to ignore North Korea as much as possible, to the Kims' frustration. NK tries to get our attention, tries to force us to "love" them, but the relationship struggles. The U.S. is not so concerned with the military threat at this point and feels it can afford a waiting game. Surely North Korea will self-destruct eventually. Their demise will not be blamed on us.

Next enter the defectors. "Let me out" folks start showing up here and there outside the nation. Their statements are not always against the Kims. After all they are brainwashed. But hungry too. Like kids who think their father has tried everything imaginable to feed them, but just can't. So they harbor no grudges. Dad tried. But for goodness' sake we've got to eat! So out they come, with habitual praise pouring out of hungry mouths. Some of course are afraid to speak against this mighty one. Some tell the honest truth. Eventually the truth sets in for all of them.

Part of that truth is that the downward spiral they have been on as the Kims have tried to create an un-matched, yea un-matchable military might on the northeastern half of the Korean peninsula. North Korea was much better off than China until the early 70's. So poor were the Chinese that they went to North Korea for aid. This explains why so many of them want to "return the favor" today.

But after the Cuban military crisis and the Vietnam War, North Korea decides it will have to compete to survive. No Yankee will be raising a flag in old Chosun. No Chinese, Japanese, Russian, or South Korean will ever dominate either. The race is on. The race has led to the grave for millions of North Koreans.

If this nation turned the wrong way, it can turn the right way when people pray. Let us allow God to show what He can do by believing Him to make all things new in Chosun.

172. somehow he survives

Credit to Jasper Becker's *Rogue Regime* for today's thoughts.

People want to know how in the world North Korea has kept on tickin' for so long. There was no question in some people's minds that this nation would fall when its first leader died. In fact, it remained, and did some pretty amazing things technologically (while its people died by the 10's of thousands from starvation). It was during this period (mid 90's on) that North Korea entered the nuclear club. How can this be?

There is an ultimate answer, involving the perfect will and timing of God, and/or prayerlessness of God's people, and/or the powers of darkness and all the rest, but today I'm looking at more surface realities (with Becker's eyes). What factors have kept the Red Korean Machine rolling down the road, if only in low gear?

1. Kim Jong Il's continued personal power over the Korean people. He forces them to do his will. And his will is that North Korea survive... his way.
2. Kim bluffs his neighbors. They thought he was about to attack them if they caused him any trouble. Would he have?
3. Foreign aid. Yes, this empire is being propped up by well-meaning nations. Aid that was given was passed on to party faithful and the government-chosen elite, producing even more loyalty from them.
4. China stopped refugees from getting too far. So many would have been long gone from the nightmare if China had not intervened, and sent many of them back to a certain death either by execution or famine or disease.

Becker compares North Korea to a huge concentration camp in which the inmates are slowly being worked to death. When certain portions of the population of the "camp" are no longer necessary they are allowed to die. Less and less aid is sent to them. They grow weak, unable to rise in rebellion. They perish.

Still there are citizens who are wise to what is coming, and believe it or not, while they are strong, they do rebel. There are strikes. Takeovers of buildings. Even murders of government officials. Kim fights back, though, with the wrath at his disposal. Public "trials". Public executions. At one time he demanded the execution of all criminals was to take place within 3 months.

During reprisals, killings become more and more gruesome. Prisoners tied to a stake while relatives are forced to light the fire (as in Medieval Romanism). Stoned to death. Bayoneted to death. And crimes become more and more petty, to be sure everyone who needs to be punished is covered. Stealing 2 pounds of maize. Stealing a couple of eggs. Killing a cow. It's all state property, so you've committed a crime against the state. You die.

Enough for today. Thanks again, Mr. Becker, for your insights.

We continue to be aghast at just how low a society can be brought when Jesus is not allowed in. It's hard to "think positive" , but we must continue to pray. Without prayer, what seems tragic is more like hopeless. But God IS able.

173. a korea-watcher's Christmas Carol

Christmas, 2007.

Henry Wadsworth Longfellow. I wonder how many know he actually wrote a song that's in your hymnbook. I'm not sure if the lyrics are meant to be taken from his own personal experience, but it's easy to imagine many believers worldwide looking at the atrocities in Kim's Korea and singing words like this...

I heard the bells on Christmas day, Their old familiar carols play,

And wild and sweet the words repeat Of peace on earth, goodwill to men.I thought how,as the day had come, the belfries of all Christendom

Had rolled along th'unbroken song Of peace on earth, goodwill to men.

And in despair I bowed my head: "There is no peace on earth," I said,

"For hate is strong, and mocks the song Of peace on earth, goodwill to men."

Then pealed the bells more loud and deep: "God is not dead, nor doth He sleep;

The wrong shall fail, the right prevail, With peace on earth, goodwill to men:"

Till, ringing, singing on its way, The world revolved from night to day,

A voice, a chime, a chant sublime, Of peace on earth, goodwill to men!

I imagine Longfellow envisioned a swelling of human effort bringing on an era of peace. But that Voice he mentions is the Voice of the Lord. That chime is none other than the Last Trumpet of God. That chant is the choir of angels and the Redeemed returning with Christ to set things straight on this planet. Oh yes, North Korea will be made righteous one day. Through our prayers, the righteousness of Christ can be raised up even in our day.

Today in South Korea, a well known Christian man was elected to the Presidency. I was happy but a little jealous. It is what I have been praying for the capital city that is only about an hour or two up the road. And why not? My God topples kingdoms and kings. He crushes empires. My God sent a baby who grew up to be Lord of all the earth and the heavens too. What can He not do when God's people pray?

174. the wealth of NK

Fifteen years old! Completed only 3 years of school. Family has no shoes, no clothes but the ones on their backs. That's why no schooling. Abject poverty. The bottom rung of a ladder deep in the earth.

Desperate, she comes into China with her father and brother. Mom is gone. "Disappeared" they say. Life is unbearable. They make it over the border into China, a true "Paradise" in comparison to the sad land they must leave. In this part of the country many homes have been abandoned. They find a house and move in.

One week passes. Only one week. Arrest and forcible "repatriation" to North Korea. Not welcome here. But this incredible girl refuses to shrivel up and die in her homeland. She returns. By herself.

Thank God for the church of Jesus. All over the world God has sent His people, and spoken to them to win the lost, to help the hurting, to remember the prisoners. It is a group of Christians that notices this brave teen when she comes back to China. They bring her to Hunchun City. They tell her of Jesus, of prayer, of the state of the lost. They plant in her a desire to go back to North Korea when the time is right, and share the Good News of Jesus.

She begins this stay in China with a North Korean woman and a Chinese man. Her life is work and study. She studies Bible in the morning and Chinese in the afternoon! She starts to look forward to the day when she will go home and spread God's Word.

The day of the interview is the first time she has left her home. Two reasons she has been locking herself in: Deathly fear of re-arrest and being sent back to Korea, and, she really enjoys studying God's Word day after day.

So there it is before you again, Western believer. A girl with absolutely nothing and absolutely everything. Would you like to rush in and give her sweets and music and movies and fancy clothes and shoes and a nice house and a driver's license and - and - and... the Western way of life? Would you not destroy her with your gifts?

My hunch is that she would like to give you something too. Because she has so much more to give...

Soon I must stand before God and give account to a crucified Saviour of what I did with my incredible American liberty and wealth. If I even think about boasting or complaining or offering excuses, perhaps he will call to the witness stand this 15-year-old girl. To my eternal shame. God forgive me. God have mercy on the Western Church.

Today's story adapted from refugeesinternational.com and their series of interviews of North Korean refugees in northeastern China. You may access them all and download them for no charge.

175. December 22: Hope for NK

It's December 22. One of my favorite days of the year. Yesterday was the shortest day. Today there will be more minutes of light. And tomorrow even more. In my strange way of thinking, spring is already here. The light has dawned. In almost no time the world will be new. God promised the seasons would remain constant. And this year will be like last. Spring will come. Spring *has* come. No wonder the ancients believed that their god, the sun, was born around this time. No wonder the Christian "church" played into the mystery and agreed that this just *must have been* the time when the Son, Jesus, was born also. Though Jesus Himself left us no clear evidence about the time of His birth. A special Mass was held, and voila! Christ-mass was born too.

But I digress. As old folks normally do. Someone surely must be waiting for the North Korea tie-in. Yes? Here it comes. Before December 22 is symbolic for me of the winter of humanity when all is bleak and dark and worse and worse. North Korea experiences this winter all year long, as does every other nation to some extent. Things are not right in the world. The snow of sin covers the planet. Cold hearts drive us to take cover. We are not free. And we think this condition will last forever. Things seem to get worse every day.

But there is hope. December 22 means hope . I see the snow, but in my mind I see spring birds flying over it. A bluebird has made its nest in my front-yard tree that has no leaves! The flowers rise, though my neighbors can't see them as they slush toward their car and begin to sweep off the night's offering.

Rotting and starving in a Hoeryong concentration camp or a Yoduk or a Chongjin, a man in whom Christ lives suddenly says, "Hey, this is not my final state. Winter shall not be always. *Christ shall come*. This regime shall fall. It will not always snow and be cold. Nothing but the newness of an eternal spring is headed my way. Don't you feel it, fellow-prisoner, do you know what I know? It's the 22nd! Christ is here and is coming!"

And so Lord Jesus, our prayer this winter's day is that hope will be firmly planted in the hearts of your suffering loved ones in North Korea. May they see the promises of God and believe them. May the joy of what is coming be sufficient to give them the grace to endure what is here. And if in Your perfect plan it is best that North Korea experience part of its deliverance before You come, what joy that would bring to the earth. But set Your people free one way or the other. And may we who remember the prisoners keep remembering them without fail, relating to their pain, bearing their cross, hoping with them for Your return and Your deliverance.Amen.

176. *always winter but never christmas*

Thus it was spoken of the land of Narnia in the C.S. Lewis classic. The unthinkable, for a small child, and for bigger kids too, is an unbroken winter. Such is the plight for these many decades in North Korea. Surely there are bright moments. And Christ Himself has entered this heart and that. But in the main, the land is in darkness. That was the thought going through my head this morning as I prayed for North Korea. A Scripture formed in my thinking and I realized I was in Isaiah, chapters 8 and 9.

This is the classic passage of Christ coming to Galilee, and to the world, bringing His dazzling Light to a desperate planet. It was desperate when He first came, it will be even more desperate when He comes again. And a picture of that desperation is daily painted for us by reflecting on ancient and modern Chosun. It was North Korea that I was seeing as I heard these words inside. They are spoken from the vantage point of a future time, when the regime has changed forever...

(8:22) Then they will look to the earth, and see trouble and darkness, gloom of anguish; and they [Chosun] will be driven into darkness. (9:2-4) The people who walked in darkness [Chosun] have seen a great light [Jesus]. Those who dwelt in the land of the shadow of death [Chosun] , upon them a light has shined. You [Jesus] have multiplied the nation and increased its joy. They rejoice before You according to the joy of harvest, as men rejoice when they divide the spoil. For You [Jesus] have broken the yoke of his burden and the staff of his shoulder, the rod of his oppressor..

(9:6-7) For unto us a Child is born, unto us a Son is given. And the government [of Chosun and the world] will be upon His shoulder. And His name will be called Wonderful, Counselor, Mighty God, Everlasting Father, Prince of Peace. Of the increase of His government and peace there will be no end, upon the throne of David and over His kingdom, to order it and establish it with judgment and justice from that time forward, even forever. The zeal of the Lord of hosts will perform this.

We may not know God's timing, but we know His heart, His zeal. This message is hated by most present world leaders, who can't accept that they and their dynasties are limited by the hand of the God they spurn. But when it's all over, only Jesus reigns! Lord haste the day! And preserve Your people until then.

My Christmas thoughts for Chosun.

177. merry christmas, mr kim

Kim Jong-il has got to be a little befuddled on Christmas morning as he views at least 1/3 of the world's population giving some sort of nod to the Christian's God. "Christmas" may not represent the truest form of the Christ life but one cannot ignore the fact that Jesus is brought to the foreground in many people's thinking. The antichrist to come will be sure to change "times and seasons." The Christmas season, the whole "B.C.-A.D." thing on our calendars. it will all go. As it has gone already in many lands of the Earth.

Mr. Kim certainly cannot write all the excitement off as a "Western" thing, as he sees so many millions of his fellow-Koreans in the South, increased thousands upon thousands of Chinese, Russians all around him, inhabitants of the lands of Southeast Asia all giving a place to the Star of Bethlehem.

So Merry Christmas, Mr. Kim. We do hope you can figure all this out eventually, and in time even be among those who, like the truly Wise Men of earth, will come and bow low before this Jesus Christ, the very Son of the very living God.

We give our best greetings to the true believers inside North Korea, also. For yes, they do exist, and they prosper. But alas, they have no tree erected but the cross of Christ, no gifts to offer but their suffering and tears.

I wonder what would it be like should we suddenly be whisked away from our own trees, to meet the North Korean believers in a neutral place for a short time of gift exchange? American Christians may cockily think the North Koreans would be ashamed that they have nothing material to give, while we would pour on them appliances and fine clothing and rich foods and furniture and car keys and deeds to fantastic homes. But if they then would show us their scars and tell us of their bereavements and imprisonments and relate to us what they had to eat all day yesterday, all because of loving Jesus, who would feel the most shame?

Ah! I mean no guilt or condemnation this happy morning! We are what we are in Christ. We have travelled thus far in the light we have been given. May the fulness of His light dawn upon us and take precedence over all the lesser lights we have valued until now. Eventually Christ will bring us all into the perfection that only He knows how to accomplish. I only pray that from this time on I will find "under the tree" where Christ already burdens himself, my own hunched body . For as Paul says, "If one died" - and He did - "then all are dead."

Christ we salute you above all this 25th of December, and ask your grace to join the North Koreans in carrying your cross.

178. why hwang left nk

Introducing Hwang Jang Yop, the "architect" of North Korea's governmental/economic spin-off from Communism. Thomas Belke has dedicated an entire chapter of his book *Juche* to this man. As has been my custom on this log, I give merely a taste of what he said, in hopes you will read the entire treatise.

Who is, and was, this man, and why is he important? He was born in 1925 in what has become the center of the evil results of his work, Hamgyong Bukto, the far northeastern NK state that houses incredible poverty to this day, as well as the infamous Hoeryong Concentration Camp, among other atrocities.

During World War II he is actually studying in Japan. Then to Pyongyang for more schooling. Here he becomes a Communist. He furthers his studies of Marx at the Kim Il Sung Universtity, achieving acclaim as Pyongyang's number one student of and crusader for the Communist way. Then comes the Korean War. Off to the Soviet Union for yet more study. There he becomes Doctor Hwang. Upon his return to Kim Il Sung's school, he is elevated to head lecturer of philosophy. Later he serves as that school's President.

More advancements follow. Chairman of the Supreme People's Assembly for 3 terms. Chairman of the Foreign Affairs Committee of the Supreme People's Assembly. Worker's Party Secretary for Ideological Affairs. Chairman of Foreign Diplomacy. Co-chief Secretary of the Worker's Party Central Committee. Vice-Chairman of the Fatherland Peace and Unification Agency. And from 1993-1997, Secretary of Foreign Affairs.

And in 1997? Last February we celebrated the tenth anniversary of Hwang's dumping of the DPRK. Yes, he just leaves. After all the study, the labor, the educating of thousands of North Korea's young, and after contributing to Kim literature to the extent that he is known as the "architect" of Juche, the "self-reliant" philosophy of the NK Kingdom, he just vanishes. People to this day are not sure why.

The forever optimistic- some say naive- argue that North Korea is just plain evil and any thinking man will eventually get out. But that doesn't explain why myriads of other thinking men do not get out. Why this mastermind? Why now?

Others, a bit more cynical, conclude that Hwang was about to be "purged" in 1997 because of his growing awareness of "the truth". Perhaps a slip of the tongue or the pen had him in hot water. He really remains a committed Communist, they say, but he is scared out of his mind and fled to safety.

We cannot discount the thinking of the conspiracy theorists either. Not totally. Stranger things have happened. These folks believe that none other than Mr. Kim himself set up the whole affair. the "escape", the "defection", the speeches after the "conversion." For those speeches were filled with warnings to the South that an invasion was surely near. True psychological pressure being exerted by one who specializes in such things.

Mr. Hwang's presence in the free world reminds us of the evil that stalks, seeking someone to devour. The fact that we do not even know the truth about one who has come out from the paranoia of North Korea, lets us know that the world is not a safe place to be these days. But then it never was. If ever the gift of discernment was needed, it is now. It has been promised to Spirit-filled believers who want it. I offer that as the prayer suggestion of the day. Oh to know the good from the evil. Oh to know the excellent from the good. Oh for the power within to choose the excellent and not be content until it is ours.

God says He will judge all liars. Their lies will be exposed also. May there not be found one hiding in us.

179. *it didn't end at rome*

So says "Voice of the Martyrs", the Oklahoma ministry that has reached into the depths of the Suffering Church worldwide, including North Korea. Yes, the vicious hatred of the Enemy for the church of Jesus Christ has been well documented in every generation. Yet the church is alive and prospering and determined to march on to its final destiny.

Consider that North Korean group for a moment: A South Korean pastor spoke at a missions conference in Germany last March, and gave us some insights into the almost unreal dedication of our dear family in Chosun. He said that at their secret gatherings they have begun to recite, alongside the Lord's prayer, the following five principles. How meaningful might this be at your assembly?

1. Our persecution and suffering are our joy and honor.

2. We want to accept ridicule, scorn and disadvantages with joy in Jesus' name.

3. As Christians, we want to wipe others' tears away and comfort the suffering.

4. We want to be ready to risk our life because of our love for our neighbor, so that they also become Christians.

5. We want to live our lives according to the standards set in God's Word.

I can imagine some fundamentalist groups in our land giving the nod to number 5, and isolated believers throughout the nation amen-ing the others, but by and large the North's "principles" may as well have been written on some other planet. It is not where we are. It is not what we do. We cannot comprehend this way of life.

If you are a Western believer reading this and in serious disagreement, please write to me soon and correct me. Tell me the story of how your church is being persecuted and your people are rejoicing in it. Let me know of the ridicule and scorn you are receiving for Jesus' sake. Tell me of tears and suffering on the behalf of Christ, and serious efforts to bring neighbors to Jesus.

I will be glad to publish your stories here. We need more of the North Korean spirit in our midst, and your tale could help us get closer to it.

Meanwhile, please take some time today to love North Korea in prayer.

180. imagine a mexican

I really don't want to get into the whole illegal alien thing. Whether they are justified or we are right and all that. Some of my best friends fall into that category. Finest people I've ever met. Just wanted to work. To earn money. To eat, etc. But I'll leave it there.

I was struck though by the very stark contrast between a Mexican "migrant" and one from, say, North Korea. Imagine a Mexican being not only sent back to Mexico, but being brutally tortured or even killed upon being sent back. Imagine a Mexican being charged with leaving his home village as though it were a criminal offense. And in North Korea it is a criminal offense. Imagine a Mexican being tried in court for not showing up at work. Imagine the accusation of "leaving the country." Leaving the country is an internationally guaranteed right, assuming of course that the other country is willing to receive another citizen or tourist.

After being found guilty of all of the above, imagine a Mexican being sent to a short-term (2-3 years?) labor camp where there is below subsistence-level food rationing and high possibility of death and the hardest of labor. Imagine grueling interrogations geared at determining the poor hungry soul's dedication to the Mexican regime.

Hard to imagine in this hemisphere? But everyday stuff in Chosun, aided by China's supportive hands. Whenever possible the Chinese police, expecting a bonus of some sort, send North Koreans back to their own land. Of course, it's not always possible. As here, "illegals" are quite often assimilated into the culture and the economy.

But part of that economy is slave trade "over there". Imagine that. A Mexican risks his life to get to a place where there is food, and is trapped at the border by a citizen of the host country. He or she is sold into sexual slavery, or forced into a marriage to some desperate American...

Again hard to imagine, but very common at the Chinese border.

Imagine local businesses in America being raided from time to time, as illegals are swept out the back door like so much vermin and sent back to Mexico (I know some have proposed this). Imagine Mexicans having been treated so poorly here, and punished beyond words in their home land, actually attempting to make the trip here again. Imagine that a trip to the United States may mean the killing or imprisonment of all their family in Mexico.

Imagine that during interrogation at home in Mexico, the Mexican is asked if he went to a Christian Church.

Imagine that with a positive response to that question he is executed. Imagine a Mexican begging the interrogator to kill her so as to avoid any more punishment.

Imagine a Mexican who has become pregnant in the States being forced to abort her child, or kill her already-born infant, so that the holy ethnicity of the Mexicans can remain intact.

Can't do it, can you? Can't imagine such horrors in our part of the world? But David Hawk in his *Hidden Gulag* (available free online) documents that all these things and more have happened in Chosun.

I ask you once more to pray with me for North Korea. Fervently. Daily. God will hear us. God will change North Korea and the men responsible for damaging the Korean people.

181. *korean war miracle*

1950 is a long time ago. Very few living Americans- or Koreans for that matter - remember the Korean War. Following as it did on the heels of the "Great" war it is easy to relegate it to an unimportant footnote of history. But destinies of many nations were determined on that horrific day when the Communists, who had been put in place by Western powers in the northern part of the Korean peninsula, swooped south in an attempt to unify Northeast Asia under Communism.

Thank God they failed. No really, thank Him every day. Imagine a Korea with little or no Christianity. Totalitarian. Communist. The largest church in the world would be somewhere else. The mission-sending power that Korea has become, Korea would not have become. The economics and politics of such a situation are mind-boggling also.

But they failed. Kim Joon-gon was one who witnessed this failure, though through several reverses of fortune. According to Hefley's *By Their Blood* Kim had first suffered persecution under the Japanese who took over Korea in the early 20th century. He had become a Christian and refused to worship at one of the many Shinto shrines set up by them. Then World War II ended with its clear message to the Japanese. They left. But the Koreans had seen nothing yet.

The Koreans themselves out-did the Japanese for cruelty when they became twisted in their thinking by the Communists and the one that ruled them, Kim Il-sung. In 1950 the North made their move and Kim Joon-gon, his wife, and his daughter fled to an island. But the Communists took over that island, and he was trapped. In October his turn came to be arrested. His crime was friendship with American missionaries, who in paranoid Communist thinking had only come to conquer Korea for the U.S. After he denied such foolishness and was given more threats, they ley him go. He had not denied Jesus or His people.

When he arrived home he found his wife busy preparing white martyrs' clothing, in Korean tradition. She fully expected to be with the Lord soon. She was not disappointed.

Kim, wife, and father-in-law were arrested in the cowardly Communist style, at 2 a.m. next morning. With a trained mob as in Jesus' trial, the Communists intimidated and beat the father and the wife to death. Kim himself passed out from the beatings, and did not awaken until dawn. He stumbled away from the tragic scene left by his oppressors to the house of a neighbor woman he presumed to be still an interested friend. How wrong he was.

She called the Communists. They came and were going to kill him at once in the house. The woman protested, asking only that they at least take him outside. Kim escapes death again.

Outside a debate began as to the best way to dispose of this troublesome Christian. As the argument continued people from the village approached and begged that this man, who had only taught them good things, migt be spared. Life spared yet again.

There was a pause. And in the midst of the silence a sudden shout from other soldiers down the road: "Americans!" Kim was forgotten in an instant, as it became clear that the UN troops were on the way. Once more, no death for Kim.

A man so marvelously allowed to live must surely be grateful and determined to serve Christ all his days. So it was. First the business of forgiveness. When those who killed his wife and father were brought to trial Kim insisted that His Lord wanted him to show mercy. And mercy was shown. And news of that mercy spread across the island. Communists repented and came to Christ. The enemy had been conquered by the King of Kings.

Next Kim became principal of a High School and pastor of a large church. The message was passed on to many hundreds more. In 1957 he came to study at a famous American seminary, met Bill Bright -founder of Campus Crusade for Christ- and returned to Korea to direct CCC's South Korean work.

Oh it's not always like that. Remember, the faithful wife died on the spot. As many others. But Christ will have His will in each of our lives as He pleases. Thank God for the life of Kim Joon-gon and may the Lord raise up many such men out of the rubble still being created in North Korea by those who do not know God or true life. We certainly cannot understand the way things are now, but one day we will look back from Mt. Zion with Jesus and all the elect and say, "Lord, You have done all things well! Be praised forever! Amen."

182. stop that prayer

"Dear Lord, Bless the North Koreans today. Give them enough food to eat. Put a roof over their heads. Put clothes on their backs. Miraculously heal their bodies. Give them what they absolutely need..."

Wait a minute! Is that how we pray for ourselves? "Enough food to eat" or cupboards and refrigerators overflowing with food? "A roof over our head" or many hundreds of thousands or even millions on a unique mansion made just for us? "Clothes on our backs" or clothes filling our many closets, attics, basements and garages? "Heal our bodies" or help me believe you to pay my medical insurance? "What we absolutely need" or every little thing our hearts desire from the "Grandpa" in the sky who wants all of his people to be healthy and wealthy and living like "King's Kids"?

We can't have it both ways you know. Either our prayers for the North Koreans or our prayers for ourselves must radically change. I will leave individual readers to decide which alterations will take place, but for today the message is, Hey, we're no better than they are!

What has given us the feeeling of superiority is the naked fact of our prosperity. We have assumed what the Bible never assumes, that "gain" means godliness. But we forget that there are many rich men who are evil. Not even saved. We assume that long life must mean God's favor. We forget the men among us who have died young after having accomplished more with God than we will in 100 such lifetimes. Jesus, for one. Stephen the martyr. Oh you know there are a lot more.

In our hearts we know that a North Korean who is released from his prison-land, finds Christ, and deliberately goes back to NK to tell friends and family about Jesus at the risk of his life, and dies a pauper at the hands of evil men, is far ahead of an American Christian who never once sacrificed for the cause of Jesus. We know that. But we somehow still look down at these "poor" believers.

May God show us our utter depravity. Our abject poverty. Our total inability to please Him in the flesh. May He show us Who owns all the riches of the world. The Giver and Taker of life. Above all may He raise His cross before our dying eyes, and when we come back to life filled with His Spirit, may we be willing to see things as He does.

"Social Justice" is not our plea. The world is lost and going to Hell. Their 50-60 years of "equality" is not our concern. Eternity is. The Oneness of the Body is. The coming judgment seat of Christ when all will be equally discerned by Him who knows all, that *definitely* is.

Well, back to the prayer closet.

183. the Lamb that was slain

"MAY THE LAMB THAT WAS SLAIN RECEIVE THE REWARD OF HIS SUFFERING!"

It was shouted over the waves as the ship passed out farther and farther from the world these Moravian missionaries had known. They had just sold themselves into a life of slavery for the sole purpose of bringing the Gospel to an island of slaves where the Gospel was forbidden. Motivated not by glory or money or power but only by the Worthiness of Him Who died on the accursed tree, these men made eternal history on that day as their haunting cry reaches deep into the caverns of our own selfish hearts still.

Why do we love North Korea and the victimized people there? Why should we daily pray for them, send money on their behalf, go to visit them via Bibles or tracts or our own person? Is it because they are worthy? Is it because we need "something to do for Jesus" ? Is it because they are in pain and we have seen their needs? Because we want to make them happy in this life? Why, any pagan with any kind of a heart at all can feel sorry for a North Korean. How is the Christian motivation different?

The answer that comes resoundingly back from Heaven was voiced so exquisitely many years back by Paris Reidhead, missionary, preacher, and much more. Brother Reidhead tells in the classic sermon *Ten Shekels and a Shirt* of his own experience of human compassion on the "poor Africans" and his desire to "improve on the justice of God" by giving the heathen a chance to go to Heaven. Well, these are not motives to be spurned. We all understand the call of missions, and videos of lepers and dying children that grip our hearts. But it is not enough.

The preacher was spoken to in the depths of his soul one night, as he was complaining about the fact that these "monsters of iniquity" had no interest in the things of which he spoke, and asking how could God have sent him there in compassion when they cared not one whit for the light of the Gospel?

God simply said, "I didn't send you here for their sakes. I sent you here for My sake."

Try that on in relationship to the subject at hand, Christians working for the North Koreans. God sends us to these precious souls, as lost as the Africans, many of whom have no desire for any more light than that which Kim allows,

I say, He sends us not for their sakes, but for His own. He died for them. He deserves a hearing. He deserves their obedience, their devotion, their forever love.

It was God who hung on the cross. Never can man understand or repay this wonder. Never can man suffer more than did the God of Heaven murdered by His own creation. Our sympathy must be turned to the Creator and what He did, and not focused on the hurts of the created. And that includes our own hurts.

I can feel this message as deeply as I have ever felt anything in my life. I cannot say that it has permeated my being and changed all my personal desires. But oh! how I want it to. Let the plaintive call go forth in our hearts every day...

"May the Lamb that was slain receive the reward of His suffering!"

184. carefully taught

Hyok Kang's *This Is Paradise* relates how Communist youth in North Korea are twisted early in their thinking about Americans and South Koreans and Japanese. Before the child can grow and form his own assessments about the nations of the world, Government-sponsored propaganda has whittled down acceptable people groups to a precious few, with the star being of course their own nation. We Westerners understand patriotism and national pride, but we also like to give the benefit of the doubt to a host of countries that are not exactly the same as our own.

Math problems similar to the following have been included in North Korean textbooks:

Our "People's Army" has just been fighting the American imperialist dogs and the South Korean puppets. We have taken 14, 892 prisoners.

There were 1543 more American [another insulting term] than there were South Korean puppets. How many American dogs + South Korean puppets were there altogether?

A wonderful little girl who is a part of the Young Pioneers, has been chosen to be a messenger to our patriotic troops fighting against the occupying Japanese. She is asked to bring a message in a basket. In the basket also are five apples. But she is stopped by a Japanese soldier at a checkpoint. The wretched Japanese actually eats three of her apples! How many are left?

During the Korean War 487 Chinese soldiers join up with 63 Rusian soldiers and 913 of our own patriotic fighters from the DPRK. Their mission is to repel the invasion of the puppets of South Korea. How many have joined together for this monumental effort?

That's carrying "practical" math a bit far, don't you think? Our constant prayer is that North Korea will soon have an invasion of Truth led by none other than The Truth Himself, Jesus the Christ. He in His people cannot lie. Truth brings light and power and a whole lot more to a society. Lord, pour mighty doses over this land!

185. will somebody stop and help

Behold one cup of rice. During the dark famine days, and in certain portions of North Korea today, in certain people groups and ages, this is the rationed amount for an entire day. Eight ounces. Eight or nine hundred calories. Every day. Until you die by starvation.

The international minimum standard for calories per day is said to be two to three times that much . North Korea sets the standard at 1,600 calories per day, about 450 grams, less than two cups per day. Some people in Korea actually are given that much. In fact Party faithful are given up to 900 grams, twice the standard set by the NK government. Some receive as little as 300. Perhaps less.

That's one topic. The amount of food the government expects one to live on. The other topic is, even with the low NK standard, will North Korea have enough food to meet its goals? If the state is now giving, as I have read elsewhere, 550 grams per day to its adults and 300 to children and elderly,that's 15 million persons times 550, and 7 million persons times 300. Therefore, 12,000 + tons of grain per day, or nearly 4 million tons per year.

Can North Korea produce 4 million tons per year? It hasn't always. During the famine years of the 90's it was about half that much. No one is daring to say that the situation has improved dramatically, only mildly. Free markets have popped up here and there but if the rice isn't there to sell, the proper economy means nothing.

And don't forget the recent floods. And don't forget how donated foods are still misdirected to feed Kim's loyal ones. There is still so much to do. In fairness, there are projects scattered over the country attempting to right the problem. But so far no one has come up with a workable solution.

No, we're not out of the rice fields yet.

On the way home tonight, the car in front of me on the freeway suddenly veered to the center lane and almost crashed into a truck. Then a hard right and off went that same car went onto the shoulder and beyond, finally turning on its side and sending up a stream of smoke. I was shaken. I pulled over, got out of my car, and since I do not carry a cell phone, I began madly waving my arms to try to get people to stop and/or call 911. Many did, both. And creative Americans found the way to get the needy victim taken care of. They smashed a window. Pulled the man out, as it was obvious he was not only conscious -though bleeding- but quite aware of what was happening and willing to cooperate. He'll be fine now.

Perhaps I philosophize too much, but it occurred to me as I climbed back in my little car, shaking but thankful, that there are some of us, due to age, due to lacking skills, etc. whose only job is to wave our arms and hope that God will send help. Maybe there's some creative prayer warrior, some gifted financier, some talented economist, who will get on over to North Korea and start doing what needs to be done. Surely most of us don't have things on our agenda that are more important? I mean, I wanted to get home tonight after a day at work. But this man who was possibly dying in a car...

Anybody out there? These daily blogs were not written to make people cry and sigh, but to motivate them to action. Chosun is in serious trouble. Dying as a nation. Almost totally without Christ. Doomed therefore forever. Hidden from the light and the truth found in Jesus Christ alone. There's got to be something you can do. Will you pull over and help a vehicle spinning out of control?

186. remember?

You were terrified. So was your mate to be. But in front of all those witnesses you exchanged your vows and your rings, and even your affection. Remember? You had thought for days, weeks, months, about the plans and just what kind of person this would turn out to be, and the progress of your career and the number of children and the house you would some day buy. You thought regularly about all the ways your combined life would give glory to God and His Kingdom. Remember?

And what does your remembering do for you? There are tears of gratitude. Tears of regret. Memories. New resolve. New vision. Remembering is powerful. It leads to action.

I remember the night oh so many years back when I thought I'd try out my neighbor's advice. "Try God", she said. She knew my dad was an alcoholic and was missing again. She knew my mom had emotional issues that were destroying her and that she was in the hospital. She knew that the family that had moved into my house was abusive... She saw my sad little face often, and simply said, "Try God."

I remember that night on the way home from school when I "tried" Him. I knelt down in a wooded area and prayed as only a child can: "God, if you're really there, I want to hear from my dad tonight!" It had been a long time. Months, I guess, since Dad had called in. Oh how a little boy needs his daddy. But I had no reason to expect that call.

I remember what the clock was saying when I got to the fence around my house: 5:45. I remember that as I was walking in the door, the phone was ringing. I remember my sister handing me the phone and telling me, "Bobby, it's your dad calling." I remember thinking, "This is God! He's really there!"

I remember it so clearly, 50 plus years later. And remembering helps me to get my perspectives in order. Remembering clears out a lot of the junk in my life. Oh yes, it's powerful to remember.

Jesus told us to take some bread and some juice and remember. That's all. No elaborate ritual with specified speeches, uniforms, lights, smoke. Just bread, juice, memory. And into that scene comes Christ, crucified but alive from the dead. Power. Sheer power.

That's why He later told us to remember the prisoners. And with His dear friends in prison He adds this bit of instruction: "Remember them as though you were there with them." (Hebrews 13:3)

First call them to mind. Give them the place they deserve in your thinking apparatus. In your imagination. In your emotions. Let the Christ in His Body fill you full.

Then let one more thought in: You are there with them in prison. You are chained. You are doing hard labor in the fields or the mines. You are separated from your family. You are about to be beaten. You have just been beaten. But you will not deny Christ. You are hungry. You are oh so cold. You are roasting from the heat, and there is no ventilation or plumbing in your cell. Go on and on. "Remember" them. Put them in your brain deliberately.

Then rise up to act upon what you have experienced in those moments. For all of our life is nothing more than acting upon that which our mind has absorbed and processed. So process this: There is one body of Christ, and it is in great pain, and you are part of that body. Feel it. Now what do you do?

What? An entire article without mentioning the name of a certain country? Indeed. But I am confident that when God's people meditate on the suffering Body of Christ, He will Himself speak that country's name.

Remember...

187. nk history: a slow and painful death

There is no doubt about it. In the '80's and on into the '90's North Korea was free-falling into a real mess. This is the testimony of most historians of the period, including the one we have been following, Bradley Martin.

From a Christian perspective, it is hard to ignore some of the spiritual connections to the decline of Chosun. It had been drilled into the population that the first words to be spoken every morning were, "Oh Great Leader Kim Il Sung." The first word a baby learned was "Kim Il Sung." Before every meal, "Thank you, great Kim Il Sung." With this man trying deliberately to take the place that only God can rightly claim in a man and nation's life, why should God honor this nation with prosperity?

Little by little, a Joseph-like famine (as in Genesis) began to take over North Korea. Before it was over, a job in the food industry was the best deal going. Coal disappeared, and citizens trekked to the mountains for wood fuel. When the trees were gone, the dirt had no place to go put down, clogging the rivers, slowing the water supply. A curse slowly enveloped the land.

Those looking for human causes want to dump all guilt on the present leader, who took over when the famine was getting to its worst stages. But some of Dad's policies, linked to the unchanging nature of the Communist way, not to mention some Confucian stubbornness, must share the blame. Things had gotten pretty bad by the time Kim Junior took the throne.

One side effect of deterioration was the eager desire of many to get out. In Siberia, North Korean men were drawn to a job opportunity that involved incredibly hard work in a frozen wasteland. But here was food. And a certain amount of dignity . Not only that, there were "free" people, relatively speaking, in Siberia. Off they went.

Those who stayed behind were increasingly vulnerable to a slow painful death. It is estimated that 80 to 90 percent of NK's people developed stomach ulcers. When the digestive juices flow, but there is no food in the stomach to be digested, the acid has no place to go but through the wall of the stomach.

Trees on mountains, food in bellies, simple little things we all take for granted. All denied to these descendants of the "morning calm." Many still suffer. But even more to be pitied is the man or woman whose hungry soul shall perish without Christ.

What shall we do? Is God calling you to act?

188. unbroken succession

How is a dictator formed? Some say it takes a people who are conditioned to receive him. Surely the Korean people were so conditioned. Centuries of harsh rulers have been permitted to hold sway over the minds of the citizens of Chosun. Take Emperor Zhu Yuanzhang (pictured). He was the founder of the Ming Dynasty that ruled Korea from 1364-1666. He required absolute obedience. He was the law and the source of all laws. When he died, generations after him were forced to sit under lectures mouthing his philosophies. As people must sit and listen to the founding father of the present dynasty.

Over a thousand years earlier much of the peninsula was ruled by the Silla kings. In those days a man's hereditary position determined his place in the social standing. Top aristocracy did not have to sign up for the military. They went instead to the top administrative offices in the land. A practice carried down to today's Korea.

Later came the Koryo State, equally conscious of rank, whose "caste" system rivaled that of modern India and persists in North Korea as well. One third of the nation was actually a slave class in ancient Koryo. This practice was only outlawed in 1894, but was quickly picked up by the occupying Japanese, and of course, by today's labor camp mentality . No one considered it unusual. This is how things had been "forever".

Caste continued in the final Choson dynasty. The different groups wore tags that branded them as high or low in Korean standing. Today's system has changed only in name, and involves 50 or 60 ranks according to class background. There are families that fought the Japanese, veterans of the Korean War, poor peasant farmers etc etc. One's rank determines where one lives and how much one eats and if one lives or dies.

There are many other intriguing similarities between the present oppression and the oppression of his predecessors. North Korea is starved for liberty and truth. Starved.

Can Koreans be free? Where shall we look for hope, for faith that things can ever be different? That's easy. South Korea, and the God upon whom so many South Koreans call every day. South Korea is the constant argument against feudalism, brutal monarchies, Communism, Juche, and the government of the North. Koreans really can be free, given the proper God and the proper leadership.

For this we pray.

Jasper Becker's Rogue Regime *was the source of many of today's facts.*

189. including the cornhusks

From Refugees International another interview from their online book, *Acts of Betrayal*. I give the summary of a conversation held between an RI representative and a recently escaped North Korean refugee.

This victim is a 27-year-old man who came from Undok, North Korea, to China in June of '03. As with all the refugees, his chances of survival in North Korea had come to the near-zero mark. So he left parents and siblings and made the trip by himself into an all new world.

His first impression of China was the stark contrast between it and his home country. How prosperous the Chinese! Then he began wondering what he will do in this foreign land. His family members are farmers. At least they work for farmers, much like slaves on the old southern plantations of the United States worked for farmers, and were "permitted" to live so they could keep prospering the farmers. His family of six was allowed to keep only 150 kilograms of food... per year. That includes the cornhusks. That's 330 pounds divided by 6, or 55 pounds each. If my math isn't faulty, that's one pound of food per week. Just ounces per day.

This gentleman claims there is no other way to get food. He says that if they don't finish planting, and don't have enough food, the manager will give them a little corn and allow them to buy some food. But if they have no money to buy food, they can't expect the manager to show any generosity in terms of cash.

So it's off to the mountains, to join the many other desperate North Korean souls who are collecting medicinal plants to sell in the market place. This is seasonal work, up to half of the year. It's possible to collect maybe a kilogram in a day of working. 2 pounds. 2 pounds will sell for 450 won. In today's market, that's about 50 cents a day.

Speaking of medicine, three of his family members have serious illness. But there is no serious medicine available. Even if there were, they have no money. And they can't sell their goods for some quick cash because they have no goods.

What does this family have? Hope. It seems that there are varying degrees of hope in North Korea. One hope that this family has latched onto is the outbreak of war and the overthrow of the present regime. Things cannot remain as they are. The aid being sent in is being diverted to the government and the military. "Everybody knows this," he says. That's why the military is willing to give its life for the present dictator.

And the common people are constantly bombarded with invitations to love their leaders too. From baby to adult, North Koreans are educated about the Kim family. 3-4 hours of a typical school day is given to learning about the Kim family. That's if a child is even allowed to go to school. Quite often, students are left at home to "battle for crops" on the farm.

One must decide whether these students are the lucky ones, or the others.

Tonight let us be grateful for all God has richly supplied to us, and work

190. the great music of juche

I was raised on Sinatra and Crosby. If you don't know those names, it's because they're pretty much off the radar of this generation, except maybe at Christmas. I graduated to the Rogers & Hamerstein musicals, then musicals of all sorts, Pat Boone, etc. Along the way I was introduced to the great hymns of the Christian faith, some of them passed down from the Reformation and before. Great stuff, all of it. Lots of variety in theme and style was my musical life. I still sing and listen to these old tunes, with joy, and sometimes with tears.

That's why it is difficult for me to understand the plight of the North Korean. As so very often. The girls pictured on my original blog were actually among the thousands who have been privileged to leave the slavery of North Korea.

They were musicians. At first they were glad just to get out, but now they seek for "stardom" in the South as a singing group. But they've had to change their lyrics quite a bit. In the North, the monotonous theme of their songs was the Kim government in all its glory. I give you from Thomas Belke's "Juche" some of the songs from which they might have chosen:

Glory to the Dear Leader
We sing of February Holiday
Song of Comradeship
Let Us become General's Army
We Began in the Debris
We Will Advance Confidently
Toward Decisive Battle
Let Us Hold High the Red Flag
We Will Defend the Headquarters of Revolution   With Our Lives
The General, Son of Guerrillas
Socialist Paradise

Granted, some of the umph! of these song titles may have been lost in translation, but it seems to me the musical life of an average NK citizen is rather limited.

And that's not all. Please continue to pray today for North Korea's freedom. For, whom the Son sets free is really free! Wait until that nation in the north is singing the great songs of Zion. It will be a sound heard around the world for ages.

191. of north korean police brutality

I've been sharing with you the eyewitness accounts of prison life in North Korea, using David Hawk's *Hidden Gulag*. I'm about to wrap up my time in this book, which is available online free. I thought I would share with you today a summary of the "torture" testimony, given by Mr. Hawk towards the end of his book. I understand that not all these prisoners are in jail for their faith, yet it is important for you to understand the climate of prison life, lest you forget that your brothers and sisters are truly suffering. Oh please pray for them!

From 1967 until into the 2000's there is an unbroken chain of evidence that North Korean prisoners are tortured. Here is a short list of eyewitness proof:

- Detainee beaten unconscious for hunger-related rule infractions. 1997. Chongjin City.
- Detainees beaten with shovels if they did not work fast enough. Chongjin City.
- Detainees regularly placed in undersized punishment boxes for 15 days, unable to stand up or lie down. Danchun.
- Prisoner subjected to motionless kneeling and water torture, facial and shin beatings with rifle butts, leaving permanent damage to ear and eye. Pyongyang. 1994.
- Separate punishment cells from which few returned alive. Yodok.
- Prisoners beaten to death by work-unit leaders. Danchun. Late 80's.
- Former guard reports that in Hoeryong Camp there were so many beatings from guards that they were finally reprimanded.
- Male prisoners beaten by guards. Chongjin. Mid-2000.
- Detainees compelled to beat each other. Onsong.

- Detainee reports that his fingers were broken, he was kicked and beaten on head and face until ears, eyes, nose, and mouth were bleeding. 1997. Onsong.
- Out of 6 persons in adjoining cell (Pyongyang, 1997), prisoner says 2 were carried out on stretchers, 2 needed guard assistance to walk, only 2 could walk by themselves.
- Prisoners ordered to be motionless who moved, were handcuffed from the upper bars of their cells with their feet off the floor.
- Detainees who talked when silence was commanded were ordered to slap and hit each other...

The list goes on and on, but I will stop. Go to http://www.hrnk.org/ for more, including the "ethnic infanticide" victims.

If we are so grieved, we know our loving God is too. He will arise. His enemies will be defeated. Oh that it might be soon, Lord!

192. when a nation chooses Christ

With the help of the authors of "By Their Blood," James and Marti Hefley, I've traced a very brief outline of Korean Church History in the last few months. With this post I end this particular series because in fact so much of what you will find on other of my posts regarding the persecution of believers in North Korea, is their history now.

This final word. After the Communist attacks in the 50's, one victim of which I described in my last post of this series, North Korea was closed once and for all to the Gospel. South

Korea was devastated for the longest time also. Four million refugees trying to get out of Kim's "Paradise" crowded into the South. Tens of thousands of orphans and widows. 20,000 amputees. One-third of church buildings destroyed. 500 pastors dead. Most every Christian family had lost a loved one.

But at least in the South, liberty. And a purging of the past religions and ways to such a degree that Christ was raised up before the Korean people and given the chance He desires to rule in the hearts of men. Missionaries came. Korea was empowered with training and finances and prayer. South Korea's church today is alive and vibrant with some of the largest churches and most dedicated saints in the world. The Christian message has permeated the entire culture, and missionaries now go *from* there all over the world. This is the most Christianized country of all Asia.

And in the North? Turning in on itself and being made to deny its Creator, it has shriveled up into a nearly lost nation. We have documented elsewhere the attempts made by God's people to penetrate this darkness, not the least of which was a 90's visit by Evangelist Graham. Kim Il-sung was given a Bible and a copy of Billy's book, "Peace With God." Son Franklin has had similar opportunities to present the Gospel to Son Jong-il.

There are "indications" everywhere that change is coming. But it has not come. The painful life of believers continues to this day. The Church worldwide is in prayer even now for a pastor that was just arrested and confined... North Korea's history goes on. Let us go on with these dear ones, our very family.

193. something in the air

Remember Jim Jones? The guy that brought a whole church to its death in Guyana back in the 70's? Remember the images of his people working in the fields listening to him preach and sometimes just rant, over giant loudspeakers? Day in, day out, that was their background music. Jim Jones.

Jim has become Kim. Jones is Jong. You know the rest. We ask as respectfully as we know how, is this the best way to get people to follow? Consider the Christ. Yes, people voluntarily want to hear more and more of His message once they catch on to how wonderful it is. You'll see believers with ipods and radios and computers pouring out the Gospel message into their souls. We understand the need for "hearing the message."

But when it is force-fed, involuntarily, what kind of creature is created, with what kind of worldview? Surely Jesus has never forced Himself on anyone, though His followers have been insistent at times, knowing the cost of leaving this world without sins forgiven.

Hyok Kang relates in *This Is Paradise,* "as we hoed, sowed, or harvested, we were subjected to a continuous flood of revolutionary songs, always very cheerful, broadcast by a propaganda lorry [truck] equipped with enormous loudspeakers."

Kang says there are very few vehicles in Onsong, North Korea. But three propaganda lorries. Besides hearing the propaganda in the fields, he had to listen all the way to and from school, and even at certain times *during* the school day. It buzzed through his head even when he wasn't hearing it. It was *life* for this youngster growing up.

Holidays were especially Kim-filled. Special days like the birthdays of the two Kims, "Foundation of the Party" Day, "Foundation of the Army" Day, and some of the more tradional celebrations, caused the lorries and speakers to proclaim the virtues of Juche *all day long.*

It is especially difficult for North Koreans to shake their attachment to their government even after escaping. Only the tragedies that have befallen these people added to the grace of God can overcome a life of one monotone message. That makes the salvation of a North Korean something special. And when such a citizen desires to go back to his land and preach Christ, as numbers have, the miracle increases.

Let's continue faithfully to pray for our bound brothers and sisters.

194. the mills of God and history

Today we continue our trek through modern Korean history (via Bradley Martin).

We're in the 80's. In 1985, North Korea signs the "Nuclear Nonproliferation Treaty." We promise not to encourage this sort of weaponry any longer, they say. But no one is allowed in at first to see that they are really keeping their promise. They do actually process uranium during the 80's and in 1991 it is clear that North Korea is testing weapons.

And in their thinking, none too soon. Here comes the first Iraq War. The North must have had a jolt during this time, watching equipment similar to theirs being chewed up by America's power.

1992: North Korea continues to lose support from and ties with Communist countries. Even China normalizes relationships with Seoul! Thus comes the idea of "economic zones." From 1990 the economy has been shrinking. Maybe 30% in 1992 alone! China and Russia are demanding hard currency settlements to some seriously outstanding debts. Up to half of NK's factories have shut down. Energy is shrinking by the day. The pressure is on.

It is obvious that capitalistic enterprises will bring in the cash flow. But in a Communist country? The government solves this dilemma with the opening of "zones" of free trade and business. Tiny sections of the country , as the east-coast Rajin-Sonbong sector, are essentially cut off from the "mainland", and enterprising capitalists from other countries are allowed to come in and have limited growth. Investors are lured in to help save the day.

In the midst of all of this restructuring and chaos, Eastern Europe falls. Dictators are assassinated or run from power. North Korea panics. Though some inspections have been allowed, by 1993 NK withdraws from the NPT altogether, and Kim Jong Il is basically in charge, with Kim Il Sung serving more as advisor than anything. The son soon turns the government from being a Communist Party dictatorship to being a military dictatorship.

Someone said "the mills of God and of history grind slowly but exceedingly fine." Who could have foretold such a long and drawn-out history of a nation such as North Korea? Yet slowly and surely God has His perfect will in this land. The evil will be judged. The saints will be perfected, purged, made white. They would tell us they are content with Jesus.

And yet we are commanded to "Remember the prisoners" and so we do. Remember those who have been caught up in this massive machine of war and strife and political enigma. Remember that for naming the name of Christ, our brothers in this historic land suffer greatly.

195. the romanian connection

Twenty years ago my heart reached out to Romania for the same reason it is reaching out to North Korea today. The church there was oppressed. Rampant disease and few medical solutions.Deep financial trouble. Communism and a cult of personality led by its dictator. The Romanian people rose up one day in 1989 and sent Mr. Ceausescu (pictured), their not-so-dear leader, to the next life.

According to Jasper Becker in his *Rogue Regime,* Ceausescu and his wife Elena visited North Korea in 1971. They were thrilled. The huge crowds everywhere, all assembled to pour love and praise on their own and Romania's leader, the exquisitely choreographed programs, the complete surrender of a nation to one man. It was more than they could comprehend. But it was something they wanted. Upon their return home, they decided this was just what Romania needed. A cultural crackdown ensued. The transformation began.

The closest I have ever been to cult-following North Korea is cult-following Romania in the mid 80's. On my two visits there before Ceausecu's fall, I was impressed with the fact that nowhere could you go in the land without seeing the dictator's face. Of course, anti-American posters. Typical Communist invitations to more and more work. The phony worship services, the certain knowledge that everyone was working for the secret police.

But central to it all, the praise and obedience to one man. How much he learned from Kim Il Sung I do not know, but the information available about North Korea today suggests the Romanian and Korean cultures were *very* close.

Becker also notes that both country's economies collapsed in the mid-80's, after having been relatively strong for some time. Kim failed to tell him that this cult worship is pretty expensive. Ceausescu paid the ultimate price.

North Korea remains in the grip of Communist-Stalinist-Jucheist leadership, with only faint signs that things may be easing. Other reports point a different direction. One still hears of crackdowns and suffering saints. We believers then need a crackdown of our own. No time for letting up. If there is a hairline crack of light, let us exploit it in prayer until the structure is totally broken and people can breathe free again.

Our God is able.

196. Jesus in the Korean War Years

"The church of Jesus Christ is the one bright spot in the present dark picture of Korea." That was said 54 years ago by missionary-author Arch Campbell as he wrote of the devastations that followed the North Korean attack of the South. He offers many examples of this brightness.

The sounds of people praising Jesus from inside a boarded up house, "Yesoo, Yesoo, kweehahn Yesoo...," ("Jesus, Jesus, precious Jesus...").

An amputee proudly showing off his push cart store that allows him to make a living. He received an artificial limb, and thus the ability to run such a business, at the Christian Amputee Center.

A little "church building" made of scrap lumber from the packing boxes of the American army. The roof, rusty corrugated iron, thoroughly penetrated by bullet holes. The remains of a mighty North Korean church now reduced to refugee status and maybe 20 people. But faithfully carrying on, joyful to be serving Jesus.

Orphans, like the ones pictured above, found by the people of God, embraced, loved, brought into God's kingdom by the thousands, as slowly the Christian world hears of the awful tragedy and insists on being included in the healing.

I don't know a lot personally about the "innards" of North Korea today, but I venture to say that "the church of Jesus Christ is the one bright spot in the present dark picture of [North] Korea." That's just how Christ is.

Somewhere in the mountains outside Hoeryong a man of God secretly ministers to God-hungry prisoners in a concentration camp there. I'm sure of it. And life is passed on, and many go into eternity rejoicing that they found life before they found death.

In a village in the Northeastern section of the country, I am confident that citizens returning from a stay in China, where they were confronted with the claims of Jesus, now pass those claims on to brothers and sisters and aunts and uncles and more.

Somewhere in a field, a child runs across a bright orange balloon covered with Bible verses or a huge bag of tracts for distribution by her parents. Others receive radios whereby they can plug into the Gospel story. All because Jesus will not allow any nation to perish in the darkness without affording some light.

All we ask in our prayers is that that light be allowed to shine a little brighter. A few more transformed lives, a little more of the glory of God on a few more faces. And then a little more. Eventually, night becomes day.

We love you, North Korea. We'll keep praying for you.

197. return of the arduous march

That's what they are saying in some quarters. The "Arduous March" has returned. Arduous, as in "characterized by toilsome effort to the point of exhaustion." More like, to the point of starvation and death, in North Korean terms. The official "march" was said to have taken place when the Korean people were led through the worst famine in their history -some say anyone's history- back in the 90's, around 1994-2000 to be a little more precise. All the reasons for such an event are not clear, but governmental mis-management is never ruled out except by Pyongyang.

During the "march" years, the Public Distribution System suddenly stopped. People ate more grass than rice. Thievery increased. Death abounded then multiplied. Hunger kills. Two to three million ,they say.

But in spite of recent pronouncements from the capital that by the year 2012 (Kim Il Sung's 100th birthday), North Korea will become so great a power that it will "dwarf all the difficulties" and solve all the problems it has been having, the people who know best say it aint necessarily so.

- some homes had less food last year than during the "arduous march" years.
- the longer some people live there, they say, the less hope they have of living.
- ordinary laborers say that 2007 was the very worst year yet, at least regarding food.
- in 2007 laborers were forbidden to farm on their own.
- once again, more and more people are turning to lives of thievery to survive.

- now the thievery is turning to members of their own families.
- many North Koreans drift away into the mountains, never to be seen again.
- people are working hard all year, but the food crops last only a few months.

No one knows the future. Maybe by 2012 North Korea really will be a rich and prosperous nation, and powerful too. I'd say they'd have a much better shot at that if they will open up to the Creator of the harvest. Right now they are being told He does not exist. Though some know otherwise, the big breakthrough of spiritual and material uplift that comes when Christ is free to be preached nationwide, is still in the future.

Our job as believers is clear. Pray, pray, and then pray some more.

198. hyok's big mistake

Right around the year 1995 in the northeastern section of North Korea lived a 10-year-old boy named Hyok. Hyok later escaped from this land and gave us his story in the fascinating *This Is Paradise!* But in this particular year on an especially boring day in school, Hyok made a serious mistake.

Now it's pretty easy to make a mistake in North Korea. The government takes the place of God but has created rules that the true God never dreamed of inflicting on His creation. In fact, Jesus said, "Come to me, all you who labor, and I will give you *rest*." Unfortunately this Scripture and all the Scriptures were strictly forbidden to young Hyok, and to all the people he left behind to this day.

Hyok knew it was a terrible thing to do anything disrespectful to the government's "Great Leader." He would never consciously have tried to ridicule this man-god. But when you're bored, you're bored. Looking at the badge on his chest, the compulsory one bearing the image of the nation's former dictator, Hyok began to doodle. Well, a little more than doodle. He began to re-create the picture that he saw. Slowly, carefully, the badge's surface was reproduced on his paper.

The little boy sitting next to him probably didn't want to hurt Hyok. But instinct told him that something was awry here, and that if he didn't report this incident, he himself would be in trouble.

"Teacher! Hyok is insulting the Great Leader!"

Now, before I unveil the scene that ensued, imagine a similar scene in the United States. Alright, we're a pretty disrespectful nation, let's be honest. So let's suppose it is a strict Christian School down South or out West. You're bored in class. You start drawing. And from pictures you've seen on TV, you start to create the likeness of our President on your paper. Your neighbor sees you. Questions:

1. does he report you or try to draw something even better at his desk?
2. supposing he does report you, what does the [good Christian but strict] teacher do? Imagine the worst.

Now that you've imagined the worst America might offer, let's revisit Hyok in 1995. Here's what happened, according to his own story:

- He was made to stand in the middle of the room, where
- For five minutes the [female] teacher literally beat him all over his body in front of his peers.

- During this time she yelled at him hysterically to make him realize how utterly awful was the sin he had just committed.
- Hyok was then sent to the back of the class where he was to stay - on his knees - the rest of the day.
- As a final "blow" he was asked to write several pages of confession of his crime, showing his true penitence.

That was one of Hyok Kang's childhood memories. The kind of scar that only Jesus can heal properly. Lord we pray for Your saints in that land, but also ask that You use the hardships of North Korea to continue to draw unbelievers to the rest that You freely give. Amen.

199. kim il sung's final days

The years just prior to the death of Kim Il-sung (pictured) were times of growing oppression by his son, or so states Martin in the history text we have followed through the Kim dynasty.During this time, more and more word was getting out that life in South Korea and the West, and even China, was richer and better than in North Korea. Saying so publicly could get you a 1-month sentence in "camp."

Knowing that Dad could not be around to protect always, Son had put together his own honor guard in case there was a coup, had created an airstrip with personal planes for a hasty exit, and had dug tunnels the 25 miles from Pyongyang to that strip.

Martin relates an incident that occurred in 1993, when Jong-Il was eveidently fearing an attack. He was reportedly nervous, and had a serious horseback riding accident in which he fell and broke all his teeth and injured his head and arms.

Dad was only technically in charge at times, yet he was still visible and especially so in June of 1994 when Jimmy Carter was sent over to have a chat with the Korean patriarch. The outcome of the talk pointed to a freeze of NK's nuclear program and resumption of dialogues with Washington. Father was bent on reform, even in what turns out to be the last year of his life. Martin says that his son, the present ruler, interfered with this process, made his father angry, and perhaps hastened the day of his death.

Whatever the cause, the 80+ year-old dictator did actually die. We all do, unless the Messiah of Israel and Saviour of the Church returns first. Death is usually not a welcome visitor, and it seems odd that we hail it now as one, but if a regime can change in this way, let it be. Unfortunately the change in 1994 was in a different direction than had been hoped.

Officially and publicly Kim Jong-Il encouraged his people to weep over his father's death. In fact, when the public mourning seemed to end after only three days, Son began punishing people if he saw them straight-faced and nonchalant about this horrific death. So they cried on.

Next time in this cycle we will talk about life after the "Great Leader", or if there even could be such a thing in North Korea.

I encourage you to go back and study the other articles in this history chain, to get a stronger picture of the evolving of a nation that so desperately needs our attention in prayer.

200. *nk: 7 million dead*

One final look at Becker's *Rogue Regime.* I strongly suggest that you pick up a copy of this book for an in-depth look at the real North Korea, as opposed to the politically correct image that is surfacing and being swallowed by some.

In his afterword, Becker suggests a number of conclusions to the shocking facts he has unearthed for his readers. First he reminds us that seven million people have perished unnaturally in the north since the current dynasty was installed by Russian Communism and later propped up by Chinese Communism. Three million civilians died in the Korean war itself, the conflict begun by the northern regime. Quite possibly three million died in the famine. One million have died as political prisoners. None of these deaths had to occur. None.

Becker is saddened that so many "statesmen" have visited with the North Korean leaders and come out praising them, setting the stage for even more abuse. All persons put on their best manners when they have important "company."

Further, Becker reasons that genocide is normally the killing of the people of a different race, but that it could be argued that genocide is taking place in North Korea with no help from the outside. He feels something should be done about it. Yet who can "interfere" with the inner workings of an independent sovereign nation? Indeed. Thus, who can protect the Korean people who happen to be born north of the 38th parallel? The world has pampered the leadership, catered to its every whim, tried to "understand". And seven million people have died.

When is it enough? When is it proper to protect not only my own family but the family of the guy next door who is abusing his wife and children? Who makes the rules? Becker believes passionately that the present ruler should be forcibly removed from power. That should be the feeling of every man in whom an instinct for liberty, truth, and compassion flows.

But as Christians we stop short of advocating violent means to humans. The world is not our province of judging. Not yet. We shall rule and reign with Christ one day, and during that 1000-year reign, such tyrannies will not have a chance to flourish. All will be peace and perfect submission to Christ.

But what about now? How did the apostolic church deal with the tyrants of its day? Simply, the call was to obedience to government except in matters pertaining directly to the Gospel. And of course the call was to prayer for all rulers, that we might live a peaceful life in Christ.

Such is our call today, though I must add that it is easy sitting here in my comfort to glibly mention these standards. Nevertheless obedience to rulers is a Bible rule. Then, faithfulness to our mission. Preaching, building the church, worship, prayer. Finally, prayer for the tyrant himself, though he be a Nero or a Hitler. Let God bring him down when He is ready. They all eventuially do come down. It is hard to imagine a man more unstable and evil than the Roman Emperor Nero, yet the Scriptures are silent about any violent dealings with him.

Following Christ means offering one's self to die with Him on the cross. This we cannot forget though like David and all God's warriors we sincerely desire the defeat of evil men.

201. nk refugee in awe: china is beyond description!

Time for another interview from refugeesinternational.com . I appreciate the work done by this organization, because the situation in North Korea cannot be denied when it is corroborated by so many independent witnesses.

Today's witness is a 29-year-old woman from Onsong who first arrived in China 5 years ago. She left her husband and 3-year-old daughter in North Korea to find a way to make some money. She tried one day as a waitress in a Chinese restaurant. But she doesn't speak Chinese. So at the time of the interview she was living in Yanji with relatives.

Earlier in her life she had worked in a coal mine and in a market making snacks. Her brothers and husband are coal miners too. If all the daily quotas are met, a person can make 1000 won a month mining coal. Not bad? I don't know the exchange rate back then, but now 1000 won is $7.00 . $7.00 per month. And that's if the work gets done. More like seven or eight *hundred* won. Five bucks. And with that kind of money, of course she couldn't afford enough rice to live on, so she'd go to the mounatins and clear out a small field where she could grow corn. Still not enough. That's why she took the risk of an illegal visit to the north.

Now she is in China, though soon she must return. China is beyond description to her. "Chinese eat rice every day," she exults. "There is no hope in North Korea." She laments that NK is not open as in other countries. She is willing for anything to happen to open her country. She even would take an Iraq-like war if it would mean her people would be liberated! That might mean she does not buy the propaganda about the evil Americans.

"Give me your tired, your poor... the wretched refuse of your teeming shores... send these, the homeless, tempest-tossed to me," Americans used to sing from the heart. So many have abused the privilege of coming here that that song has gone a little sour.

But Christ Jesus still says, "Come to Me all you who labor and are heavy-laden, and I will give you rest." Please join me in praying that this invitation will soon be heard by every North Korean.

202. happy birthdays, unhappy birthdays

February, 2008

'Tis the season of love again. In America everyone is rushing out to buy flowers and candy for their beloved "others." People thus loved can endure the rest of a bitter winter and blossom with the flowers of spring. That's the idea anyway. And it's all voluntary and fun, as true love ought to be. Our own Heavenly Father delighted in loving His pathetically needy creation so much that He surrendered the best He had for us.

In North Korea, there is little of this voluntary impassioned personal sort of love, at least when it comes to "loving" those two men who are supposed to be on the receiving end of all such devotion. In their case, devotion is quite often forced and punishable if not lavish enough.

Of course "lavish" is not a term one sees much in NK. There aren't a lot of birthday presents to go around the family, much less to be given up to the head of state. But the magnanimous leader graciously accepts a minimum of three flowers from every child. Not just any flower, mind you. The specifics of size and type are delineated, and children are sent to the nearby florist to be sure the order is met. If they have the wherewithal to purchase three flowers. If they do not, children are left with some stark choices. They can steal. Or they can refuse the gift, saying truthfully that they could not afford to buy three flowers.

Hyok Kang [*This Is Paradise*] and his friend decided one year they would just have to take their chances. They showed up in class empty-handed. It turns out they were not alone. These poor unfortunates were asked to line up and face the consequences of their horrid actions. When it came to be their turn, the children were beaten with a cane or the teacher's fists about 10 blows. On the head, in the stomach, in the face. Then it was silence the rest of the day in a nearly impossible position, as "at attention" on their knees, or hands up in the air in surrender mode.

Senseless beatings do not cause little ones to love but to hate and fear. And normal leaders do not demand this sort of "love" anyway. It is so difficult for us to imagine our national leaders, or church leaders, or our Jesus, behaving in this way. What a price the North Koreans pay just for being born there.

Won't you do something for them tonight?

203. the iron grip

In other pages of this blog collection I have documented often the ravages of the Korean famine. Though we have come to that period of time in our study of modern history, I will refer readers to other blogs for most of the details.

Words cannot possibly describe the period. Even the favored military were not being fed well. They began to steal from civilians. And no one could stop them. The citizens of North Korea are akin to a child in the womb in their vulnerability to evil in the modern Korea.

The long-expected "reunification" that surely had to come before August 15 of 1995 (50 year anniversary of liberation from Japan) didn't come. Horror came in its place. All morale was gone. Had not friendly nations, and those not so friendly, shown compassion, North Korea would have become a historical tragedy. Gone forever.

The present leadership endured the decade of tragedy, but not without constant tension and fear. Bodyguards were in great demand. Over 3,000 were in use in Pyongyang's government way back in 1976. Then Ceaucescu was assassinated. Within 5 years there were upwards to *70,000* bodyguards available for service.

Political repression increased in this time also. At one time, perhaps even today, 25-30 concentration camps dotted the landscape of North Korea. One can be assigned there merely for saying something disrespectful about the government, or because a member of the family committed an offense.

By the year 2000, the NK leaders decided they needed some European friends and so, for public consumption, addressed human rights issues. But when acceptance was gained, some say the situation got even worse.

In that same year, the Presidents of North and South Korea got together. Seoul promised to invest in the North. In return Pyongyang would allow families to reunite. Clinton would relax sanctions. Strange isn't it? Trade and aid open up, and the North's only response is to do something that should have been done all along.

In another similar negotiation of the period, North Korea demands from the US one billion dollars a year for NK's gesture of suspending its missile efforts. Demands are made of Tokyo, in fact ten times as much, since Japan still owed them reparations from the War years.

North Korea keeps demanding, the nations keep bowing, as do all the subjects of his domain. How long?

Pray today that North Korea's leadership will one way or another lose its grip. Our God is big enough to do that in a moment.

204. danger, where?

Where is the greatest danger for the Christian believer today? If you could choose to live in a place where you, the church, the world perceive the greatest threat to your personal safety, your character, your soul, your eternal relationship with Christ, where would you go?

I do not suggest that it is given to us to decide such matters. The Lord of the harvest must send this one here and that one there. So it's good that we not necessarily respond to our decision as though our thinking process is what makes the church go 'round.

But where would you go? I have portrayed North Korea as one of the most horrible places a Christian, or anyone could live. No liberty. No church, at least above ground. Tortured and tormented for naming publicly the name of Christ. Abject poverty. No modern conveniences except near Pyongyang. Big Brother alive and well and watching every move, and reporting it too. Oh my! Dangerous!

But out of North Korea come saints who walk with God. Not because American missionaries come in and out of that nation;they're not allowed. They don't thrive on American dollars and conveniences. Our gifts are mis-directed and hoarded by the inner circle. How do they possibly thrive without American riches and ingenuity? What drives a refugee who has finally escaped the nightmare, to turn around and walk right back in with Bibles, tracts and personal testimonies, to share Christ with neighbors and family? Yes, it happens in this dangerous land.

Danger you say? I agree. Yet when these souls pass on to the next life, it is all soon forgotten. These suffering saints are received in Christ's embrace and eternity begins in His arms. Makes North Korea look a little safer after all.

Consider fellow-nation USA. Safety everywhere you say? Oh, I agree there also. No guns. Well, actually lots of guns, but most people can move freely to places where guns aren't an issue. No persecution. No problem with church attendance. Why, a church on every corner. Plenty to eat and drink and enjoy. A comfort zone if ever there was one!

The dictator of North Korea has deceived his people into thinking that he is a god. Fear of failing this god has created this nation. But Americans are convinced of lies just as serious. Even Christians. They are convinced, for example, that a bag of air carried from one end of a field to another by a highly paid athlete, or a rawhide sphere slammed by a stick over a wall is gravely important and worth whiling hours and hours away as their safe little nations sinks deeper into its sins and faces the wrath of God.

Where are the heroic saints emerging emerging from this land? Believers who still go to church better not be asked to stay over an hour per meeting. The prayer meeting has all but died, and its format has been dead for a long time. Music is worldly, messages are miniscule, and evangelism has stopped in so many of these period pieces. Soon the world will speak of post-Christian America as we speak of Europe today.

Did we say this is a safe place? Not for the soul. Temptation is all around.

The answer for most of us is not to move to North Korea. But to repent. And to be such odd ducks for Jesus here, for holiness produces such, that the persecution will follow us too. Where is the cross in this nation? Surely Jesus has one for you, and it's not that sore toe or rheumatism. The world can boast of all those things.

It's the sold-out devotion to a living God that brings the wrath of the Enemy. Without it, our facing of eternity may be more hazardous than we had bargained for.

"Must Jesus bear the cross alone, and all the world go free?

"No, there's a cross for everyone, and there's a cross for me."

205. the romanticizing of pain

They say that a word that means too much means nothing at all. So it seems to be with the word *romantic* . It can mean one who belongs to the Romantic Movement which thrived in the 18th and 19th centuries in the arts. Wagner in music, Browning in poetry, etc. Emotional architecture.

Or, more to our purposes here, it can be a more generalized term applicable in any generation. It can have to do with amorous romance or just idealism and idealism's cousin, unreality. It is this branch of the word's description to which I refer.

We love our movies. Most of them are filled with fantasies that grab our attention because they offer ways to escape. Recently they have become a bit too real, and cause us a different set of problems than the old "romantic" movies that brought us into the middle of a romantic relationship or a heroic deed in just 90 minutes or so.

We have all known people that will sit and bawl over these heart-warming stories. Something stirs in the soul.

Then we take a deep breath and walk away. We know it wasn't really ours, except for the moment.

This romantic pain may have its place but I fear it may have affected us all too much. Someone said that such pain could be cured by a good toothache, a dose of the real thing.

Which is where my thoughts are finally headed. (You knew I was going somewhere with all of this, I hope.)

I am deeply concerned today about the gut-wrenching stories that have been coming out of places like North Korea for these many years. I am glad that someone found a way to get the truth to us, but I wonder how easy this pain is to forget. It feels a little like one of those musicals, albeit with an unhappy ending. We watch, we cry, we go away. It's not really ours after all. It's something we can take or leave.

For us, it's a good show.

My plea to readers and hearers today is to listen with ears of the Spirit to these messages. Our God would not allow His people's pain to be exposed to us so that we can have a good cry. These brothers and sisters, our family just as surely as the ones who bear our name, are truly hurting, truly in need, and the Spirit is screaming to us of the agony in Christ's Body.

Oh, let us hear the cry. Then to our knees for instructions as to what to do. Surely if the situation were ours we would be so humiliated to know that others only watched and cried and walked away.

Remember the prisoners as though chained with them-those who are mistreated-since you yourselves are in the body also. (Hebrews 13:3)

206. paradise. a garden in a city

A preacher once told me, when you're trying to show how crooked a stick is, just find a straight stick and lay it beside the crooked one. I haven't followed that wise advice on this North Korea site. I've often contradicted Kim Jong Il, who claims that his version of Korea is a Paradise. Communist propaganda has shared that imagery often through its history. The worker's Paradise.

Have you ever chuckled when you realize that these founders of atheistic states use Biblical imagery to describe their strange concoctions?

Today I lay before you and Mr. Kim and the workers of the world the straight stick. The real thing. The Bible's description of Paradise. Those who are averse to Biblical literalism will have trouble with this. But I believe in a literal God who sent a literal Saviour into a literal world to save literal mankind from its literal sins. A literal reward is in store for them, totally out of this world.

The presence of the tree of life in the middle of the garden called Eden in Genesis 2:9, ties Eden to the place that John calls Paradise (Hebrew, *Pardace,* "forest, orchard") in Revelation 2:7, where the tree surfaces again.So anything that can be said of Eden can be said of Paradise. Not only that, but the descending city of God called the New Jerusalem in Revelation 21 and 22 likewise contains that tree. That's three names for the same incredible capital of the New World. The Bible actually speaks much of this place, enough to make us desire it with all our heart if we are His.

The original man and woman were placed in a simple garden. But they encouraged an unwelcome guest there, and defiled the entire place. God could not allow them to partake of eternal life in their sinful condition. They were cast out.

Paradise was then hidden from man's view by angel guards who to this day do not allow any unauthorized persons to enter. Can a garden be uprooted and taken into the sky, or was this place somehow disconnected from the mainland to begin with? That seems to be the greatest mystery, one which we will thoroughly understand when we need to.

Meanwhile, Jesus says that in His Father's house are many dwelling places (John 14) and that He has gone to prepare a place for us. We assume he has been building this city, house by house, over the years until now it is a luscious place that combines the finest architectural styles of heavenly beings with the natural wonders of the original "park" (the oriental meaning of *Paradise*).

Did Jesus really believe in a place called Paradise? Oh yes. He would not have lied in His dying breath - or any breath. He promised his cross-fellow that on that very day, after the pain, after the shame, they would be together *in Paradise* (Luke 23:43).

Other famous house guests include the apostle Paul, II Corinthians 12:4, who became a believer in a literal Paradise one day when he was suddenly whisked up to the place himself. His fleshly pride would not have been able to bear the talking about such splendors that he saw, if he had not been given from then on a grievous thorn of reminder, 12:7.

Oh it's real. It's coming. Just as we have always heard. Jesus promised it to all just as He promised it to the thief, in Revelation 2:7, " To him who overcomes I will give to eat from the tree of life, which is in the Paradise of God."

Pray for North Korean believers today. Pray that they will *overcome* the Satanic torment that follows them into concentration camps and hunger and loss. Pray for Western Christians too, that they will *overcome* riches and comfort and lukewarmness.

For the city with the garden is only for overcomers.

207. God puts things in writing

Just how important is the written word? Most of you already know.

- Complain out loud at work and not much will happen. But put in writing that you're strongly considering another job, and your post can be filled immediately.
- Try getting a loan from the bank with a smile and a please and a thanks. But sign your life away, and the money flows in.
- You can say you were at the meeting, but when the boss sees your signature on the sign-in sheet, it's a done deal.
- The government can say they want to lower your taxes, but laws to do such must be in writing.
- They can say the new machine is easily put together, even show you a picture of what it is supposed to look like. But a written set of instructions is what makes the difference.
- Government leaders can promise their counterparts that they will not attack, but a written document eases everyone's fears.
- You say this car is yours? Where's the written title?

Have I made my point? The old song goes, It's real for it's written. Yes, when it's written down is when truth becomes something we can take to the bank. Christians have been hearing good things from pulpits for many years, but how many true believers will stick around if the preacher doesn't prove that what he's preaching is written?

Oh how wonderful that our God is an author, a writer. Wonderful that He breathed His Spirit on 40+ writers over 1600 years and through them gave us a Book. Yes, it was 66 books, but the unity is so great that we have always thought of it as one book, *the* Book.

Brother Peter says that the prophecies of old were of Divine, not human, origin. Men were moved along by the Spirit. So the written word has come down to us. II Peter 1:20-21.

God's promises are sure. He wrote it down, and passed it on.

Our brothers and sisters in North Korea and other suffering nations need to hear the precious promises of God. He saves. He forgives. He heals. He comforts. He guides. He is coming. Eternal life. Joy. Peace. Love. It's all in there. And it's all true. They deserve to see and believe it for themselves. Who will get the Word to them?

Will you join me in prayer to that end?

208. priceless treasure in a flower bag

The North Korea saga goes on.

Just yesterday I was talking here about the importance of the written Word, especially the Book God gave His people. How marvelous that Word! How priceless its message. Eternity is bound within its covers.

Yes, and people will still risk their lives for it to be shared with others.

Story goes that about a year ago, several employees of a North Korean company heard the message of Christ from believers in China and the underground North Korean church which is alive and well. The love of God filled their hearts and they longed to share their faith with others. Through their Chinese connections they purchased 200 Bibles and several hundred Christian CD's.

To get their precious cargo across the border, they placed everything in a shipment of flour bags. The mission accomplished. But not without a huge price. The leaders of this project were discovered and arrested and severely tortured. The vice-president of the company, fearing for his life, escaped to China.

But the Bibles and CD's were circulated. How and to whom we will not know for a long time. Except for one Bible, and one CD. Ten college students somehow got possession of these items and began to read and watch. They passed them along to friends. And were caught doing so. And also arrested.

And that's all we know. Should be enough to keep caring Christians up praying tonight. Pray for their release, and the release of those originally locked up. Pray for the fugitive. For those who heard the precious Word of God at their hands. For the government that makes all this secrecy and torment so prevalent. For a people waiting for a break.

Oh, and pray for the West again, for your church and mine, for a fresh appreciation of the Book God gave us.

209. no saint left behind

How strange is the new doctrine that states that those saints who arrive in Heaven during the last years of Earth as we know it are not really the church. These believers, living as they do through earth's greatest trouble time are, in the modern teaching, *Tribulation Saints*. They got left behind because of their backslidden condition. Jesus took His real church to Heaven for banquets and parties and allowed these dregs of Christian society to fend for themselves and get to glory only by death at the hands of the antichrist.

Let that sink in awhile. The true church is Up There enjoying all that life can give to a believer, when suddenly a Tribulation Saint dies, is funneled upwards, and, and what? Crashes the party? Is kept in a back room for even more shame? Oh my. I think modern theology is just as shallow as it is widespread.

My Bible shows a different picture altogether. Revelation 7, verses 9-17, paints an unforgettable image of these Tribulation Saints. First, it agrees with the title being attached to them today, they are the saints of the tribulation period. But it does not suggest by any rule of logic or communication that these saints are different in species from the saints who walk the earth in our non-tribulation but very troubled world.

No, they look very familiar. They are from every nation, as the church today is. They are clothed in white, as Jesus had promised to *all overcomers* a few chapters earlier. They are crying out praises to their Saviour. That's what church folks do, you know. The Lamb receives them, wipes away their tears, welcomes them tenderly into the joys of their Lord. Oh, this is the Body of Christ, the Church. And they did not get there through an escape route. They walked straight into the mouth of the lion and found in his interior eternal life. No rebuke. No hardness. Jesus is so happy that they have arrived. And the party will not start until the last saint is home!

Now I readily confess that this group, upon whom the evils of an antichrist are thrust, are a breed apart. They are akin to saints suffering even now in North Korea and many other places on the planet. This is why we in the West may have trouble recognizing them. This is why we have assigned to them only this horrible tormenting, this lowly backslidden unworthiness, this implication that persecution is really punishment upon those who have earned Christ's frown. Surely, we say, he smiles only at the prosperous on Earth, who have made something of their lives.

Oh how God's people need to be reminded that the cross of Christ is not a spanking at all. That, in every generation and in every life, the cross is a personal daily choice. It's not your sore toe or your rheumatism or the boss's displeasure of your ways. It's not your lowly house or slow car or your location in town or your skin color. It's Christ in you, working visibly through you, and causing rejection of you. It's a pathway to death. But a death that leads to the arms of Jesus.

"Jesus...suffered outside the gate. Therefore let us go forth to Him, outside the camp, bearing His reproach." (Hebrews 13:12-13)

210. kim il sung and the foxtail millet

Rodong Sinmun is North Korea's propaganda headquarters. On a daily basis there is a stream of strange-sounding information, or mis-information, emanating thence. Recently I picked up there another entry in the large collection of Kimmian mythology. This one is about the annual birthday celebration of the [deceased] grandmother of North Korea's present leader, i.e., Kim Il Sung's mom. Fascinating North Korea speak.

The writer introduces this maternal figure not as a mother or grandmother, not as someone's wife or descendant. No, Kang Pan Sok is "an indomitable revolutionary fighter and an outstanding leader of the Korean women's emancipation movement..." Doesn't it warm your heart? Wouldn't you love to be snuggled close to this cuddly mommy if you needed some solace?

Once upon a time, when this mom was very critically ill, soldier son Kim Il Sung, forever battling the pesky Japanese, took a break in his endeavors to buy some foxtail millet and bring it to her, as it has certain medicinal value. She was touched inside, but would not allow her son even to mention her sickness. Instead she wanted to talk about political topics. Japan. The struggle. The revolution.

At least, that's how the story goes.

In response to his spending the night, gathering firewood and such, Mom said, thanks for being a good son, but you really need to get back to the great cause of Korea. She gave him some seriously-hard-earned coins, and sent him on his way.

The story ends as it begins. The author indicates that what the mother had shown was not "simply motherly love. It was true revolutionary affection..."

Our hearts ache over a people who have sold out natural affection for military-political ideals. We hurt for those who honor nation above family, society above the individual soul. We pray for those who give their lives away to start a revolution and have never heard of the revolution Christ began here centuries ago. And we grow weary of hearing stories like these being told as historical fact.

Yet, there is something about this story, even this perversion of NK history, that is worth taking away and contemplating. No less than the Christ Himself has called us to a comparable life, has He not? Did He not say that those who follow Him are to love Him more than mother, father, brother, sister? Did He not call us to lay down our very lives for the sake of promoting the Gospel Revolution that He ignited?

So, on second sight, we do not necessarily disown every feature of the dismal lifestyle of the North Korean, but rather we object to the target of Korean affection. We desire for One worthy of all this pain and suffering to be honored in this way, One Worthy of the daily sacrifice, One who will richly repay, not with more restrictions and more poverty, and more famine and death, and international shame, but with everlasting life, with joy unspeakable and full of glory, with the unabashed delight of sins forgiven, all items that are not within the NK government's power to offer.

Lord Jesus, we pray that Your message will permeate the darkness. Show us our part. Amen.

By the way, the real history of this revolutionary mother of North Korea indicates that she and her husband were faithful members of the local Presbyterian Church.

211. what i learned from a hoeryong prison

Such presumption. To suggest that I actually suffered in North Korea and have returned to tell you about it. How arrogant and insensitive.

But I have learned something from the sufferings of others there. I've learned to obey the Biblical mandate to "remember the prisoners." I learn from the saints there to trust God one day at a time in my own negative situations. I'm seeing that one must wait for God to open prison doors, but that one must continue to be faithful while waiting.

I hear them teach me that God's grace is sufficient.

I learn from Hoeryong that carrying the cross is not for a selected few, but for all who would follow the crucified Christ. I learn that *things* don't matter, but people do, and One Person in particular. I am learning that I actually need the cross, and I need the North Koreans more than they need me.

It is certainly a romantic notion that I actually desire what they have, though I want to believe that I do. I have seen my grumbling ways over the smallest of difficulties. My tolerance for pain or even discomfort or inconvenience is near zilch. Yet the spirit touched by God that He is making me, reaches out to the fellowship of His suffering and ignites a burning of the heart. There is a sweetness about it somehow. The days I spent with the suffering church in Romania were among the most difficult yet the most blessed ever.

I think that in seeing these saints move on in spite of the pain, in viewing their patience, their selflessness, I have seen Christ. It is Him I desire after all. But how shall I ever attain to this vision? I who have lived in a land of plenty, where balance is a virtue, and the quest for security is downright heroic. Very few have ripped off the mask of these two impostors to see that one is lukewarmness and the other is the love of this present evil world.

I invite my readers and listeners today to visit each page of my site and gather more information with which to approach the Father. May we not be swallowed up with distractions. Jesus is still in great pain.

212. a *prison without bars*

I commend to your attention today, a production of the United States Commission on International Religious

Freedom, published in March of 2008. It is *A Prison Without Bars* , *refugee and defector testimonies of severe violations of freedom of religion or belief in North Korea.*

As another work from which I quoted extensively on this site, the present work is simply and factually written, giving the stories of refugees as they were reported to the interviewers, of course translated into English. And as then, the facts are enough.

The USCIRP team interviewed 32 persons who fled to China from 2003-2007, and 6 former NK security agents. The story they tell is amazingly the same as stories which came out a decade ago and before. Refugees are still subjected to interrogation and punishment when contacting religious groups or South Koreans. Those who confess to either crime can be tortured.

If there is change, some of it at least is in the wrong direction. There is increased police activity in the NK area bordering China. Agents interviewed told of their being sent into Korean-Chinese churches, posing as pastors so as to gain information about "traitors." Still others formed fake house church groups in North Korea to entice and expose true believers.

Protestantism continues to grow and be a threat to the security of the Korean government, or so it is perceived. Shamanism in the form of exorcists and fortune-tellers is also on the rise, and draws a cross section of spiritually hungry Koreans, all the way into government circles.

In spite of all, *Kimilsungism* and *Juche* continue to be the guiding light of the Korean people. The proper attitude toward the Pyongyang power center is the only ticket to success in the land. And so most everyone complies.

Human rights abuses in North Korea continue to be so great as to call for the authors of this and other reports to ask for a U.N. Security Council intervention. I'm not sure how potent such a move would be, given the U.N.'s dismal record of non-success in the nation so far. But intervention they need, for sure! We are asking God individually, and in groups, and in whole churches, and by offerings, and by missionaries, and by sending of Christian literature, and a host of other projects, to set North Korea free.

213. nk 2008. the state of religious freedom

Hear from the recently transcribed voices of those who have just escaped the madness that is today's North Korea - for one who would follow Christ:

"Even though North Korean law guarantees freedom, it's only a slogan. People in North Korea are not familiar with the concept of religion... God is interpreted according to Communist standards."

"Religion? Not at all. You cannot say a word about it or three generations of your family can be killed... We can only serve one person in North Korea."

"If you say the word 'religion' you could face consequences."

"... religion... is considered a threat to the system, a hotbed of security problems, and opium..."

"If one says anything about religion, one immediately gets killed or jailed. There is no freedom of speech..."

"One cannot even say the word 'religion.' North Korea does have Christians and Catholics. They have buildings but they are all fake... the government does not allow... religious organizations because it is worried about the possibility that

Kim Jong Il's regime would be in danger, because religion erodes society."

"Worshipping God... would make one a political criminal. Christianity is not allowed... The Christian church is the last thing that the North Korean government would permit. The government believes that the Christian church is an anti-national organization."

"In North Korea we are educated and taught since childhood that you can never believe in religion. Even if we go to China on business, it is unforgivable to attend a church.We are taught that if one is involved in religion, one cannot survive..."

"In reality, there is no freedom of religion at all. Not even 0.1 percent. For example, recently, many North Korean refugees have Bibles with them when they are repatriated. If they are caught carrying a Bible they are punished. In North Korea you can get away with murder if you have good connections. However, if you are caught carrying a Bible, there is no way to save your life."

The nighmare continues. Don't stop praying now.

All quotations from free 2008 online book: *A Prison Without Bars , refugee and defector testimonies of severe violations of freedom of religion or belief in North Korea.*

214. if i could be born again

I have met only two North Koreans. Both times it was a great honor. On the last occasion, I proudly shook the young man's hand and promised to write to him. He does not know how much I owe him. He cannot comprehend the message he conveys to the West by his mere existence.

According to his testimony, there are several other things he does not comprehend. Like family, and friendship.

Well, you'd have trouble with these commodities too if you had been born and raised in a Communist concentration camp. If the only life you knew was the animal-like existence of underprivileged humans whose only role in life was to keep the NK machine rolling smoothly for the dictator. If your parents were so abused by their "superiors" that they abused you in turn.

That was his life. Somewhere down the line someone truly offended the Dear Leader and his regime. So the family of that someone was considered a threat, and kept in a labor camp. Those who were given husband-wife privilege produced more slaves for the government. He was so produced. But there was no family life, no warmth, no affection. Parents, yes. But no parenting. Only work, beatings, eat, sleep, die.

One day a fellow laborer was talking about the outside world, and the thought of such a thing began to consume him. He had to escape.Through a series of incredible experiences he was able first to get to North Korea, then China, and eventually to South Korea.

He is still a young man, but has lived many lifetimes. Family members executed. Torture to his own body. The absence of friendship and nearly everything humans come to value as they exist here. Seemingly hopeless.

But here is where Christ comes in. Here is where He is shown to be mighty and truly different from all others who deal with us. "Come to Me, all you who are heavy laden, and I will give you rest," He says.

One of the saddest moments of the young man's presentation was in response to a question about what he would like most. He told of seeing a mother in Seoul holding the hand of her daughter. That simple image captivated him.

He told the questioner, "If I could be born again, I would like to have that."

And he was talking of being the child, not the parent. He simply wants to understand by experience what it means to be loved by another human being. Yes, it is the cry of all our hearts. How much more one who still cannot even comprehend it?

Will you pray that this young Korean man will know that love? And the love of friends, and the love of a woman, and the love of children, but above all the love of God that will communicate to him that all his offenses have been wiped clean, forgiven, erased. That he truly can be born again. That life can start over.

Here is our chance to personalize all this affection we feel for the Korean situation. Here is a chance to make a difference. Let us pray.

215. the churches you cannot see

Once hailed as the "Jerusalem" of this part of the world, North Korea is barren in spirit now. The nearest real North Korean-founded church is in Seoul (pictured), South Korea. There are a few show-churches in Pyongyang, and of course the true Body of Christ sprinkled throughout the land, in homes, prisons, even government edifices. Christ has not been kept out. But Americans walking the streets of the capital or other large NK cities, after a lifetime of seeing churches on every corner here, are in for culture shock of the highest order.

On this subject of religious activities, *A Prison Without Bars* from which I have been borrowing these days, produces 16 quotations from recently escaped citizens of North Korea. You are free similarly to print out this online report of 2008, where the evidence is overwhelming that not much has changed in the Hermit Kingdom. Here are a few samples of their testimony:

"I have never seen any... Christian churches... in Wonsan... I did hear about one old [Christian] lady."

"... I saw the Bongsu and Chilgol churches in Pyongyang. When the church was under construction, I saw two old people kneel down at the construction site, praying 'Thank you God. Finally we can have a church in North Korea.'.. They were not taken right away because foreigners were recording the scene. But nobody knows what happened to them later."

"If you hide religious books well during the house searches, you won't be in trouble. If not, nobody can tell where you will be taken away at night."

"It is unimaginable, no one can even say a word about churches... in Hambeung... Those who believe in God [are thought to]invade other countries. I was taught that the U.S. penetrated culture first by sending missionaries..."

"There was a 44-year-old man who lived in Secheon, Hoeryeong who had lived in China for two years. He became a believer there... and he was said to preach salvation by Jesus. He escaped to China after being reported... I thought he was crazy..."

"In Bakcheon... there was an old site of a church. Part of it remained... but it is now a house."

"There are churches... in Pyongyang... built only for... foreigners to attend... I never heard of religious books until I came to China."

"A friend of mine... owned a Bible. I read a little because it was interesting... and asked my friend about it. He told me not to read the book. I did not report my friend to the authorities."

And so on and on. The testimony is clear and conclusive. Visible Christianity is essentially non-existent. But Christ lives there in His people. His Word is circulating. Please pray for the success of the Gospel in a land where Good News is at a premium.

216. refugees confirm: kimilsungism lives

The virtual worship of the present leader of North Korea, which is inextricably tied to devotion to his father, is truly alive and well. Children learn to say "Thank you Father Kim Il Sung" as they learn to talk. They move on eventually to "mandatory adult education classes held in the workplace or shrine-like buildings called 'Kim Il Sung Revolutionary Idea Institutes' " Here is documentation: excerpts of refugee interviews from the new book *A Prison Without Bars* by the U.S. Commission on International Religious Freedom (free online).

"We call it the Kim Il Sung Institute of Revolutionary Ideas. Attendance is mandatory... the history of Kim Il Sung's life is displayed on the walls with his pictures. They use chapters and verses like the Christian Bible... I used to be a section leader. We used to burn our own clothes... in order to keep meeting because there were not enough candles."

"We often spend some of our own money... we decorate rooms with red-colored wallpaper and pictures...When I was young, I used to wear my best dress and bow my head in prayer before the portraits [of the Kims] on occasions such as national holidays. Your family members force you to do that. It's like your religion... When people experience miraculous happenings... they come in first in a race or don't get hurt from a fall, we...say 'thank the General Kim Il Sung and Kim Jong Il.' "

"If you are absent... there are political consequences..."

"It's mandatory [the Kim Institute]... you go or your ideology will be questioned. However, nobody will go there voluntarily. We don't do it at home, ... It's ridiculous."

[The difference between North Korea and the final world ruler is that antichrist will have access to technology that will permit him to enforce his ways at home, too, through the ever-present television or computer screen.]

"[The Institute] is located in the best place in every village... From birth North Koreans are educated to think that they owe Kim Il Sung ... their lives and existence..."

"One is not allowed to think about the reason why people have to obey."

"Everyone wears the Kim Il Sung badge on their chest. Otherwise, the person is a political offender. Even saying a word about the difficulties of practicing *Kimilsungism* can make the person a political offender. To show loyalty, North Koreans participate in study meetings, repentance (self-criticism) meetings, and lectures..."

"The purpose of hanging the pictures [of the Kims] is to worship Kim Il Sung and Kim Jong Il. There is a ritual done before the pictures, [part of which says] 'If a fire breaks out, people would show their loyalty by running into the fire to save the portraits. Anyone who gets burned doing this would win commendation.' "

"When I was a child, I was taught that [Kim] was a 'god of the sun,' so I thought he really was a sun."

"If a person openly complains, then that person disappears the next day. Kim Il Sung and Kim Jong Il are god. They are deified and they should be considered as an ultimate."

Here is truly a picture of the coming antichrist . "Anti" is not just *against* but also *in place of.* Satan's method in North Korea is a flagrant act of defiantly replacing the Lord Jesus

Christ as Lord of all. It is no accident that what you just read reminds you of our own Christian practices:

- Teaching children to worship at the earliest age possible
- Some of the finest buildings in the best areas set aside for worship and study
- Books that have chapters and verses like the Bible
- Self-sacrifice, financial sacrifice for the cause of the Leader
- Judgment for the disobedient
- Dress up for meetings
- "Repentance"
- And from pagan religions: worship of pictures (icons), the "god of the sun."

Kim is not very subtle. How he came to hate Christ so is not clear, but we do not despair in our prayers for his government and his land. Christ truly can do anything. Let us keep believing for the huge victory that one day must come. Jesus alone is worthy of all the praise and all the worship and all the obedience. He will be glorified!

217. the show church

In North Korea there are churches that have been opened by the government, just for show. I was pondering recently over the situation in America. One wonders how much of what we Christians do is for the same reason, show. How many churches are run by the bulletin instead of by His program? How many have an agenda that must be kept at all costs?

Order is essential in a congregation, we understand. But when the meeting becomes predictable, or when the flesh dictates that order, one has a show church.

For example, today many pastors refuse to wear ties, in deference to the unpopularity of that item of the male wardrobe. It is assumed that the donning of casual dress will attract casual people. This is fleshly thinking.

In many churches, the desires of the young have been placed over the wisdom of the elderly. Music is one of the victims of this decision. For generations the church has passed on a rich tradition of in-depth majestic hymnody. The great teachings of Scripture have been put to music, and passed on decade after decade. As new songs have come along, those of wisdom have slowly added them to the collection.

But now, the collections are set aside en masse. Entirely new collections are in place, and weekly there are new songs added to the list. A man who has been a Christian for 50 years can sit through a meeting totally a stranger to the music portion of the fellowship. And he can think he is a stranger to the church, being left behind. This has not been true in every generation. It is sadly true in this one.

Often, standing before such elderly saints are young rockers, who have been granted sanction in this fast-evolving scene, authority to lead, not only worship, but devotion, prayer time, up to half of the meeting. Certainly we honor the new believer, and want him to learn leadership skills a bit at a time. But the wholesale turning over of pulpits and platforms to the young is not a Biblical precedent. It is more fleshly thinking. And it is destructive to all concerned.

The thinking is, We will let these people get involved, and then they will stick around. We used to think of such a process as bribery. What if they are not given heady leadership roles, and attention? Will they drift away? Is this what the framers of the New Testament saw as a likely scenario for church growth? Is this how we progress?

Or is this a show church? A church that hopes to grow by having the best show? Should not a warning be posted to the ones responsible for shepherding God's flock, that those who neglect the ancient landmarks in the interest of attracting those whose motives are fleshly will produce a fleshly church, a la Rome? When the saints are set aside so that the world can be promoted in God's holy church, is that church holy any longer? Is that church God's? When the sheep are bleating out their pain at the hijacking of their fellowship by those who only seek ambitious fulfillment, shall not the Shepherd take action?

Evangelism is to be by testimony, not by show. Not the best building in town. Not the best performance in town. Only the purest Gospel, the most defining of standards, preached all week by its members. Raise the bar high. Let the world know that without help from above they cannot reach the wonderful ways He has given us.

Is that not how we were raised? Oh there were those who became "all things" to us. There were youth leaders who drew us in and made us feel comfortable. But there was also a higher plane to which we attained. There was a corporate meeting of men and women to which we aspired. The elderly men stood before us, and by life and word led us to better things. Who is leading now? Certainly not the men, in more and more churches. And certainly not the elderly.

I fear that these later inventions will be exported to North Korea when it is finally open to the Gospel. So many Koreans are in America drinking in American ways. And so many want to take this brand of Christianity to the North. May God help us to understand that the brand of Christianity already in North Korea is what they need more of, not our brand.

There, people come to Christ because they love Him. No one else in his right mind would take the journey to certain suffering. They need not rock music, modern ways. They already love Him more than many of us. They don't need to be bribed. Sprinlked throughout this barren nation are pockets of believers worshiping and learning of the Master, serving Him alone.

They have found the way of the Cross. The way of the Cross trumps the way of the show.

218. refugee interview confirms the underground church

Quoting again from "A Prison Without Bars", a March 2008 collection of interview updates of the North Korea situation, I bring to the stand witnesses who know personally and have witnessed the workings of the underground church. When these neutral escapees were asked what they knew about the existence of a Christian underground, they offered the following responses:

"In 2003, an underground church called 'Yuseon' was uncovered. Ten to 14 people were said to be church members..."

"North Koreans pray for healing to God rather than Kim Il Sung or Kim Jong Il..."

"I know many people who pray. There is no organization. When I traveled to the rural area as an oriental doctor... my friend showed me a Bible (in 2004). It was a book with a red cover... I didn't read it thoroughly... I told my friend, 'You should be careful because the NSA officials said that people who have or saw the Bible should confess...' My friend said, 'Since the police talk about it, I'm assuming many people have one because even I have one.' "

"...My relative by marriage was caught while giving away a Bible, so the entire family was taken to prison 22 [in Hoeryong]. They were taken there under the category of religious spy."

"[In the city of] Hoeryong Mr. Han preached the Gospel to my husband and me in 1997... There was one underground church which was a decoy... This church was started by the NSA [National Security Agency] to host all those people who came back from China after becoming believers, who wanted to pray..."

"There are underground churches. I heard about spying activities regarding the underground churches at a drinking meeting, from my relatives who were executive Party members. [They said] three to five people got together to worship."

One interviewee talks about how sad it was for him personally to catch Christians, when he himself was a Christian. But, he reasoned, I stay in my position so that an even worse person is not in my place harming believers.

Another talks about how nearly impossible it is to have over a handful of people at a time. He tells of one man who tried to worship with 20 people, but was caught...

And one says, "I've seen a trial and public execution [of religious believers]. They weren't executed for believing in God. Instead they were executed for not following the One and Only Guidance System. It was in 1991 and five people were executed... notice for the public execution was posted in the market."

I encourage you to find this important document online, and copy it for yourself. And of course, let us keep praying.

219. eyewitnesses of nk christian persecution

More from *A Prison Without Bars,* 2008 interviews with escaped North Koreans. Free online.

We who speak of Christian persecution within the DPRK are not guessing or exaggerating. Eyewitnesses see it all. Here is today's collection of quotes for you to peruse and consider for serious prayer:

"My relative brought a Bible from China and gave it to some close friends. But the rumor spread...the police heard about it. His entire family was taken to the prison camps... I don't think they will ever be released."

"There was even a case of a child (16 years old)... They made that kid stand on the platform, in front of gathered parents...There, the kid's entire family was arrested in order to show an example... That kid had learned whole Bible Scriptures by heart and that was the reason he was arrested..."

"A person was shot to death...I asked why... and they said, 'A person from Musan took a Bible from South Korean [church leaders]."

We used to talk about how there are so many Bibles gathering dust in American homes. Now it is sad to say that Bibles are similarly unneeded in many churches. In this electronic age it has been discovered that verses appropriate to the service can be flashed onto a screen. Gone is the fumbling through Bibles trying to catch up with the preacher. Gone is the confusion of various translations giving people fits trying to follow along. Gone also is the bringing of God's Book into God's House.

Don't I sound old today! Well there's no doubt I have seen much younger days. But there's also no doubt that some of this talk about the good old days... is totally true. A church without a Bible is heading in the wrong direction. Just ask a North Korean.

220. refugee living, nk style

It must seem that the tales I tell here from day to day are pure fantasyland. But eyewitnesses declare they are true. I am quoting from the free online report published by the U.S. Commission on International Religious Freedom, Prison Without Bars. This is a series of interviews with those who have escaped the nightmare existence in North Korea. Today's subject : the condition along the NK/China border for one trying to escape. Each paragraph is a separate interviewee.

"Religious groups provide a channel to South Korea by connecting North Korean refugees with a broker. However, if you have a pretty face, the broker might want to sell you as a bride instead. It's scary... you don't have any choice since he can decide your life... "

"Most women refugees I met in the Korean-Chinese church told me that they had that kind of experience [sexual trafficking], except for those who had relatives in China... For male North Korean defectors, trafficking cannot be an option because so many of them are ferreted out and are repatriated to North Korea. In the case of male North Korean defectors, they conceal their identities and work in farms or coal mines, or at construction sites... [but] finding that kind of work is not that easy."

"Many young North Korean women [like me] who marry old Chinese men are so abused that they run away leaving their husband behind."

"I know a case where a North Korean sold five North Korean women in cooperation with the North Korean army. Chinese people were waiting on the border... Male refugees have more difficulties. Chinese police treat male defectors more severely because they think they are more threatening to Chinese public security. If a male defector says that he served in the army, then he is immediately shackled..."

"North Korean women are usually sold to Chinese people. Once a woman is sold, they guard the woman so that she can't go anywhere. There are also many cases where women actually wish to be sold of their own desire because their situation is so difficult. A 20-year-old woman is sold to a 70-year-old man... Women are not sold to rich people but to very poor or handicapped people. They are sent to rural towns. Prices vary depending on the age of the woman. It is just like trading goods... they are sold and treated like slaves."

This is the situation that has been created by Communism and the Juche government of North Korea. It is time for a change. God is able. Let us pray about it!

221. when you get sent back

Some of the countries to which North Koreans flee are not keen on keeping their new guests. Pictured is a Thai attempt at sending them back to North Korea. China is the most serious offender in this regard. What happens when Kim Jong Il's government is handed back its own citizens, fleeing to escape starvation? Here are eyewitness accounts gained from interviews, and published in the free online report, *A Prison Without Bars.*

One interviewee was sent with his older brother to prison for 15 months. The brother killed himself during that stay. How was he treated? "Just like animals. An animal without a name..."

Another was asked the normal questions about why she went to China and whether she had had contact with a church or missionary. During the interrogation she was forced to kneel the entire day. Whenever she moved, guards beat her. This guard asked prisoners to hit each other. If they disobeyed, the guard would hit them. Her brother was sent to jail for 10 years after admitting he had contacted Christians in China.

Another victim states, "They didn't ask whether I had encountered Buddhists but asked whether I had contact with Christians. I was kicked and struck severely. I had to stand all day long and I was not permitted to move or speak. It was impermissible to raise my hand or to walk. If I went to the bathroom, a guard followed me..."

Interviewee 23 saw it this way: "I was beaten up and ate nothing for three days after being detained... They knocked my head with an iron hook. I was hung head down from the prison bars with shackles on my legs and I was beaten with an iron hook. My shoulder was also beaten. Those sufferings resulted in the rupture of a capillary. I had to sit and could not make a motion all day long from 5 a.m. to 10 p.m., which continued for six months..."

"When I was sent to Onseong, the officer said to me, '... I'll beat your face!' and they poured cold water on me and kicked me. There were about 50-60 people in a cell, so we had to sleep in a seated position because there was no room to lie down. There was one toilet in the cell... Many people died of colitis because of the polluted water. There were so many lice. We got a mouthful of overcooked noodles three times a day."

"I really thought that dying would be better," said yet another. "There was a woman who gave birth in the cell, but the guards took the baby away. It seemed like in my cell about 10 people out of 80 were believers. They kept praying. So I started to pray with them."

And let us start to pray too. Daily. More if possible. Let's gather groups to pray with us. Let's plead with God for the souls and the soul of this nation, horribly defiled by Communist ideas and worse. And one more prayer request this time. Let's ask God to take away the fear that the North Korean government has of Jesus' people. Something tells them that believers are dangerous. Let's pray that they will receive a vision of the One who healed sick people, forgave sinful people, and preached good news to poor people.

222. famine once more looms in nk

I summarize this information from the Korean Central News Agency:

Evidently the global warming phenomenon has not yet hit North Korea. Maybe not enough SUV's? For that matter it hasn't been all that warm in my Chicago either. Whatever, it's been over 5 degrees colder this May. If you go into the far Northeastern sections, that translates into freezing temperatures, and crops that will not grow.

The weather set back rice transplantation anywhere from 10 to 15 days. It has "affected the growth of maize crops on a vast acreage of fields, cultivation of rice seedlings and the striking of roots of rice seedlings in the west coastal areas, the granary."

North Korea's food supply was already dangerously low. The deficit of 2007 was about a million tons. This year the prediction is closer to twice that amount. This came about for a couple of reasons: Floods and politics.

Last year's devastating floods are now showing their effects. Wikipedia says, "The flooding submerged, buried or washed away more than 11 percent of the country's rice and corn fields. The North is especially susceptible to bad weather because of a vicious circle where people strip hillsides of natural vegetation to create more arable land to grow food - increasing the risk of floods. On August 16, 2007, Paul Lysley, spokesperson for the WFP Asia, has estimated the damage to crops alone at 450,000 tons. Some 223,381 hectares of farmland were damaged, with about 20 percent of North Korea's paddy fields and 15 percent of its corn fields flooded or washed away."

Then came Myung-bak Lee. A popular new President has taken the reins of South Korea's government. One of the platforms on which he ran for office was a get-tough policy with North Korea. Most of us can understand and agree with this long overdue stance. But Kim Jong-Il of the North is not so happy. And in keeping with his ways, Kim has decided to shame this new leader by not asking his help.

Very smart. "Hey, you don't like me? I'll starve my whole nation!"

The U.S. is still in the game. As you recall NK, US & others are involved in talks after which Mr. Kim will politely lay down his (nuclear) weapons. Just after he has "allowed" everyone to bail him out of this latest crisis. 500,000 tons of food will come from our shores. But it won't be long before this crazed regime will begin cursing us, and reminding us that we owe them not only this shipment but many more.

An impossible situation. Ruined crops. Ruined people. Ah, but God is able.

We must continue to pray now for North Korea's greatest breakthrough. If hard hearts are not swayed by the Gospel or the hand of God quickly, we will once again be reading of the horrors of a genocidal famine in a land that lost 2-3 million of its citizens not too awfully long ago in the same way.

God save North Korea!

223. former nk agent confesses: we targeted Christians

For days now I have been sharing with you, topic by topic, the interviews found in the new report *A Prison Without Bars.* Today's subject is "former NSA (National Security Agency) and PSA (Public Security Agency) agents, their roles and methods." Yes, the ones who do get out have interesting tales to tell.

"The NSA officers in charge of a district...know everything about an individual's life and family history. We find this out by informants... There are risks and rewards of being an informant. If an investigation fails or the NSA officer defects, his informants can be executed. When an informant finds something useful, that person will be compensated for his service with a mark of honor... he could be exempted from his bad family background, get a better job, or he could even be moved to Pyongyang for his safety."

But how are informants chosen to begin with? Well, first, a very flawed person with poor background -we would say he has "skeletons in his closet" - is singled out, taken to the NSA office, and beaten severely. He is then asked to write bad things about himself. His writing is challenged, accusations are made about facts omitted, and he is threatened with a three or four year sentence. When he begs for mercy, he is given mercy Juche style: "Sure, we'll forgive you if you inform for us."

"In the past, there was a group called the Northwest Youth Association. I was in charge of tracing the group. They were all executed. Things like possessing religious books, sharing one's faith with others, or preaching cannot exist because they undermine the Kim Jong II regime. All we need to arrest someone is one bit of evidence such as the Bible with someone's name on it. If the Bible is found, the NSA leaves it until the real owner shows up."

"...North Koreans are classified according to their background in the residents' register [document formed by NSA after intense investigation using informants etc.]. Families of POW's are listed as Number 43, families that have been exiled and were brought back are listed as Number 49... Religious people are not classified because they were supposed to have been liquidated after the revolution. A Ms. Kim has a mother who was a Protestant evangelist. Her husband had an important post in the Party and she wanted to join the Party, but because of her background, she could not. She visited me to eliminate the record of her mother, so I took her name off the list. Confirmation of seven people is required to make a document that a person's ancestor was a Christian."

"There were lots of religious people in [several North Korean towns listed], so people in that area are still prohibited from moving to other places and no executive party members are selected from that area..."

"North Korea is a prison without bars. The reason why the North Korean system still exists is because of the strict surveillance system. When we provide the information like 'this family believes in a religion from their grandfather's generation,' the NSA will arrest each family member. That is why entire families are scared of one another..."

"The NSA officer who investigated me knew Christian terms and... seemed to have read the Bible. [Another agent] said he was being trained to uncover religious people according to special directions from the NSA. He was supposed to look for things such as a person who remains silent with closed eyes... or when habitual smokers or drinkers quit smoking or drinking all of a sudden. These people should be targets to be watched closely."

North Korean agents learn that religion is a drug. It can destroy a regime, they are told, as Gorbachev of Russia learned when religion penetrated his nation. "In this way, all threats are related to religion."

So again we have encountered the feared Christ. Let us continue to pray that North Korea will discover the Christ who is not to be feared at all, but welcomed with great joy.

224. along the china-nk border

Just a couple more sessions with the new book put out by the U.S. Commission on International Religious Freedom, *A Prison Without Borders.* Remember that the book is available online, free. I reccommend highly that my readers avail themselves of this opportunity.

One item upon which this book of recent interviews sheds light is the punishment for North Koreans who are found "in church." It is now alleged that "simple attendance at a Korean Christian church in China [after having escaped North Korea] may not be considered a 'political' crime." Some refugees claim that "they found leniency when insisting that their affiliation with South Korean groups or churches was temporary and needs-based."

One interviewee, a former guard, expressed it this way: "If a repatriated refugee insists that they went to church because they were hungry... we let them pass and tell them not to tell anyone that they went to church."

Nevertheless the fact remains that those who had other reasons for staying in church faced inhumane torture. Here are three more eyewitness accounts:

"There are no preliminary hearings when religious people get caught. We regard them as anti-revolutionary elements... the NSA officers surround the person and kick and beat the person severely before interrogating. When... interrogated, they are first asked whether they had gone to a church in China. North Korea is very concerned about religion. However, no question is asked on Buddhism. Most of those repatriated... pretend to know nothing of religion... However, if they get caught during the interrogation, they are turned over to the NSA..."

"We usually just ask them general questions like 'Did any South Koreans give you money?' and 'Is God good?' to test them... Interrogations are more difficult now since too many refugees have been to church in China. If a repatriated refugee insists that they went to church because they were hungry... we let them pass."

"If [the repatriated] confess that they have met missionaries or deacons... then without any further questions, they will be sent to the NSA and they are as good as dead...In order to find out the truth we interrogate seven-eight times...If we don't find out what we want during interrogations we let people go hungry for about three months, then they inform on each other naturally. In prison, we give two big spoonfuls of bean-mixed rice and it is comprised of 20 percent beans, 70 percent corn, and 10 percent rice. If they behave well, then we give a full cup of soup and they can at least fill their stomach with water. We don't give enough water. Also because the place is cramped, the prisoners are seated in two rows and are not even allowed to raise their heads."

I think of those people in the life of Jesus, like the man born blind, who while poor and needy offered no challenge to the reigning powers and were left alone. But given their healing at the hands of the One who scared them so, the government trembled, and sought to humiliate not only the Healer but the healed.

So it is in North Korea. Be born and raised in Kim's regime as a pauper with a disease, and you will be left alone. Go for food, get healed, have your life turned around, and you face death in several new ways.

How our hearts grieve for this nation.

225. what can i do for nk?

THERE ARE SO MANY THINGS A CARING PERSON CAN DO FOR NORTH KOREA. As you begin working on this list, I believe God will show you even more! Please let me know what other things I ought to add...

1. PRAY. First and foremost, let's obey the command of God in Hebrews 13:3, "Remember the prisoners as though bound with them." Then pray...

Get up earlier and pray
Encourage others to pray.
Go to meetings in your area to pray.
Start a prayer meeting of your own.

Create a special place in your house to lock yourself in, prison-   like, and pray.

Create a prayer map that includes the concentration camps of North Korea, and known ministries.

Go to jail in the Spirit with them every day.

What to pray?

> Pray for all believers to remain faithful unto death even when being tortured or starved.
>
> Pray that aid will get to the hungry and not just to the government and the military.
>
> Pray for the spread of the Gospel from within and for saints to get in from the outside.
>
> Pray that tracts and Bibles and workers will flood the nation.
>
> Pray for the salvation of many and the opportunity for salvation for all.
>
> Pray for ministries worldwide that support and bless North Koreans.   ·
>
> Pray for refugees in China and elsewhere, that their lives will be changed forever by the truth and a loving reception.
>
> Include Kim Jong Il [Kim Jong Oon] in your prayers.

2. GATHER INFORMATION.

Find Scriptures that relate to your brothers' and sisters' suffering.

Read current books, magazines on North Korea.

Subscribe to newsletters.

Watch videos.

3. SHARE

Give donations to groups that specialize in North Korea.

Check them out carefully: there are frauds in this business, as in   every endeavor.

Visit http://biblesunbound.com/ and find how you can send New Testaments into North Korea!

4. WRITE

Write letters to prisoners at prisoneralert.com, which often features North Korean prisoners and how to contact them.

Write letters to the North via e-mail.

Search the net for such addresses.

Write a "letter to the editor" of your local newspaper, regarding   the treatment of North Korean refugees by China. Or other   topics.

Write to the United Nations High Commision for Refugees,   pledged to protect all persons of concern, but seemingly   paralyzed in its attempts to help North Koreans.

Write a letter to the South Korean Embassy, in the U.S. and/or   Seoul.

Write a letter, send an email, or make a phone call, to the North   Korean ambassador to the United Nation

Write a letter, send an email, or make a phone call, to the South   Korean ambassador to the United Nations.

Write to the China embassy regarding repatriation.

Write a letter to the State Department's chief negotiator with   North Korea.

5. RELATE TO NORTH KOREANS

To relate to famine-stricken Koreans, ask God about starting to   eat less meals in a week's time. 21 meals-per-week at present? Try for 20. Or cut meals' size in half. See how far the Lord will   give you grace to go.

Exercise more.

Stop complaining about *anything* in this bountiful land.

Cut back on foolishness, such as over-doing secular TV/movies.

6. VISIT/MOVE

Once you're in touch with these people in the Spirit, and in your   lifestyle, you'll want to start looking around for a way to get   *physically* closer to the people, if God allows. Yes, *there are doors open* into North Korea and surrounding areas...

Consider being an English teacher in Northeast China.

Meet a refugee. Your life will never be the same.

226. political offenders, foreign spies: aka refugees

Refugees who confess to religious belief or who are suspected of spreading Christianity are viewed as having come against the fragile government of North Korea. Pretty incredible. But true. They are subject to harsh penalties, the harshest available, including hard labor and lengthy imprisonment. These facts are quoted directly from *A Prison Without Bars.* I have spent several days to bring you excerpts from this serious work, a compilation of recent interviews that prove the North Korean situation has little changed if any. I encourage you one last time to "Google" this entire work online, and download it free!

Here are the actual words of interviewees on today's topic. Each paragraph is from a separate interview.

"...The fact that a person keeps a Bible means that this person plans to believe in a religion in the future...The most severe punishment is applied to those who are engaged in new religious activity [as opposed to those who have Christianity in their family history]: those who carry the Bible from China and those Christians who help North Korean refugees in China... When they [officials] mention a religion, it is mainly Protestantism rather than Catholicism or Buddhism. I went to a fortune teller many times... North Koreans consider Buddhism as [superstition] different from religion... The target of the search is Protestantism... Protestantism... is related to the United States... and is considered spying... Spies are executed..."

"Protestant religious organizations are considered political offenders and traitors attempting to overthrow the government... If we [guards] find Buddhist [believers], they...do [only] forced labor for about six months. We just consider this a superstition... Buddhist monks are actually members of the party..."

"Christians are regarded as spies. If you meet a Christian, it is considered the same as meeting a South Korean intelligence officer. Spies and Christians... are treated equally. Most people who are Christians or who met Christians are sent to Yodok to serve sentences of between four years and life. People who spread Protestantism - instead of just believing - are sentenced to life sentences."

"Many refugees carry the Bible with them back to North Korea because they would do anything for the money. If caught they are sent to [prison]. The authorities have rarely executed political offenders lately because human rights in

North Korea became an issue worldwide... but now they are sent to inland mountain areas where living is difficult."

"Everything except Christianity is fine. When a person is caught carrying a Bible, he will be punished because he has brought an external influence to North Korea. A person caught carrying the Bible is doomed... and his whole family may disappear."

"Buddhists tend to keep their religion to themselves, but Christianity spreads fast... Christians don't pray alone, but try to get together in numbers and also they spread fast. Kim Jong Il is more afraid of his own people than the United States. The great god of North Korea is Kim Jong Il and if that changes to a real god, it can stir up people."

There you have it. The lie abounds. The Truth suppressed. We are praying for a turnaround of that. Let us meanwhile be sure that the Truth abounds in our own life, in the midst of the corruption that inundates this nation. May God have mercy on all His people that call upon Him with the whole heart, wherever they live.

227. *Crossing*

The following is reprinted from the Washington Post, May 31, 2008. It is a review of a movie that I trust every North Korea lover will go to see.

Some of the most tragic experiences of Yoo Sang-jun's life have made it into a major new South Korean feature film, but now that the results are on the screen, the North Korean defector is too traumatized to watch them.

"I don't want to think about my past," Mr. Yoo said in a phone interview, the day before a special screening of "Crossing" was held for reporters in Seoul. Some viewers, familiar with Mr. Yoo's personal tragedy, wept as they previewed the film yesterday.

"Crossing" stars Cha In-pyo, one of Asia's top actors, as a North Korean miner whose undernourished, pregnant wife contracts tuberculosis. With no medicine available in the impoverished nation, Mr. Cha's character leaves his wife and 11-year-old son to travel to China to work, earn money and buy drugs.

While away, his wife dies, and his son, played by Shin Myung-chul, becomes a wandering orphan. The starving child attempts to escape to China, but is captured and placed in a re-education camp - where the film's most harrowing scenes take place. A bribe arranged by his father, now in South Korea, breaks him out of the camp. The film's jarring finale takes place in the Mongolian Desert.

Avoiding the melodrama of many South Korean films, "Crossing" is relentless in its detailed, docudrama approach. A cross-border trader and his family are seized by secret police in a midnight raid. Ragged orphans beg in destitute markets. Camp guards kick a pregnant woman in China in the stomach.

Kim Tae-kyun, the film's director, said he did not retain Mr. Yoo, a high-profile defector, as a consultant for fear of creating a political incident while filming in China. Last year, Mr. Yoo was imprisoned there for four months after assisting North Korean defectors. Half of the film's proceeds will go to help North defectors, Mr. Kim said.

The life of Mr. Yoo, now a Seoul-based Christian activist, mirrors much of the plot of "Crossing."

After losing his wife and a son during the North Korean famine of the late 1990s, he escaped to China with his surviving son, Chul-min. Despairing of making a living, and in fear of deportation - Chinese authorities routinely send North

Korean defectors home, where many face terrible punishment - Mr. Yoo put the boy into foster care while he attempted to escape to Seoul.

He reached South Korea and worked as a laborer, earning money to pay smugglers to bring his son out of China. In 2002, Chul-min set off from China for Mongolia to reunite with his father. In the barren frontier between the countries, lost, weak and exhausted, the child died from exposure.

Yoo Chul-min is buried under a wooden cross in the Mongolian desert. He was 10 years old.

German human rights activist Norbert Vollertsen, who briefly knew Yoo Chul-min, has arranged for the film to be screened in July at the European Parliament. He said the film took him back to his time working as an aid doctor in rural North Korea.

"People will see this film so they can see places where they cannot go, and see things they cannot see," Mr. Yoo said. "I hope the film can help the world know about North Korea."

"It would be pertinent if China's leadership watched this film," said Tim Peters, an American activist and friend of Mr. Yoo's who attended the screening. "With the stroke of a pen, they could stop thousands of tragedies."

228. the day Jesus looked up to a man

Being tall is a limited option for the North Korean. Due to ongoing malnutrition caused by flood , famine, in many cases inhumane treatment, and of course Communism itself, there is a significant height difference between North Korean citizens and their South Korean counterparts.

For example, take the adult population in the South between 20 and 40 years of age. The average male is about

5'8", and the average female, approaching 5'3". But in the North that same-aged man would be a little over 5'5" and his wife just over 5'.

Will the shortness continue, maybe even worsen? Without God's intervention, alas, North Korea, they say, could become a separate race of humans altogether. Although near miraculous growth can take place when one escapes to the South, in the North the situation is so bad as to have forced the government into changing the military's height requirement.

Does God care about short people? Yes, especially when they are not stopped by their predicament as they seek for Him. I was reading just this morning the story of a short man who knew Jesus was in town. It's found in Luke 19. The man is Zacchaeus, and what he lacked in physical stature he more than compensated for in cleverness. By his own admission, his cleverness had led him into great sin, cheating the people of his day out of their hard-earned wages.

But then Jesus came along. Zacchaeus had heard of the wonder-worker and the sin-forgiver and the One claiming to be Messiah, even God. Using one last burst of clever thinking, as the old Sunday School song relates,

"He climbed up in a sycamore tree for the Lord He wanted to see,

And as the Savior passed that way,

He looked up in the tree, and He said,

'Zacchaeus, you come down,

for I'm going to your house *for tea*.' "

Well, the British had not taken over that part of the world by then, so we can debate the "tea" part of the song. But suffice it to say that before that day had passed, short

Zacchaeus was a new man. Jesus had looked up to Him, and he had looked up to Jesus, and found eternal life.

I could not help putting this story into the context of our short friends in the top half of the Korean peninsula. Through no fault of their own, they have become the spectacle of the world. Small in stature. Small in diet. Small in privilege. Small in standing. Small in opportunity.

But no matter. Jesus is passing this way. When Jesus comes into view, the small can become great and those who think they are great can become small. In an instant. I'd like to see that, wouldn't you? Pray with me about it! Jesus, pass through North Korea, today and every day.

229. NORTH KOREA RESOURCES *Want to learn more about North Korea? There are a lot of ways.*

1: Books.

Amazon.com has literally hundreds of titles on North Korea, including many listed below. I have listed the books first in chronological, then in alphabetical (by title), order.

Child is King of the Country, Citizens Alliance for North Korean Human Rights, 2009

Lives for Sale, Committee for Human Rights in North Korea, 2009

Escaping North Korea, Mike Kim, 2008

I'll Cross the River, (novel) C. Hope Flinchbaugh, 2008

Famine in North Korea, Stephen Haggard and Marcus Noland, 2007

North of the DMZ, Andrei Lankov, 2007

North Korea: The Paranoid Peninsula, Paul French, 2007 (latest edition)

Escape from North Korea, Paul Estabrooks, 2006

Inside North Korea, Edward Harris and Bruce Cummings, 2006

Living With the Enemy, Inside North Korea, Richard Saccone, 2006

North Korea 2005 and Beyond, Philip Yun and Gi-Wook Shin, 2006

Rogue Regime, Jasper Becker, 2006

This Is Paradise, Hyok Kang, 2006

Under the Loving Care of the Fatherly Leader, Bradley Martin, 2006

Aquariums of Pyongyang, The, Kang Chol-Hwan, 2005

Comrades and Strangers, Michael Harrold, 2004

Idiot's Guide to Understanding North Korea, C. Kenneth Quinones and Joseph Tragert, 2003

The Tears of My Soul, Hyun Hee Kim, 2003

By Their Blood, James & Marti Hefley, 2002

When My Name Was Keoko, Linda Sue Park, 2002

In the Absence of Sun, Helie Lee, 2002

Extreme Devotion, Voice of the Martyrs, 2001

Juche, Thomas Belke, 1999

Decision at Dawn, Chulho Awe, 1965

The Grass Roof, Younghill Kang, 1959

The Yalu Flows, Mirok Li

The Christ of the Korean Heart, Arch Campbell, 1954

From Voice of the Martyrs ministry, the classic about Christian persecution:

> *Tortured for Christ,* Richard Wurmbrand/Voice of the Martyrs, 1967

From Open Doors ministry;

> *Escape from North Korea,* Open Doors/Paul Estabrooks, 2006

For books actually published within North Korea:

> North Korea Books. http://www.north-korea-books.com/

2: Special Reports

All available free online. Just click the title:

> Prison without bars, 2008 The United States Commission on International Religious Freedom

> Concentrations of Inhumanity, 2007 David Hawk

> The Hidden Gulag: Exposing North Korea's Prison Camps David Hawk

> NK Freedom Watch (Human Rights in North Korea) Freedom House

> Acts of Betrayal interviews from Refugees International

3: videos.

Amazon.com DVD collection:

> *Crossing,* 2008

> *On the Border,* Chosun Ilbo [newspaper], 2008

> *An American in North Korea,* 60 Minutes, 2007

> *Inside North Korea,* National Geographic, 2007

> *The Hermit Kingdom,* 60 Minutes, 2006

A Rare Look Inside North Korea, Nightline, 2006

39 Years 6 months 4 days, 60 Minutes, 2005

North Korea- A Day in the Life, Pieter Fleury, 2004

Kim Jong Il, A & E Biography, 2003

The Forgotten War, History Channel (Robert Stack) 1996

Documentaries from VeryMuchSo Productions:

A State of Mind, Daniel Gordon, 2003
website: http://www.astateofmind.co.uk/

Crossing the Line, Daniel Gordon, 2000
website: http://www.crossingthelinefilm.com/

The game of Their Lives, Daniel Gordon, 2003
website: http://www.thegameoftheirlives.co.uk/

Other:

Hidden Shadows, 2000. 52-minute documentary of refugees hiding in China. Aired in 3 parts later by ABC's *Nightline.* from journeyman

Seoul Train, Lisa Sleeth & Jim Butterworth, 2004 http://www.seoultrain.com/ or purchase ($25.00) from Open Doors

From You Tube. Click and watch online.

"Escape from North Korea"

"Free NK Radio" mini-videos

Welcome to North Korea

LINK's 2006 montage of NK news,

Just how bad is it in North Korea? in Korean language.

Clip from National Geographic video, "Inside North Korea"

North Korea- Secret Victims , about
abductees
Source for Video and DVD Published in N K:
http://www.stores.ebay.com/northkoreai
mports
4:Pro North Korea websites. In English:
North Korea Times
North Central News Agency
Korea Today
Korea Friendship Association
From North Korea (Korean)
Rodong Sinmun
And from South Korea, for contrast (English) :
KBS News
Korea Herald
5:miscellaneous
FREENK , defectors speak out on the
radio.

[attention. this list is from 2008]

230. nk prayer challenge: hoeryong concentration camp

It is embarrassing to suggest to someone that he has family members in jail. But we do. When believers go public in North Korea they can face death in a number of ways and places. One of the camps they might be forced to enter is this place, that some call *the worst place in the world*.

When North Korean Kim Hyun Hee, the North Korean pardoned in South Korea after being involved in the bombing Incident of 1987, and her family were on official business in

Cuba her father once pointed to some land that was barely visible on the horizon. "That's America, Hyun Hee, the worst place in the world."

I have a different candidate for that description.

If Gehenna, or Hell, is the worst place in the universe from a Biblical point of view, then surely anything that is related to eternal torment must be the worst place on the earth. North Korea is a prison and a land of prisoners, where torment and deprivation have become a way of life. The "Gulag" within that nation is even more evil, and some say, the worst of the worst is the

HOERYONG CONCENTRATION CAMP

Here are pieces of the description given us by David Hawk in his *Hidden Gulag*:

> Official name: Chosun People's Security Unit 2209.
>
> Area covered: 30 x 25 miles! (750 square miles! That's more than half as big as Rhode Island, and 10 times bigger than Washington D.C.!)
>
> Guards: 1000
>
> Administrative agents: 500
>
> Prisoners: 50,000
>
> Nature of prisoners: The families of alleged wrongdoers.
>
> Annual production quotas: 400 tons corn, 100,000 tons potatoes, 50,000 tons lima beans, 10,000 tons red peppers. Many other foods produced. Much coal also mined and shipped to Power Plants and Steel mills.

Estimated deaths from malnutrition (in spite of food produced): 1,500-2,000 (mostly children)

Public executions per year: 10

Reasons for executions: Stealing food to survive.

Basic diet: Corn, potatoes. Meat only from rats, snakes, frogs, if they could catch them.

Other deaths: From beatings if quota not met. For pregnancy. Sex/marriage forbidden. Beatings for camp regulations being disobeyed.

Pay for work: 500 won ($227.00) per year.

Education: Basics of reading, writing, arithmetic, (youth.)

Holidays: 9 per year, mostly Kim Il Sung related.

Hoeryong Camp is a *Kwan-li-so*

...that is, a political penal labor camp. Political prisoners are those in prison because of their perceived beliefs, whether political, religious, or whatever. Here is a listing of some of the descriptives that apply to such camps, and therefore to Hoeryong. These items are also classified as crimes against humanity, per the new book from Freedom House by David Hawk, <u>Concentrations of Inhumanity</u>.

Those who think wrong, along with their families, just "disappear" and wind up in "family camp."

There is no judicial process followed to deposit human beings in these camps.

Most prisoners are cut off from their families and friends and any contact with the outside world.

Prisoners must eat at a below-subsistence level.

No North Korean laws cover the *kwan-li-so*.

Prisoners are regularly subjected to beatings and/or more systematic torture.

Prisoners are often compelled to observe executions and to defile corpses of the just-executed.

Female prisoners are frequently raped by officials and guards of the prison.

There are high rates of death at these camps.

Pregnancies that occur are terminated by involuntary abortion.

Infanticide takes place if a child should somehow be born.

families do their own cooking using below-subsistence rations

meals supplemented by eating grass, snakes, frogs, rabbits, rats

kept on verge of starvation for control purposes

back-breaking labor: mining, timber cutting with shovels, pick-axes, hand-pushed carts filled with ore, carrying logs down from mountains. All while half-starved.

Witnesses of the Hoeryong Tragedy

Former guard: Ahn Myong Chol remembers atrocities:

A food factory produced soy sauce and cookies and bean paste. And here the women worked between 20 and 30 years old. The women are the sexual slaves of the security officers, they are forced to wear only white thin gowns and no underwear, they are not given underwear. They make all the beautiful women work here.

The prisoners go to the coal mine along this road, in carts pulled by cows. And while they are passing through here, I was instructed to beat a disabled person by my superior, and I had no choice but to obey.

Even in the small village there is an officers headquarters, and if any prisoner disobeys, then he can be beaten here, and the officers were armed, and they would kill prisoners here.

Not only here but all other places, even in the small hills they bury bodies. And when we cut the trees down, sometimes we find a buried body. Not only here, but all around here are buried bodies.

In the hills here, if there is some flat area, it is covered with graves. And if people start to farm there, they find bodies or bones.

This area is where there are the most densely buried bodies. There are graves all over here, and we can see the graves where there are no woods. There is no particular area to bury dead bodies, but they put them all in this general vicinity, and no one can cry. It is forbidden to cry, and there is no funeral ceremony, and the officers say, "The anti-revolutionary person has died, so there is no reason to cry."

Witness statements from a report by The Guardian:
I witnessed a whole family being tested on suffocating gas and dying in the gas chamber,' he said. 'The parents, son and and a daughter. The parents were vomiting and dying,

but till the very last moment they tried to save kids by doing mouth-to-mouth breathing.'

Hyuk has drawn detailed diagrams of the gas chamber he saw. He said: 'The glass chamber is sealed airtight. It is 3.5 metres wide, 3m long and 2.2m high_ [There] is the injection tube going through the unit. Normally, a family sticks together and individual prisoners stand separately around the corners. Scientists observe the entire process from above, through the glass.'

He explains how he had believed this treatment was justified. 'At the time I felt that they thoroughly deserved such a death. Because all of us were led to believe that all the bad things that were happening to North Korea were their fault; that we were poor, divided and not making progress as a country.

'It would be a total lie for me to say I feel sympathetic about the children dying such a painful death. Under the society and the regime I was in at the time, I only felt that they were the enemies. So I felt no sympathy or pity for them at all.'

His testimony is backed up by Soon Ok-lee, who was imprisoned for seven years. 'An officer ordered me to select 50 healthy female prisoners,' she said. 'One of the guards handed me a basket full of soaked cabbage, told me not to eat it but to give it to the 50 women. I gave them out and heard a scream from those who had eaten them. They were all screaming and vomiting blood. All who ate the cabbage leaves started violently vomiting blood and screaming with pain. It was hell. In less than 20 minutes they were quite dead.'

Where is this Hoeryong?

The camp is located some 12-15 miles outside the city of Hoeryong, a city that sits on the Tumen River, opposite China in the far northeastern province of North Hamgyong. The Chinese city across the river is Longjing. It is said that Kim Jong Il's mother, Kim Jong Suk, his father's first wife, was born in Hoeryong. But far more notoriety has come to the city by way of the reputation of this camp.

General Characteristics of *Kwan-Li So* physical locations:

- located in the mountains in the remote interior
- cover huge areas, miles long and wide
- outer perimeters surrounded by barbed wire and guard towers
- multiple thousands of prisoners
- housed in scattered areas based on category of prisoner
- families live in tiny shacks, sometimes multiple families to single shack

And there is much much more...

You do have family in Hoeryong. Please remember to pray for them.

231. son jong nam awaits death

The following article is nearly a year old (from Mission Network News), but the situation is current. Please pray for this brother. Another way to help is suggested in the article.

North Korea (MNN) - <u>Voice of the Martyrs</u> has launched a worldwide campaign to free Son Jong Nam, a former North

Korean army officer awaiting public execution for being a Christian.

VOM's Todd Nettleton says this is an unusual situation. "It's actually fairly rare to have a name and a face about a North Korean prisoner because the country is so closed. Since we did have that specific information, in this case, we want to use this to draw attention not only to this case, but to the overall situation for Christians in North Korea."

Nam has been behind bars for a year and has been sentenced to public execution as an example to the North Korean people. His brother, Son Jong Hoon, made a public plea Thursday before the National Press Club in Washington D. C.

Their voices are joined by U.S. Senator and Republican presidential candidate Sam Brownback, a noted supporter of human rights for North Korean refugees. Brownback sent letters [also signed by Senators Max Baucus (D) and Richard Durbin (D) and Senators Jim Inhofe (R) and David Vitter (R)] last week to US Secretary of State Condoleezza Rice and UN Secretary General Ban Ki-moon asking them to secure Nam's release.

Nettleton says they're asking people to write letters and send emails on Son Jong Nam's behalf which will then be mailed to the North Korean delegation to the UN. Along with those letters, the group is asking the North Korean government to spare Son's life, release him from prison immediately, report on his current statu,s and deliver the personal letters to Son.

According to VOM, Son defected to China in 1998 with his wife, son, and brother. His wife died after arriving there. It was in China that he met a South Korean missionary and became a Christian. Mr. Son continued his religious studies and felt called to be an evangelist in North Korea.

However, Son was arrested by Chinese police in 2001, sent back to North Korea, charged and imprisoned with sending missionaries into his native country. He was paroled briefly in 2004 and went to China. When he returned to North Korea in January 2006, he was arrested again and has remained in prison since.

While it's an uncomfortable story, it's also a message of hope for the embattled church. Nettleton says the response can let other believers know they haven't been forgotten. He urges people to take Nam and others like him before the Lord. "Pray for this prisoner, for Son Jong Nam. Pray for his encouragement. Pray for his health. We know that North Korean jails are not safe places. I think we can also pray that he would have opportunities to share his faith even while he is in prison."

Go to prisoneralert.com to compose a letter of support and encouragement to Son.

232. pass the dandelions, please

The following report is nearly three years old (August, 2005). But the situation has only scarcely improved in North Korea, and now threatens to worsen again. No exaggerations. The article comes from the Research Institute for North Korean Society, and is easily obtained from Open Doors. Simply order the DVD "Seoul Train," and as a part of the "Bonus Features" , you will find not only this article, but scores like it, charts, graphs, legal documents, a video of a North Korea public execution, and much more. Not only that, every North Korea lover should have by now seen the excellent documentary by Jim Butterworth and Lisa Sleeth that this DVD is all about. Now, the article: [from a translation, with corrections by House of Chosun]

Food Substituted for Thin Maize Soup with Wild Vegetable - *Seturi* .

A Farm worker from the fourth unit at the Sansung Farm in Onsung County says the food situation for local farmers is being extremely aggravated.

The shortage of food urges the locals to substitute or add wild vegetation to their daily food. Boiled *Seturi* (a dialectical variation of North Hamgyung province - otherwise it is called *Se-tu-rae* in South Hamgyung province: a kind of dandelion) with a handful of powdered maize is added to substitute for a proper meal. Since there is a marked increase of the price of grain, this state of affairs for the ordinary people should persist for awhile.

Methods of Purchasing Food

People who have more money buy the food in large quantity during the harvest period when the grain cost is relatively low. The price of rice inflates as high as 1000 won during the year, but in the harvesting period, rice prices are 400-450 won (300-400 won in Hwanghae Province). Hence this is the time to buy the rice in bulk.

People who buy rice in bulk store it in a built-in storage in the house, a secret storage with iron bars. This room is disguised as part of the wall - one could not access it without going through another room of the house. Most of the families who buy the rice in bulk buy the maize and rice in 6:4 or 7:3 ratio, respectively.

Purchased rice is consumed for one's own family or some is sold at the marketplace in June to August of the next year when the price of rice is at its highest. The profit from selling the rice is then spent on buying rice in the next harvest season. For instance, the price of maize increases in July, so with the profit from selling 100 kg of maize in the harvest season, a person can buy 200 kg of maize. This is the way that some 'better-off' people are providing for themselves.

Food Situation in Booyun District, Chungjin

Families under the poverty line are mostly from the Booyun district or Ranam district. Particularly the Booyun district has infertile soil with stones so plentiful that it is difficult for any one to farm decent vegetation. Most families in the area do not even have a proper set of household goods.It almost is impossible to find a household with proper bedding, since anything worthwhile was exchanged for food long ago. People do not trade in the market because they do not have cash to begin with.

In a situation like this, seventy percent of the people in the area are consuming potatoes and wild vegetable for their major source of food. They travel 16 km to Mayang-ri in Musan County, where they get potatoes. It takes an entire day for the return trip.

A few weeks ago there was a big scare in America. Sam's Club and Costco said they would start "rationing" rice. No more than FOUR BAGS per VISIT. No matter what the size of these bags were, the comparison to North Korea and others in the world is ludicrous. Thank God for prosperity, but we have become addicted to over-supplies of everything.

It would seem North Korea is in a different world, but it really is a part of the globe that is included in John 3:16. Many of those affected are Christian family. Earnest prayer is still the order of the day.

233. escape from nk

Another resource for those who have decided to love and pray for North Korea, is a 150-page story of the "desperate quest for food, love, and life" of a single North Korean family of not too long ago. Written by Paul

Estabrooks and <u>Open Doors</u> and called *Escape from North Korea*. Here is an extended quote from his introduction (used by permission):

"In May, 1997, seven imprisoned North Korean Christians in Hambuk Province had their jaws broken by guards because they continued to pray and sing praises to God. Minutes later they were shot to death.

"Other incidents, again in Hambuk prison, took place in March and July of 1998. Four Christians were shot to death. In an effort to force one prisoner to deny his faith in Jesus Christ, guards starved him for days. When he refused to give in, he was shot to death. Three other prisoners displayed remarkable boldness and peace concerning their faith. North Korean officers beat them severely until they became unconscious. Then they were shot.

"In December 1999, two ladies were openly shot in Haesan city on charges of illegal smuggling. In reality they were faithful Christians and ministered actively. During the same month two other Christians were shot in public in Hambuk Province. One of them had every tooth broken so that he could not talk clearly. Yet he boldly witnessed and preached the gospel to the end - even as he was being dragged to the place of execution.

"These heartrending testimonies are only the tip of the iceberg..."

We Americans are used to seeing people shot to death by the scores every week on the television programs we thirstily imbibe day after day. I am grateful to God for giving me grace to put TV aside. But how I wish that the images I just shared with you from this well written book would stir me more. How I wish I had concentrated on realities rather than fantasies for these many years. How deep could my love now be?

Here is more...*Here we are being introduced to the main characters of a true story [though names have been changed], Pil Soo and Myung Hee, a man and wife in present-day North Korea. Pil has gotten home a little early today from work. Wife is not surprised. In fact he only works about 10 days a month at this furniture factory, due to a slow-down in supplies needed. Imagine a conversation like this taking place when your husband comes home from work, ladies:*

"You're home from work early again! Did you have any lunch?"

"Oh, I'm so sick I feel like I'm going to die. I left work early because my fever is really high. Maybe I'll be an addition to the fifty or so of our town's people dying today! Then you can eat my body," Pil Soo replied in all seriousness. That was a reality in their area. But no one openly talked about it. Two sons of a nearby neighbor had recently starved to death. Surprisingly, there had been no funeral. Rumors were rampant. It was too close to home!

"Nonsense," retorted Myung Hee. "You've just got a cold again, from this changing weather! Come lie down on the bed and I'll get you some hot water to drink." On the one hand, she sought to downplay her husband's condition; on the other, she inwardly fretted about his pain and fever.

"How was your day?" Pil Soo grimaced as he held his aching stomach.

"Nothing more notable than neighbors begging for food again! Of course, I had nothing for them. The Soon family thinks their Grandma may die of hunger tonight. She regularly insists her grandchildren be given her portion of food."

"Where's my mother?" Pil Soo queried as he looked around the cottage for their resident grandmother.

"Oh she's gone to the mountainside to gather grass to make porridge. The children went with her. They'll try and find some pine bark also."

"You mean we're out of corn rice again already," Pil Soo replied in a tone of frustration...

I leave you with the normal encouragement to pray for North Korea. Oh how she needs Jesus.

234. nk history lesson. the great famine

I quote again today from Escape from North Korea *by Paul Estabrooks and Open Doors. This is one citizen's first-hand perception of how the famine of the 90's devastated the nation.(pp.70-72...)*

After the death of Kim Il Sung in July 1994, the government stopped giving daily food rations to the people. From 1996 through 1998, some two million men, women and children died of starvation. In the province where we live, thirty to fifty died daily in every village. Bodies of the dead were lying on the streets.

It became so bad that a group of people, mostly men, hid in the mountains. They stole women and food from the villages.

Much of this could be traced back to the mid-1980's when South Korea was devastated by one of the worst typhoons in its history... Kim Il Sung, who had been told by some of his officials that we had enough food stored away, said he would help the South Koreans. Unfortunately, he was either deceived or the officials were inept. A tremendous amount of food was given to South Korea... our people realized that there was not sufficient food for us... starvation became worse. But what could they do? If Kim Il Sung said a pussycat was a tiger, then it was a tiger... He promised that one day everyone would be living in mansions and eating beef soup, promises that never came true.

We were taught to fear him. Even though many of us felt he was wrong, we didn't dare to publicly share our opinions for fear of being executed.

In the 1980's, a working adult used to receive 650 grams of grain daily...

In the early 1990's, people received twenty days worth of rations for each thirty-day period. In 1993 and 1994, that was reduced to fifteen days of rations per month. By 1995, a year after the death of Kim Il Sung, monthly rations were cut to five days. Some months, nothing was provided.

Before Kim Jong-il was president, the ordinary people lived on corn rice. It wasn't enough to satisfy our hunger, but at least we didn't have to work on empty stomachs. Right after [Kim Jong-il] came to power, [he] invested more than ninety percent of the government's money to cover the expenses of the military-defense program...

According to Kim Jong-il, we had the finest defense technology and military force in the world. But what good was that when people, even soldiers, were starving to death every day? The soldiers were so hungry that they resorted to gulping down oil designated for the maintenance of their artillery and other weapons.

It wasn't just that there was little food. You have to understand that there are many black hands played in the food-distribution process. The government would allot food to, let's say, the First Batallion. The overall manager there would steal some for his own use. That would leave less for the First Batallion, whose food manager would also help himself. What was left for the soldiers was never enough.

The government did nothing to help. The soldiers were told they would have to find other ways to feed themselves, so they stole from farms and looted houses. Some have robbed and killed civilians for their food. As a result, there's great hatred between civilians and soldiers throughout the country. I've even heard people say that if a war breaks out, *they*'ll kill our soldiers before the enemy can kill them.

Can any of us understand the language of suffering? May God give every reader and listener today the gift of interpretation, so that what is being said will register on the deepest levels of the heart. When that happens is when people begin to pray. God have mercy, have mercy on North Korea.And if as they say, another famine is imminent, show us what we can do. Oh hear Your people!

235. nk, here comes Jesus

For many months now I have been sharing with you all the difficult things people need to know about North Korea. We've talked famine & flood together, refugees, orphans, split-up families. I've wept with you over concentration camps, torture, public executions. But rarely have I been able to share good things with you. Well, hey, there just aren't a lot of good things to share. But today my quiver is full. Stand back and get ready to be blessed.

Would you believe it if I told you that every day of the year the Gospel is being beamed into North Korea by short wave radio, and that one million North Koreans are hearing that Gospel message? Imagine it. 30 minutes a day these otherwise destitute NK nationals get to hear readings from a North Korea dialect New Testament read by a *real North Korean*, a man we will call "Mr. Kim", living in South Korea, plus an audio drama of the life of Christ, and even a reading of the classic Wurmbrand book *Tortured for Christ* !

Would you also believe me if I related that before September of this year, 600,000 Gospel tracts will arrive by air into various parts of the Hermit Kingdom north of the DMZ? That plans are being made to increase that number astronomically by technology that will allow year-round launches of balloons carrying these fliers?

Would you still stay with me if I told you there are 13,000 North Korean defectors living in Seoul ghettoes as we speak, and that they are also being reached with a message of hope and purpose? That many of them are being trained to bless their own people with the Gospel?

And what would you say if I told you that all of the above energy and planning is North-Korea created and energized?

If you truly believed that all of this is happening, would you think what we often think when we read the papers about North Korea, that "nothing is really changing. Poor folks , they'll never make it now. More famine is on the way. Probably wipe out the whole nation..."?

I recently had to re-seed the back yard. My wife had a garden out there. Now that we're thinking of selling, we are trying to make it look a little more "normal." Unfortunately extensive gardens in a suburb of Chicago aren't considered the norm. So I had to try my hand at horticulture, or whatever it's called. I've decided after several hot days not to leave my day job.

But the work itself was not the worst part. It was the waiting. And waiting. I had decided after about a week that I had really blown it this time. I was mentally planning to re-do the whole thing. No grass! Hey, I'd planted faithfully. I'd watered faithfully. God Himself poured buckets on several occasions. In fact He helped so much that I thought the poor seeds were drowned. Forget this green-thumb stuff.

Then one morning, like that first sign of a beard on a skinny teen-age boy, there it was. The tiniest, frailest, but most beautiful green I had ever seen. This was *my* grass. I did this. I can't describe how good it felt.

Do you think Jesus might just have a morning like this soon? Oh my, SO many seeds have been planted! Oh my, SO much watering is being done. The Word of God is not bound. It keeps doing what God says it must do. Many lives have been changed forever already. The Word is getting out. Something is stirring deep underground.

What our "Mr. Kim" is preaching cannot be stopped by that other "Mr. Kim." Jong-il had his shot at stopping it for sure. But the plants are growing anyway. See the frail little seedlings sprouting, barely visible above the surface? The news media hasn't picked it up yet. But when they do, what a chance for Christ to be glorified!

For it is Christ Who is touching refugees and orphans. It is Christ Who is feeding the hungry, caring for the dying. The world will see the difference that *Christ* makes when he is given the reins. May the day come soon.

Information for the above gleaned from Seoul USA in Seoul , Korea and Colorado Springs , CO .

236. home sweet home

Yes, the West has its problems. But most of us will take those problems over the ones dumped on certain eastern nations. Take "Chosun" for example. I hope you'll find a copy of Estabrooks' Escape from North Korea *(available at Open*

378

Doors) as soon as you can. It's a fairly recent tale of the ongoing suffering of a nation. The particular couple he follows in the book have come to Christ, as so many of the escapees do. Here is a portion of their story, as they are about to make their way out of the country...

"Halt!" That single word, screamed into the night, had a spine-chilling effect. Big flashlights were trained on Myung Hee and Pil Soo, and soon they could make out four North Korean soldiers with their rifles aimed right at them. When the two were almost out of the water, soldiers grabbed them and roughly dragged them to the embankment. What the two had feared most was happening.

They were handcuffed, shoved forcibly into a truck and transported to a military base near the border. During the next three days, both were denied food as they were questioned separately for hours at a time.

Pil Soo was usually questioned while seated on a chair, soldiers shouting in his face. Whenever his head fell forward, a guard would grab him by the hair and snap it back up, several times with such force that he fell off the chair. The guards considered that hilarious. Hundreds of times he was asked to give the names of his contacts in China and of places he had been. There was nothing clever about the process, nothing that indicated any expertise about how to deal with a prisoner. Their lone strategy was to tell Pil Soo that, if he would simply give information about relatives or friends in China, they would allow him and Myung Hee back into that country so they could come back with money - bribe money for the guards. Obtaining money, that was their *real* goal in all of this.

The worst of the guards' tactics was the assortment of ways in which they administered violence. If a punch in the face did not soften up Pil Soo, then perhaps two blows to the stomach might. Or, better yet, how about three kicks to the ribs? Blows were applied to assorted parts of the body with a heavy wooden stick that resembled a baseball bat, which was why the guards referred to this procedure as "baseball game." Blood? Nothing more than another reason for howling with laughter, especially when the blood gushed out of the nose. Pil Soo was forced to swallow his own blood. For the guards, all of this was alternately high entertainment or mounting frustration at having a detainee who refused to break...

These victims, are they spies from a foreign country, planning to bomb the government offices? Terrorists intent on destroying the nation's people or leaders? Nope. Fellow-citizens of the guards, hungry, wanting to worship freely and live in liberty. Sounds like my own heritage. But they are still at the mercy of an out-of-control system that only God can break. It is our regular prayer that the break will come soon. Today, if God wills.

By the way, the story does not end here, as you can tell by the title of the book.

237. he talks to a million every day

It is my pleasure, my deepest joy, to introduce to you today radio broadcaster "Mr. Kim" of North Korea . After I re-tell his story, using mostly his own [translated] words, from a testimony he gave recently at a Voice of the Martyrs function, I will tell you how you can hear one of his daily broadcasts right here on Sermonaudio! Lord willing, this audio series of his will continue several times a week...

Mr. Kim is a North Korea defector. He now lives in South Korea with 12 or 13 thousand others in his situation. 300,000 more are scattered across China and Southeast Asia . They live as beggars. Even though Kim was a commissioned officer in the North Korean military, he joined the line of NK beggars in China when he became disillusioned by the system of that other Kim ruling North Korea .

NK defectors hide out in China trying to avoid the Public Security Bureau of that nation. If they are caught, these "national traitors" will be sent back to prison or execution. The only people they can rely on are the Korean-Chinese churches. He decided to go to one of those churches in Yanji [China].

"The church opened the door to me, but the moment I passed through the door, I got to meet a stranger known as 'God.' We were introduced in a worship service. As days went by I came to the conclusion that God was actually the same as Kim Jung-il. Both made promises about people's futures and destinies. The Scriptures quoted sounded like Kim quotations. Of course I had learned that those quotations were worthless.

"Even prayer time reminded me of how we learned to criticize ourselves in the 'Life Harmony' period every week. It made me very sad. There was even a trinity, like we had: leader, party, people. 600 songs of praise to the Kims were in our NK songbook. But the Christian hymnal I now used had only 558 songs. I felt the invisible Christian God must be weaker. I felt sorry for these people.

"The truth is, I refused God. But I could not leave because I had nowhere to go, nothing to eat. Then one day I overheard the prayers of some of these Christians. The temperature was minus 30, but they were sweating due to the passion of their prayers! They prayed for my starving people, and the defectors wandering around China . How could I criticize people like this?

"Still, when I was asked to copy the entire Bible by hand as part of discipleship training... it was too much. The pastor said he would send me to South Korea if I copied the Bible one time. But I abandoned this project, left the church. It was February of 1997. I wandered around until I found a ship getting ready to sail to South Korea . While waiting, I was arrested...

"They put handcuffs on me and forced me to return to NK due to the fact that I was a high level military officer and had tried to board a ship to South Korea . The "PSB" turned me over to the State Security Agency who began to torture me terribly as they interrogated me. All of the bones in my fingers were broken, and my mouth was torn. I came to have blood all over my body and was sent to my prison cell after less than an hour.

"After 9 days, three of my fellow officers showed up. It looked like a public trial was coming, with the resultant public execution. I began to pray to the God I had rejected. All during the three day trip to the location of the execution I prayed desperately for God's help. I told Him I wanted to live, that I would give my life to Him if he saved me. The soldiers began to ridicule me, and thought I was so crazy that they began to be a little careless in their guarding of me.

"As we neared Pyongyang , our destination, I stood up to go the washroom, thinking how I could make my break. The bathroom was in such bad shape that the officer kept his distance behind me. It seemed that maybe this would be my chance to escape. Without thinking it through I just jumped off the moving train by launching my whole body through the window frame. I must have aged 1000 years in that moment. I knew I had to risk death if I wanted to live..."

I will continue this story in my next time together with you. Meanwhile, why not listen to the very voice of Mr. Kim as he reads from the first chapters of Matthew, presents a Bible drama about those chapters, and then reads from Richard Wurmbrand's "Tortured for Christ."

One thing: It's all in the Korean language, North Korean dialect. Listen as long as you can, but please tell your Korean friends about this exciting man and his message, and yes, pray for his safety and encouragement. One million North Koreans can tune him in every day! Can you imagine how powerfully Jesus Christ is being represented in North Korea this very day? What a breakthrough! What an opportunity!

Go to sermonaudio.com, look for "He talks to a Million Every Day."

238. More of the Kim drama

Who needs TV & movies when real-live action dramas with exceptional heroes are placed before us by the Spirit of God in His Church? I speak today of "Mr. Kim", whose testimony I began in my last article. You will recall he was on a train nearing a certain death by execution for having betrayed his military calling in North Korea . He has just jumped from the train...

"As the train disappeared from sight, I was flattened on the ground, but without any harm to my body. I found myself crying out to the Lord over and over, 'God, there is *no comparison* between You and Kim Jung-il! Thank You for saving me!' And I asked Him to - please - help me escape from this hellish country, and into China once more.

"Even with my face on wanted posters, I escaped back to the church in China where I had previously been. I was a wanted man, but the church welcomed me again, unconditionally, and I began to try to lead a faithful walk with the Lord.

"People around me said, 'You met Jesus when you escaped from the train,' and other such things, but I know that I did not really meet Him and put my trust in Him until just last year, a full *10 years* after I jumped off that train.

"After I came to South Korea , I completed my undergraduate and graduate degrees and was selected as the president of the NK defectors association. I became also a National Broadcasting writer. In 2004, I founded 'Freedom NK broadcasting.'

"Then one day I met a Pastor F. and, his wife. They were devoted to NK ministry. They reminded me that I should not forget the people I left behind. So I began to develop ideas about how to minister to North Koreans living in NK.

"One idea was to start a photo studio. Here, underground believers could earn a living, share the Gospel, network with other believers. All we had to do was raise $2.00 U.S. for each worker each month. They could charge 10 cents a color photo. It wasn't a lot of money, but even this amount could give some stability to a believer give them opportunities to meet with others like themselves.

"Yes, there were still believers all over NK, many of whom had kept their faith for nearly half a century, resisting the ideology forced on them. It is also sadly true that most North Korean Christians have been slaughtered over the last 50 years. The ones who remained have been kicked out to the countryside, essentially abandoned by the government. It was some of these folks that Pastor and Mrs. F. approached about a photo studio.

"These believers were still a worshiping people. Though they ran a risk every moment, they continued to meet and worship and pray for their nation to be awakened. They even videotaped some of their meetings so that they could share with people outside their nation, their faith in the Lord. And now they had a way to share it with unsuspecting customers at their own business, a photo studio.

"One day we received word from a Korean-Chinese deacon that believers in several towns where we were working had been arrested. North Korean news broadcasts at that time, this past September 5th, announced that they had arrested spies from a foreign state department as well as spies from North Korea . They produced a "confession" of such, and even showed the equipment we had supplied for the photo studio. Those accused "spies" were our brothers and sisters in Jesus Christ.

"All of the materials I had bought and sent to North Korea through believers outside the nation were being called spy materials. Our worshiping brothers and sisters who prayed right under the nose of the totalitarian state were now being prosecuted as spies.

"I flew immediately to the NK-China border and tried to save even one of these people. I appealed with tears to Pastor and Mrs. F. and asked how we could help these underground Christians who now faced public execution. I cried out in prayer with my workers, but the only news I received was that the situation was hopeless.

"Then, in China , I received word of the final prayer prayed by the believer who had been in charge of the project in one of the cities. He prayed, "Lord, please forgive me. All the people got arrested. I cannot escape for the sake of only my life. Lord, I will remain and die in order to share your story with the North Korean government."

Like I said, you can have "American Idol" and "Dancing with the Stars" and "Lost" if it means that much to you. But as for me, I desperately need to hear and follow the Christ who is in North Korea , suffering still. For, though the price for our sins was paid in full on Calvary, the price of getting that message to the world will keep being paid until -enough is enough!- Jesus in Body and in full authority comes to take all of North Korea and all of this planet for Himself.

Until then, we go "outside the camp" to where He suffers and calls for us to join Him. As you have heard and read several times on this blog, we need North Korea much more than they need us. They understand the message of the crucified life. I don't think I do. What about you?

Mr. Kim's story continues next time.

239. Again, Mr. Kim

So, you've just encouraged a bunch of brothers and sisters to serve the Lord a little more openly. Because of your great idea for service, they all get arrested. Great feeling. That's what Mr. Kim, the radio evangelist whose story we conclude today, had to deal with when his "photo studio" plan disintegrated. From a talk he gave not long ago at a Voice of the Martyrs gathering:

"I found myself blaming God, who had permitted them to be sent to a concentration camp, though He is all-powerful and could have prevented it. I cried out so much I thought I'd go crazy, when I realized I'd probably never see my brothers and sisters again. I even wanted to curse Pastor F. who got me into all of this to begin with.

" Then Pastor F. called. I did not want to talk. But he asked me to open the Bible with him and pray. I thought, 'Pastor, these people are dying now. What does it matter if we pray for them now? No one can save them!' While I was trying to stop those words from coming out of my mouth, I heard the Word of God coming through the phone...

" 'But I have prayed for you, that your faith should not fail; and when you have returned to me, strengthen your brothers,' the pastor was reading. (Luke 22:32)

"I knew immediately that the voice and the message were from God, not from a human being. It wasn't some American pastor I was hearing, but it was Jesus Himself, and His Word became my cornerstone. Yes, I had complained about the Lord 'sitting by' while others suffered. But He said to me, 'I am the One Who set you on your feet, and I am the One Who will guard your faith.'

"That's when I was born again as a son of God. That's when my heart began to desire to share the message of love with NK defectors around me. I called on them to join me and those other brothers and sisters in laying down our lives for North Korea .

"God has blessed this group of defectors. We are in the center of North Korea missions, literally launching flyers [tracts] into the country via helium balloons, and broadcasting the gospel through short-wave radio into North Korea .

"Yes, we hear that the primary challenge facing NK is that they are starving to death. But I believe that even more they need the Word of God and songs of praise.

"Recently the NK government spent $900,000 for an 'eternal shrine' to Kim Il-sung. But they say they have no money for rice. That same government threatens the world by making nuclear weapons, yet there are mountains of dead people who were told the government could not support them. So we announce to this government and its people the living God, Who will expose their idolatry and blanket the land with hope and freedom.

"Some criticize our work, both the balloon launches and our broadcasting. You can imagine that the NK government is not too happy with these things. But a growing number of young South Koreans have begun to believe the lies of the North, and they criticize too.

"But we know that the Holy Spirit and His people in VOM and elsewhere are beginning to touch the hearts of the North Korean people. We are the first to share the Good News in the North Korean dialect. People who don't live on the Korean peninsula may not realize the huge differences there are in the northern and southern speaking and vocabulary, including even the very name for God!

" Culture differences are great too. Think of the difference between Russians and Americans, then think even more. Remember that North and South have been segregated for the past 60 years and have been carefully taught to treat each other as bitter enemies.

"But as North Koreans ministering to North Koreans, the language and culture differences do not exist. That is why we can touch their heart with the 30,000 flyers launched via balloon, and with the daily broadcast, 'The Voice of Freedom'. Sometime this very day many many will hear the words, 'Now you are hearing the gospel, broadcasting in the North Korean language through the Voice of Freedom.' Imagine it. These words daily fill the vast empty space of North Korean hearts.

"We have gone through a deadly difficult time, from 'hell' to 'heaven.' And through the ministry you have enabled us to have, we have been reborn from slaves into the sons and daughters of God. Each step we take is a testimony to the people back in our hometowns.

"Pastors, Missionaries, VOM staff, and everyone here:

"Please pray for each flyer. Please pray for each broadcast. Please pray that God will allow the NK people who are experiencing such bitter lives to come to know the Word of God and the love of God. And please pray endlessly for Pastor and Mrs. F., VOM, and all of the NK missionaries who live with the mind of sacrifice, like the pain of bone scraping against bone and skin being torn from body, for the sake of dying souls. I thank you from the bottom of my heart."

Amen and amen. Join "Mr. Kim" daily here on Sermonaudio, as we will be presenting his 30-minute broadcasts just as they are heard in North Korea daily! The name to look for is " North Korea Radio Broadcast."

240. when the time is right

Someone's been taking care of Kim Jong-il's people in North Korea. Someone has surrounded the nation with intercessions to God. Someone has found the exits for many thousands of her citizens. That same Someone has been at the other end of the journey as refugees run to China-based Christians. Someone has been sending in food and clothes and Bibles and tracts.

That Someone is of course Jesus. Mr. Kim needs to know that the Jesus he squelches and Whose Word he consigns to the flames or the garbage is the very One who is caring for North Koreans day and night. That's Who Jesus is. That's the kind of thing He does.

Do we think for one moment that our God is emaciated and weak like the starving Koreans that Kim enslaves? That He is unable to rise up and with the breath of His mouth incinerate Pyongyang in a moment? He has done too many mighty works for us to think that.

There is a show of strength that is even greater than the meting out of deserved judgment. It is the restraint of a loving God Who will do nothing before the exact time has arrived. It is a God Who waits for people to repent, as He waited for the evil Canaanites, then the Egyptians, the Babylonians, the Romans.

All great powers have been given their chance to change, but eventually judgment came. And in the midst of all their prospering, God was prospering too. Inside Egypt, inside Babylon, inside Rome and subsequent Romanism, God grew His people. Then He manifested to the world what He was doing, and received the glory for what He had done.

Someone needs to tell the Kim government that their power is granted them only for a time. God is even now growing a people inside those prison walls. Inside every concentration camp, every jail, every holding center for repatriated citizens, are some of the People of God. Their moment of manifestation will come. The government will fall. God's people will rise. History is clear. God's Word is always more powerful than the chains of men.

On an even grander scale, the Bible says that the entire planet is awaiting the manifestation of the Sons of God. We are a people in exile. We are the scum now, though a few of our people seem to shine and be acceptable. By and large our message, our Christ, is rejected, hated, beaten, imprisoned.

But the One Who behind the scenes has been our Healer, our Provider, our Comforter, will one day make not only His people appear, but Himself. He will return, judgment will fall, and we will be caught up to Him to reign over the planet.

A fairy-tale ending? Of course. Where did the fairy tales ever get such ideas in the first place? From the hope that springs eternal in the promises of God. We really do win, Mr. Kim. Evil really shall be rewarded. God's people really will shine forever.

Be patient, people of God. Force is not an option for us. Neither is defeat. Give it to God. He will bring the outward victory in His time. He will give you the inner victory this very day.

241. convicted in a nk jail

The stories keep coming in. Following is a relatively recent account of a prisoner of the Kim Jong-il regime. Much of it will seem familiar to those who have read this column often. But surely the workings of God in each North Korean are individual. Consider:

Peter [name changed], a North Korean, lived as a refugee in China, where he was found by the security police and sent back to North Korea. Oh, and he was arrested with his family, that is, with his wife and his *six-year-old daughter*.

His wife had been a believer since her days in North Korea. Her mother, likewise a believer in Jesus, had waited until she was 16 years of age to share about Jesus with her. It is not safe for a child to bear such precious information, reason North Korea's believing parents. Peter became a believer after they all came to China.

Now, anyone sent back to North Korea from China is always asked two questions:

Did you meet any South Koreans there?

and

Did you go to church there?

Peter said "no" to both questions. I ask you, reader, what would you have said? Is it not a proper thing to tell untruths to persons such as these are, who destroy lives for no reason? Read on.

While he was incarcerated, a new prisoner was brought in. He was a Chinese man who had come from inland China to North Korea for the expressed purpose of *evangelizing North Koreans*, even though he *could not speak Korean well.* Such love from God! He was arrested.

When Peter heard of the Chinese man's story, he was convicted in his heart. He realized that, like the apostle called Peter, he too was denying Christ. First he said he had not met any South Koreans, but especially, he denied going to church while in China.

He confessed his lies to an officer . The officer began torturing him saying, "Even if you would deny Jesus now, we won't let you go." Peter said, "I will continue to evangelize and will never deny Jesus in my heart."

So he told people in the prison about the Savior. And despite the on-going torture by the guard, he experienced joy and developed a hope that he would go to heaven quickly.

Instead, he was *released* and witnessed to his entire family, who have now been saved, and have started an underground church. Peter now lives in South Korea.

Being willing to die does not always bring death. Being anxious to live does not always bring life. What is important for all of us is, What is the perfect will of God for my life? Thank you, "Peter", for sharing your story with us and for being true to Jesus.

242. brother john and the airborne messengers

The following interview report came to my attention recently. It provides valuable insights as to the effect Christ's church is having in North Korea.

We [the source of my information, a Christian group

sending flyers into North Korea] interviewed Brother John, a North Korean refugee who now lives in Los Angeles. While in North Korea, he encountered several flyers [we might call them "tracts"] launched from South Korea. (These are the same type of flyers as VOM now launches.) We asked him how he obtained them, what the contents were, and his thoughts on the effectiveness of flyers. His reply is below:

"The first time I saw a flyer from South Korea was in the early 1990's at *xxx,* where I had gone to do some business. Any flyers that land on the road or in villages are supposed to be brought to the National Security Agency (*Bowiboo*). Whenever I found a flyer, I of course went to a mountain or a quiet plain to read it.

"Flyers from South Korea containing messages against the North Korean political system are common. Anyone who finds one of these must not read them. They must crumble up the flyer and put it in their pocket immediately. If they read the flyer or spread any of its contents, they will be severely punished.

"At the time, I thought the contents of the flyer were stupid. One of the flyers I found told about South Korean people eating meat, and the amount of food a person would eat in a year in South Korea. Another flyer had a picture of some defectors' wedding in a splendid place in the South. I saw those and I thought it was futile because North Korean people already know about all of these things. Also, some North Korean people who read that flyer with me scolded the defector in the picture saying, 'They are scum, because their family is still starving here while they have a feast and look like they are happy.' I took the flyer to the National Security Agency (*Bowiboo*).

"The people in South Korea sending these flyers may think these are great, but I think they are pathetic because we read them with a North Korean mindset. On the contrary, some flyers even seem to help communism."

We asked Brother John about the North's knowledge about reality in the South, and what he thinks about the flyer we are using in our balloon project. We sent the contents of our flyer. His answer is below:

"No North Korean I know of thinks that South Korea is poorer than North Korea. If there are, those people are really, really pathetic. On the contrary, NK people know about the reality in SK even if the stories have been exaggerated. I list here North Korean classes by how knowledgeable they are about South Korea's wealth (from most knowledge to least knowledge):

1. Communism Executives
2. Regional Government Officers
3. College students & Intellectuals
4. Wealthy class
5. Laborers
6. Farmers

"I will also talk about your flyer and what I honestly think of it.

"First, if the contents of a flyer are too long, it will not be effective. Second, the actual content of your flyer is really great! Lastly, I think it has the easiest and plainest explanation that I have ever seen compared to other religious flyers."

He also said: "Some missionaries who disciple North Korean people in China don't prepare them enough, but then give them some money so they can return to NK. I have never criticized this, but the problem is that money has a big influence on NK people. Almost all of the victims are poor North Korean people, especially homeless people. They want to earn money in order to live in NK. So when they hear about South Korean missionaries in China offering money, they spend time with these missionaries, pretending to be believers, in order to return to North Korea with some money. Many of these peoples' stories end with their execution by the NK government. Because of the execution of Christians in North Korea (due to their contact with missionaries in China), many NK people hate SK missionaries more than the North Korean government. So NK people (who are not Christian) think that Christians are fools because they think Christians don't consider this life as precious, instead choosing to focus on religious nonsense such as 'Eternal Life'. NK non-Christians think this is due to the 'ignorant' South Korean missionaries' teachings."

So, another prayer request: Will you ask God for wisdom regarding how and when and where to send the Gospel into North Korea? Since the Spirit first fell on Pentecost, God's people have been going into all the world with the Gospel. But that same Spirit still needs to be the guiding force in all we do. And that guidance comes through your prayers.

243. stories from mrs im

This story comes to the House of Chosun from "sources."

When the translator saw Mrs Im, she told us that she was surprised at how well she looked. When she had first met her upon arriving in SK, she was very thin, had missing teeth and her hair was very brittle and light colored (from malnutrition). When she saw her this time, she had put on a little weight, had her teeth fixed and her hair was dark and healthy looking.

Mrs. Im is a 65 year old woman originally from North Korea. She came to know the Lord in 1990. She did not hear about God from any person, but in her dreams. One of her family members died and she felt sorry and confused. She said, "One night, I dreamed of my dead family member and wanted to change the clothes that he was wearing in the coffin. When I first looked at him, I saw a rotted body. As I watched, I saw the man revive; his skin was restored and red color came back into his lips. When I awoke, I wondered what the dream meant. I went to my neighbor [Mrs. Im did not know her neighbor was a Christian] and told her about the dream because I was anxious about it and wanted to know its meaning. When I shared the dream with my neighbor, her interpretation was that that God would revive the spirit of the North Korean people. My neighbor also shared the gospel with me and I accepted it totally."

When asked how knowing the Lord changed her life, Mrs. Im responded, "Before becoming a Christian, I was afraid of many things. After I came to know Jesus, He made me strong and I was reminded that God protects His people. It was like tasting honey." Mrs. Im stated that when her neighbor shared that Jesus would be returning, she was so excited that she could not sleep. "I was so happy and simply believed."

Mrs. Im went on to share about the situation of Christians in North Korea. "The NK government searches out Christians in order to persecute them. Even one word about God, if the government hears about it, could mean that the person who mentioned His name would 'disappear'." People in North Korea also are always on guard because people are always watching to see what everyone is doing. If seen doing any of the following three things, the police are called and the person is arrested:

       1) If there is a group of people seen traveling together (meaning perhaps a meeting is going on).

       2) If people are caught giving money to someone, this is seen as suspicious especially if the person is not rich. Christians often give sacrificially to those in need.

       3) If someone looks like they are praying, this also warrants a call to police.

In all 3 of these situations, the police arrest people who they think are Christians.

Then Mrs. Im shared about several North Korean incidents . In the mid 90's she heard of an incident where the government caught a Christian group (around 300 people). One old woman was a missionary to these people. The police caught every one of them, including some as young as 19 and 20, and asked them whether they would deny God or not. If they denied God they would be free. No one denied Him, and all were shot to death. She said that believers are few in NK, but they are strong.

Another incident happened around 2000. After a very heavy rain that washed away a lot of soil, someone found a bag of New Testaments which were buried under a pine tree and reported this to the police. The police started searching door-to-door for who they suspected was a Christian. Several people were arrested and disappeared.

At a recent meeting Mrs. Im attended at a South Korean church, a SK pastor shared about the time he attended one of the show churches in NK, and how he saw people singing and crying. He was moved by them, but Mrs. Im was angry because he had been deceived; she knew these were actors.

When asked how Christians can pray for NK, Mrs Im said, "Like Elijah, who thought that he was the only survivor of all God's prophets, but was encouraged when God told him about the 7,000 people who did not bow the knee to Baal, please pray for NK believers that they would not bow their knee but remain strong and encouraged and believe God will protect them."

She worries about North Koreans who give false testimonies, telling lies about how they have been Christian living in NK. Spies for NK in SK report this information to NK, then police search for and arrest Christians in the area.

She is reluctant to share her testimony in public in order to protect Christians in NK. She emphasized that, "we must take care with NK missions so as not to endanger NK Christians." She is concerned about SK missionaries who train NKs as missionaries and send them back to NK. She thinks in general, "the missionaries don't understand enough about the situation in Norh Korea and basically send people back to NK to die."

Please join those of us who have decided not to wait to serve the Koreans, but are praying constantly for their deliverance and salvation. What a great day is coming!

244. christ of the korean heart

When my book was mailed to me, I retrieved it much like a dog who has just been thrown a juicy bone, or a squirrel who has found a choice acorn. I wanted to get away with it and savor every word. This was one I just knew I would love. I think you will enjoy it too.

Arch Campbell was a pioneer missionary to Korea from 1916. He became the president of Kei Myung Christian College and the Theological Seminary of the Presbyterian Church of Korea. More importantly, Arch Campbell loved

Jesus and the Koreans with all of his heart, and he was there during the great trials of the War Years.

The brother who wrote the foreword to this book said that "few men have the God-given combination of effectiveness in soul-winning, vision of the world's spiritual famine, and ability to tell of the pulsating events of the mission fields" as Dr. Campbell.

He goes on, "The chapters of this book are destined to awaken missionary zeal under the blessings of the precious Holy Spirit. I unhesitatingly commend it to every lover of the Lord Jesus Christ."

And I add in this day, a full 54 years after its publication date, that lovers of the North Korean people should consider this classic book as "must" reading too.

I was able to track it down at Amazon. A good Google search will be well worth your time.

Can I quote only the first paragraph to whet your appetite for more:

"Amid the rubble and ruin of Korea's blasted and burned cities (1954), in the crowded squalor of the refugee camps, in the bleak and bare makeshift army hospitals, along the dusty roads, through the narrow alleys of the hastily rebuilt mud villages, in the congested, odoriferous markets, and in the crumbling bunkers and dugouts of the stalemate-battle front walks the Lord Jesus Christ today...enshrined in the hearts of hundreds of thousands who know Him...

"...Although He treads the crowded or the lonely thoroughfares, he is not just the Christ of the Korean Road. He is the *Christ of the Korean Heart.*"

And from there, Dr. Campbell goes on to prove his point with story after story of the faithfulness of Christ during years of the horrors of men.

I do hope you will find this book!

245. a prisoner chosen of God

Following is a translation of a recent testimony received from sources I shall not name. We shall call this precious woman "Mrs. Park" and rejoice with her in what God has done.

Why is the military dictatorship on a rampage in North Korea? Why have innocent people in North Korea died without any word? The reason is that Kim Jong-il thinks he is higher than God and reigns over the land. For me, I praise and worship God, who chose me out of 23 million North Koreans , out of six billion of the world's population, and is training me.

Before, I could not find anything to be thankful for, but now I am thankful for everything around me because I have met the new Shepherd in my life.

I was born as the youngest daughter, in beautiful North Korea. My hometown was in a lovely setting. The home in which we lived was a thatched- roof house with a well that was over 10 meters deep and had really cold and refreshing water even in mid-summer.

Because I was the youngest child, people often think I received a lot of love by my siblings and parents, but this was not the case. Since we were so poor, I didn't get that much attention. My mother suffered a lot from supporting so many children by herself.

Often we were hungry. I still remember vividly when my older brother climbed a pear tree to pick unripe pears for me when I cried with hunger. The pears hit my head, and I ended up crying even more.

After my childhood, our family had to move because my father had been demoted. In fact, we had to move out in the middle of the night.

I went to four years of elementary school and then on to middle school. When my father passed away, our family moved again. I graduated from middle school and went on to college. I graduated college with the top honors in three years. I was then assigned to an elementary school. I was promoted to senior teacher with an elementary school teacher's license.

In the meantime, I met my husband and started a family. We moved because my husband was transferred. For awhile, I actually had a happy home with a son and daughter.

I worked for a time in an office job, but because of health problems that occurred from giving birth, I had to stay at home . Then government assigned me to yet another duty when I was able.

The economy of North Korea began to suffer severely. Then my husband died of serious illness. I tried hard to support my family, but if the whole country is poor, how can one family be well off?

My son was an athlete. But when he returned home from his training, he was a mere malnourished skeleton. Looking at my starving son, my heart was broken. I could not feed him even a bowl of rice.

The government stopped food rationing in 1996, so everyone was barely managing to live off the roots of grass and the bark of trees. I would hear every morning that someone's father died or someone's child died or a whole family died. There were countless human remains on the streets.

They say that "even a king becomes a thief in the face of hunger."

I had to take action. I left my crying son, who wanted to come with me, and bought him five kilograms of corn noodles, a half of a kilogram of salt, and two kilograms of radish leaves. I told him that I would come back in five days. I then crossed into China. How could I know that that would be the last time I would be with my son? I still choke back tears when I think of him.

I tried to find my relatives in China, but I found that one had already died and some had gone to South Korea. I was at the end of my rope. Fortunately, one of my distant relatives helped me find work. I experienced the saying, "It is better to be a dog than to live in a strange place without a country." But I could endure all kinds of suffering and pain motivated by thoughts of my children and my land back home.

I tried to find another job, but I was caught by the Chinese police. I was sent back to North Korea in handcuffs. I had betrayed my country and its citizens.

In a forced training camp that specializes in brainwashing and hard work , I labored from 5AM to 10 PM. I also had to sit through speeches on ideology as part of my re-education each night. They did not let me sleep and made me stand up all night if I would not publicly confess my faults. They hit me and I had to say, "I was wrong, I committed a capital crime."

I was given only a few dried radish leaves and a bowl of corn-meal soup a day.

While starving, in coldness, in the forced training camp, I found out that my son was already dead. When I received this piece of news, I fainted. I had to stay in bed for five months in the training camp.

After my release, they allowed me to recover and be nursed at home. Training camp officers came to check on me every day, and officials came and asked me who I met and what I talked about with people in China. Because of the constant harassment, I decided to escape to China again. I made my way to China, but again was caught by Chinese police and sent back to North Korea. The only thing that I had done wrong was crossing the border because I had no way to meet my basic living requirements.

I want to try to share my experiences about my time in the concentration camp, but they are indescribable. North Koreans wince at the mere mention of "work camp"...

... We ate only a bowl of corn soup which had less than 100 kernels. We had to make bricks and cement and carry stones from 7 AM to 7 PM. The manager of the work camp said that people who betrayed our country deserved to die and should not be pitied. Even dogs in the work camp lived better than we did.

People in the camps die every day and while I was there, scores of men and women died. Guards wrapped the dead bodies with straw bags. North Korea is stained by the blood of many people who have died without tombstones. I bow to honor the many deceased who while starving and exhausted, died without complaining.

Because I was extremely hungry, I ate bean leaves, pig grass and all sorts of other grasses which are not supposed to be edible. My job was to run with a stretcher and if I slowed down to walk even a little, guards would hit and kick me. They would hit me with the butt of a gun and blood would spurt from my head. There was no one to hear our complaints.

It is likewise indescribable how severely guards treat pregnant women. They would mock them saying, "You are carrying Chinese men's babies," and then kick and hit them. They even made pregnant women do the same harsh labor as the rest of us. When they gave birth, guards put the baby's face down and let them die. The pregnant women were forced to resume working right after giving birth with a bloody lower body. How tragic it is for those dead babies who had never been wrapped in cloth and had never sucked their mother's breast!

There was a family who tried to escape and was caught. Guards beat the wife in front of her husband, and hit children in front of their parents.

For others, they would tie girls' hands together and would trample and cut their hair at random. They were beasts beyond imagination. The detention room did not have any heat and there were layers of frost on the wall. Peoples' fingers and toes would become so frozen that they could not even stand up.

I was escorted from a work camp to a detention house. There , I had to get up at 6 AM and go to bed at 9 PM. All that time I had to sit, putting my hands on my knees and bending my waist at a 45 degree angle. If I moved my body just a little, guards would hit me with a square wooden stick until it broke.

I was in a death cell. Twice a month, criminals were executed by firing squad. Condemned criminals had to prepare the wooden post which they were tied to when they were shot. How my heart felt for them when I saw the criminals carrying the wooden posts and going to their death. It is something that someone who has not experienced it can understand. When the guards would come to the death cell and call the criminals' names on the day they were to be executed, my heart would freeze with terror and some people would even faint.

The criminals who tried to escape to South Korea or who were caught on the way to South Korea had to suffer more than other criminals. Even those criminals' families and relatives were forced to go to the state security department prison or were sent to an uninhabited island.

A woman who tried to go with her son to South Korea to find their relatives was arrested and sent to the state department detention house for eight months. Then, she was sent to a cell designated for life sentences and I have not heard from her since.

Finally, on February 16th, 2002, Jeong Il Kim admitted that people who tried to escape from North Korea, escaped because they could not meet their basic living requirements, not because they were rebelling against North Korea. Consequently, he ordered the release of those who had tried to escape and had been caught. As a result, everyone in the forced training camps and work camps was released .

As I look back upon that time, I realize it was all a part of God's plans.

Knowing God and loving God is now my biggest joy. It is not long till the day when God's presence will be felt in North Korea, and the people will know God, and church bells will ring. I want to live for Jesus and I believe that God will give me the ability to manage an evangelical ministry.

246. enter the baekjeong

The Koreans say "백정," that's *baekjeong* to us, or if you prefer, *paekchong*. Who are they, and why in the world am I writing about them? Good questions, and deserving of a good answer. Let me try.

Question one: "Member of the lowest class of old Korean society. Executioners (that's pretty low). Grave Diggers (lower still, but somebody's gotta do it). Butchers (no offense, butchers of the world, but in some societies meat-eating is not cool).Leather workers (same problem!). And there's another word I'm not free to print.

So there you have it. Now the answer to your second question becomes even more difficult. Why devote space to persons such as these?

Well, let's just say it's an old family tradition. Now, the oldest family on earth is God's. We can say 4,000 years old if we want to start with Abraham. And from the beginning, and all the way down to modern-day North Korea, (although "modern" and "North Korea" may not sound too well together), God has had this *tradition* of pulling up *baekjeong* from nowhere and bringing them somewhere. From nothing, making something.

Whoever said "Out of nothing, nothing comes," didn't know our God!

God loves these "members of the lowest class", these "untouchables", these *unspeakables,* these folks... well let's just say we might not invite them to dinner. But they're crowding around His table all the time. We might as well get into the flow. And what better place to begin than North Korea?

Look what God did with a bunch of southward-bound refugees on that peninsula! Back in the 40's and 50's, terrible tragedies pushed many of God's people and a whole lot of people that were not His into some new turf. For a long while South Korea hung in the balance. But Christ, at first Himself a *baekjeong* of Korea, lonely, unknown, has now become , as missionary Arch Campbell put it, "enshrined in the hearts of hundreds of thousands who know Him as an intimate friend... who love Him with a deep passion seldom found in the sophisticated West."

This Christ was preached and this Christ was accepted by these terribly poor and terribly unacceptable (by the world's standards). And now? Some of the biggest churches in the world grace that small but mighty Korean nation.

Just think what will happen when Christ is given His due place among the northern *baekjeong*. Oh my, do I want to see that!

Next week, a baekjeong story. Then you judge for yourself what God just might want to do...*maybe through you?*

247. how close can you get to a tiger?

I suppose the entire question of my entry today ought to continue... "before you get mauled?"

I started getting into tigers a few years ago when I found a Wal-Mart bigger-than-life poster of a tiger's head. That thing has been glaring back at me all these months, to my wife's regular disapproval. I've actually had to hide him in the walk-in closet. He's that intense.

Then came North Korea. Some of you may know that the Siberian tiger is one of that country's national symbols. A fitting one. Fierce. Aloof. Threatening. And beautiful. Like that Wal-Mart poster, North Korea has been staring me down, challenging me to stare back and wonder.

Next there was the Lincoln Park Zoo. Twice in the last few weeks I've made a trek over there just to get away for a day. Both times I was captivated by this very cat from the East. In fact, on one end of his area there is a place where observers can look through a glass barrier . Most don't go there because Kitty is usually prowling around somewhere else, if he's awake.

But occasionally he paces. Every time I saw him this week he was pacing. Back and forth. Back and forth. And for one magical quarter of an hour, he paced right next to the window. It's hard being my age at these times. Occasionally I actually do get excited about something, but I'm not allowed to show it. As quickly as I decently could I scrambled - no, just walked - over to the window. As people tired and moved on, I moved in, and within a short time I practically had my nose on that glass.

The tiger did better. Every time he came to where I was standing, he actually bumped his head on that window, then moved on in his circuit, 'round and 'round. I was literally one inch from one of the fiercest of all God's creation. And yet I lived to tell of it.

The people crowding in were making growl sounds and pretending their hands were paws, you know the drill. Mothers were teaching their children. Teens were impressing their friends with noises and gestures. Ol' Bob stood there in awe.

If the friendly cat had bumped that glass a little harder, and the smallest crack had formed, we all would have been lunch for pussy-cat. As it was, we were just an audience being entertained.

It hit me days later that many of us are involved in a spectator sport when it comes to North Korea. We read the stories, we visit China and South Korea, we give our money, we even pray, and we might even think we understand the animal on the other side of the glass. But we don't.

There is no way to know what people who live in a "tiger's" world feel, on the other side of a zoo window. "Remember the prisoners as if bound with them" may be one of the toughest commands ever issued. How can I really feel what they feel? Skip a meal? Pray a little more? Wear old clothes? Beat myself? Abandon all media?

Who among us dares to enter other worlds, as did our Lord? Who goes beyond the glass and suffers whatever consequences there might be? Until we do, we may be good story-tellers, good fund-raisers, teary-eyed romantics who feel imaginary pain, but we must not conclude that therefore we have taken up the cross which Jesus has our brothers carrying.

I trust I am not being too harsh. Zoos are for looking, and looking is a good thing. But eventually we must, I believe, shed the zoo mentality, go out into the field, and confront a tiger. Mauled or not.

248. escaping nk

In January of 2003, Mike Kim, successful Korean-American businessman, left for China on a one-way ticket. He moved to the border of North Korea and dug in for the next four years, determined to learn and report what was happening there. The result of his labor is *Escaping North Korea* [not to be confused with *Escape from North Korea* put out by Open Doors, which we have also featured], an exciting and up-dated tale of the ongoing tragedy we call "Chosun".

Mike has given me permission to quote excerpts from his book, and I plan to do it. But I'd like to recommend that you just go ahead and buy the book for yourself before we begin enjoying it together. It's one of those "no-doubters", if I may borrow from baseball terminology the reference to a ball that has been hit so well that the crowd knows it's a home run.

I do not say that you will enjoy the book. Books like this should never be enjoyed. You will be troubled by it. But the story it tells needs to be treasured in the heart, and its contents poured out to a loving God Who alone has the answers to this land. With that in mind, let us begin a journey together using Mike Kim, Korean, as a guide.

I challenge my readers to try what Mike tried, a visit of your own. See if it affects you in the same way it affected Mike. On a preliminary trip to China-Korea, Mike...

"...returned to the States a bit shaken from what I had experienced. I distinctly remember sitting across from clients talking about mutual funds, retirement plans, and insurance while feeling disengaged from it all. The 'underground' house churches in China and the North Korean refugees weighed heavily on my heart."

He began praying for the land, and eventually had to go back for a much longer visit. Something about the place gets to you...

His report begins by examining the North Korean mind, the whole subject of brainwashing that this blog has frequently covered. While taking *tae kwon do* lessons, his North Korean teacher told him of anti-American games played in class:

"Sometimes the teacher hung up a picture representing America. Then when the teacher signaled, all of the children in class took a sharp object, charged at the picture screaming at the top of their lungs, and then ripped it up. During wintertime, I remember the teacher telling us to make two snowmen. On one snowman we wrote 'America', and on the other we wrote 'Japan.'.. " Screaming, with sticks in their hands, they would charge at the snowmen and break them.

Hatred, pure hatred. A taught life-style. Let us continue to pray that God's love will be allowed into North Korea, that His message will shatter the darkness and bring a new day.

More of Mike Kim's stirring stories soon...

249. *we lead very happy lives*

If a North Korean citizen said that to you, would you believe it? I guess I've read too much. I wouldn't. But countless people in that nation have either been brainwashed into believing it, or say it from fearful obedience to their "Dear" leader.

So I read in Mike Kim's new book *Escaping North Korea* . Used by permission, I quote several other examples of propagandized minds... men, women, and children whose brain has been stolen by their government.

"When visiting North Korea, at every turn you will find some sort of propaganda posted on the streets...signs... 'Hail Great Kim Il Sung!' 'If the Communist party decides it, we will do it,' 'Let's beat America with a big iron stick.' "

I remember similar smatterings of poison when I visited Communist Romania in the 80's. No surer way to befoul a scenic drive...

I have shared with you in this blog some of the outlandish stories that are passed along as truth. Mike adds to my collection...

This first one is via a tour guide in Chongjin: "Shortly after winning our independence from Japan, Kim Jong Suk came to this spot [where the tour is standing] when she was 30 years old, two years before she died. All the people gathered and said, 'We have heard that you are a good shot. Will you please demonstrate for us?' Do you see that big memorial stone over there? If you take a close look you will see a hole in the rock made from a bullet. Kim Jong Suk once came to this spot when she was thirty years old and shot five bullets at that stone. There is only one bullet mark because the first one hit the stone and the other four bullets hit the same exact spot."

A member of the group, not quite convinced, suggested that another way to look at it was that she missed four shots. The group enjoyed that one. The tour guide didn't.

My favorite story in this chapter concerns a meeting in Seoul between two diplomats, one from the North, the other from the South. As the two were riding into Seoul, the NK diplomat noticed "the city bustling with construction and traffic."

His astute observation: "We're not stupid, you know. It's obvious you've ordered all the cars in the country to be brought into Seoul to fool us." His South Korean counterpart, known for his sense of humor, replied, "Well... that was the easy part. The hard part was moving in all the buildings."

Fed on lies, you will deceive others. Given the Truth, you spread that. Our constant prayer is that the Truth of the Gospel will keep permeating this ever-so-needy land.

250. out of the shadow of death

If Jesus and the disciples were baekjeong, *(outcasts, lowest dregs of society, worthy of misery and death) why am I not? I say I love Him, know Him. But even if I travel to a restricted country, I am usually honored in some way. If these thoughts are beginning to irritate you at times, maybe you are being called alongside the* baekjeong *of our own day, like this one in modern North Korea:*

I was a boy living in the shadow of death, starving and despairing in North Korea. Before I escaped from that land, I lived with my parents and a younger brother. But without rations or food, my family was about to starve to death. So my parents left home to make money. They said they would be back in a couple of days. They never returned. My 14-year-old brother started to cry out for food.

I stayed home and sent my brother to our grandfather's. But he soon had to come back when grandfather died of an illness for which he could do nothing. Shortly after, my brother also died after suffering in the house with no parents present. My heart wrung. I felt it unfair, so I wept a lot. The world seemed pitiless and my parents, reproachful.

Left alone, I waited for my mother and father, but eventually had to wander around for food, begging sometimes, picking anything off the ground that might be useful. I drifted into various towns by train. One day, I got off at a station, and decided to go over to China.

On a dark rainy night in 2001, I crossed the river, very hungry, leaving my parents behind in their miserable situation. I was so weak from hunger and illness, that I started to be carried down the fast-flowing stream. I closed my eyes, thinking that I would die trying to save my life! I'd never see either my homeland or my parents again. But no, I narrowly escaped death. I crossed over something solid, and when I laid my feet on it, I found it was a rock. I came back to myself and reached shore. When I look back, I see that God saved me so that I would spread the Gospel to dying North Korea, and show His love and grace.

After I survived the river, I begged for food in China. At one Chinese-Korean home, they said they didn't want to see North Koreans anymore, and threatened to report me to the police. My opinion of China soon changed. I have always heard that food is abundant in China, but I was being rejected, turned away. It seemed so unfair.

I had walked for a long time when I met an old Chinese-Korean couple. I begged for food. They asked if I was from North Korea. When I said yes, they took me home, gave me food and money, and told me to go to church. I thanked them and walked to another town instead.

I met North Korean kids there, and started to live with them. We sustained our lives by begging for food from Koreans at parks and bridge-heads. This is illegal activity. One day, my friends and I got caught. While in jail, I met a Christian defector. I thought it absurd that he would be praying and singing praises in a prison, but he was.

It was the first time that I had ever seen someone praising an invisible being. Oddly, I felt joyful and strong whenever he would sing. He asked me where I was from and told me to believe in Christ. He said that these hardships would not happen if North Koreans would trust God. He gave me an address and as soon as I was released, I went there.

That is how I came to the house of the Lord and accepted Christ. But the story does not end there. My illness re-appeared and since then, I experienced God's love and grace even more, as I have come to fellowship with this Jesus who died for us and gives us grace to endure all things...

Our young brother goes on to tell his desire to serve this Jesus and tell others of Him. Aren't you proud to know the baekjeong? The earth is filled with them. One day Heaven will be too.

251. one way to heat a home

I've been taking you through Mike Kim's *Escaping North Korea*. The following anecdote is used by permission.

In October, '06, Mike is talking to a recent defector, asking how he managed to heat his home during one of North Korea's harsh winters. The answer is astounding.

"We used wood for heat. Since people don't have money to buy wood, they go to the mountains to get it. The distance to the mountains is about eight miles, which takes us around five to six hours to walk. We'll leave at about 5:00 to 6:00 in the morning and arrive in the mountains around 10:00 a.m. We get back home around midnight."

Why so late, Kim wants to know. It's "only" five-six hours, after all.

"In North Korea, you need a permit to go into the mountains to get wood or you have to pay. We returned home late at night to avoid the police."

He goes on to explain that because there is such a shortage of wood in North Korea, it is illegal to cut it without a permit from the government.

"We're probably twice as fast as people here [in China]. We walk fast so we are able to do the hike in five to six hours. We see people walking on the streets here in China and wonder why they walk around so slowly. We each took a log about two meters long and dragged it back home. We made this trip every two or three days and we took turns going two at a time. So, thankfully our family was able to have heat every day. It was easier for us because we lived near the mountains... In big cities like Chongjin, you have apartments where there is no heat..."

Full time work, going to the mountains to get wood, Mike Kim queries?

"There's no work to do in North Korea. Even if you do work, they don't pay you. So why work?"

Sigh.... God give us grace to hear. To care. To pray. God save North Korea!

252. *he slept in a stairwell*

Let's continue looking at Mike Kim's *Escaping North Korea*. If you haven't already bought it by now, and I hope you do, here's a story, used by permission and re-written a little, that will melt you. Melting is not the goal here, but while you're melted down, why not remember North Korea in prayer...

North Korean children are by and large mal-nutritioned. That happens when you don't eat. Mrs. Yoon is a former NK citizen who "still cries when she thinks of a six-year-old boy named Chung-Ho whom she met on the streets in North Korea."

She was making her regular rounds at the food market when she saw a boy sitting on the ground, pounding the floor with his fists, with a desperation that one might expect from an older person who has tried everything to meet his needs and is now giving up on life. He wailed at the top of his lungs, "Why was I born into this world? Why did my mom give birth to me?"

He actually cursed the day he was born. Like old Job.

Mrs. Yoon had pity on Chung-ho. He was quite a sight. As many of these orphan children wandering the land, he wasn't even wearing shoes, but had wrapped his feet with cloth.

She approached him, and he told his sad story. No home. No parents. All alone, living by himself, sleeping every night in a stairwell. Already this day he had been caught trying to steal some food and had been beaten by the store owner.

"I felt terrible for the boy, so I bought him some corn gruel," she said with tears. "I cried a lot with him. He was so hungry that he ate the bowl of corn gruel in one gulp. After he finished his meal he got on his knees and bowed to me, touching his head to the floor over and over again, saying, 'Thank you, Auntie. Thank you.' "

Can you see Jesus right behind that boy adding His own thanks? Don't you want to hug that little guy? So does Jesus. Don't you wish he knew about the One standing behind him, the One Who made the worlds? So does Jesus.

Sometimes we think alike, don't we, Jesus and us? So what is keeping us from making it a regular habit?

253. God at a railway crossing

This testimony is fresh from the Korean peninsula. God continues to work and move to do His will among those who will seek Him. From SeoulUSA, used by permission.

Let me tell you about the first time I came to China. It was with my brother-in-law. He has visited for several years and has been helped through his friendship with the church. Often he tried to persuade me to have faith in the God he met. But I ignored his encouragement.

Well, I have many questions about God. Does God really exist, like my brother-in-law always is saying? Hey, if God exists, why does he let North Korean people stay so poor?' If God really loves humans so much, why does He let North Koreans die by starvation? Also, Just how big is this God? Does He even have the power to help humans? I didn't believe God, but I had a lot of questions. On this China visit, I began to get some answers.

You'll never believe what happened as we made our way from NK to China. Around 4 a.m., we tried to cross over a railroad passage into China, but we were just frozen. We somehow went the wrong way, and passed up the train tunnel. Suddenly we saw 2 NK guards. There was just 40 meters between the guards and us. It was light out, we couldn't do anything.

My brother-in-law prayed to God, "God, please help us!" The prayer was really quiet and very simple, and he prayed it again and again. And then he said "Let's go." I couldn't move. Not even one step. I shook my head, but he began to walk.

I couldn't believe it! We made clearly audible sounds with our steps, but the guards never even looked at us! What was happening?

Brother said God had heard his prayer, and made the guards blind and deaf to us. I couldn't say anything. I couldn't understand such a thing with common sense, but it had happened. I began to believe in God's existence after His amazing help.

With this experience, I decided to believe God. I accepted Jesus as my Savior, and my Lord.

God is my salvation, my shelter. Jesus is my joy, my hope.

Thank you, God. Thank you Jesus.

One at a time He builds His glorious Kingdom. Thanks for praying.

254. refugees without borders

Mike Kim is our source of information today. I'm still quoting from his recent Escaping North Korea, *a must-buy for NK lovers, especially those who want to pray knowledgeably. The subject: Recent trends in regards to defecting from North Korea. Mike writes:*

There are a number of factors that have made it increasingly difficult for North Koreans to defect. For one, the North Korean regime is trying to clamp down on defections.

In August 2006, it executed three North Korean soldiers for taking bribes and allowing North Koreans to defetct to China.

In addition, the regime is handing out harsher punishments for border-crossers. Traditionally, a repatriated refugee could hope to be released after spending three to six months in labor re-education facilities. Human Rights Watch reported a policy change in the summer of 2004, however. Refugees are now being punished with longer and harsher sentences.

A final challenge for would-be defectors is that Chinese villagers are becoming increasingly hesitant to help North Korean refugees. In the past many people would gladly open up their homes for a night and feed refugees, but this is no longer the case. One reason is that the Chinese government issued an edict stating that it would fine and potentially arrest anyone guilty of feeding or housing a refugee. A sign in the border region posted in Chinese reads, "It is forbidden to financially help, harbor, or aid in the settlement of people from the neighboring country who have crossed the border illegally."

A second reason is the increasing number of cases where refugees assault and steal from Chinese people (especially the elderly). If you visit some Chinese border villages, you will see signs warning people against helping North Korean refugees...

Thanks Mike. A lot to think about. Christians know they must preach the Gospel illegally. Would you break the law and risk arrest by taking a refugee out to a restaurant? What does our theology teach about that? And would you still want to give to someone who tried to steal from you?

Pray, pray, pray. That much we understand.

255. the trafficked women of nk

Suffering comes in all sizes and shapes... and genders. Mike Kim's new Escaping North Korea *documents the specific tragedies faced by females. I shall not be overly graphic, nor was he, so there is no need to fear the completion of this article. But I can safely say that none of you would want any of the following for your daughters. By the marvelous grace of God, many of these "trafficked" ladies are rescued, saved from sin, and become wonderful testimonies to God's grace. We continue to pray for the rest. Now, Mike (used by permission):*

On March 6, 2006, a Crossing Borders staffer testified at a U.S. congressional hearing:

"North Koreans are in the ultimate position of vulnerability with the only alternative to following a [sex] trafficker into China being starvation, suffering and possibly death. Knowing this, traffickers take advantage of the dire situations of young North Korean women and coerce them... Many of the promises of a 'better life' are never fulfilled and many of the... marriages are to physically disabled or alcoholic husbands with the end result often being abandonment or physical abuse."

After women are met at the border and forced/tricked into a "marriage", quite often -though not always- the abuse begins. Again, Mike:

... described the physical abuse she endured at the hands of her "husband" after she was sold: "He had a mental impairment. When I refused... him, he hit me. His mother and sister also hit me. I would rather die than [have an improper relationship] and fought the family for seven months. I received severe beatings... I cried every night."

Having grown up in North Korea, [another trafficked woman] had never heard of God before but in a moment of desperation she found herself uttering a prayer, "God in Heaven, help me!" [She] was sold to a home near a house church. There she met a deacon who helped her escape. She believes that being sold to a house near a church was an answer to her prayer.

In the end, Chinese authorities capture and forcibly repatriate many trafficked women.

... remembered: After I had been there for a month and a half, someone came knocking on the door in the middle of the night. It was the police, five men and one woman...They said they were taking me to register as a Chinese citizen... I followed...

The end of this particular story is not too pretty. The very end is worse than that. She is taken back forcibly to North Korea where she is treated as an animal. (Whoever called North Korea the "people's" rebublic?) She escapes from the prison. Defects again to China. Arrives at a Christian refugee center. And dies of cancer shortly thereafter.

Well there you have it.Two bad stories, one good one. We need more good ones. We desperately need more good ones. Can you help?

256. with Christ in Communist NK

The following article comes from the secular press. It covers matters that are secular. Except for one thing: the places described below house Christians. "Political" prisoners are those who threaten Kim Jong-il's grip on power in some way, and Christians, with their talk of King Jesus and a better way of life, do just that. So though you will not find the name of Jesus anywhere in the following article, know that Jesus is very much a part of the horror being experienced. I ask you to pray when you have finished reading...

Hyung-Jin Kim - The Associated Press

SEOUL, South Korea -- The condemned inmate, his body torn apart by guard dogs, slumped unconscious as the three executioners fired. The bullets shattered his skull, splattering blood near other prisoners forced to watch.

His offense: trying to escape from the remote prison camp in North Korea.

"People were seized with fear but no one could say anything," former prisoner Jung Gyoung-il said, recalling the 2001 execution. "That's worse than the way animals are slaughtered."

For a decade, North Korea has denied such accounts from defectors, and South Korea has shied away from them to maintain good relations with its wartime rival. But now, under new President Lee Myung-bak, South Korea is investigating alleged abuses, including the prison camp system. South Korea's state-run human rights watchdog is interviewing defectors and is hosting a two-day international forum this week on the issue.

Meanwhile, President Bush has made the push to crack down on rights abuses in North Korea one of his last missions before leaving office in January. He signed a law promoting the U.S. special envoy on North Korean human rights to ambassador and making it easier for refugees from the North to settle in the U.S.

The focus on alleged abuses has infuriated North Korea, which dismisses the accusations as a U.S. plot to overthrow its government. The country's Central Committee of the

Democratic Front for the Reunification of the Fatherland called Seoul's moves proof that South Korean officials are "sycophants toward the U.S." and "maniacs" who risk confrontation with the North.

North Korea runs at least five large political prison camps, together holding an estimated 150,000 to 200,000 inmates, according to the U.S. State Department. The gulags remain one of the Stalinist regime's most effective means of controlling its 23 million people, analysts say.

Last week, the U.N. investigator on human rights in North Korea said large numbers of people remain in prison camps. Satellite images show the camps in valleys tucked between mountain ranges, each covering up to 100 square miles.

Former prisoners say the camps are encircled by high-voltage electrified fences and have schools, barracks and work sites.

Offenses meriting banishment to a prison camp include everything from disparaging North Korean leader Kim Jong Il to trying to flee the country, defectors say.

Former prisoner Jung said he spent three years in Camp No. 15 in Yodok, about 70 miles northeast of the capital, Pyongyang, on charges of spying for South Korea.

Jung, who was working for a state-run trading company, claims the charges were fabricated by security agents seeking promotion. After months of torture, Jung said he acknowledged the charge. By then he had lost nearly 80 pounds.

Shortly after his release, he fled to South Korea in 2004 with his wife and two daughters and now works for a civic group on North Korean prisons.

At Yodok, Jung said, the 400 inmates in his section subsisted on 20 ounces of corn each -- the equivalent of one medium-size can daily -- while toiling at mines, farms and factories for 13 to 15 hours a day. Many died of hunger and diseases brought on by malnutrition, he said. Some managed to trap vermin and insects.

"People eat rats and snakes. They were the best food to recover our health," said Jung, 46, adding he still suffers from ulcers, headaches and back pain.

One inmate, Choe Kwang Ho, sneaked away from his work for 15 minutes to pick fruit. He was executed, his mouth stuffed with gravel to prevent him from protesting, Jung recalled.

"I still can't forget his emotionless face," he said.

Life at the four other camps was even worse, Jung said. A former North Korean prison guard said only two inmates have ever escaped from the camps known as "total control zones."

"Inmates there don't even have time to try to catch and eat rats," An Myeong-chul said in an interview in Seoul.

An said he served as a guard and driver at four camps before defecting in 1994. If a female inmate got pregnant, he said, she and her lover would be shot to death publicly. Then, An said, prison guards would cut open her womb, remove the fetus and bury it or feed it to guard dogs.

Forced abortions are common, and if babies are born, many are killed, sometimes before the mother's eyes, defectors say. Grandparents also may be punished since whole families are imprisoned.

"We were repeatedly taught they were the national traitors and we have to eradicate three generations of their families," he said.

An, 40, defected after his father, a former Workers' Party official, killed himself after being accused of criticizing the government food rationing system as inefficient. Now working at a bank in South Korea, An said he pushes for the abolishment of North Korea's prison camps as the least he can do to offset his work as a guard.

Public executions are not limited to the gulags.

Before he was imprisoned, Jung took his eldest daughter, then 8, to the execution of a prisoner in 1997 in the city of Chongjin. She watched solemnly as the inmate's skull was smashed to pieces.

"She asked me, 'Hey Daddy, is he vomiting?'" Jung recalled, a bitter grimace curling his lips. "I should not have taken her there."

Associated Press writers Kwang-tae Kim in Seoul and Edith M. Lederer at the United Nations contributed to this report.

On the Net: U.S. Committee for Human Rights in North Korea report: www.hrnk.org/HiddenGulag.pdf

257. *born and bred in the briar patch*

Remember the marvelous tar baby? Joel Chandler Harris's "Uncle Remus" tales were part of my childhood too. One came winging its way back toward me recently. This snippet occurs after Brer Rabbit gets stuck in the tar baby and is about to be finished off once and for all by Brer Fox... (translated from original African dialect).

"Skin me Brer Fox," says he [Brer Rabbit]. "Snatch out my eyeballs, tear out my ears by the roots," says he, "But please, Brer Fox, don't fling me in that briar patch, " says he. Of course, Brer Fox wanted to get Brer Rabbit as bad as he could, so he caught him by the behind legs and slung him right in the middle of the briar patch. There was a considerable flutter when Brer Rabbit struck the bushes, and Brer Fox hung around to see what was going to happen. By

and by he heard someone call his name and 'way up on the hill he saw Brer Rabbit sitting cross-legged on a chinquapin log combing the tar pitch out of his hair with a chip. Then Brer Fox knew he had been tricked.Brer Rabbit hollered out, "Born and bred in the briar patch. I was born and bred in the briar patch!" And with that he skipped out just as lively as a cricket in the embers of a fire.

Martyrs are the most honored of all God's children. Those willing to give their very lives for the One Who died for them shall be honored throughout eternity. The church began with a backdrop of persecution that granted this glorious status to many of God's finest. We were *born and bred in a briar patch*, a place that looks like certain misery and finality but in fact opens the gate to immortatlity anf fellowship with God.

Men like Kim Jong-il of North Korea create the perfect breeding ground for saints and martyrs. Though he cannot possibly comprehend what he is doing in his present darkness, he is working ultimately for the purposes of God. Mis-treated saints have gotten the attention of believers worldwide. Now the church arises, sending in missionaries, Bibles, tons of food and other aid. The Gospel is being preached as never before by air waves and balloons. A "closed" nation isn't closed after all. Every soul that passes from this life for Jesus' sake taps others on the shoulder and invites, "Follow me as I follow Christ."

We pray and work for the deliverance of God's people, of course. But perhaps some of our pity is mis-placed. Poor "Brer" Kim Jong-il. An anti-Christ if ever one lived and breathed, but that to which he is giving his life is totally wasted effort. He has helped create a pure church that is a standard of excellence the world over.

Please, Brer Kim! Don't fling me in that briar patch!

258. of hunger pains and small spoons

This NK thing isn't going away. Not today anyway. I feel compelled to continue sharing the horrors of Kim Jong-il's nation, though there is a chance we will grow hardened to it by hearing it so much. Today we'll follow Mike Kim once more, in his new Escaping North Korea, as he describes hunger in a prison setting:

Young-Kuk, a 19-year-old refugee who spent a year in prison after being repatriated, recounted:

"We had to work extra hard, especially when they were watching us, and we put some bounce in our step hoping that we would receive food at the end of the day. But for three days, they didn't give us anything to eat, and I didn't even feel the hunger pains at that point... Sometimes they would give us pieces of Chinese bread, but we didn't have appetites, so we gave away our bread and only wanted to drink the water. I lost a lot of weight. The soldiers hit me severely and starved me for three days while I was detained. They worked us really hard in the freezing cold and didn't feed us... We were bound together by the wrists in pairs, and it was very difficult to maneuver around. We were in a place where there was flowing water from a river, and because it was winter and we were so fatigued, we drank from the stream. But at night, I would suddenly start shaking and feel my insides going crazy from hunger and fatigue."

Out of all the North Korean prisoner survivors I have interviewed, only one person has ever said that they were fed sufficiently while in prison... she said,

"In the beginning there wasn't enough food. There weren't enough spoons either, so they would place only a certain number of spoons per group. I sat at the very front. All the newcomers had to. The front was the coldest, because the guards left the windows open for ventilation. Those who sat near the windows felt the freezing wind blowing on them. Only small spoons were given because the guards feared the prisoners might commit suicide by eating a spoon. We had to use small spoons like that. Others had to use their fingers to eat..."

Thank you Mike. Now we know. Now we pray. Now we listen for God's ideas about what can be done. Surely something can be done...

259. the soul of korea is gone

Early 20th century Korea. The Japanese, long antagonist of the Korean people, have finally pushed their way into authority and have annexed Korea to their own island nation. Koreans from top to bottom of the peninsula are in agony. Hear the grief expressed by author Younghill Kang's uncle as he receives the dour news. From The Grass Roof:

That night I went into my uncle's studio and lay down on the mat, crying miserably. By and by I heard [my uncle] walking around and muttering in the next room. With my wet finger I made a hole in the paper door and looked through. He stood there at the outer door and just shook his fist in the face of the sky.

"Oh, stars and moon, how have you the heart to shine? Why not drop down by thunderstorm and cover all things up? And mountains, with your soul shining and rustling in the green leaves and trees and grass, can't you understand that it is over now? This national career of the people who have lived with you all these many ages, who have slept in your bosoms, whose blood you have drunk, whose muse you have been for the countless years? You spirits of waters, you ghosts of the hollows, don't you see how death has just come to this people established among you for the 4,000 years since the first Tan-Koon appeared on the white headed mountain by the side of the Sacred Tree? Don't you know the soul of Korea is gone, is passing away this night, and has left us behind like the old clothes?"

Was Korea ended then? A pristine country, contemporary of Homeric times and of Golden Ages- far, far removed from the spirit of the Roman Empire and all later modernity until this day... I cried and cried myself to sleep.

No, Korea. It was not the end after all. The Americans came. The Russians came. Two Koreas were formed from the ashes of World War II and the subsequent Korean War. And still she survived and survives. Her soul? Not dead, but seriously damaged. But in honesty one must add, this was a soul given to idolatry, as the above passage points out quite well. Korea has had to pass through the fire, but perhaps only long enough to burn out of her that which does not bless the one true God. Korea can be born again, in a very literal and wonderful way, if Christ is given His rightful place in the Korean heart. Something to pray about.

260. hitler lives. in nk

I am so very grateful for the liberty given me by the author of Escaping North Korea, Mike Kim, to quote freely from his book. It is a gold mine of pertinent information, and I heartily recommend that you buy your own copy soon!

Today's topic is the Nazi-like meaningless lives lived within concentration camps in modern day North Korea. You remember the Nazis? They were the ones from whom the Communists "freed" places like Romania and Czechoslovakia. Similarly, Kim Jong-il is freeing North Korea from the Japanese, the Americans, the Chinese, the Russians, the South Koreans, and the entire civilized world. To do this he has instituted elements of Stalin and Hitler and Ceaucescu in his pretty mix of poison.

And I do not speak of history here. This is what is happening as I type. Says Kim:

The regime depends on forced labor for every industry imaginable... prisoners are given strict quotas, and if they don't meet them, they will not receive food that day.... An MSNBC report indicated that products made by North Korean prisoners might end up in U.S. stores having been "washed" first through Chinese companies that serve as intermediaries.

Repatriated [sent back from China] refugees are worked the hardest of all the prisoners. Young-Kuk explained, "They would work us harder because we ate so well while we were in China. They made us carry heavy loads, and when they beat us, they would use all sorts of things with which to hit us..."

Mrs. Park, a refugee woman in her forties, described what her days inside a North Korean prison were like. "We started our physical labor early in the morning. We began working at 6:00 A.M. and then ate breakfast at 8:00 A.M.... we had to cut wood... Oftentimes we worked straight through the day until dinnertime... Even if there was no work for us to do, they made up meaningless work for us. There was a big pile of large rocks. The guards would say, 'Separate the rocks! Move all the big rocks to the right side and all the small rocks to the left side!' "

Then the directions would change. Put the rocks back in one big pile. Move all big rocks left, small rocks right, and so on and on... Kim reminds his readers that this is exactly how Hitler broke the spirits, and not only the backs, of his own people. Prisoners there died not only from exhaustion, but from "the purposelessness of their work."

May God clarify our own purposes. For me, I want to give myself to Christ and His people in North Korea. Occasionally I hear from some of you who have made a similar decision. There is still so much to do...

261. kim vs kim

So many Koreans are named Kim. I speak of the present dictator regularly on this site, Kim Jong-il. For the next few days, another Kim, a victim of Jong-il and of his father, Kim Il-sung. He arrived in South Korea seven years ago in the way described here...

I was born in North Korea in 1956 and lived there until 1986, when I defected to China. Sixteen months later, in 1987, I was arrested and sent back to North Korea, via a bridge between _____, in China, and _____ in North Korea.

The reason I defected was that people are not treated equally there. In North Korea, not one single crime or accident is made known publicly. And although its official name is the Democratic *People's* Republic of North Korea, there is absolutely no freedom and the land is not the people's at all. I no longer wanted to live in such a place.

My faith in God began in April 1987 through a Christian church in _____, China. I had heard about God but did not have detailed knowledge about Jesus or Christianity. I had not even had a chance to read the Bible.

In those days I was working in a mine. I got a copy of the Bible and began reading it, but I did not understand very much. Then I was arrested by the Chinese police. They packed up all my things and sent them and me back to North Korea.

When I arrived, I was questioned about the Bible they had found in my possession. I denied any knowledge of it. Though the interrogator thought I might really not have known, his boss would not be able to be convinced, so he demanded a better answer from me.

So I confessed that I obtained the Bible to read, simply because I wanted to know more about God. Then the interrogation heated up so they could find out where I even heard about God to begin with. Then I was sent to Yodok Political Prison Camp under the charges of "disturbing Party policy", committing "national treason" by illegally crossing the border, and "anti-revolutionary activities" by which they meant my reading of the Bible!

Much severe torture followed, and more interrogation, for eight long months. Then I was imprisoned without a trial there in Yodok. That was 1988.

Next time: details of the interrogation process...

Mr. Kim, citizen of North Korea, dares to leave his country to find freedom and food. He finds that and more. He finds the Bible, and God, in China. But he is arrested and sent back to that other Kim, who reigns over the chaos of the northern end of the Korean peninsula. When his new-found faith is discovered, he is interrogated and imprisoned. He shares now some of the details of that ordeal...

Interrogation

I suffered from the torture of "motionless sitting" during interrogation. Anyone who moved, however slight the movement might be, was handcuffed and chained to high grids with arms spread wide, and then beaten. They employed an iron rod that is normally used for cleaning a gun, to hit bones such as the wrist, knee, or ankle. In this way they could inflict extreme pain with little effort.

Detainees were often not allowed to sleep and forced to stay unclothed even in extremes of temperature.

The sanitation level of cells in the detention facility was horrendous. When detainees were forced to sit still, lice crawled on their faces. And one could not wash his face until sent to prison or released.

If two people talked, they were ordered to stand facing each other and forced to slap each other's face.

Interrogation was such a painful process for me that I decided to injure myself to escape it. I swallowed a nail, hoping I would be sent to a hospital for surgery. The painful stay in the cell made me think that the pain of a surgical operation would be nothing by comparison. If only I could stay away from the cell, even for a few days! You can imagine my disappointment when the nail came out in my stool.

Political prison camp

I was imprisoned in No. 15 political prison camp, which is in Yodok County, towards the northeastern part of the country. It was March, 1988.

Though my health was very unstable due to malnutrition, I was forced to do hard labor. In April

I was ordered to carry humus soil down a mountain, using an A frame carrier. I was very weak, and I put less soil on the frame than some other prisoners. Seeing this, a "lead" prisoner kicked me hard, making me roll down the mountain. As I cursed at him, I got dragged to the guards' quarters, where I was severely beaten with oak-wood clubs. I was knocked unconscious due to the brutal beating and was brought back to my cell later by fellow prisoners...

There's more, and we'll pick it up again next time. I couldn't help but think, as I was typing this story, what was it like when I first decided I wanted to follow Christ? My mother, a Roman Catholic, was not going to allow me to be baptized in water. But I fussed a little, and she relented. There were a few friends that I never made due to my faith, I guess, a few opportunities that closed. But I simply cannot relate to this Mr. Kim. Can you? Regardless, will you pray for him? He continues to follow Christ and wants only to bring the Gospel to others. May we follow him, as he follows Jesus...

262. Kim vs. Kim, part 2

We've been talking about "Mr. Kim", one of many Mr. Kim's *in North Korea, and his struggle inside the NK system created by that other Kim, Kim Jong-il, the dictator. Please see parts one and two that tell of his arrest after fleeing to China for food, his interrogation, and the beginning of the relating of his prison experiences. Here is more of that prison tale:*

It was August of 1989. I was again carrying something heavy in an "A" frame. I had to stoop a bit, as I was trying to balance the weight. As a result, I failed to notice a guard on patrol who was passing by me at that moment. I did not make the required bow to him.

Later, I was asked to report to him to receive my punishment. He and 7 or 8 of his colleagues brutally beat me. After the beating they stripped off my clothes, handcuffed me, and made me stay standing in the middle of a courtyard. Though it was August, it was extremely cold late at night. I learned that cold is even more painful than being beaten.

My wake-up call next morning came from the heavy foot of the lead prisoner, letting me know it was time to go to work. Work at that time was building bulletproof walls for security guards.

About that handcuffing: after the cuffs are on, guards step on the hands to tighten them. The hands go black very soon.

Another form of punishment was to force me to sit on top of quicklime when it was raining. Now, when water is added to quicklime, due to a chemical reaction the lime gets very hot, maybe 100 degrees C or more, and it exhumes gas. My buttocks were burning, but the guard forced me to sit there. Because of the burns on my backside, I was not able to lie on my back for about a month, and I suffered severe pain when relieving myself at the washroom. I couldn't even put trousers on for awhile. The watery discharge from the sore stuck to my pants and gave me an excruciating pain.

In the fall of 1990, I was caught by a prison guard named _____. My crime at this time was baking corn while i was on duty in a cornfield. He relentlessly beat me in the legs with burning wood. To this day the burn marks on my legs still give me shivers.

In a political prison camp in North Korea, one should forget that he or she is human. There are things one must do to survive. I carefully watched a dog so that I could steal its food. I ate snakes, frogs, rats, and anything that could be a source of nutrition.

Of course I was not the only one there, suffering. I met a lot of people. I saw people who cut off their own finger or pretended to be insane because the brutality of the forced labor was so unbearable. A man who had been beaten with a shovel had to have one of his arms cut off because it rotted due to tetanus. So many people spent 20-30 years in the prison camp simply because of some ludicrous crime their grandfather committed...

We will conclude next time. May our hearts reach out to those who so much need to experience the wonderful love of Jesus...

263. Kim vs Kim, part 3

Today I conclude my re-telling of the story of "Mr. Kim", a resident of Kim Jong-Il's North Korea no more. Though all men love their native lands, people by the thousands have tried to get out of the Kim "Paradise" simply so they can eat. This Mr. Kim tells of the brutality he faced for having found food and God in Communist China...

My prison cell was extremely cold. I had to sit up holding my legs with my arms, because this position made the chill a bit more bearable. But for that simple action, a warden stripped me and kicked me on the face. I started bleeding from the nose and got very dizzy. So the guard put me into a flea-infested room. As I tell this now, I shudder thinking of the pain of being in that room. I begged to be put into a room without fleas. In response, the same warden came back with a bucket of water and poured it over my body. Imagine the pain of the entire body being frozen. Even today, whenever a streak of cold wind hits me, making me sneeze or have a runny nose, the memory of this cell of freezing haunts me.

I survived this living in hellish conditions until 1992, only by the grace of God. In 1997 I once more defected from North Korea. Even the risk of being caught did not take away the joy of being out of North Korea. I could worship God and read the Bible as much as I wanted. Then in 2001 I came to South Korea through Mongolia. Under the blessing of God I am studying theology at Chongshin University.

In closing, I want to tell you one more incident that I witnessed when I was in the prison camp. Of course, in the camp you must follow the guards' orders, and you can't confide in anyone, because there are spies everywhere. The camp authorities constantly feared collective action by the prisoners and so kept tight control. Still, in May of 1989 a couple of brothers in the camp started a fellowship group. There were about seven members, including me. One day four of the group were arrested.

Though I was a member, not everyone knew I was. Only two did. Now, one of my responsibilities for the camp enabled me to secure food and supplies for our little group. But soon after I became a member, one of the group founders broke the news to me that we had an informant, a "Judas" among us. He assured me that the other members didn't know my existence, and also that we should not meet each other again.

Later, this leader was interrogated, when they discovered that he knew about God. He was asked to disclose who told him about spiritual things. His answer: " Do you know that the sun gives warmth because someone told you to feel that? No. It is because the sun warms us up. I know God exists because he reveals himself to me."

When he was relocated to another part of the prison a few months later, he did not have his right arm . The interrogator had not liked his answer and had beaten him with a shovel. When he tried to block the blows, his arm was damaged beyond repair.

We have met once since that time. He told me that I should not sway from the path of spreading God's words once I am released.

May it be so, Mr. Kim. Go with God. And may we be bold to go with you...

264. how much is enough?

Is it wrong to want the suffering to end? Will the Father's perfect will not be worked out if suddenly North Korean prisoners go free? I cannot answer this, but thankfully I do not have to. The command is real. "Remember the prisoners as though you were bound with them..." Hebrews 13:3. Let the analysts and pundits speculate. God calls His people to pray and do... Here's something to pray about, from Mike Kim's new book, Escaping North Korea *, used by permission.*

If North Korean prison walls could speak, they would tell horrific stories of beatings, torture, and death. One North Korean prison survivor wrote to me of "the cries of the North Koreans as they're beaten... their tears of hunger... moaning in pain that doesn't end... their dark faces with no smiles... I picture these faces and I see a picture of the shadow of hell."

Women, children, and the elderly are all subject to beatings and torture. Mrs Lee..."When it comes to beatings, they don't look at men and women differently." Ms Lim..."However, it is only the men who are electrocuted with cattle prods. Women aren't electrocuted, but we are kicked,

hit with sticks, and have our hair pulled out until we bleed."
Another former prisoner showed me a bald spot on the right
side of her head. "I was hit on the head repeatedly with a
hammer, " she said.

"...They swear at you and beat you relentlessly...
Sometimes, the guards would demand that prisoners put
their hands on the floor. Then they would step all over them.
I would hear horrific cries. I've seen people lose all their
fingernails like this."

...a young teenager told me "Some people think kids
don't get hit in prison or that they get hit less. This isn't
true... Sometimes kids get hit more." A 16-year-old
recounted, "My punishment was sitting in a chair every day
for 15 hours. From 7:00 A.M. in the morning until 10:00 P.M.
at night, I had to sit perfectly still in a chair. I wasn't allowed
to move an inch or say a word... if one person moved,
everyone was beaten..."

Mrs. Kim..."There was another person arrested together
with me. She was beaten so much that it made me sick to
watch it... They repeatedly hit and poked the woman with a
sharp stick. They kept on hitting her until her flesh ripped..."

Pastor... reported..."It is known that the prisoners in the
central prison are fed with glass debris embedded in a bowl
of rice. This happens quite regularly and is not a one-time
incident..."

A former prison guard recalled, "They trained me not to
treat the prisoners as human beings. If someone is against
socialism, if someone tries to escape from prison, then kill
him. If there's a record of killing any escapee, then the guard
will be entitled to study in the college..."

I will end my verbal beating. It is difficult writing and
reading these things. But such images may be necessary to

disturb us sufficiently to pray. Oh that the Comforter will come to North Korea. May we never stop praying...

265. 3 incredible stories

There is a good chance you have never heard the name Yi Sun Shin. There are great men in every culture of which Americans are unaware. Understandable, but here is one you would truly have profited in knowing. Easily equal to the likes of Sir Francis Drake and Lord Nelson - some say superior to these western naval stars - Yi towered above the petty power-seekers of his day and became a hero beloved of all.

Imagine it. Twenty three major naval clashes with the Japanese who had invaded Korea in the late 16th century. Twenty three victories. After the Japanese landed and destroyed village after village, even to the taking of the capital, the first positive news that came to the King of Korea, in exile, was that of Yi's first battle that crushed a fleet of Japanese vessels.

So you expect me to say that Yi's popularity landed him titles, riches, honor. In fact, jealousy among the ranks led him to *prison* in the midst of his finest triumphs. That, to me, is the most unbelievable and awe-inspiring part of his story. The seeming failure in the midst of all the triumph.

Consider one Jesus. Healer, comforter, gentle Teacher. Blind eyes made to see, broken hearts forgiven, hungry mouths fed, all by His compassion. Anyone who had faith to receive something from Him, did. Victory after victory. Never defeated.

Then hung on a cross.

Hmmm. That last line doesn't seem to fit either. Seems like we should rip that part of the story out, as Peter tried to do before it even happened. "Not you, Master! Stop talking negative things!"

Incredible stories, these. Yi Sun Shin, Jesus Christ. No, they are not in "the same boat" in terms of significance, I know. Yi Sun Shin's resurrection from prison to return to the battle front and continue his unbroken string of victories is great history and very inspiring, but cannot be compared to Jesus' rising from the grave to give life to all who will receive Him *forever and ever*. But the parallel is there.

But my title promises *three* incredible stories. Stories of persons who were incredible in their feats, incredible in their defeats, but somehow rose again. The third story is being lived out as I write. It's going on in North Korea, among those we label the "baekjeong", the low class, because we do not have the same sense of high and low as Heaven does...

The lowly Christian believers of that land do exploits every day. Finding enough food to eat. Working long and hard hours in a mine for money that is not sufficient to support their families. Worshiping carefully and hidden, so as not to incur the wrath of a hostile government. Hiding Bibles and guests. Yet victories. You would expect that someone somewhere would honor these folks and call them heroes.

Unfortunately they are called by at least two governments traitors and criminals. Escapes are often tragic in outcome. Many end in death. All end in some sort of wrenching separation. Even coming to the "free" world can mean enduring suspicion and persecution by those who ought to know better.

So why call this an incredible story along the lines of Yi and Jesus? Because those who are faithful will be raised up with Christ. Their story is not yet complete. It is the lowly for whom Jesus came. They are the only ones who will see thier need of a Saviour and continue to the end. High-born materialists have only a slight chance of making it, according to Jesus.

High, low, baekjeong... Do we really know what these words mean? And "incredible".. Can your story and mine be called *incredible* when compared to the ones I have described? Have we known the experience of defeating the enemy during a long and difficult war? Have we seen the Power of God move through us to change our sphere of influence? Have we then been sent to further humiliation instead of the reward we expected?

May we search our hearts daily, and always be a friend to the lowly Christ Who still works His wonders among us in the form of Baekjeong...

266. starry-eyed, beware

So you've been reading my columns and other columns and books, and watching videos and newscasts... and you've finally decided: You've got to get to North Korea, one way or another! If you can't get in, at least you'll go to the border of NK and China, just to experience the atmosphere, touch a hurting brother somehow, meet a wandering refugeee, make a difference. May you do it! But be sure to count the cost... Mike Kim's new book *Escaping North Korea* relates his own experiences along those lines.

"As I reflect on the people in my life who have displayed the most courage and the qualities of a warrior, I realize that I met most of those people at the China-North Korea border. During my four years there, I met an amazing group of individuals. The border draws courageous souls. If I were to put together a list of heroes in my life, the people I met in Northeast China would be at the top of it.

"[Besides an incredible array of Koreans] The China-NK border also attracts fascinating people from all walks of life: activists, missionaries, reporters, businesspeople, professors, English teachers, and government workers. Because of its proximity to North Korea and the presence of North Korean refugees there, it has become a melting pot for intelligence activity. Government workers, activists, missionaries, and agents flock to the border to get the latest word on North Korea. North Korean [espionage] agents there try to gather intelligence, infiltrate networks, and sabotage the work of activists and missionaries. These agents will sometimes employ extreme measures, even abduction and murder. Pastor Kim, an elderly pastor with many years experience operating in China, once visited me there and warned of imminent danger: 'You think you're safe here? You feel safe? Right now, living here and with all the work you're doing, you have about a 50% chance of getting caught and kidnapped by North Korean agents.' He reminded me that the area was a hotbed for spies and tried to convince me to move further inland."

Are you able? Remember Jesus' question? Remember the disciples' answer, to a man? And remember the Garden of Gethsemane?

Far be it from me to discourage NK ministry! But let's be sure we are being led by God's Spirit and the purest of motivations. Getting caught up in spies and intelligence and mystery fantasies will take our eyes off Jesus, Who continues to cry out to us for help from over the border. If we try to help in our human strength alone, guided by Western pre-occupation with thrill-seeking, and disdain the connectedness of the Body of Christ with its authority figures

443

to guide, we could become another of the horrible statistics that KJII is producing daily.

Martyrdom is available. But all in due time, and that time is His time.

267. baekjeong* like me

His name was John Howard Griffin. Middle-aged. White. Male. 1959. Mansfield, Texas. He was a man dedicated to the end of racism, and was so passionate for his cause that he underwent medical treatment to turn his skin black, temporarily. What he experienced as a "black" man became the classic book, "Black Like Me." And what did he experience? "Nigger." No jobs available. Can't cash your check. No public restroom. Slowly Griffin became hopeless and defeated, as were the people he was portraying by his courageous act. He eventually allowed the medication to wear off. He was White again. His report went out and brought him adulation throughout the world. Except in still-very-racist Mansfield, Texas, where he was abused and threatened for favoring the African American cause.

In this weekly letter we deal with a similar situation, the *baekjeong**. Behold the North Korean. But wait! Are we sure it is a "North" Korean? Add a few pounds and a few centimeters. Clean up the dirt of the coal mine or the hue that comes when clean water and good soap are not available for washing. Put a few good clothes on to replace the ragged cloth you see. Let his smile break. Stand him up straight. Teach him how to walk with dignity again. Is it not now a *South* Korean? Can you tell? Does it matter?

For so many, yes, it does matter. In South Korea today, North Koreans are herded together and placed in a "special" neighborhood. Their churches are separate. Their lives are suspect. Depression experienced for long years under Kim Jong-il's government gives way to a similar dejection created by the elite and rejecting South Korean government. Stomachs are fuller, trappings are nicer, but the inner separation continues.

Yes, not totally fair. Many South Koreans, there and here, love and cherish the Northerners. I'm sure there are even members of the SK government who have opposed the stringent policies that hurt rather than help their long-departed family members. Nevertheless, the situation remains.

And in this situation lies a wondrous opportunity for the church of Jesus Christ. For when folks are weak they are really strong, if God has a chance to get hold of them. That's a Paul-ism, straight from the Spirit's mind, recorded in your Bible. What if those weak and sickly ones rejected by this world -as was Jesus Himself - were called to strength and salvation and eternal glory? What if they were raised up to incredible worldwide service to the Master? What if mission stations were directed by these for whom hope was lost, and what if their very *message* was "hope!"

Ah! That's an in -your-face to the Enemy, don't you think?

*baekjeong: considered Korea' lowest class of humanity.

268. *romance revisited*

Last June I posted here an article about the romanticizing of pain. It's a theme that wends its way back every now and then, and is pricking me this morning.

A nasty struggle goes on in this old brain as I contemplate spending a summer in Korea this year. There's a voice of some sort, I won't call it the Lord, as so many rush to do. Perhaps conscience. Perhaps common sense. But maybe the Lord is speaking too...

"So," the voice says, and I loosely translate the impressions I receive, "you really think you have something to offer these Koreans!"

"Yes, sir, I have felt their pain so strongly, that I must do something."

"Felt their pain, you say? Felt their pain? You?! Exactly what pain have you felt?"

"You know, the pain of their suffering and their rejection. I feel it in my gut!"

"Oh you do, do you? I'm wondering just which part of their suffering you feel. Is it the hunger? Do you fast often, or have you been unable to afford food, or have you been on a low-vitamin diet so long that you are developing a sickness of some sort? That kind of pain?"

"Well, uh, actually I eat quite well. I do skip a meal now and then to keep my weight in line. I've even been known to fast and pray, but not too often, really..."

"Then perhaps you have lost your job? The economy even here is sinking, and you've joined the thousands who are now unemployed? That would surely help you feel the pain!"

"Hmmm, no, my job still seems to be intact. The education sector has not been affected as yet. Not so much as missed a paycheck, and there's even a bonus now and then. No, it's not that."

"You've been in jail, then? A political prisoner, arrested because of your involvement with Jesus, locked up away from your family, with a few beatings thrown in?"

"No, the only times I went to jail I was just visiting. Never been seriously persecuted for my faith."

"Then what kind of pain can you possibly be speaking of? You're not talking about the bravado the disciples displayed when they vowed they would die for Jesus? You're not talking about the tears you shed when you saw that NK video? Call it any number of things, but don't call it pain! How dare you compare your snivelings to the North Koreans' prison sentences and say that you now know their pain!"

"Uh, well, I, I guess I..."

And this smothering exchange of comments keeps reminding me of how fully and totally inadequate is any external preparation for such a visit as this. Through the months I have asked God for His preparation, though, and some things that have surfaced are promising. Since my decision to go, I have had to face nights - long nights - of personal fears and doubts. I have had major and minor procedures done on my body, where - in my imagining way - I despaired of life. I have been a victim of ineffective drugs. Attacks have assailed me at my work place. And more...

When we lay our comfortable little lives at the foot of the cross and say, "Show me the rest of the story, let me feel, not just romantic 'pain,' but the pain You felt on the cross, and what You want me to feel on my own cross, and the real pain of your people, so I can relate..., " things begin to happen. Life unravels, a bit at a time, and our sham hypocrisies are exposed. Even we realize who we are after a while, and cry out with Isaiah our unworthiness, "I am a man of unclean lips..." Only then are we fit for this service.

It may start with tears, but it ends with the real thing. And on the way, there will be constant re-calculating of the cost, many chances to say, "Hey, I just can't afford this. I never knew..."

The apostles, filled later with the Holy Ghost, decided the cost wasn't that high after all, and are in bliss with Jesus as I write. May we be able to see what they saw, and decide what they decided.

Hey, romance is OK at the beginning of a relationship. That's the natural order. We "fall" in love. But eventually there is the rising back up again, to commitment, marriage, hardship. Are we ready to be wedded to His cross? Is He worth it? Is His suffering Body worth it? Is the lost world worth it?

269. Fax attack on NK

Ever heard of a "fax invasion" ? Use your imagination. Think of a country that is hard to get into. It's in desperate need of information and news. Essentially no internet. You can't pick up a phone and talk to someone. Visiting the place is almost unheard of. So you grab a fax machine after you've found here and there a whole bucket-load of fax numbers, and you fire away.

If you're thinking North Korea by now, you're with me. And if you're also thinking, Hey, what a way to preach the Gospel, too! you get a bonus! Yep, invading North Korea by Gospel fax. That's just one of dozens of Seoul USA projects geared to show that there are no closed countries after all.

Oh by the way, I just happened to have the latest Seoul USA fax, written by a Korean mission intern... imagine you are a North Korean bureaucrat, and your fax machine signals you that a message is coming over the wire. In perfect Korean, it says...

Recently, US Secretary of State Hillary Clinton visited South Korea and China. During her visit, she commented several times about North Korea. She mentioned about the secrecy of the NK government and the possible power struggle that may have a hugely negative effect on many people when Kim Jung II leaves his office as head of state. Clinton said that there is no direct line of communication with NK so it is very hard for the US to understand what is happening inside North Korea.

There are speculations about who will be Kim Jung II's successor. And the uncertainty about this important issue is causing great concern for NK's neighboring countries , not to mention the very people of North Korea. NK needs a leader who is willing to sacrifice himself to save the nation from the widespread poverty and many other difficulties that the country is facing. A leader must promote the good of the whole country and its citizens, instead of upholding his own prestige or supporting a few people who are willing to offer loyalty in return for a favor.

We hope that the next leader will be a person who has the courage and boldness to face the challenges that North Korea is facing both externally and internally, and who will be truly benevolent enough to look after the orphans and widows who are abandoned in remote areas of the country away from Pyoung-Yang and other relatively affluent cities.

Someone said the following about the greatest leader the world has ever seen:

"The people living in darkness have seen a great light; on those living in the land of the shadow of death a light has dawned." These words were said about Jesus Christ even before he was born. Everyone is living in darkness whether living in a comfortable house in the West or starving in a barren land. No human being is able to give this light that opens the eyes of the heart, apart from Jesus Himself.

Many leaders throughout history claimed that they could deliver their people but every one of them failed to keep his promises and had to submit to death. Jesus *conquered death and rose from the dead*. He is alive today and he continues to help and comfort the downcast and the lowly. While the leaders of the world focus on keeping power and wealth for themselves, Jesus is looking for the helpless to strengthen them with eternal hope and life.

He is interested not only in the neglected people of the world but the rich and the powerful as well. All we need to do is ask him with humility to help us and change us. He can and he will change our heart to be humble and loving toward God and our fellow human beings. Just ask him from your heart to come and change you. Ask him to give you the eternal light of life. He will surely come and change your life from within. He promised.

With that simple blast from a fax machine, Jesus is preached. Now someone has to ponder a decision regarding Jesus! Will you back up this project in prayer so that more and more of those decisions will be positive? Imagine Kim Jong-il surrounded by an ever-growing coterie of Bible-believing, praying lovers of Jesus Christ. Incredible thought!

270. a prayer guide for nk

Today I begin a series of articles drawn from our new 30-day prayer manual for North Korea. You can get your free online copy by going to http://baekjeong.com/ and clicking on the appropriate link. You can also subscribe there to a free weekly North Korea newsletter. The manual is also available in the original Korean language.

The first entry I want to share from the manual is taken from the introduction. It begins with this praise poem... (All words in italics are directly from the book.)

"The air that I breathe, The sunlight that shines on my body

"Is completely filled with your love.

"I find that love in the hallways of my house, In the upper stories and the lowest floor.

"Your love is stacked in endless layers.

"By your forever-treasuring, Your warm encouragement,

"By your merciful love

"That wants to give to all again and again, I am astonished,

"Wondering how love can be so grand.

"Having been kept so long from love Only today, at threescore and ten

"Do I cry, though late, Finally comprehending.

"Ah, dear comrade Jung-Il Kim, You, man of passionate love,

"Are the incarnation of the greatest love."

Does this poem wound and offend you when you realize to whom it was sung? Then try for a while to understand the heart of God the Father Who has been offended by so many years of idolatry in this land. As long as the Enemy draws such praise, North Korea must be a frozen wasteland with no hope of deliverance.

Yes, *this poem was dedicated to Jung-Il Kim, the leader of North Korea, by Mr. Li In-Mo who had returned to North Korea after spending 34 years in a prison of South Korea. In this work, one can notice the writer's boundless devotion for Mr. Kim.*

By the time our prayers are answered, the North Koreans will sing songs like this to One Who is worthy to receive them, Jesus Christ.

271. kim jong il, mother of NK

You read it right. Over 30 years ago, Kim Jong-Il, dictator of North Korea, ordered official song-writers and poets, all of whom must be Party and Kim loyalists, to compare himself to a mother figure ! So they had at it. Poem after song after lyric feminized the Dear Leader. Here is a typical song describing North Korea's mom (translation makes it a little stiff, but you'll get the picture):

My mother

"Are you too warm or too cold?" She looked after me.

"Is life too painful and too difficult?" She held me to comfort

Mother, mother, benevolent mother,

I will honor her forever and ever .

With warm heart she watches over the road I take,

Even on the bright path she carefully watched over me.

Mother, mother, benevolent mother,

I will honor her forever and ever.

You were full of concern raising us up,

And still pour out love on your grown-ups;

Mother, mother, benevolent mother,

I will honor her forever and ever.

Well now, Christians couldn't just let those words stand. All praise belongs to God, the Father. So one believer in North Korea decided to tweak the original version just a leeetle bit. Out came the following poem. I personally prefer it...

My Father

The arms that hold my faith and future;

"Are you too warm or too cold?" He looks after me.

"Is life too painful or too difficult?" He holds and comforts me.

Love that I never knew before, great as heaven,

With all my heart I will serve him forever and ever.

Though I forget his loving grace and his embrace,
His love remains with me like the sunshine.
Love that I never knew before, great as heaven,
With all my heart I will serve him forever and ever.
The arms to which I committed all my dreams and future,
They are the eternal place that I will live after death;
The One Who holds my fate and my future,
Ah, my Jesus, I will serve Him forever.

Just another look at the baekjeong way of life in North Korea. People considered low-class by the government are taking government songs and making them into high-class praise. To One Who is worthy to receive them.

272. How the Gospel came to NK

Our second look at the North Korea prayer guide comes from Day 2, and features a history lesson. You can get your free online copy by going to http://baekjeong.com/ and clicking on the appropriate link. The following has been translated from the original (North) Korean.

The history of Protestantism in Korea started with the blood of martyrs although the good work hadbegun before that. In September 5, 1866, a Presbyterian missionary, Robert Thomas, arrived at the Dae-Dong River. He was captured and executed even before he began his missionary efforts. Before his execution, Thomas passed on his Bible. This bore the seeds of Christianity in Korea.

Following this event, John Ross, a preacher from Scotland, arrived and did evangelical work among the people of the Majo province. It was then that the Bible was translated into Korean for the first time. In 1885, the evangelical work of Horace Underwood and Henry Appenzeller helped continue the spread of the gospel. The

Jangea-hun Church was created on January 6, 1907. It contributed to the adoption of missionary work nationwide.

With the coming of Japan's rule over Korea, the church was slowly being forced into difficult times. The self-imposed Japanese government enacted a policy on September 9th, 1938 that forced all churches throughout Korea to follow the *Shinsachamvae*. This doctrine forced churches and followers to betray their loyalty to their faith by worshiping a false Deity. The Presbyterian Church was resistant and was the last institution to change.

Religion in Korea experienced a darkness that impacted the church for quite some time. Only ten years after the Japanese decree, communism was established in Korea. And in yet another ten, September 9th, 1958, the Kim Il-sung government ordered that all churches in North Korea must be cut off. Around 3,000 churches officially disappeared with that order. Only the hidden works remained.

But God Himself initiated the largest missionary efforts ever seen in North Korea as starvation plagued the nation. Ever-increasing numbers of refugees secretly fled to China, and were helped by the Christians in place over the river. People believed that if one were able to find a church in China, they would be saved from starvation. Most Korean refugees received help from the Christian churches and were baptized, in many cases being saved from even more than their hunger.

Sometimes there was no reaction when they first heard the Good News because of the education they had been given. But as they kept being exposed to the Truth, to praising, and to praying, they began to believe and repent. Some quietly met Jesus Christ through the work of the Holy Spirit like a dove, and some met Him through the work of that same Spirit like fire. One girl quickly met Jesus after she had heard the Good News for only 10 minutes! She is still following God. One secret agent of North Korea who was working on capturing Christians repented of his sin and cried, "God, I am a sinner! I have killed many Christians!"

Some people who met Jesus Christ devoted their lives to the mission of reaching their people. One missionary conveyed the words of Nehemiah to a 16-year-old North Korean refugee boy. "Nehemiah prayed God to forgive him and his nation after he realized that they were falling because of sin. It is due to idolatry that North Korea was devastated and so many people died there. They discard God. We should shoulder responsibility for the sin of North Korea and repent." After the boy heard these words, he started crying. Repenting the sin of his people along with his own sins, he prayed to God that he might be used like Nehemiah.

One girl who was trained in China for one and a half years confessed , "I want to be a servant of God like Moses and be one who prays for my people to repent and come back to God. I want to go out to the world following the call of God and proclaiming Jesus Christ so that many people can meet Him and become a people of praise, who honor and please God." God heard these prayers and did His work.

And He will hear our pleas too.

273. How to use propaganda for Jesus

All praise belongs to Jesus. The North Koreans have been grabbing songs of praise and commitment to Communism/Kim Jong-Il, and turning them into messages for God's people. How we love their boldness and creativity. Here are numbers two and three of the series. Remember that these are translated from the original North Korean.

This is a propaganda song asking North Korean young people to offer their lives for the Communist Party and the country. In mid 1990, Kim Jung Il complimented this song, saying that it combines literary and artistic qualities. It is commonly sung by NK people.

> What is Life? (original NK version)
> If somebody asks what life is,
> We will answer like this:
> It is the past on which you can look back with a smile
> At your last moment.
> As the streams gather to form a river,
> Each day gathers to make a lifetime.
> Who can blame if it is short?
> Eternity has nothing in common with time.
> If somebody asks what life is,
> We will answer like this:
> It is the moment that was given to the country
> That will never be forgotten with time.
> What is life? (new Christian hymn version)
> If someone asks what life is,
> We will answer like this:
> It is the way of following the Lord
> Who suffered for our sins.
> If someone asks what life is,
> We will answer like this:
> It is the way of living only for the Lord;
> That is what eternal life is for you and me.
> If someone asks what life is,
> We will answer like this:

It is the way of serving only the Lord,
The One Who gives us faith and hope.
Wait for Me (renamed Song of Faith)
This song was the title song for the movie "Away From the Headquarters" which was to glorify Kim Jung Il's mother Kim Jung Suk. The place mention here, "O San Duk" is the birth place of Kim's mother in the northern part of Ham-Kyoung province.

Wait for Me (Original NK version)
Let's not cry when we depart from each other;
Let's not be sorrowful when we walk on the thorny road.
Wait for me, wait wait for me.
We will meet again when the day of independence comes.
Song of faith (new Christian hymn version)
May the love we share never change;
May it never change though time passes by.
As the flower that follows the sun,
May our love for the One never change.
May the hope we share never change;
May it never change though we walk the thorny path.
Like the sun and moon that lights the dark world,
May we live tomorrow as a beam of light.
May the faith we share never change;
May it never change though the storm is heavy.
Though it may be lonely to walk till the end,
May you and I live eternity in faith.
Amen. Thank you again, North Korean believers! You inspire us so much!

274. creating the new human being, NK style

Here are some facts about NK's educational system from one who lived there. As is increasingly true in our own land, education there is geared to making robots for the "system." This piece is from our new 30-day manual.

Education in North Korea is categorized into preschool, elementary, secondary, and "higher". Preschool is a two-year program that has low level (first year) and high level (second year). Elementary includes a four-year primary school and a six-year middle school. Higher education is similar to the University system in South Korea. The undergraduate program is held in a technical college (three-year program), a college (four-years), or a university (four to seven-years). After the undergraduate program, there are research and PhD courses (two to three years).

The nation believes it has made a country where "anyone can learn." The purpose of education in North Korea is to create competent people who will work for their government. On May 5, 1977, North Korea, using the words of Kim Il-sung, announced the heart of their view of education: "All students must be educated not to follow individualism and egoism but to devote oneself for the benefit of society and government and its revolutionary actions by the law of collectivism." North Korean constitutional law also mentions in article 43, "We educate and foster a new generation who will be innovators struggling for their society and people. We will create a new communistic human being who has knowledge, virtue, and a sound body." It is clear that the purpose of education in North Korea is to train the revolutionary, armed with communistic ideology by reconstructing human thoughts.

In the six-year middle school program, there are subjects such as *Revolution history of Kim Il Sung*, *Honored leader Kim Jong-il's revolution history*, *Korean language, algebra, geometry, physics,* chemistry, biology, Communism and ethics, music, physical education, English, Russian, and Chinese. Not only in specifically political subjects, but also in all the others, the contents of the textbooks and the lessons are strictly geared toward the praise of socialism, patriotism, communism, anti- Americanism, anti-imperialism, "anti-puppet government-ism", and anti-religion.

However, in these days, North Korea seems to be attempting to focus on fostering competent and talented persons. For example, they started an elective course system so that students can choose what they want and learn what they actually can use. Also in October, 2002, they brought up new rules to revise their educational work to meet the current trend of the Cabinet council. Since then, North Korea has been upgrading contents and the quality of their education through innovative changes.

God is preparing to do His work and to enlarge this nation through education. We pray that only God's will may be done in North Korean education.

Join your faith to this positive-minded North Korean, that one day normalcy will come to the land, as Jesus is allowed His rightful place in human hearts.

275. don't leave me in prison alone!

Jackie is a teen-aged young lady who lives in our Midwest. With a growing number of people all over the world, she has caught the fire inside of her that cries out for an outlet. She is the reporter behind this tale - a true one of course - from North Korea. May God keep raising up the youth, and the old guys like me, and everyone in between, to tell the stories of NK, until that land is totally surrounded by the love of God and His transforming power.

When Sun Lee defected to China in 2000, she believed she was leaving her native North Korea forever. Yet, while studying at an underground church seminary in China, the Lord began to impress upon her heart the desire to go back to her loved ones in North Korea and share with them the love of Jesus. But North Korean spies had been collecting information on her, so she was quickly arrested upon her return to her hometown. She was sent to Pyongyang for one month and then turned over to the Bowie Bureau, a special organization whose purpose is to protect Kim Jung II. "The most difficult punishment," Sun Lee says, "was when I was required to sit in one position for twenty-four hours without moving." She described it as worse than a beating.

Sun Lee knew there was a reason she was imprisoned, but she couldn't see what it was. She prayed, "You brought me to China to get educated, and I believe you brought me to North Korea, but please do something!" Six months into her prison term, at a time of depression and still wondering why she was there, the Lord answered her question and her prayer. A new prisoner, named EJ, arrived. EJ soon learned from other prisoners that Sun Lee was there for religious reasons and even though prisoners were not allowed to talk with each other, EJ began whispering questions about God to Sun Lee. Sun Lee realized that God had brought her to prison so that she could share the gospel with this tortured soul.

EJ was a spy for the Bowie Bureau in China before she was caught trying to defect to South Korea. Suffering from guilt for sending so many families to prison, she wanted to know if God existed and if He could ever forgive her. Sun Lee told her about 1 John 1:9 which says that if we confess our sins He is faithful to forgive. She also shared other verses from memory with EJ. Though the process was slow, God was working in EJ's heart. EJ confessed all her sins before the Lord and then prison could no longer keep her captive; she was free in Christ.

One evening EJ had a dream and in her dream the Lord said, "I will bring Sun Lee out of prison." EJ was terrified and cried out "What about me? I cannot make it here by myself." Sun Lee asked the Lord what she could do for EJ before she was released. He directed her to write down some Scripture. There was no paper, so she used what she had on hand, toilet paper. She didn't have a pencil to write with either but EJ was able to smuggle one from the investigation room. Thus, Sun Lee began to write some Bible verses for her. She wrote out the Lord's Prayer, Isaiah 41:10, some hymns she had memorized, and some other verses that God brought to her mind. In all, she was able to write about ten verses.

When Sun Lee was finished, EJ attempted to return the pencil, but it fell from her pocket and the guard saw it. He was angry and he started shouting. EJ was weak from three days of fasting and she fainted during his tirade. She was taken to the doctor and eventually returned to the cell without injury. Sun Lee had been afraid that EJ would confess about the paper, but she had not. When Sun Lee asked her why, she replied, "You have risked your life to give it to me, so I will carry it with me wherever I go." Sun Lee asked God to forgive her for doubting EJ.

EJ feared Sun Lee's imminent release, so Sun Lee asked God to show Himself to EJ in a dream and help strengthen her faith. He did and in the dream, two angels showed her a book, which was the Bible. They also showed her that Sun Lee's time of release was at hand. Sun Lee received a similar dream. She prayed for her release in one week's time if it were the Lord's will. Because of the dream EJ had, and the incident with the pencil, she was ready to let Sun Lee go. Her faith had become her own. The end of that week came on a Sunday, a day that no business took place. However, on this particular Sunday, the Superior Bureau people came and prepared papers for Sun Lee to sign (agreeing to be mute about her time in prison), and after she signed them she was released. It had been one year.

During her time in prison, God gave Sun Lee the desire to speak to the free world about the corruption in North Korea, and after defecting to China again, she waited for God's leading. She received a call from a pastor asking her to come to South Korea, and she prayed for God's direction. Three days later, a broker the pastor had hired called and said it was time to go...and she left within a few hours.

Since arriving in South Korea in 2006, Sun Lee seeks opportunities to speak her testimony and share the plight of the North Koreans with others.

The Bible says that the word of God is quick and powerful, sharper than any two edged sword. God also says through Isaiah His prophet "So shall My word be that goes forth from My mouth. It shall not return to Me void, but it will accomplish that which I please, and it will prosper in the thing to which I sent it."

These verses bring such a promise of hope because we know that whenever we open God's Word, God has His divine hand on that moment. Anytime we feel discouraged or we want to know more about what God has for us, we can easily pick up God's word and begin to read. This best-seller of all time, this life-changing book, the very words of God (!) ... at our fingertips.

This book so easily placed in our hands is almost entirely unavailable to North Koreans. Every page placed within their hands is a treasure that must be read in secret, memorized, and prized.

Sun Lee didn't have a Bible to share with EJ; she didn't even have one to read for herself. Everything she had was from her memory, and everything that EJ had rested on a piece of toilet paper. Unfortunately, this is the status of most Bibles in North Korea. North Korean Christians long to have God's word in their hands to study, to disciple others, and to share with others the hope of Jesus Christ.

Well, thanks to the partnership of Seoul USA and SDOK, this dream can finally be a reality. These two ministries have collaborated to print and distribute the first North Korean dialect Bible ever-completed for mass production.

During the 1970s, a North Korean Bible Scholar created a complete translation of the Scriptures in the North Korean dialect. This translation is widely regarded (by the United Bible Societies, the Korean Bible Society, and the Korean Language Scholars Society) as the best Korean translation of the Bible, but it has never been widely distributed. This Bible will be edited and reduced in dimensions so that it can be printed in portable and conveniently-sized copies. This will be the first time a full North Korean dialect Bible will be printed in mass quantity.

This project will directly benefit five thousand Christians in North Korea, and five thousand North Koreans visiting China on business or relative visas, as well as an estimated fifty thousand underground Christians or potential Christians in North Korea whom these original recipients will either teach or impact.

Imagine the power of God's Word sweeping the nation, touching lives, and shining forth the truth. The lives that see the light can never be the same again. Pray that many are reached and that God will accomplish a great work in North Korea and in the lives of those who serve Him.

"Oh how sweet are Your words to my taste, sweeter than honey to my mouth" are the words of David the Psalmist. He also says "Your words are a lamp unto my feet and a light unto my path."

Lord, let Your sweetness permeate North Korea and let Your light and Your word chase away the darkness and illuminate the way for those in the shadows.

"The grass withers and the flower fades but the words of the Lord last forever." Amen

276. tears for pyongyang

Today's entry is yet another song meant to bless North Korea's dictator, but intercepted by an enlightened North Korean, and made to praise the God Who alone can deal with praise, since He deserves it. The following is translated from the original (North) Korean.

Fly, Dove

This song was praised as one of the best works that artistically describes Kim Jung II's heroic reign. As you will see below, now the dove is proclaimed to be God's Holy Spirit.

Spreading the wings of hope in the blue sky,

Flying freely dancing forever;

Dove, Dove fly higher,

That the blue sky of my mother country may not become cloudy.

Loving my home Pyongyang so much,

He flies, dancing, holding the twilight on the wings;

Dove, Dove fly higher,

Your wings filled with happiness, even the fiery cloud won't stop you.

With our desire for loving peace,

Flying into the future against the storm;

Dove, Dove fly higher,

That your song may resound forever in this land.

Fly, Dove (New Christian hymn version)

Above the sky far far away, the Dove flies with our hope,

Above the sky of my home,

Dove, send this song to the throne of the Lord:

My love, willing to offer my life for this sinful land.

Sorrow heaped high on the street and villages,

Tears make ponds on the dry ground;

Dove, send this song to the throne of the Lord:

Our prayers, filled with stories of brokenness.

Dove, Dove fly higher.

(Spoken prayer) "Do not make an idol for yourself. Do not make any image of anything that is in heaven or on earth or the things in the seas. Do not bow down to them and do not serve them." You said this, Lord.

Lord, Pyongyang, which was once called the Jerusalem of the East, is turning into hell. Where the first church in the Korean peninsula was built 100 years ago, Kim Il -Sung's 60 meter tall statue now stands, alongside the 38,000 idols and the writings and songs for this "Great Leader" that blanket the entire nation.

Now let this be a time when we discern how this poverty came about. Help us to realize where the whole thing went wrong for these powerless people. Help us to repent and cry before this terrible reality my country faces where the worst idolatry is practiced as a nation.

I pray that no more people from my home will die of starvation. May my children in my homeland no longer wander the streets with hunger, and may my beloved sisters no longer sell their purity for a bowl of rice. Send food to those who have none, send the warmth of the sun to those who shiver in cold. Let those who are jealous, envious and grumbling realize that love, faith and hope are the gifts of God.

Your people also live in North Korea. Please look down upon those whose eyes are upon you. Please help these people who bow down their heads here. Plant in their hearts the calling, courage and wisdom to step forward to save the brothers, the country and the whole nation.

I will become one seed to share the hope,
I will keep this faith passed down by blood;
Dove, send this song to the throne of the Lord,
My love, willing to offer my life for this sinful land.
Dove, Dove fly higher

277. the deadly politics of pyongyang

Hyun-jung Hong, North Korean, is the name associated with the following translated narrative from our new 30 day prayer manual. Do you have your manual yet? It's free, and available at http://baekjeong.com . For a small fee you can order that book in its original Korean, at the same website.

The description of North Korean politics that follows is given by a refugee out of her experience. By reading it, you will understand better how North Korea controls its people and with what kind of ideology:

It is well known in the world that North Korea is governed by one man. Kim Il-sung's dictatorship which is unique in the world has been continued by Jong-Il Kim and his tyrant government. North Korean politics is so abnormal that this kind of political style cannot be found even in any other Communist country. Since 1980, the economy in North Korea has fallen rapidly. These days, Kim, who does not have any other way to recover the economy, is enforcing absolute loyalty to himself. He also forces his people into the Red Flag Spirit.

The Red Flag Spirit is like a life-decree which is, you win if you follow the Communist way, you die if you don't. It terrifies North Koreans who are suffering poverty and destitution. One of the most verifiable series of events related to it is the public firing squad and shooting on the spot carried out from October 1996 to March 1997.

The six-month shooting events happened all over North Korea , in Pyong-Seong, Soon-Cheon, Hoi-chang, Seong-Cheon, Mu-San. The charge was always, "National Traitor", and people who were shot to death were charged that they ate well like the people of property, while others starved.

Among the shooting events that I witnessed, there is one scene that is before my eyes now like a nightmare, even though five years have passed. It is the dead body of a mother who had been shot in a train station. They say she was from a rural village in Hwang-Hye do. She was trying to sell 30 bullets to the Chinese which she carried on her person. She was caught and searched by a non-uniformed security staff. Scared, she started to run, her pursuers shooting at her ruthlessly.

She got hit and fell down on the cement ground... with her baby on her back. People around who did not believe that they would shoot her were extremely shocked. They came to assist her, but she was already dead. The bullet had gone through her head. The baby on her back was crying and could not open its eyes as Mother's blood was all over its face. People shivered when someone pulled the baby away from the dead body.

This is shooting on the spot. It is not widely known how much of this has happened during the years. Even in the feudal age and Japanese imperialism age, innocent people like the baby's mom were exempted from shootings. Why in North Korean society, which says that it considers human lives so important, can someone take away another's life so easily? Powerless and sometimes innocent North Koreans live like dead people because their precious lives are not guaranteed in society.

The whole world saw how serious the situation was when Jang-Yeop Hwang, the godfather of the Juche Ideology, and other high-ranked government personnel, got out of North Korea and became exiles.

Then came the "Food Decree". It was issued by Kim to North Koreans who were eating rice roots and arrowroots as their meals. The decree allows for shooting a person on the spot if he steals an ear of corn. As a result, North Koreans started to escape to China. Jong-Il was embarrassed. His fascistic and dictatorial politics were revealed to be a very low-class methodology. The world was watching, by means of North Korean refugees.

With the cooperation of the Chinese government and the North Korean secret military agency, the number of refugees who were sent back to North Korea was as many as 3000 in the winter of 1998. For punishment, they had to wander here and there on bare feet, beaten, holding signposts saying, "I am a betrayer of society and our people," in the severely cold winter.

When we hear Kim's accusations of these tormented citizens, we're supposed to be angry, not sad. "Why did they desert their country? Why did they leave their hometown and relatives and move to foreign countries," citizens are supposed to say. The obvious truth is, if the North Korean government had provided enough food to keep people from starvation, they would never have left their beloved home. History cannot be dressed up in new clothes nor taken off like old ones.

Jong-il and other North Korean rulers are trying to do anything to keep their government from falling. Internally, they are threatening their people with guns and knives. Outwardly, they are telling other countries that North Korea is an "invincible Democratic People´s Republic of Korea" with its chief, its party, and its people as one.

The aged In-mo Lee was a war correspondent and a non-converted long-term prisoner in a South Korean P.O.W. camp. He changed his mind and wrote songs such as "the incarnation of love" and "the incarnation of faith" to support the ideology of North Korea. Please, who would want to call Kim Jong-il an incarnation of anything except misery? He and those around him have made a huge number of his people starve to death and wander to other countries to save their lives.

The North Koreans called Il-sung their "gruel general" and Jong-il their "grass general". An old saying goes, *The mind of the people is the mind of heaven*. The North Korean leader who is cursed and accused by his people should not be allowed to rule anymore. He must fall if he cannot give any hope.

As the firm Jericho castle was collapsed by God's words and power, many pray that this dictatorship is demolished like snow melting in the spring.

While reading this chapter, I came across an event which took a big portion of newspaper space. The article was about a scene from a firing squad in North Korea. It was taped in secret and released to many countries including South Korea and Japan, in March, 2005. Since then, they have set alarms and are hunting down refugees around the boundaries such as the Hoe-Ryung area. Also, North Korean secret agents have come into areas near the China boundary. All of this shows the reality of North Koreans suffering, a suffering initiated by their own government.

Well said, and thank you Hyun. We'll be praying.

278. nk economy: lies and pride.

This excerpt is from Day 13 of our NK prayer manual. Please go to http://baekjeong.com and order the entire pdf book.

Following is part of a book about the economic crisis written by a refugee mother from North Korea. Though a few people live comfortably, the majority of North Koreans have suffered because of the economic difficulties. This article may help you understand NK's economy:

North Korea is confronting an economic crisis due to the deficiency of food, raw materials and foreign exchange. Since 1990, the breaking down of Communism in the Soviet Union and Eastern Europe followed by a similar breakdown of the trade system of North Korea, has created a decrease of the amount of imported raw materials and energy sources which are so absolutely important formanufacturing. This has caused the economy to shrink dramatically and the situation, especially the shortage of food, became even worse after the '95-'96 flood and the drought of 1997. At present, less than 10 % of the factories of North Korea are producing goods. Most medium and small-sized businesses have stopped operating altogether.

Due to the continuing drought and food scarcity, continuous power supply became impossible. Of course, that also affects the railway system. It is accepted as daily routine for trains to stop in the middle of the route or for service to be suspended one or two days due to a power shortage.

Kim Il-sung, ruler for North Korea's first 50 years, said in his greeting statement of the New Year, 1992,

"It is my heart's desire that every North Korean may be able to eat beef broth and rice, wear silk dresses, and live in tile-roofed houses." But Kim's 50 years' promise died out with his own death, and North Koreans are seriously starving even without being provided so much as corn and bean-paste soup. So now it is the heart's desire of the North Korean to have food, clothing and housing of any kind.

North Korea's poor situation has been known through many problems and in various ways to the outside world. The pain can be summed up in just two phrases: "economic crisis" and "financial panic." People live without essentials of life like shoes, socks and undergarments. Maybe people should not be concerned about what to wear, when there is such a shortage of food. But, think about it: There are actually a lot of North Korean men who cannot afford "inner wear". Women have to mend theirs or even have to live without any because so many textile factories and clothing manufacturers have been closed.

Yet, Kim Jong-Il spent eight hundred-ninety million dollars for preserving his father's body permanently in the same form as when he was alive. Since there are about two million tons of food shortage annually, that eight hundred-ninety million dollars could have been used for feeding North Koreans for three years. Kim Jong-Il chose to spend the money to satisfy his own desires and to keep his dictatorship, at the cost of millions of starving people's lives. Another outlandish expense is the ongoing "war expenditure" against a non-existing invasion threat from South Korea.

There was one poor woman in North Korea who borrowed some money from her neighbor to start a small business. She became a peddler in an effort to feed her children. She bought some products and took a train to transfer them. Since there were too many people on the train she couldn't stay inside.

So she climbed on the roof. A guard followed her and tried to steal the products she had bought. She couldn't believe it. And if she lost them all of her family would starve to death. So she begged and begged in tears. But the guard was stubborn. The woman was so desperate that she gave up everything and she grabbed a high-voltage cable above the train while holding the guard.

Both were shocked. The woman died instantly with a hole near her neck and the guard lost consciousness. Such sad accidents occur often due to the economic collapse.

The crisis of North Korea is not due to the economic blockade by foreign countries, as Kim claims. It is because of medieval style personal dictatorship. Kim Jong-Il advocates a so-called self-supporting economy which is about blocking foreign funds and trying to elevate North Koreans' life quality by only North Korea's own production ability and natural resources. But his false policy has been driving the North Koreans into crisis.

In these days, the majority of coal mines or steel mills in North Korea are just empty buildings. Most of the important machines or accessories inside were sold to Chinese smugglers a long time ago. In 1997, when the food shortage was so critical, almost every North Korean family sold all their metal such as copper, iron, lead, and zinc so that an excessive amount of metal was smuggled abroad. Not only was the typically metal-rich north exhausted of its supplies, but throughout the southern portion of the country, in places like Ja Gang-do and Sin Ei-ju, vast amounts of metal were traded.

The government tried to stop it in many ways. They used guns, forced confession, and all the rest. But what do the people care about all that when they are confronted by starvation? Death is death.

North Korea's economy is totally devastated and has failed. The only way of overcoming the crisis is for Jong-Il and his followers to repent of what they have done before God and the North Korean people and return to God and his words. I am praying that the North Korea economy is recovered so that joy in each family is revived and the North Koreans' wish of life is resurrected in the name of Jesus.

279. korea's bible men

Here's something that was sent to me by Seoul USA, a ministry that is reaching North Koreans wherever they live. It is an explanation as to why Korea's church is so Bible-based. May it ever be. And may those north of the DMZ (38th parallel) get more and more a taste of the solid Rock upon which many South Koreans have been established. This was written and translated by Koreans, with just a little English assistance from yours truly...

The Korean church grew rapidly after the Sino-Japanese War and the Russo-Japanese War. In 1894, missionaries from the American Northern Presbyterian church had 235 baptized believers and the Methodist church had 221 registered and "probationers" in the church. But by 1905 the number of Christians increased to 30,386 and 7,796 each. This was partly due to the Russo-Japanese War but perhaps moreso due to the growth of faith resulting from the distribution of the Korean Bible.

The believers were aware of the evangelical power of the Bible from their experience and they put all their heart into distributing it. This was influenced by Ross and Nevius who emphasized Korean independence.

The Korean aggression in Bible distribution is brought out in this article by the British Bible Society, reported in 1899:

"The Bible society has not employed as many Bible men in some areas as we should have. This is because the Korean people are doing it themselves. In Pyoung-An province the local churches are taking this responsibility so seriously that within three years there will not be any more villages or cities left that needs to be reached with the Bible."

The Bible society withdrew their "Bible men" from the areas where local churches were eagerly distributing the bibles. At Eun-Yul church which was under the supervision of missionary C. E. Sharp, the Bibles were stored in the church building so that believers could take them along to a market place or neighboring villages to evangelize.

In addition, Korean churches employed the Bible men independently and supported them. "Won-San Southern Methodist church and Mok-Po Southern Presbyterian church each supported one Bible man per year." And the Korean Christians had huge interest in their report when they came back from their trip. "Bible men's ministry continued with a great interest and passionate prayer from our church. When the Bible men return to their home at the end of each month, the saints gather in their houses to hear the joyful news."

In the year 1899, Korean churches even chose one Sunday in May as "Bible Sunday" in order to spread the Bible, and by 1902, almost every church in Korea celebrated this special day.

There you have it. Well, not all of it. There were Bible WOMEN, too! Next time...

280. korea's bible women

As promised, here is the sequel to my last blog. How often God has used women in His program is beyond counting. I trust that no one who has ever read my literature on the subject of "women in ministry" has ever come away thinking anything else. There is truly a place, and this article, written and translated by Koreans, is one of those places...

Bible Women

When the Gospel reached Korea for the first time, there was strict segregation between men and women. The Bible men could not approach the women with their Bibles and that is why the Bible women came into being.

Mrs. Adamson who was working in Bu-San, employed one Bible Woman in 1896 and perhaps this lady would have been the first Bible Woman in Korea. Even if the only place of ministry for the Bible Women would be the kitchen, at least that place was opened for them.

Some of the Bible Women were from the gentry class, like Kim Sarah, but most of them were widows or mature women from believing families.

One of the essential qualifications to become a Bible woman was that she had to be able to read. But women who could read were very rare. Apart from some lady from a well-to-do family, hardly any women knew how to read. For this reason, if the candidates met other important criteria, they were recruited and taught how to read first.

During the period of 1898 to 1904, about 15 to 30 Bible

Women were employed. They were paid by the Bible Society, but they were under the supervision of female missionaries. Sometimes, they were partially supported by other mission organizations and churches apart from the Bible Society. In that case, they spent a proportional amount of time selling Bibles.

Their main task was to visit women's quarters and read to them from the stories of the Bible and explain the truth. One of their major responsibilities was to teach "Han-gul", the Korean language. Women during this period did not know how to read and write, thus they were not interested in buying the Bible. So when they finished working during the day, the Bible Women gathered women to teach them during the evening.

A "Mrs. Jones" who supervised the Bible Women made the following comments about the effect of the Bible Women teaching Han-gul: "Finding how many people who have learned how to read gives me the greatest joy...three years ago, in our church here in Kang-Hwa, we did not have anyone who could read, but now I can see 29 people who are reading their Bible."

So Korean women learned to appreciate the Bible by learning how to read. Around this time, Bible study meetings opened up in many places for women, and most of the women who came to the meetings believed in Jesus and learned how to read. Of course the Bible Women's book sale record was far behind that of their counterparts, but the truth of the Gospel and Christianity that they preached gave new freedom and joy through Jesus Christ to those women who were poor and marginalized in society.

Education was provided for the Bible Women to improve the effectiveness of their ministry. In the report to the American Bible Society written in 1901, Mrs. Skrinton said that the Bible Women were doing a great work but were not meeting the demand. So, she decided to start a Bible Women's School. A Bible class began in 1897 and a Bible study class and college started in 1905.

The English term "Bible Woman" also came to mean "Evangelist" woman. Now when mission organizations and churches use this term, it almost always means female Evangelists. When it is used by the Bible Society, it means the Bible Women. However, during the early days when there was great shortage of female workers there was not a clear distinction. And when the churches grew through the 1910's the number of women evangelists grew but the number of Bible Women decreased. This means that the emphasis moved away from Bible sale to evangelism toward non-believers and Bible study.

And now you know.......... the REST of the story!

Whether by men or by women or by boy or by girl, may God now get His Word back to North Korea. What great things are in store when this happens!

281. one big unhappy family

How does the Confucian-based family fare in Kim Jong-il's version of Korea? Can we believe that his ripping apart of the social structure can leave a blank slate upon which Christ will be allowed to write?

The following is from Seoul USA's 30 Day Prayer Manual for North Korea, Day 14, "Family."

Since communism started to reign, North Korea has built a new concept of family supported by their communist ideology and replacing the traditional idea of family. On

September 1, 1946, the government abolished the traditional family registration system and, also traditional, the concept of kinship through the 'Revolution of family' policy, claiming that they are remnants of the feudal age.

Instead the government started the *citizenship system*. During the 1940's, Pyongyang broke down the family-centered economic foundation through socialistic revolution policies such as abolition of private ownership of land and the inheritance system. They then made the family into a control unit of the Communist Party and as an intermediate group which promotes the achievement of tasks that the Party gives out.

In 1946 came the "law of the right of equality of genders in North Korea," by which they secured women's social-political roles and positions. This law clearly gave women the same rights as men in voting, getting jobs, receiving wages and being educated. But women in North Korea have now even more burden than before, because this law drives them to the sites of severe labor, formerly allocated to men.

Even though the equality law was established, in reality the traditional patriarchy, with husbands and sons in the center, still survives. Wives are still in a subordinated relationship to their husbands. The old traditions are so widespread that husbands still have a lot of power in the family, and in fact commonly use violence against their wives.

Many restrictions apply in NK marriages. For example, an executive member of the Party or even a candidate for Party membership cannot marry a woman whose background is not firmly based on Communist ideology. Workers whose jobs are in places like an armament factory, have trouble marrying a woman on the "outside" due to security issues involved.

The government also controls the education of each family's children. Babies whose ages are between 30 days and 36 months are left to the care of a government-sponsored day public nursery. When babies turn four years of age, they are sent to pre-school where they are educated systematically the way the government wants. All children are supposed to be raised to become devoted to communism and fascism. But actually, after all the economic difficulties, it is hard to expect people to support this program. The serious financial crisis has destroyed many families, and their love for their nation.

The above was given to us by North Koreans raised in the NK system, true authorities on the system. We encourage your persistent prayer in the light of these somber facts.

282. child is king of the country

I didn't say it. The Bible doesn't say it , that I know of. Some parents do spoil their kids a bit, but Christian ones teach the Kingship of Jesus. No, it was Kim Il Sung, the father of North Korea's present dictator, that said it. Kim began a dynasty that looks now like it will reach its third stage in the son of Kim Jong Il. But that's another story.

The statement I use as the title of my blog today is first the title of a new book put out by Life and Human Rights Books, the publishing arm of the Citizens' Alliance for North Korean Human Rights. It is not specifically a Christian book, but for its thoroughness of research of the plight of the child in North Korea, it is unmatched.

The title is given not to promote Kim's philosophical theory, but to show just how far away from this lofty ideal the Kims have come in their treatment of children in the

DPRK.

The book, however excellent in reporting, is tragic in its content. I cannot imagine a place on earth where children's rights are more abused, unless it be so-called civilized nations that foster out-of-control abortion policies. Nothing is more despicable than the murder of an innocent child quietly resting in its mother's womb. But that too is another story.

One thing the book brings out is that school authorities and teachers of North Korea often benefit from children under the guise of helping the state economy. For example, children are forced to the mountains to gather a specified quota of acorns, pine nuts, herbs, supposedly to earn foreign currency. The quotas are high, though, and many do not reach them. These unfortunates must make up the difference using their own food, such as peas or corn, or even with cash.

Children in Korean schools, further, are asked to buy all their school materials, even those that have to do with maintenance or furnishings or education tools. But the outside world is told that North Koreans, products of socialism, have free education. As America heads down the socialist road, consider the amount of our taxes that goes to Washington spending on educational measures. This is for America's "free" education! And those who decide to go to better, and Christ-based, schools must pay tuition too... but *again* I digress!

In the winter is the worst of it. Young children must gather boughs and twigs from the mountains to heat their schools. Middle School students are to carry along axes and saws and cut down entire trees, help load them on trucks... Accidents are commonplace.

Then there is the requirement that certain students bring in raw materials such as metal pieces, rubber... children unable to cope with this request are kept from joining certain youth organizations, and subjected to other discrimination. Children thus motivated resort to any number of ways to hold their own, including outright stealing.

Families that cannot keep up with the constant series of demands are forced to leave education behind. Low attendance rates is a growing problem in this nation of many problems.

As always, this material is provided that you might pray for God's wonderful Light to shine in Satan's awful darkness. Oh that they can see the alternative to the Kim Jong Il way of life!

283. why don't you visit pyongyang?

Today I once more give my column over to North Korean writing, as found in the 30-day prayer manual you can receive free at http://baekjeong.com . This is from Day 19.

Some people who visit Pyongyang get a little sentimental, like Yoon Suk-min, a famous composer for student activists' songs in the 80's and 90's. He visited Pyongyang in 2003 and composed a song entitled "*Why don't you visit Pyongyang?*" on the return flight:

Why don't you visit Pyongyang when you have hard times?

There are people who live with smiles despite the hard times,

There are priceless people.

We must feel a type of brotherhood when we see North Koreans. We must be able to see the future of the beautiful and bright Pyongyang. But we must also see the *veiled truth* of the city. Most of the fugitives who have fled from North Korea know the veiled truth. Many South Korean are not able to see the truth and easily fall into the sentimental approach of the composer.

But we must take a look at the dark side of Pyongyang. We will love them when we see it. We will have a consistent heart-love for North Korea. Here is some of the "dark side" of which I speak:

1. A city for show. Pyongyang is a place for showing a good face toward foreigners, since there are some in the city who live quite well. NK Citizens living outside this metropolis must receive, often with great difficulty, a special pass to travel there. North Koreans want to be in Pyongyang at least once in their lifetime.

And yet, at least one foreign businessman who lived in North Korea for a while said that Pyongyang is not North Korea, since it was built simply for show to the rest of the world.

2. The center of Idols. Pyongyang is the city where the "greatness" of North Korea and Kim Il-sung and Kim Jong-il are broadcast to foreigners, much as in Nebuchadnezzar's Babylon. Visitors are brought to the statues of the leaders and all the historic monuments.

3. The center of waste. We can feel the struggle of famine and poverty-stricken North Koreans at famous places where huge outlays of cash were expended, including the pagoda of the Juche ideology, the Man Kyung-dae Home, Kum-kang-san Palace, and Youk-yung Hotel.

Incredibly, as mentioned on another day, the government spent eight hundred nine million dollars to build up the Palace where they laid Kim Il-sung's body in state. This amount of money is equal to 600,000 tons of imported corn.

If they had spent that money purchasing food, upwards to 300,000 lives might have been spared, some estimate. Therefore, many North Koreans think Pyongyang is a city to be disdained, not admired.

We must be able to see the shadows of Pyongyang inside what is being propagandized for the world. Even then, we do not judge, but rather pray. We ask God to forgive us, as we witness a city once called "Jerusalem" become a place full of sin. Let us call out to God that He will change the city back to its former glory.

284. the korean war rolls on

Syngman Rhee refused to sign.

It was July 27, 1953, and U.S. President Dwight Eisenhower went to Korea in hopes of ending this bloody and long-standing "conflict." Both sides of the Korean peninsula had tried everything imaginable to be the ultimate victor, but nothing was working.

The North had invaded first, a now-documented fact still denied by that nation. North Korea had provoked the South, just as it is doing as I write these words today, but when all was said and done, it was a pouring over the artificial border by zillions of North Korean troops that started this awful slaughter.

The surprise and brute force involved pushed the South farther and farther back until only the southeastern tip of the nation, near Pusan, still stood. It seemed that within days the world would be talking of Communist Korea, much as it does now of Communist Vietnam. What a different region if not world this would be if things had not turned around.

In the providence of God, American General Macarthur was empowered to launch an attack at Inchon, behind the troops of North Korea. Trapped and startled, they eventually made their way back into the northern regions, with American-Korean troops on their heels. Back across the "line", the 38th parallel, and farther. On to the Chinese border.

Then another surprise. China, the sometimes loyal mother of the Korean people, not wanting a free American-based nation on its border, sent hordes of troops down into Korea and countered the American offensive. Back down, down, to where everything had started. The line.

The line still stands. One of the few differences of the boundary line is that it now comes south of what once was the capital of all Korea, Kaesong. It is firmly in North Korea now. And it was at Kaesong, where at this writing a South Korean is being held hostage, and where the dread of more such hostages hovers as a joint North-South business venture fails in the wake of a pending war, here that the truce was signed on that fateful day 56 years ago this July 27.

Well, that is, North Korea signed, America signed. But Syngman Rhee, Korea's first President in the South, would not sign. In his eyes, all of Korea was one, the war had been a horrible waste of life and time, and this was an unjust settlement. Fight on until this thing is settled.

Dear Mr. Rhee, equally praised and villified by historians, may soon get his way. Kim Jong II seems poised for the continuation of hostilities, armed with nuclear capabilities and the seeming inability of the "great nations" to stand in his way.

What Mr. Kim has always failed to realize is that the Korean War will roll on with or without him. This is a war being fought in the heavens, as are all wars of men. God's will, not Kim's will, will be done. The Koreans will hear of

Jesus, Kim or no Kim. They will be called to Eternal Life, Kim or no Kim.

God enlists soldiers for this war even now. Prayer warriors must position themselves and dig in the trenches on a daily basis to uphold this land. They must listen to the Commander in Chief for strategic ideas about how to get the work done that needs to be done.

"Listeners" to date have been involved in sending the Gospel into this ravaged land via balloon, fax, Bible smuggler, and a lot of other ways. Jesus will not be denied His place. The Korean War is His to win. Let us march into this hell with Him.

285. lives for sale

As I write, the world awaits the verdict of the North Korean trial of two American journalists, apprehended and imprisoned with the charge of "hostile acts" toward the North Korean people.

What they were in China - Yanji to be exact - to do, has been done by many, and will continue to be done as long as certain issues remain unresolved in North Korea. Issues like sex/marriage trafficking.

I have talked on this blog before of those evil men who wait at the China/NK border for desperate North Koreans looking for a new life, a decent meal, a little hope. They are offered all three. The price is pretty high, though: a lifetime of slavery to the sexual or marital needs of some lonely Chinese or ethnic Korean man.

In honor of those two who are under lock and key, while many pray for their release, I offer a story from the new HRNK book, Lives for Sale (2009). This is a book filled with personal accounts of women fleeing to North Korea. Like Ms Kim in China's Jilin Province: I quote directly from the book, page 33.

"I was married in North Korea and had two sons. My father died from an illness in 1996. My husband worked in a coal mine, and I worked in the restaurant of a motel. I was not in a good relationship with my husband and finally we divorced.

"My sister-in-law and her husband left North Korea in 1997 and went to China; she was caught and sent back to North Korea, where she was put in a detention center. After she was released, she persuaded me to go to China with her.

"In January 1999, I crossed the Tumen River with my sister-in-law. She was taken in by the same Chinese family she had been sold to before the arrest. I went to Tumen in Yanbian and stayed in the house of an old ethnic Korean woman who owned an orchard near the house. I worked in the orchard. There were a few more North Koreans staying there.

"One day, a friend of the old woman came to visit her and said she would get me a decent husband. A few days later, a couple who were ethnic Koreans living in Heilongjiang Province came to the house. Then, the five of us all took a train to Heilongjiang.

"We arrived at a house where I was introduced to a man who was about 30 years old. He was just smiling and speaking to himself. It turned out that he was the younger brother of the couple and had been mentally ill for the last ten years. Even the old woman who owned the orchard in Yanbian and had brought me there was shocked at seeing him.

"Nevertheless, her friend took 3,000 yuan from the man's sister and they went back to Yanbian leaving me there."

Unfortunately North Korean women in China often have no option but to marry Chinese men in rural areas, most of them poor, some elderly, where they become entrapped in the poverty, hardship, and unhappiness they left Korea to escape. Some are beaten and badly mistreated...

Do I need mention to you believers in Jesus, that North Korea continues to need our desperate prayers?

286. what happened when i moved south

Seoul USA has published a 30-day prayer manual, in English and Korean, for those whose love for Korea demands a greater outlet. You may order yours at http://baekjeong.com. The following article, about Korea's "settlers", written by a North Korean, is from Day 23 of the manual:

Most North Korean refugees, when they hear the truth about South Korea, want to go there. Since 1998 the number of North Korean refugees entering South Korea has increased every year. There were 1,894 North Koreans who entered South Korea in 2004. This number decreased to 1,383 in 2005. The total number of *saetŏmin*, that is, North Korean refugees settled in South Korea, reached over 8,000 in June, 2006.

Since these thousands of North Koreans are totally accessible to the West, we need to be prepared in prayer and knowledge of them. We need to understand what kinds of problems they have when they reach South Korea, what causes those problems, and so on.

First, Saetŏmin, are by and large very frustrated. They

had thought South Koreans were their very own people. But they feel betrayed when they are virtually ignored by the South. I heard a settler say he wanted to leave South Korea after he was so humiliated, so ignored, and so abused by his employer. He believes that the discrimination would be less in other countries.

Second, these displaced Koreans are confused and feel lonely. They are living in a place with a totally different mind-set from their old ways of thinking. For example, one settler complained about his wife who seemed to be copying the ways of the South Korean women. She began to talk back and be disrespectful, like she had never been before. So some change is negative.

But there are positive changes that are a challenge also. Some are just not able to change their life style with which they grew up. They simply don't want, and don't try, to learn some new way of living. Some even want to avoid contact with South Koreans altogether.

Third, only a few defectors have a good job. In the NK group of which I am familiar, a full 80% are unemployed. Some are involved in job training, but the percentage is way too high. Consider also that the defector population is largely in the 20's and 30's age bracket. Finding a job is their worst problem.

Fourth, many *saetomin* students study under great stress. Most of them are not allowed into their proper grade, because of the time lost in travel and readjustment. This can actually be several years in some cases. They simply fell behind. Many of those students, out of shame, just give up public school altogether. Some are able to enter a private institution or simply find a GED course so that they can get ready for college.

Fifth, and finally, many who gained faith in China, came

to South Korea and slowly lost it. Why? Unfortunately, it is because they take a look at those who call themselves Christians, and are turned off. Also, some are concerned about the constant demand for offerings, and the rigid organizational structure of the South Korean congregation. Some even complain that the service is boring.

If the South Korean church is going to help its northern visitors, it must learn to love them aggressively. The church must be, among other things, a safe and friendly place to go. Its message must encourage their faith and point them to Jesus. Fortunately, there are some churches, even large ones, that have caught this vision and are beginning to understand the need.

Hmmm. That will "preach" in America too. Thank you again NK, for your deep insights, purchased with your pain.

287. a new look at the dmz

Captain's star date NK2009, 06-22.

Now you may think it's an exaggeration calling this trip a Star-Trek-like journey. That's because you probably did not have seaweed soup for breakfast. It doesn't crunch at all like my cereal at home. You probably haven't had to sit on the floor and eat using two sticks either. Korea has modernized a lot, but we've been going traditional quite often, seeing things that many don't see. Speaking of that, we took a trip to the DMZ that most do not take...

The DMZ (demilitarized zone) is a 3-4 mile wide space that entends roughly across the 38th parallel, the western-fabricated line that has divided the Korean peninsula into two countries since the end of the Korean War. It is 50 miles north of Seoul.

An armistice -not a peace agreement - was signed on July 27, 1953, and the conflict, though occasionally punctuated with clashes at the border and on the Seas surrounding Korea, was put on hold at that time. The DMZ , filled with land mines and soldiers from both sides is the silent but threatening testimony to the fact that peace is very fragile here.

The DMZ is the most fortified border in the world. It is especially scary at Panmunjeom, where the original peace talks were held in 1951. There angry-looking soldiers will intimidate their counterparts on the other side, and visitors too if they can.

Though the tour was originally scheduled to visit tunnels around the DMZ, dug by North Korea and discovered and filled by South Korea, and though the normal visit includes Panmunjeom, our group was forced at the last minute to take a third alternative, the Dora Observatory, the nearest point to North Korea from South Korea.

From our vantage point, we did not see angry soldiers trying to stare us down with intimidating affects. Instead, the only sight of soldiers we had was some that were in a field farming the land. The group was ushered into a theatre to be briefed on the whole DMZ lay-out, then on our own we assembled outside for prayer.

What a joy to plead for North Korea's soul from this place. Will you join us from your place in these pleas? The Korean national wish on both sides is unification. God's wishes are even greater. He wants to bring them into His Everlasting Kingdom, united with Christ for eternity.

More when I can write again...

288. Kim tells me his story.

I think you know by now that I'm in Seoul for a few weeks. Meeting some very fine people. Let me tell you about a few of them. This brother, whose name I have changed, is a man whose failures far outweigh his successes. But all his exercises in futility lead him to the only success that matters after all...

Kim Yong Sang was born in the late 70's in the most remote province of a most remote nation. Stripped of its natural resources and its original beauty, this land is the worst of the worst that the enemy of our souls has done in Chosun.

At an age that is far too young to be experiencing such things, his mom and dad succumb to the pressures of life and are divorced. Though he stays with father where there is less of a problem for his survival, his heart reaches out to Mom, who moves to the mountains to see if she can eke out an existence of some sort. Most Korean sons cannot see their mothers in such pain.

Against his own personal longings, yet in accord with Korean tradition, he picks up the family mantra of farming, and gives money earned to his mother.

In 1980's North Korea, when his farming life begins, a one-year portion of food is a mere 50 kilograms of corn. The government graciously provides a certain area of land, available for a small rental fee. Production must be reported to the "landlord", and of course that same entity grabs its share off the top.

Did I say 50 kilograms? Clumsy of me. After processing, the actual weight is more like 30 kilograms. And if the corn is not ripe, the number drops even further. And yes, I did say, one year.

It is hard work, especially for a growing boy, but the temptation to miss a day now and then is far off-set by pressures from various organizations who become aware of the shortcoming. In the ever present Communist youth clubs, children must take an oath to serve the dictating Kims forever. And serve they do. Like machines serve, without soul, without joy, except that which is pasted on by those who watch for smiles.

So to miss work is considered a sin in a nation that doesn't even know of the One who defines that word properly. Meetings akin to our church services are held weekly, and a major portion of the time is spent in criticism. Not Biblical or textual criticism. Self criticism. Public personal condemnation of one's own faults, faults being those imperfections that hinder the progress of Communism, and the North Korean version of same called "Juche."

Even though one is hungry, he goes to work to avoid those meetings.

Whether the farmer son, or the father , of a different calling, it is considered normal to put in a full eight-hour day combined to three or four hours of overtime. From age ten. Anything less is considered a blatant show of disloyalty.

In a good year, reports Mr. Kim, there is no extra food offered to the worker, only to the government coffers. Still, throughout the 80's, he is doing well enough. By the turn of the decade, a sudden drop in the oil supply of the nation has a serious affect on farming machinery. Oxen are used more, but this does not meet the need. And though less and less is possible each year, the quotas remain the same. Uncle Kim Jong Il gets his, but our Kim and his family see their corn ration dwindle to starvation levels.

Now the entire farming community has to head for the hills, looking for edible plants, wild vegetables. This, added to the meager amount of rice, allows for a thin soup meal each day.

Seeing his income, and thus his means of helping his mother, evaporate, Mr. Kim escapes the farming area, and finds his way to a hospital where goats are raised. He is brought on board, and starts a new life as a goatherd.

When it becomes clear that he cannot both survive and send things to Mom on this income, he starts an extra-curricular business in the mountains. Securing his goats firmly in a place where they can eat grass much of the day, he climbs into the higher elevations and creates his own farming plot. This of course is illegal. No ownership, no privately run enterprises are allowed in North Korea. Only the government can own. If the police hear that a citizen is making money, they do an investigation, confiscate the money, and send the creative person to jail.

Though Kim knows all of this, he continues on, even adding to his list of jobs a carpentry business. He makes and repairs farming equipment, using his experience as a farmer. Then he finds used and old furniture, refurbishes it and resells it. He is only 18 years of age.

His string of luck begins to run out. As could have been predicted, one day the Police do indeed come and and ask why he is doing all this, and he is forced to give profits to them, so much so that he cannot continue this line of work. Thankfully, he escapes a jail sentence.

In 1998, as the now-famous North Korean famine has been raging for several years, he follows a steady flow of refugees out of North Korea into China with his mother and sister. His intent is not to live there, only to visit awhile until things get a little better.

*Next time I will tell you what happens in China...
Meanwhile, my oft-repeated plea to pray for North Korea.
Prayer is the only hope that nation has, but it's a great one!*

289. failed but not a failure, part 2 of the Kim story

*This is the second of three portions of a story I heard
first-hand in Seoul. "Mr. Kim" is a dear brother in the Lord
whose story cries to be heard. I pass it on to you in hopes that
you will pray for the thousands he represents who suffer
now...*

*We were talking about how he got to China and what
happened there.*

His mother's sister is a Christian in China. During his
stay, auntie brings them all to church. This is a novel
experience. Seeds are planted.

In the providence of God Kim meets an old High School
acquaintance who convinces him not to go back to his
homeland, ever. He listens to the wisdom, but still in China
there is constant fear of going back whether one wants to or
not.

Church is not the only novelty that greets Kim. He listens
to the radio on a channel not fixed by the government. He
hears the truth about the place of his birth. Through
programs such as the Voice of America, and the whole
network known as Korean Broadcasting System (South
Korea), he begins slowly to understand the concept known as
freedom. What a jolt. What a glorious surprise.

Time passes. The fever of freedom running high, he

decides to go to one of the (South) Korean embassies in China. Why not? These are his people! Surely they will understand his plight and bend over backwards to help.

The meeting of refugee and consul takes place. Not exactly a backward bend. A smile perhaps. An acknowledgemnt of the problem. But no help.

Four months later he goes to another Chinese city to talk with the officers of another consulate. He is again refused. What he does not understand - nor does the entire civilized world - is that the Chinese do not believe that North Koreans who leave their land because Kim Jong Il will not feed them, are refugees. No, they are just hungry.

What the Chinese do not understand is that even hunger is a crime in North Korea, if one tries to satisfy that hunger by crossing a country border. Being sent back to North Korea is certain imprisonment, and if connections have been made to the church, certain death.

What we wish we did not have to tell the Korean refugees is the other fact. The other fact is that South Korea would rather not be bothered with these folks either.

Blissfully ignorant of the craziness of modern governments, burning with a dream to be free, he refuses to give up. This is the man who has given his whole life until now to serving his mother's needs. Farming. Goatherding. Businesses. He will not allow men dressed in suits and ties to thwart this passion which drives him.

His mother now marries an ethnic Korean in China. His new step-dad is connected to a company which soon hires Kim. But when the boss finds out he is a defector, he is fired and it becomes increasingly difficult to find another job. Failed again. But not quite finished.

He sells food for a living. Step-dad says, not enough money. Get out. The irony is that the stepfather's other two sons, the "real" ones, do nothing but gamble, lose money, and replace their losses with free handouts from Dad. That means that all that food money and company-paid money that Kim has been dutifully turning in for his mother's sake is being turned into games of chance by his step-siblings.

Angry, he and his mother plan to explode step-dad's house with dynamite. The plan is not to kill the father, only to get his attention. But though Mom sympathizes and plots, eventually the plan is cancelled. And she will not leave this new man. Against all his heart's leanings, Kim is forced into leaving his dear mother, to begin a new chapter in his life.

First stop, the nearest airport . He has no ID, so he will not be flying in the normal way. His plan is to find a way to get into the cargo hold somehow, and smuggle himself into South Korea.

He goes over a fence fifteen minutes before departure . He positions himself close to an airplane, and hides in a luggage cart. But once more he is discovered, reported to police, arrested.

Their first reaction is to inform him that they will send him back to North Korea. But he begs for his life, and gets off with a few years in prison, in hopes that the NK situation will change. He accepts the Chinese offer.

When the case is brought to court, he is charged with terrorism. His honesty will not allow him to accept such a thing, and he denies it in court. This throws a monkey-wrench into the plan, and he is told there will now be an adjournment until morning. The next day, instead of hearing, Let's now continue this case, he hears, The verdict is...

And the verdict is "guilty". Guilty of terrorism. Case closed. He asks if he can appeal, but even Chinese citizens cannot have this luxury. Who does he think he is, they wonder.

Good question. Who do North Koreans think they are? Should they believe what the governments around them have decided, or can we offer them some better answers? It's part of what we are doing in Seoul this summer.

290. Failed, but not a failure, part 3

I offer today the final installation of the story of yet another "Mr. Kim." His life is proof that failure must be a term defined only by God, and only on that day when we meet him. Judging from appearances in his life, many would have written Mr. Kim off a long time ago. But his story, like yours and mine, continues on until the last chapter.

We had just received the verdict of his court case...

And the verdict is "guilty". Guilty of terrorism. Case closed. He asks if he can appeal, but even Chinese citizens cannot have this luxury. Who does he think he is, they wonder.

As a North Korean, discrimination is evident in prison. He is made to wear a special uniform. He has less opportunity for exercise than the others.

Prison life soon begins to wear on him. He clashes with guards, who tell their supervisor, who creates even worse pressure. He becomes so obnoxious that he is forced into solitary confinement for 50 days. He loses the desire to live in this 6 x 2 box. Yes, that's about coffin-size.

Even the non-solitary imprisonment is nothing to write home about. It's a basement, there is no sunlight, it is damp, it is cold. He is fed corn soup in the amount of about a half a cup, 2 times a day. He has no energy, no body-heat, serious skin problems, and more.

It gets worse. Ruffians are sent into his cell to fight with him. He becomes angrier still.

Eventually, suicidal thoughts stalk him daily. In one attempt at ending it all, he tears up a bed sheet. Avoiding the camera, he hooks up the sheet to a pipe on the ceiling. The hanging begins. When he wakes up, the distant rumble of a headache informs him he has failed in this enterprise also. He opens his eyes. He is on the floor. Someone has cut him down.

Forever the persistent one, he tries again. This time he asks for some razor blades from a fellow-prisoner. Acquiring this new treasure, he cuts himself 17-18 times. Blood gushes out. Surely now he is a success...

Yes, but not like he imagines. He sleeps. Hears noise. Wakes up. Oops, that means, alive. The blanket he has used to cover himself from being discovered on camera has actually stopped the blood from flowing.

Just how long will this train of failures continue?

The Chinese police do not treat his wounds except to wrap some gauze around his arm. Perhaps motivated by appearances more than compassion. Oh, and he receives 40 days more in solitary.

So where is God, he questions. He knows there is a God now, but he doesn't know how to pray to Him. For so many years he has denied God's very existence. Yet, these strange failures at suicide. God must not only exist, but He must have a purpose for my life. This could not have been a coincidence. Grasping at the little bit of Christian revelation he has taken in, he goes from that awareness of a merciful God Who gives meaning to life, to the even more fascinating idea called forgiveness. He tries it out.

The first persons he wants to forgive are the guards. Done. The police. Done. Friendships develop. Eventually help is received.

He now reasons, God has brought me this far and He will not let me be harmed even if I have to go back to North Korea. He prays every day. His fighting days are over. He complies with the guards' demands. His sentence is reduced.

As I listened to this story first-hand in Seoul, I could not help but hear, "If any man be in Christ he is a new creation." Who can change a heart like Jesus?

The statement of his case is not sent to the North Korean government. He tells them simply that he has robbed and fought in China. Though he is apprehended by North Korean police on his return, God sends him friends at this time who help him escape their grasp.

In December of 2007, when the Tumen River, dividing China from North Korea, is usually not yet frozen, Kim finds to his delight that the weather is a bit different this year, and he walks across on solid ice into China. Thence through a series of other exciting events, he finally comes into South Korea, where he now resides.

To this day he gives God glory for what He did, and he loves to tell his story to all who will listen. And we surely were listening.

Now let us go to God where we always have a ready audience, and ask God's blessing on this brother who must continue on with his life despite all the memories of trauma and pain. God grant him victory and peace, and a ministry that will touch many!

291. a westerner reflects on persecution

Being around those who suffer, or are threatened suffering, puts some new perspectives in a man's heart. Brings questions to the foreground that often are buried.

There are two questions in particular.

1. Am I really willing to carry the cross when there is persecution? I don't like pain and inconvenience. I have found out this summer how really frail I am in a lot of ways. What if this minor affliction I experience now were made permanent, and added to? Would I eventually flinch? Would I follow Jesus no matter what? Oh Jesus, pray for me like You did for Peter, that my faith fail not in the hour of trial.

2. Until the above is a reality in my life either by a special calling of God or a general persecution that comes to my nation, another question needs to be dealt with. Am I willing to carry the cross in the midst of plenty? When others are eating a lot, will I choose to eat a little? When others are going to the world for their pleasures, will I be willing to stick with the people of God? When others are trusting television, will I spend time with God? When others are looking for fashion clothes, will I be satisfied with just covering my body? These decisions are forced on the persecuted. We who have a choice, what will we choose? In persecuted lands, mother and father and child can be separated against one's will. Am I willing to lay all these people on the altar and follow Christ regardless?

The American team from Portland, Oregon is gone as I write blogs now. What a blessing they were. One morning we visited a traditional early-morning prayer meeting. Literally hundreds were present. It was good to see that people of a western persuasion are still willing to get out of bed early to feed their souls.

I must say though that the preacher's message was a bit troubling. And I'm told that there is much of this in South Korean shepherding. It goes something like this:

Christians are now leading our world. Obama is a Christian. Korea's new president is a Christian. Follow Jesus and you too can be a huge success. Consider Colin Powell as another example. He is a Christian, and God has blessed him with this important position. God wants Christians to rule and to have power.

No one can doubt that Korean churches are successful in this regard. The largest churches in the world are Korean. This church has 100,000 members, and 150 pastors! The Korean church has nearly as many missionaries as the Uunited States already. They will have more in the next decade if the trend continues.

So we surely don't want to knock success. But is Western Christianity in general too hung up on numbers, and too little hung on the cross Jesus places before us? Is our calling to build great churches or great Christians? Is the Kingdom now, or after Jesus comes?

More questions than answers today. Please pray for North Korea...

292. on a mountain in seoul

Our Seoul saga continues. Had thought I would give you a travelogue about all the interesting things we are seeing. But the thing that really interests us is the people we keep meeting and the stories they tell us. Here's one, for example...

Much, though not all, of the now-famous *Crossing* movie about North Korean refugees is based on the life of one Yu Sang Joon. The American team visiting Seoul in the summer of 2009 was privileged to be audience to this special man. Then my wife and I were blessed to be invited to his apartment later in the summer.

He was born in July 1963, in Chongjin, Hamgyung Bukto province, North Korea. Thirty years later he escaped to China with his son. He worked there two years seven months. Then he made his escape to the South. Not in his public testimony nor in our private interview did he ever mention family again. Even an innocent query into his earliest days and how his family life was then, brought only a one-sentence reference to the fact that there was no joy in that life either. His was a poor family. Both his parents have long since died. And the events that were in some way covered by the movie are hidden deep inside. Such pain.

In 2001 he was granted South Korean citizenship, and gained employment at a company there.

In 2003, he felt the inner call to help other North Koreans to come to safety. Eventually this sort of activity got him arrested. That was in 2007. He had been assisting some to get to the Mongolia border. Government assistance from America, Europe, and South Korea helped in his release.

We asked him why he continues to assist others in these dangerous places. His comment was that what people do depends simply on how interested they are. Interested people simply do these things. They may not be all excited about it. They just do it. Those who don't care, don't do. Echoes of the Biblical sentiment that "perfect love casts out fear."

He has often considered working in a regular job again, but friends who need his assistance in the ministry keep saying, please help us! He responds to the call and in spite of what seems to be failing health, greatly desires to be in this ministry and even be a bridge builder for other ministries.

Though wanting to see effective ministries, he himself does not participate with a particular group, preferring to work alone. Some things he has seen in the ministry of the church and para-church has turned him off. He feels that some are in it for the money, or the reputation. A bitterness has crept in. He's not into groups that "show off" or simply "talk."

Mr. Yu lives alone now, and much of his life has been characterized by this aloneness. Though he tells me that as many as 70 North Korean defectors live in the immediate vicinity, he rarely fellowships with them. There's an unrelated grandma that lives next door, calling him and other neighbors over for coffee almost every day. It happened while we were there. She also cares about his house and his plants when he must go on one of his mission trips to bless North Koreans in some way. Or when he is in prison.

He lives near a mountain that he climbs daily to start the day. He took his two American visitors on the trek that afternoon even though he had already been there himself that morning. We got, according to his estimate, about 1/5 of the way up before we cried for mercy, sat on some chairs that suddenly and happily appeared, then began the happier trek down.

For him, the mountain is essential to health, physical and mental. He gets away from the noise and traffic of Seoul and sits and walks alone for hours at a time, letting the cooler air ,the birds, the greenery, bring healing to a soul that has felt the winds of hell.

Mr. Yu struggles still in the area of faith. Your prayers are appreciated. In 1998 in China, while doing some farming work, the owner's aunt gave him a tract. His first reaction, a thought formed through many years of indoctrination, was, "This is superstition." He only believed what he could see.

In North Korea, there is a visible god, after all, false or not. There are pictures and statues of Kim everywhere. But who could ever believe in an invisible God? The thought that this unseen one could create the world, the whole concept of "Heaven," it was all too much.

But in 1999, in the summer, a Korean American

missionary saw his living condition, formed a friendship with him, and gave his personal testimony. In addition, he left a booklet and a tape.

As he thought about this man praying for him so seriously, and for his son too, he was thankful, and his heart was strangely warmed.

He looked at the booklet, a description of South American missionaries. My, Christianity looked better than Communist philosophy. And the tape, it was about thankfulness, and loving others. Incredibly he felt very comfortable with it, realizing he had discovered some very good news. The missionary returned often, prayed with him, sought to win his heart.

The battle continues to rage, as he contemplates the realities of the heavenly world vs. the only world he has known as a citizen of North Korea. Though he attends a local church, it is only once a week, and his involvement in it stops there. His life, his cause, is North Korean ministry.

Mr. Yu coughed during his entire presentation and to a lesser degree with us. He does not present at first as one who is vigorous in physical or other health. (But don't try to match him in a mountain-climbing contest.)He has lost his family. He struggles with God. Yet he continues on striving to bless those who suffer as he has suffered.

The group here prayed for him. My wife and I prayed again, even brought him some medicines. Now we pass on the prayer request to you, that he will truly discover God and trust His Son fully. We believe that somewhere in this man is a statement about Who Jesus is and why He is a friend of the *baekjeong*.

293. *an anniversary gift for the nk gov't*

June 25 was the anniversary of the beginning of the Korean War, a war that continues without a settlement, without a true peace accord.

On that particular day this summer, the American team from Portland and Chicago had a gift to offer the present government. You might call it an anniversary present. Though it was unwelcome to the Communist rulers, it surely was a boon to others throughout the nation.

It was 80,000 tracts sharing good news about Jesus.

It started with a bus ride to Incheon, famous for critical invasions. The briefing on the bus as we approached the port city was somber, even scary. We were given words to repeat should we be approached by anyone on the boat or even before we boarded:

1. I am carrying an American passport. and/or
2. I am here observing the launch.

And nothing more. Nothing, nothing more.

Thankfully we never needed to perform our lines. All went nearly perfectly. One hour by fishing boat into the sea, up towards North Korea. We were accompanied by two patrol boats and had a KCIA (Korean Central Intelligence Agency) man on board. Just in case. None of this escort was requested by us. What we were about to do was perfectly legal but typically raises important eyebrows when it is done. You just never know what might happen.

I saw that KCIA man doing two interesting things. He helped to feed the black-tailed gulls that followed us all the way. And he made a call on his cell phone when we arrived within the proper distance of NK. I'll let you guess which event had me shivering just a little extra. (Hint: I'm an avid bird-watcher and had never seen a black-tailed gull before today.)

No, I don't know how close we came to the controversial waters where fishermen and others have been threatened by North Korean vessels. I decided not to ask. Doesn't really matter.

What matters is that within 30 minutes of our arrival at the "spot", eight balloons were filled with hydrogen and began sailing up into the sky and out over North Korea. Their payload: 10,000 tracts each, to be time-released all over that land, announcing from the heavens that Jesus Christ is the leader that is needed there.

Happy Anniversary, Mr. Kim and company. God have mercy on North Korea!

Thank you Lord, for the reminder that

"Jesus shall reign where'er the sun doth his successive journeys run,

His Kingdom stretch from shore to shore, 'til moons shall wax and wane no more!"

294. aquariums of pyongyang: an update

Thirty plus years ago a 10-year-old boy entered a North Korean labor camp with his family. He lived to tell about it, the first story of its kind: The Aquariums of Pyongyang, *by Kang Chol-Hwan. There's probably not a serious North Korea watcher who has not read* Aquariums. *In a now-rare public appearance, Mr. Kang addressed our SeoulUSA team a couple of weeks ago. For those who have wondered what happens to refugees once they have their dramatic escape, this talk was certainly informative.*

Kang Chol Hwan is doing his best to live a normal life. Can anyone imagine how abnormal his life was, by any standard the world over, living in a labor camp in North Korea?

Once settled in South Korea, he graduated from Hamyang University. After all, his former study, in prison, was limited to survival tactics and knowledge about the Kim dynasty, not far removed from the education afforded the entire nation. he needed the real thing, and got it in Seoul.

He was then employed by the Korea Electric Company for three years. He is working now, and has been for nine years, as a reporter for Chosun Ilbo, the well-known Korean daily newspaper.

Nevertheless, he has not completely severed his ties with the sorrowful past of his life. He is a well-respected member of the North Korean Democratic Movement. The Council of Five upon which he sits includes men like Voice of Freedom's Kim Seung Min and Juche architect Hwang Jang Yop.

Later editions of his book trace his journey to faith in Christ after his experiences. For the last fifteen years he has attended a Baptist church in Yeoido. For those who may remember, this is the church Jimmy Carter visited on a diplomatic trip to Korea.

Kang continues to grow in his understandings of faith, and life itself. He came to South Korea with what he describes as a "messed-up mental state." He left family in the North when he departed. The sons of North Korea are all given a legacy of misery and emotional chaos.

As he pointed out, in a democratic country, there are many choices that determine one's fate. In an un-liberated nation, the choices are already made. That puts a lot of responsibility on the free.

Taking his responsibility seriously, he -as he says - *accidentally* went to a church at one point in his searchings, but *deliberately* got on the right path when the message he heard captivated him.

Next time: a trip to the Office of the President of the USA.

295. Aquariums update, part 2

The author of "Aquariums of Pyongyang" intrigued a team of Americans with his testimony in Seoul this summer. He doesn't go public often these days. Trying to live a normal life. But the call is still upon him to work, and work he does. Here's the rest of the story of Kang Chol-Hwan.

In 2005, the George W. Bush White House invited him for a 40-minute private session, where he was able to tell his story, and offer a copy of it to the leader of the free world. Such honor. From such misery. He gives God the glory for this incident, one which deeply affected the President as well. It was such testimony as Kang's that helped Mr. Bush properly to discern the character of this rogue nation and its rogue leader.

Does Kang desire democracy for North Korea? Absolutely! But without hesitating he will tell you that he wants the Gospel to go there even more! Kang claims - and the claim is not without contest in some quarters - that North Koreans are finished with Juche, that is, the political philosophy of the Kim dynasty, and further that North Korea will fall soon.

Most would agree that at least inwardly, a multitude of North Koreans have soured on this evil regime, and that eventually it will end. If Kang has spoken in an extreme manner only out of a consuming hatred for what he has seen, who can blame him?

But even so, he says, we need a plan. We are not ready now to evangelize or disciple properly the masses of citizens that would be set free in a total failure of the government.

The people of North Korea need to know the right path of life or they won't know what to do when everything dissolves, he affirms. They simply cannot adjust without the Light that comes from knowing the Lord.

He should know. Seventeen years ago he came to South Korea, uneducated and without a clue. Well, he had one clue. It was faith in Christ. And through that faith he has been able to progress.

He documents many who came over at about the same time, bright, strong, but faithless. They fell apart in this new world.

So faith must get to North Korea before North Koreans come south in an avalanche. But the Book that contains that faith is a sure way to get more Koreans killed. If one is caught with a Bible he can be killed instantly or at least sent to prison.

So Kang suggests that broadcasting is the best way to give the Word to North Korea. In keeping with this he has been given 1000 radios by Far East Broadcasting Corporation for distribution in North Korea. He delineates at least three methods of media distribution, which I must leave to your vivid imagination.

Kang believes that Kim Jong Il is afraid. He will not change, but his people can. Hearing over and over the truth via the media that has been the pathway of lies is the salvation of this country.

Even the United States State Department is supporting these projects. For this reason, among others, he is regularly followed by the Korean CIA. These are serious matters. Kang says that being a Christian is a more severe crime than espionage. Put the two together, though, as NK leaders do for some reason, and you have a target that the NK government eyes regularly.

Though he continues to desire the "normal life" that every man seeks, Kang Chol Hwan has been touched forever by two dynamic forces: the darkness of the Kim Jong Il Empire, and the Light of the Kingdom of God. These things war in him daily, and in that sense, for the Christian, he has entered into a sort of normalcy after all. Is that not your conflict also?

Will you pray for your brother Kang today, and often?

296. Mr Lee. marked for life

We continue on, reporting the story of one of the finest men I have ever met. What grace to know such folks!

The first sight that greeted us as we entered the Lees' high rise apartment was a collection of clear plastic bags, filled with thousands of fliers. We knew exactly what they were for and for whom. Kim Jong Il would be receiving a downpour of blessing as this brother and his colleagues would soon be launching helium-filled balloons carrying a payload of tens of thousands of messages for time release in the unfriendly skies of North Korea.

Lee and his wife have been here several years now, attempting to make the difficult adjustment from one country to another. *South Korea is not North Korea.* With all its conveniences and liberties, the new country is never the old. Separation anxiety is not just a human to human event. Being wrenched from one's land is an awful, tormenting pain.

Brother Lee comes from a city that received much Gospel on the Korean Peninsula in the early days.

Unfortunately, by the time of his birth that fact was lost on the population.

His earliest memory is of Mom working in a restaurant to support the family in a North Korea that was surviving, though not wildly prosperous. And of Dad. Not such a pleasant memory there. One day Dad is just gone. Disappeared. Lots of such magic takes place in North Korea. Here one day, gone the next. Dad is careless in his speech one day. Dares to speak favorably, or so it seemed, of the Americans of the Pueblo incident. That was the 1968 event wherein North Korea accused the USS Pueblo of straying into its waters, killed one of its men, captured the rest, tortured them...

To favor in any way the American side of things, that's all it takes in Kim Il Sung's Korea effectively to end one's life. Dad is reported. He is never seen again by his family.

Lee is eight years old. The government confiscates all their belongings and sends the family packing to the countryside. No restaurant income now. To the fields for sustenance in backbreaking all-day work. And where is the rest of the family during these dire straits? All under pressure because of those same comments by Dad. No one dares to help these outcasts.

Even his older sister, married some time before, won't be getting a visit from Mom any time soon. She's not allowed to travel. Can't obtain the necessary paperwork to go from here to there. Travel passes are required of all North Korean citizens. No pass, no passage.

The mark that is on young Lee continues through school days. Discrimination is his partner for many years. He is elected, because of his considerable abilities to a foreign language institute, but a friend is chosen over him. A friend not quite his peer in talent, but who is politically more sound.

His mother in tears has to explain what happened. She does not defend her husband. That is not permitted. She merely warns the son of her love, that he needs to be very careful. He must work twice as hard just to keep up.

The advice is followed. But he is still not allowed to join the military, go to college. One stray comment has done all this.

It is unpleasant to note here that in the first 18 years of his life, our Mr. Lee has never heard the name of Jesus. Mother occasionally talks about the "sky", a place where one might go, or at least a symbol for better things. But not the Bible's "Heaven." Lee suspects though, that since his city was such a well known spot for Christianity in the years not too long before this, that Mom probably knew, and felt she had to protect her son from imprisonment by keeping silent.

It is probably in the mid 70's that a major turn in Lee's thinking occurs. Surely he has to suspect before this that something is rotten in Pyongyang, but it all comes into focus when his friend, like his father, disappears. This particular ally is the captain of his classroom, the main man. His father is a professor in the University. One day, comrade captain does not show up for class. Very unusual for him. Lee stops by his house after school. It is empty. He finds that every member of the house has been taken to a prison camp.

Yet this is a good man. He thinks of his own father. Why entire families made to suffer? He is shocked, angry. All his other classmates had rejected him, but this one had not. He asks his mother for more details, for more information about Dad, his character, his philosophy. He finds that his dad had been arrested many years before his birth in the famous Sinuiju demonstration, for which he had been sent to Russia for several years. Dad always spoke his mind.

He begins to think positive thoughts about his father. Surely Kim Il Sung is wrong about that one. And, he knows that Americans are wealthy. Something his government denies. Two strikes against the truthfulness of his "god." He then considers all the political prisoners out there in much worse shape than is he. He begins to turn his heart toward them. They're all good people, he believes. But they're cut off. Why? Kim Il Sung looks worse and worse.

Lee goes to work in the metal industry, and then another turning point. Kim Il Sung makes a monumental decision as the decade of the 80's begins. He reasons that even the low-class folks who may have made a mistake somewhere down the line, deserve a chance to be embraced by Communism and his Utopia. Why not let them work their way back into his favor?

In a general amnesty of sorts, Lee is now given schooling opportunities, if he is willing to work, work, work. He is. He goes into the study of Chinese traditional medicine. While in college though, he is not allowed to enter the "Party," gateway to all privilege in a Communist country, for the same reason as before. Mother becomes worried that after college her son too will make a mistake, and end up like his father.

True, his views have changed. He finds himself increasingly taking the side of anyone who is opposed to his government. Seeing a *Nodung Daily* article (North Korean newspaper) criticize the *Chosun Daily* (from South Korea), he assumes the SK paper is correct.

And when that same North Korean daily criticizes France for demanding younger beef and protesting against the government, Lee sees only, "Hey, the French can actually eat beef!" And his frustration with things as they are continues to grow.

After graduation from the medical program, Lee is allowed to enter for a couple of years into a job in a hospital, followed by more doctors' training, and yet another hospital. During all this time, he never makes public statements against the government, though he does allow himself to confide in relatives from time to time. He says things to them like, "Wouldn't it be great to go into a school classroom and write on one of the chalkboards there just how evil the Kim government is?"

But publicly he is so careful that even on one of his frequent trips to the countryside he refrains from picking up one of the multitude of air-dropped fliers he sees on the ground. There the truth keeps flying in, but citizens are forbidden to know it.

And where is the message of Jesus now in his thinking? Twenty years have passed in his story. By now he has heard the message! Clandestinely, via shortwave radio. Good news, yes?

Sadly we hear the words of the Ethiopian eunuch of the Bible story, "How can I understand unless someone helps me?" Not a bad question when a Philip is standing by to expose the Word. No Philip. So no Word. Frankly, he tells us, the program is meaningless to him. Not a clue.

Please check in next time. I know personally that this story turns out well. What a treasure of the grace of God is this Mr. Lee. He and his wife still desperately need your prayer, but they overcome daily...

297. mr lee, part 2

There are marks left on our souls by men, and other marks by God Himself that overrule men's plans. Mr. Lee is a marked man, for sure, but he bears now the mark of Jesus.

Quite apart from politics and religion an event now occurs that is the catalyst for the rest of his ongoing adventure. Borrowing a friend's boat, he goes to China to sell some merchandise. A price is agreed upon, the deal is settled. Supposedly.

Upon arrival, Mr. Lee is told that they need to weigh the shipment before they can pay him. Leave the merchandise here. But a week later, when payment should have been forthcoming, and a month later, and longer, there is no money to be had. He stays there in an inn, waiting for the matter to be resolved. Finally it is found that the man who has taken the merchandise has gone. It is December. The little wooden boat is frozen at the dock. It is going nowhere as is its temporary pilot. He stays until spring.

Now, Mr. Lee has relatives in the part of China he has been visiting. Some of them long ago made their way to South Korea, and, left with a lot of time on his hands, Lee decides to check out the stories of his people. But his inquiries are reported. People are becoming suspicious. And then he hears that eleven of his friends back home have "disappeared." A case is mounting inside of him to use this opportunity to get out of North Korea altogether, and just stay in China.

He moves to another city, and lives the life of a refugee, sleeping on concrete floors, eating little food. He begins to think he will never make it to South Korea. His family will now be in danger.

His fears are realized as he is approached by Chinese police, whose questions, in Chinese, he cannot answer. After release, he lives in fear of a long-term confinement and his family suffering an even worse fate. I must stay alive, he insists to himself, I must go South!

For five long months he works at anything that is available.

Meanwhile, his distressed wife back in North Korea is constantly being asked questions of the police, questions which she of course cannot answer. A rumor begins to spread now that he has simply run away to China and will never return.

He goes to China's capital, short wave radio in hand. Hears the Voice of America, among other fascinating programming. Here is posted all sorts of information about defector routes and methods. He listens intently and decides to go the Spanish Embassy, a place that many NK defectors seem to frequent.

He goes to a Korean hotel there with his false Chinese I.D. He asks the innkeeper, How can I get to the Spanish Embassy? The innkeeper's response is a bit disappointing, for he challenges Mr. Lee instead to go to church, and meet a pastor. Write a letter, he says, expressing your intentions and give it to the pastor.

Not exactly what he is expecting, but certainly the hand of the Lord is in it. Lee innocently follows this advice, prepares the letter, goes to the church, and gives the letter to the pastor. But the pastor refuses to receive it.

Disgusted, Lee throws the letter on the floor and leaves. But God is not through. A phone call comes to him at the hotel. It is a church deacon. "Come to the church again." Nothing to lose now, he goes again.

The church deacon asks him all about the North Korean government, why he wants to go to the Spanish Embassy, etc. A thorough and careful testing. Satisfied with his answers, he now gives Lee the advice that will change his life forever:

"You can't go to the Spanish Embassy. It is guarded too well. Go to the British Embassy. There, you will encounter a high fence, but you can somehow get over."

"I will try," Lee affirms. "If I die, I die. Give me the address."

Done. Along with a series of instructions. Lee is not to look around, but to walk straight ahead. He is to buy a chair. Here is some money.

Lee arrives on the scene shortly afterwards and walks around the British Embassy three times. He is measuring the distance between guards, and the height of the fence. Then to a store for some gloves, razors, and a chair. He will do this thing the next day.

The fence is about 8 feet, topped off by barbed wire. It won't be easy. He practices climbing elsewhere. When it is time to sleep, he cannot.

It is at this juncture at his life when he begins once more to think about the things he has heard about God. God, the Heavenly Father. He puts out his cigarette and begins to pray, "I don't know how to talk to You. But I know that You know me and my family. Father, help me climb over that fence."

Sleepless night. Decides to wait another day, so he can study things a little more. He sleeps all day, waking up in the late afternoon. He decides that a chair isn't going to do the job. He'll need a folding ladder. He also prepares a concoction of red pepper powder and flour, and sticks a container of it in his pocket. If a guard pursues him, he will throw this in his face.

For the barbed wire, he'll need a small pillow. More practice. More measurements. Fifteen meters between policemen. He will need 7-8 seconds for the climb.

This night he sleeps two hours.

At 6:00 a.m. he begins his walk toward the guards,

positioning himself between two of them with ladder at the ready. A pillow protrudes from his back pack. He quickly begins the climb, reaches the barbed wire, and then... and then...

As Mr. Lee told us the story he suddenly went blank. There was no memory of the barbed-wire portion of the climb. The next memory is of falling into the British compound, technically a free man.

The Brits handcuff him immediately and take him into a basement where he is ex-rayed and his belongings thoroughly examined. The razors. Why did he bring the razors? His answer is simple. He takes an imaginary razor and slits himself on the throat. He intended suicide if this mission failed.

The Brits think this is funny. Of course, it isn't.

Kim wants to call the American Embassy, but a meeting with a South Korean consul convinces him that the way to America is long and hard and possibly fruitless. So although he knows he can say more to more people about the abuses of North Korea from an American platform, he resigns himself to South Korean citizenship.

Thirteen days later he takes up residence in the southern part of his peninsula. And through use of a broker, his wife is joined to him only one week after that! His assumption: "God did this!"

His relationship to Christ and His church grows after this, other connections are made, and soon he is a member of that select group of North Koreans who live in two lands at once. They are legal residents of South Korea, but refuse to forget that out of which they have come, and give their lives to serving Christ in their home land.

In Lee's case, he also desires to find a way to bring those other, very special, members of his family to the south.

Mr. Lee, you will recall, always wanted to go into a classroom and post bulletins on the boards there about the North Korean government. In his present life, he shall have that opportunity on a grander scale than he ever thought. His messages will be posted in the skies over Chosun, and on internet sites around the world. You are looking now at one of the desires of his heart. Do I even need to ask you to pray for this dear man and his family? May his very life bring you closer to Jesus.

298. note from a kotjebi

A missionary who works in China along the North Korean border was in the same office out of which I am working for a couple of weeks recently. We talked a lot about the situation there and he was eager to pass on stories and letters from people on the other side. I was eager to receive them. This one was especially meaningful to me. Please recall that this note is from a real person. And that the story is only weeks old. The nightmare known as North Korea continues on unabated and so much demands our prayers!

I lived as a wanderer in North Korea. Living like this was sometimes fun but other times it was sad. My dad and mom died when I was 8 or 9 years old. My sister and I had to live as "flower swallows". The North Korean term sounds like *kotjebi* in English. It's a colorful word but only means street orphans. We were named after birds because of the way we flit from place to place looking for food and shelter.

Without a house to stay during the winter season, we had to find lodging in the apartment alleyways, train stations, bus stations or on the streets. In order to survive we had to steal from other people's houses things like shoes, clothing, and whatever else we thought necessary to sustain life.

At the market, I used to pick pockets or tried to steal from food stands. It was fun at times but it wasn't too fun when I was beaten by those from whom I stole.

An 18- year old boy that I used to hang out with was beaten with a rifle by one of the security guards. What happened was that this older boy stole three kilograms of pork. He was caught. After the beating, he had to crawl for about a month. My sister and I now went to the market and stole food for this temporarily crippled boy .

Living like this was bitterly sad because of the hunger, but also because of the pain that comes from having no parents. When we heard people describe us as *flower swallows* we so longed for our parents. And when people described us as dogs and pigs, well, can anyone imagine this degradation?

I did not know the whole truth about China. In North Korea, I heard rumors that the Chinese sell North Korean people as slaves and they also might even cut off one's hands and feet. Because of these rumors I didn't dare go to China.

At least for awhile. Desperation changes people's minds about a lot of things. After a while, I found myself in the place I said I would never go. In China, I found so much food! From then on, I went across to China almost every day, just as if I were visiting the next door neighbor. Whenever I was hungry, I asked my friends to go over with me.

During early winter, the river freezes slightly and to cross safely, we all grab hands as we walk over the thin ice. Walking on the Chinese territory with bare feet was so awful that I actually lost my toes due to frostbite.

Last November, five of us boys planned to spend the winter in China. After my birthday, we went to an old couple's house in Jang Baek. They were like grandparents to me. I heard about church before but I never heard about God. From there, I came to know God and learned that He looks after even people like kotjebi.

I like much better hearing that the God of all cares about me, than that I am some animal or bird.

We have received love beyond our imagination. It is hard to believe that we are actually now living in China away from North Korea. The fact that we can live and hide here is unbelievable.

Above all I am happy and honored that I came to know the Lord. And I am equally grateful that other NK exiles have accepted the Lord Jesus too!

I am very happy that God helped me to know about the kingdom of heaven by bringing me to the church of Jesus Christ, out of North Korea where people serve Kim Jung Il and Kim Il Sung. When I grow up I want to be a servant of God and be his lamb. I will live like Isaac in the Bible.

I am now hoping for a lot of things I could not hope for in my own country:

1. I want to attend school.

2. I want to go into business, and use that as my cover for traveling back and forth from China to North Korea. While I am there I want to help build a huge church for Jesus.

3. I want to know the Bible well.

4. I want to be able to speak Chinese and English.

5. I want to have a permit to stay in China so I can move around freely.

Maybe there are people who can help me. Surely you can pray.

Father God, I thank you. By the help of many people, You have brought me from place to place safely. You have allowed many NK exiles to live a happy life. Thank You for your grace, Lord. Please lead me so that I can go to NK in the future and spread Your Word well. And also bless many grown ups who have helped me. I hope they will enjoy good health and that You will bless their steps. Thank you Lord and I pray in the name of Jesus who saved us from our sin. Amen.

Thank you friend. Brother in Jesus. We're with you.

299. refugee meets Jesus

This story is from a missionary to China with whom I worked while here in Seoul. I've heard similar tales to this for quite some time: Desperate North Korean meets Jesus in His people. I am compelled to tell it again. This unnamed but very real person is one of the thousands whose stories must be told so God's people will pray.

I came to China with my cousin by crossing the Tumen river. Because of the poor living conditions in North Korea, we came here in spite of the great danger in order to find our aunt who escaped to South Korea earlier.

It was actually in North Korea that I heard that the Christian church would help us. I found a missionary's phone number from a friend and was able to meet with him. When I told him my story, he found someone who said that he knew my aunt. He was living in Yanji, China, and for safety reasons, the missionary sent us there by taxi.

However, that Yanji person did not help us.

He said he could send my cousin to South Korea without any cost. When I asked him to send me as well to Korea with her, he said it was not possible. I became suspicious about this man and I called the missionary on the phone in secret. When I told him about the situation, the missionary said that the man could be a smuggler who sells young North Korean women. He told me to run away from that place immediately. So we looked for the right moment and ran away in the dark of the night.

When we escaped that night, having nowhere to go, the missionary contacted us and arranged for someone in the area to come and pick us up. We were able to spend the night with the helper. The next day the missionary came to Yanji and took us to Kae San Tun. We were so thankful to him: he put himself in great danger for us.

During my stay here, I came to learn about what "church" is and what God is like. Within such a short amount of time, I cannot say that I know much about any of this, but I will say that even though I was not able to meet my aunt, I am so happy that I came to know God and met him in my heart.

The church is just the opposite of what I was told by the communists in North Korea. Christians have been so kind to us. How can we express our gratitude well enough!

They gave us some money, with many medicines, and about 40 MP3 players. They also prepared enough food for us. This is just unimaginable in North Korea. We are especially grateful to the Kims who were so kind to us. When we return to North Korea we are planning on spreading the gospel when we have the opportunity. I want to tell the others about the love that I have received.

This trip is so full of unforgettable memories and I give thanks to God for his love.

Don't you just want to stand up and cheer, "YAY CHURCH!" Or rather, "YAY JESUS! for filling Your people with Your love where it is needed most."

There's not a people group anywhere on Earth that matches the called-out sojourning Kingdom people, the true Church of Jesus Christ. I ask you again to pray for the North Korean situation, including those believers on the NK border, in China, who are ready and waiting to bless the suffering who come out to liberty.

300. while i this vale was in

I close my summer of reporting from Seoul with yet another entry given me by a missionary to China. It is a letter written to him only weeks ago, from one who came out of North Korea and gratefully blesses God for his physical and spiritual deliverance. I can think of no better way to summarize the things we have seen and heard for the last six plus weeks.

We have a few more classes to teach, and Lord willing that will be followed by a trip to one of Seoul's Prayer Mountains, to seek the Lord's blessing before we return. I have more stories to tell, as God leads, when I return to the computer in a week or so.

Thank you for praying for North Koreans. Here is one of the results of your prayers, no doubt...

My name is....

I used to live in North Korea, and now I live in China. I'm writing this letter of thanksgiving to those South Koreans who have treated us in such a humane way.

When I was in North Korea, I didn't know anything about Christianity, not the real thing. What little I heard caused me to consider it a vain and foolish idea. Who could believe in an invisible non-existent being?

When I came to China, I went to church and heard Christians praying for the first time. I was exposed to their writings, books from Americans, from the Chinese. I read of heroic men who spread this Christian faith everywhere. I read of a powerful Holy Spirit that fills men.

My viewpoint began to change. As I considered the nations of the earth, it seemed to me that those nations that believe in God and those that do not are so obviously different from each other.

I began receiving ever so much help from the teachers God sent us. Every verse helps me understand a little more. Though I personally have very little knowledge and capacity to understand what the Spirit is doing, the teacher guides me along verse by verse.

I have now read the entire Old and New Testament, the whole Bible! In the future I want to read it again in much more detail. I want to go deeply into Christianity, because this faith is committed to the law of God. I can see that, and I desire it.

This is especially meaningful to such a person as I have been, who did not know God all his life, did not know how to control his emotions, now one who has come to this foreign country. Such a worthless sinful person! People like us are on the margins of life.

But God, in these teachers, treats us as precious. They take us in with a warm heart, and they nurture us.

I'd like to become a child of God, like the Christian people who have warmed our hearts.

I read this in Pilgrim's Progress, a poem that it seems was written just for me!

"O world of wonders, (I can say no less,)
That I should be preserved in that distress
That I have met with here! O blessed be
That hand that from it hath delivered me!
Dangers in darkness, devils, hell, and sin,
Did compass me, while I this vale was in;
Yea, snares, and pits, and traps, and nets did lie
My path about, that worthless, silly I

Might have been catch'd, entangled, and cast down;
But since I live, let Jesus wear the crown."

Lastly, I once more thank you that you showed us God's mercy and generosity in this difficult circumstance.

Sincerely....

301. *7 weeks with korean defectors*

Funny thing happened the other day. Several things actually. I took a shower in my bathroom and the entire floor did not get wet. I sat on a chair at lunch. I used a fork. I got in a car, turned on the ignition, and drove down the road. I saw the sky. I slept through the night.

That's right, we're home. Seven weeks of mission concluded. We are absolutely exhausted but hope to recover with your prayers.

We met them. We have *persons* in our hearts, and not just imaginations now. They're pretty ordinary folks who have suffered super-ordinary things. They're the greatest, just like we thought they would be. We captured their stories as they captured our hearts. We did some teaching, some learning, some interviewing, some traveling, some visitations. All that we said we would do.

Now we return to the constant documentation, posting of true tales and sermons, prayer, giving. We had planned a meeting for August 15, but that will be on hold for awhile.

Thanks be to God and to His people for an opportunity of a lifetime. Thanks to Seoul USA for setting it all up.

We feel we understand some things we couldn't have comprehended before. Like, being in another country, even a nice free one, is excruciating. Like, being on the outside of a group is simply not as fun as being on the inside. Like, sometimes life does not seem fair. But through it all, God's grace is sufficient for those who will call on the name of the Lord.

We learned that the cross given "us" is not like the one given "them." Trying on other people's crosses is an exercise in frustration. We learned that He will never give us more than we can bear. So we continue to have passion but not panic for those who suffer. God is in charge. When we pray, much happens. The world is not ours to save on our own.

We continue to bless the other side of the world while not forgetting our side. The friend, the neighbor, the co-worker, the church member... they all hurt sometime.

I personally learned how woefully low is my spiritual energy and ability to cope when coping is sorely needed. I developed a hunger for God and all He is ... I learned how wonderful the simple things of life are.

That's some of the stuff we picked up among hundreds of other things. I can only hope that those we "went to teach" picked up something from us.

302. my father was a south korean

Though we are back, the stories have not all been told. I'll keep posting what I have until you get the full picture of our summer. Her name is not important to the story, so please excuse that omission. My wife and I received this directly from a trainee at the Underground University.

I was born in 1960's North Korea, in the northeastern province of Hamgyeung Bukto. I was the oldest child, but not the happiest. Happiness seemed impossible for me growing up.

Much of the reason for my sadness centers around my father. My father was a South Korean. That's a pretty serious thing in my country.

During the Korean War years, when my dad was in his teens, the Chinese attacked his home town and arrested him. They took him away and eventually brought him to a North Korean military base.

"Where are you taking me?" he cried out, "My mom and dad are waiting. I must go home."

"You cannot go home any more. Take this gun , protect this country."

And so it was. He never returned to South Korea. And from that time on, the North Korean "CIA" was always watching Dad. All of my childhood was shadowed with the knowledge that we were being watched, very carefully watched.

I could not even go to college. I actually blamed my father in my younger years. How could I understand such things, the bitterness he had toward his new "home," his homesickness for the land south of us?

Though I too had a growing resentment toward the land of my birth, I could not express my anger toward the North Korean system. I was well aware that three generations of people could be hurt by saying the wrong thing.

I loved and married a man. I think now it was the wrong person. He was a soldier. He was a very loyal soldier. The kind of soldier who could take a picture with Kim Il Sung. Tension grew between my husband and I because of my father. I began to understand him, but I wanted to please my husband too.

Both of our parents had been against this marriage, but we were in love. However, by the time my daughter came along and reached the age of ten, we divorced. Now, divorce in North Korea, at least in those days, was not a common thing. Technically it was forbidden. But in this case, the government actually stepped in and made the separation occur. My loyal soldier husband was valuable to the Party. He was in line for a promotion in fact but my father's South Korean heritage did not look so good on his resume. I had to go. I moved back to my mom's house.

In the course of time, my old acquaintances came over to see me. Lots of chit-chat, renewing of friendships, etc. We talked about a lot of things, like the fact that some of those friends have relatives in America.

Strange. The friend with whom I had that discussion suddenly disappeared. After her disappearance, a man working in the North Korean CIA confronted me, and let me know that tomorrow I would be arrested! I discovered later that the reason was that people imagined that somehow I was the one encouraging this person to go to America and had even set up the trip!

But I didn't know that at the moment. I was shocked. Why did they have to take me? I thought it was because I was selling antiques, actually running a forbidden business on the side.

Someone randomly asked me, "Did you help your friend go to America?" When he said that, I knew I had to leave right away for China or Korea!

Yes, I had had a lot of rage against the system when I was growing up, but I had my family to think of. I could not even think of escaping North Korea. But when he asked me that question, at that moment, all my feelings bubbled over. The injustice of it all! How dare they think this! I must go!

I asked for some money from my brother, added it to all my savings, took my daughter, and crossed the Tumen River that separates China from my land.

I gave the guard a bribe, and was able to cross over in the middle of the afternoon. People often ask, how do you know who to trust when you are offering bribes? Will the guard betray you? I can't speak for everyone, but the word at the border is that a bribe *always* works.

I didn't know what to do when I got to China. I saw a handicapped man working around the Tumen. I found only later he was a trafficker. I approached him:

"I have just come from North Korea, can you show us somewhere to go?" He invited us to his house, and called someone on his cell phone. We got a taxi and headed for a nearby Chinese city.

He put us in a house, and started inviting a number of men to come and "check me out." I realized something bad was going on. I told him, "Look, I am thankful to you but I know you are trying to sell me to a Chinese man. I promise you I will find a way to escape if you do this. Please just look for a job for me. I am not going to live in China. I want to go to my father's country."

With that, I gave him some Chinese money. He went somewhere for a day to think about my proposal. Thankfully, he agreed to find me a job. He sent me to a construction company to bake bricks. There were four other North Korean women there.

For the next couple of weeks, I went off to work each day, and left my daughter in "day care" at the house. I had just enough to cover our needs and the day care expenses.

It was after noon early in the third week that someone from the house came to the construction company with bad news for us North Korean mothers. All of us immediately ran home. *Our children had all been arrested by the Chinese police.*

In China to this day there is a reward system set up whereby any Chinese citizen discovering and turning in a North Korean can receive a handsome sum of money. Such had been the fate of my daughter.

For two days I did not know whom to call, to whom to report . All of us were out of our mind with grief. At least two of them had married a Chinese man. I had no one. We literally grabbed the grass, as mad women, crying morning, afternoon and all night for three days.

Eventually we heard there was a man trying to find out what had happened. He discovered that that they had been taken to a city one and a half days away by train. But they had traveled by truck. Military truck.

I heard from the man that one of the Chinese husbands had connections. But I had none. The pain inside became too intense. I got out of my room and saw a container of DDT. I noticed that the bottle had a little left, maybe 5-6 ounces. I drank it all.

I passed out. When I awoke, I was in the bed of a pretty bad hospital. A doctor informed me that if I had had much more I would have been killed, but that I had taken just enough to throw up everything. I was spared.

The treatment was not good. If you can imagine it, I was "flushed out" with a simple water hose...

...and there we must leave it for now. Final portion next time, but enough to pray about.

Oops. Got taken away from my desk a few days. That's a story worth telling some day, but for now let's finish up with the anonymous North Korean girl whose life was disrupted because of her father's heritage...

After I got out of the hospital, there was no place to go. I was still very sick, my stomach and intestines totally a mess. Such misery.

It was so very cold, in the month of December. I didn't have enough clothes. I could not go on. Once more I fainted, in the street. I woke up in a hayfield, where I guess someone had thrown me to die.

I suddenly remembered there had been money in my pocket. But it was gone. I wanted to find the Korean woman who had been with me before I passed out, but I was unsuccessful.

Wandering around the streets I came upon a greenhouse, and stayed there one night. I was discovered by the owner, who asked me what was wrong, and a third time I passed out.

This time when I woke up, I was in an old lady's house. She had had no clue I was a North Korean, and so had ordered some men to take me to her house.

"Please let me stay here several days," I begged. But the woman was afraid when she finally realized who I was. Harboring a North Korean refugee would bring fines she surely could not afford.

She tried to feed me. But all of my mouth, my gums, were split open. I could hardly eat anything.

The lady placed me on the back of a tractor and took me to a Buddhist Temple. After talking to a monk there for 30 minutes, it was decided that they could take me in. They fed me. They took care of me the best they could. I stayed in this temple one month.

After healing some, I worked awhile in a Korean-Chinese market area. As I got stronger, three months later, I began laboring in a factory that made women's accessories. Then in a Korean restaurant for one year.

Of course, during that time I never stopped thinking about my daughter.

It was in this situation that I was first introduced to the church. I even found a place where North Korean defectors gathered and were sent on from there into South Korea.

I attended this little group for two weeks. Then one day I was about to go there again, when someone standing at the corner warned me, "Don't go there. Yesterday six people were arrested in that place! For the next three years, I never went to church again, out of fear.

I stayed in that Chinese city near Shanghai for six years. One and a half years I worked in the accessory factory. But I also learned to do work on the side. I saw South Korean vendors coming in and out. I got an idea. With the money I had saved up from restaurant work I was able to start a little business with these vendors.

I was not alone in this venture. Another Korean woman worked with me. It would normally be hard for a North Korean woman to have a successful business in China, especially at a port city. But my friend was a citizen.

Before I came to faith, I was a drinker. I did a lot of visiting of bars in those days, and began to make some friendships with men who offered to protect me. They were not exactly law-abiding citizens, but they were a strong bunch of men, and I needed their help.

These connections kept my business safe for three years. Then things began to go down, and I had to move to yet another city. I worked successfully there another three years.

It had been six and a half awful years since that fateful day when my daughter was arrested. Through a series of circumstances I was able to make contact with people who knew the truth about what had happened. The truth I discovered was that my daughter, only a young teenager, had been powerfully kicked to the floor in her jail cell by a cruel guard. She had not survived that blow. My daughter was dead.

Somehow I had to carry on. Somehow I had to carry on.

But the rain continued to pour down on me.Things seemed to be getting worse. Someone became jealous of the prosperity of my business, and I was reported.

The ever-present North Korean CIA found and started following me again. One of them actually approached me and asked me, "Can you translate this note into Chinese?"-a test designed to prove that I was not actually Korean Chinese but rather a North Korean defector. Of course I could not translate the note. I began to run. I ran so fast, that I did not even know where I was going.

I got on my cell phone and contacted one of my "protector" friends. "A North Korean man is following me, please come and help!" Almost immediately, some motorcycles appeared. They rescued me. "Where do you want to go?"

"Take me to a plastic surgery hospital!" In three hours I knew I could have eye surgery.

But that wasn't going to help enough. I had to get out. Through this gang, a broker was found that could get her to South Korea immediately.

But this broker only took six people at a time, and he was already full for this trip. A call was made, an exception was allowed for, and I was on my way. I gave up all my merchandise, my business, and seven days later I left China.

I took the route that so many before me have taken, hundreds and hundreds of miles, over four months, to take a trip that should only be a couple of hours.

When I arrived in South Korea the Korean CIA questioned me for a full month. I had to tell the truth, since they knew most of the story anyway!

In that four-month ordeal, sitting in a country in Southeast Asia, I had some serious doubts about the whole God thing. Even after I got here and was encouraged to go to seminary to learn more about the things of the Lord, I wasn't so sure. It seemed like they were pushing their denomination and their viewpoint.

But as I have become a part of Underground University, my faith is growing. I know I have been so very blessed never to have been caught. God has guided every step of the way. I am trusting that God is going to work everything out.

303. pyongyang to seoul, a world away

This is the story of Mrs. Kim, received firsthand in Seoul just weeks ago. It will sound somewhat familiar. But in Heaven it is known individually and cherished with all the rest. If a sparrow doesn't fall unnoticed by the Heavenly Father, how much more these tragic ones of the human family are noticed and attended. Please add your prayers.

This is part one:

Mrs. Kim gratefully acknowledged up-front that she has learned a lot from the new Underground University, where she is a regular student. Her experience in this Seoul-based training institute is a far cry from her beginnings.

She was born in Pyongyang. Her father was a soldier. She had one brother and five sisters. She had an early longing to follow her father's line of work.

In 1945, after Korea's independence from Japanese rule, her father easily transitioned into the labor party. Because of the dual protection of his service and his party membership, life was not all that difficult for the young girl.

From 1972-80, she actually was a part of the military and even gained an officer ranking.

Mrs. Kim recalls that when she was young, Pyongyang was a fairly wealthy city. There was an abundance of seafood in the markets, along with all the other marks of prosperity.

But by the time she left the army, stores' supplies had been depleted. Life was on its way down.

After her military career, Mrs. Kim worked in a seafood market for five years. Three children were born to her during this time. Though the family prospered, her husband did not want her to continue that extra job.

But duty called from other directions. She was appointed by the government to be district administrator for her area of thirty-five families. She "took care" of them. What that meant in actuality was that she reported their every activity to the party. We call that spying. She was to see if anyone visited them, if anything unusual occurred. Extra spending was noted. Mrs. Kim was accorded much power in this way. She could if she desired get people sent away. Her neighbors for whom she "cared" became very nervous when seeing her in the neighborhood.

Even by the middle of the 1980's things were not so bad. But then came the electricity power outages. Less rations . Hospitals started saying, you must buy your own antibiotics. When your children are sick, you must treat them on your own. Hospitals were powerless to help in any practical way.

As part of her inspections, she went to every house, opened kettle lids. If she saw there was no grain at all, she reported this to the government, and they would be permitted to receive some grain.

But by now, even she had no rations. She sold her belongings to receive corn. Then ran out of food altogether. For three awful days, nothing. She slept on a cold floor.

Unlike others, because of her official position, she could not run a secret business "on the side." Far too risky. So she went to the countryside, cut plants, and fed her children. But it made them sick. Their bodies swelled up. So much so that those trying to give injections could not find blood vessels for entry. Her son went to the hospital for one month. He requested and was given a pill that helped him sleep for 3 days. He improved. But it took twenty days for the swelling to subside.

Pyongyang citizens, because of their special placement near the seat of the government, were given candy and other delicacies from time to time. They immediately would take it to the countryside, and exchange it for corn.

But from 1996, there was no ration whatever.

Many, many others tried eating plants, but some plants were not meant to be eaten. People were getting skin disease, as her son. Situation worsening.

Mrs. Kim finally realized she could not live like this. She asked her first daughter to go to the north and try to sell what they had. But the daughter was gone for one month. She had to go and find her now. When asking for a pass to travel, she was denied, as so many were seeking to go that direction all of a sudden.

She grabbed her second daughter and went anyway. She gave her husband and son a food supply, and promised to be back in one month. 30 kg of grain. She thought it would be enough.

The train took twenty-three hours to get north, on a normal day. There are no normal days in that part of the world. The trip took a full week because the electricity kept stopping. What an awful trip. Every time the train stopped, everyone attacked whatever market appeared. People snatched others' food. Kotjebi, wandering youth with no home. were everywhere, stealing to survive.

She saw a woman with a fire making a little rice. You have no house, she asks? No, we sold it to buy food. She saw 14-15 year olds, dirty and black, covered with thin blankets.

Women begging for food. Kotjebi hanging on to the steps as they tried to travel... and more...

Our story concludes next time.

304: Pyongyang to Seoul, conclusion

These stories are for the strong in heart and faith. Because they are true, and because they are - in the natural - awful. Yet this one has some joy attached. Read on, and then please pray!

So, *Mrs. Kim loses two daughters - or does she ?*

Her first daughter, it turns out, went to China and a trafficker sold her. She had to decide to go back to Pyongyang or go to China and look for her. She decided to go to China. Over the Tumen River border.

But while crossing, her hands slipped. Her daughter was somehow lost in the middle of the river. She cried out to whatever God there might be, Help Me! Struggling for awhile, they hit rocks on the China side of the bank. With some first aid, all arrived safe, She decided to continue asking God for help.

She went into the village with her daughter. Someone threw them a blanket. It was October and already cold. The food offered her was very hard for her to eat. She told whomever would listen that she came here to find her daughter.

She gave out names. But her daughter could not be found with just a name, as there were so many traffickers, and so many victims. What could she do? She put an advertisement out.

Even the person she had been talking to was a trafficker. He offered her a job as a housekeeper. Five North Korean women were there in the same house. The owner there was selling women.

Next she witnessed violence there during her stay. One young girl was violated. She realized she has to move on, quickly. But when she went to the market and came back home, her second daughter had disappeared. Then they lied to her, saying she was looking for her mother and had simply left the house.

After a serious argument, she left, wandering around looking for her daughter, who was only 16 and very helpless. Everytime she saw someone looking like her, she thought it was her.

She had no place to stay now. She met a young girl, a citizen of the area, asked where she was from, told her she had no place to stay and asked for asylum. The girl agreed. She stayed there three days, began to relax, and came to her senses.

How can I find my daughter? There is a neighbor who now visited, heard of the situation, and offered to solve it. He was Chinese-Korean. He offered marriage, with the promise that as her husband he would find the two missing daughters.

People listening to the proposal encouraged her to take it. She must do anything to find her daughter. She went ahead with the marital arrangement. Her new husband went to a house he knew of, and immediately began to threaten the owner.

This brought out some truth, but still the connection was not made. Three months later, there was communication back from her daughter. The girl had been sold to a twenty-some year old man. But by this time she was nearly crazy and wanted to go home. No one could tame her, so they left her at his grandmother's house. The new husband took money there to buy her back.

Regrettably, some Chinese people buy North Korean women married to Korean-Chinese, and sell them to Mongolians in need of this commodity. In fact this is what had happened to daughter number two.

She had been threatened, "If you scream, I will kill you." She resisted, and tried to fight. Next door, police were called, an arrest was made, and all who belonged there were sent back to North Korea. Even Mom, who managed to get to the scene of all this madness. But Mom escaped from North Korea three days later.

Mrs. Kim went back to her new husband, and the second daughter escaped only a few months later. Then, kidnapped again! This time traffickers tried to sell her to Inner Mongolia, but they were all arrested by Chinese police, and sent to North Korea yet again!

She went to a North Korean prison. Once more an escape. She walked across the country to where her sister lived. Back to the Tumen River. She moved out of the border area to a somewhat safer place in China. She advertised in a magazine that so and so mom was looking for daughter so and so. One year later, the match was made again. She had found her first daughter.

Then she heard news that her son had arrived from North Korea! All children found, she decided to come to South Korea via the long route of thousands of miles that so many have taken.

It was in Cambodia that Mrs. Kim began seriously reading the Bible. She wanted to learn more about the Lord. And though she had some bad incidents in the South Korean church, she started coming to the Underground University, met up with others of like values and backgrounds, and her life has taken off from there. One daughter came to Christ in China.

People want to know what happened to that first husband: The food ran out. He could not eat. He could not work. He was sent to a reeducation center. He starved to death in one year. Her son was a kotjebi for six years. Her second husband was afflliated with the gangs of North Korea and could not be considered the father of her children. He had agendas of his own.

Her future? She definitely wants to go back to North Korea when it opens.

Mrs. Kim's story has been recorded at a U.S. Senate hearing. It is well known. But it is an unfinished tale. Though she appears bright and cheerful, and Christ is making His mark on her life, won't you take some time to pray for all the scars, left by this horrid way of life, to be healed? Some memories take a long time to go away, and will need help from the grace of God.

305. all in Christ's family, part 1

Shall we continue telling the stories I heard this last summer? Sounds good to me! Here's a two part episode sure to warm your heart.

Imagine four generations of Christians in one North Korean home. My great grandfather was a believer who paid for his faith in a much earlier Korea. He was arrested. I do not know all the details, but he did pass on the faith to his children...

My grandparents on my father's side lived under the harsh days of the Japanese occupation, in Pyongyang. Grandpa died early, but his wife, who knew the Lord, passed that knowledge on to her six children. Yes, times were tough, but it was still legal to share Christian faith with your children.

After the Japanese left and the Communists took over, she continued to tell them Bible stories, albeit secretly. She actually had a worship service in her home: Herself, another relative, and of course the six children. A fairly large congregation compared to North Korean groups today.

On my mother's side, my grandfather, also a Pyongyang resident, was asked to do something on his job that he could not conscientiously do, so his job was taken and he was sent to the northeastern province of Hamgyong Bukto, the very place where my paternal grandfather now lived.

The message the children received was, "Don't believe in Kim Jong Il & Kim Il Sung, only believe in God, because one day if you believe, you will go to Heaven."

My father was a "made to order" tailor, visited often by customers who came to our house for measuring. It was relatively easy to have worship gatherings under the guise of customer service. "Buyers" would come on Saturday, sleep over, and have Sunday worship the next day.

Now, under Kim Il Sung, North Koreans could go to China with a one to three month visa. It so happened that my aunt's mother-in-law actually lived in China. She attended a church there, whose pastor was ethnic Korean. The strange message came to that church that in North Korea there really were Christians, a fact not widely known then, so she and the pastor's wife came to visit our house.

Aunt and "somanim" stayed for about a month, then went back to China. Later, the Pastor came over with the aunt. His reaction, Ah! So there really are Christians here! He was so delighted.

His delight turned into actions... concluded next time. Meanwhile, please continue to pray for North Koreans in trouble...

306. all in Christ's family, part 2

A Korean pastor living in China is delighted to find that there truly are Christians in North Korea. God's Word is not bound. The Gospel will go where God wants it to go, oneway or another. We conclude the story of a North Korean defector, gained firsthand this past summer...

He had heard from his wife about a huge collection of large individual sheets of paper, upon which had been laboriously copied the Holy Scriptures. That was the family Bible, and when necessity demanded, it could be very hard to hide . He was very touched by all this, and brought with him a Bible. A small Bible.

When my father was caught later, that Bible was found. Yes, he and the other several worshipers were arrested in the mid 1990's. Unbeknown to all, his customers, the real and the worshiping kind, had been recorded by means of a microphone planted in the house. Beyond that, it seemed strange to the secret police that certain people had tailoring needs at the same time every week.

Grandmother passed away two weeks later, from the trauma of it all.

Then it was that we found that that Korean-Chinese Pastor was looking for us. It happened in this way:

Some North Korean refugees came to his church in China. Kim Il Sung had died. The situation in North Korea was deteriorating.

"We came here because we are hungry," they said.

"Where are you from?" he asked.

They answered, and the pastor gave the refugees some money, with the instruction, "I know some people in that city. Do you know this family? I heard that a bunch of people got arrested for spying. If you see them, have them contact me."

Some of the refugees came to stay. But when he found people who were going back, he sent them to her house, with a cell phone and the invitation to call. When they showed up at my house, I denied any knowledge of the pastor, and also denied that I needed any assistance. I did not want to implicate myself in any way. My area was under surveillance constantly. I thought these people were spies.

But this happened several times. The pastor kept sending the same person my way. Finally, with nothing to lose, I admitted, "We are the ones you are seeking." I took the cell phone and headed for the top of a mountain, because the signal does not work any lower, and a phone meeting took place.

I was told that there were a lot of people who are going to die of hunger in North Korea. "Come to China!" The pastor told me that because I was young. I had a great opportunity to be educated and used.

And so my sister and I did indeed leave for that land, with Mom's blessing. We stayed in the pastor's house three months and then headed for South Korea, via the typical long route that people use. Then later, my mother and brother came also.

But my sister, well, we don't know. When crossing the Mongolia border, she was caught and sent back to North Korea. I had waited for my mom and brother three years. I was hoping my sister would come along with them. But she didn't. And my dad too has been out of our lives since that tragic day many years ago.

The story ends abruptly. No happy ending. Though happier than some, I imagine. She still has some family around her. And she glows with the Lord Who is in her. She will make it. But it will not be easy. Your prayers will make a big difference in her life. Really.

307. living in heaven, now

Those who have trouble with miracles in our day, with manifestations from Heaven, may find this story tough going. But hers is not the only account we received this summer of a God Who visits with His creation, and especially with His children. Can we rejoice that God is actively involved in North Korea?

Before Yu Byung Soo crossed the Tumen River that separates North Korea from China, she had never heard the name Jesus Christ.

She comes from a mining area in the far northeastern regions of North Korea. She lived there all her life, a faithful citizen, absolutely loyal to the Party, an exemplary servant of the Kim dynasty.

To her, the Kims were god. But her god of those years provides a monthly paycheck of 52 won. 52 won can get you a kilogram of corn back then. Almost.

She has few belongings, few clothes, little food. But most of those around her are living this way. She goes with them to the countryside looking for grains on which to exist. A story oft told.

But like so many, enough becomes enough eventually. With four others, Byung must make her escape. She must leave her teen-aged sons behind to fend for themselves.

Life until now is becoming nothing but breath. Her husband has already breathed his last in these mid 90's famine-stricken Chosun.

She can never imagine how the simple crossing of the Tumen River will change her life. Only God knows, she tells us, how wretched and miserable are the people she has to leave behind.

She begins her wanderings around China. Korean-Chinese in the know inform her that her best bet is to meet a South Korean missionary. How like the Lord to be stationed where life's hopes are dimmest, offering His beams of hope.

A man takes her to a mission house, and soon shows her a Bible. "If you read the Bible, you'll see where the Lord Jesus says a soul is more precious than the whole world!" She hears other astounding truths, that men are to love each other, and more. She begins to wail with joy rising from the depths. All her life loyal to the Party, but never loved like this, never heard such gracious words as these!

She finds it all so hard to assimilate. How can people love each other in this way? She learns how to pray. She hears the grand stories of the Word of God. Eventually she wants to meet a God who can say things such as these. She begins intense prayer.

Because of some forged passport issues, Byung is arrested at an airport along with several others. It is during this critical moment that she meets the Lord in her heart. Christ comes in. Though by nature a light sleeper, she actually sleeps normally in jail, feels totally calm. Those who have known nervousness or fear can say already that God has worked a miracle in his servant. Word is, she actually snores in China. That takes some peace!

The others are sent back to North Korea. But not she. Connections have been made, friends have been procured. God has other plans for this lady.

She is searched by female police there who discover a bottle filled with poison. When asked by the policewoman the reason for the bottle, she lets her know that her plan was to take that poison should she be arrested. When the arrest finally comes, though, she does not even think about the bottle, and is soon in touch with her new peace-giving Friend.

The policewoman gives her three things: pity, a hug, and some milk. No, it doesn't always happen that way, but it did this time.

Connections are made with a pastor who is a friend of her son, who is in Seminary in China. He wants to help. A guard is paid. Seven days later, at 4 a.m., she is quickly waved out of her cell along with a Chinese-speaking fellow-prisoner.

Through what has become the NK to SK thoroughfare, thousands of miles of hard journeying through a number of countries, led by guides and forged passports and lots of money, she eventually makes it to South Korea, where she has lived peaceably for many years.

Not end of story.

To live peaceably in a foreign land is no easy task. My own stay of 5 weeks plus in South Korea so far has been most difficult. I come from a free nation and South Korea is equally free. I come from a land of plenty, a land of many churches, South Korea ditto. But home is home and it is in us and is hard to replace.

So the story of North Korean refugees must be told beyond the time when the plot is hatched and carried out. Happily ever after does not often occur on the other side of the border. Refugees are mistrusted, unwanted, ignored, often unemployable, and sadly lacking in cultural information. A most unpleasant way to live.

In Byung's case, God Himself seems to have intervened, and for this we must pray more earnestly for others coming out.

She has gotten into the nightly sleeping pill habit. She can not calm down. She is constantly ill.

One night she simply calls out to the God she has met in prison, "God, if you are alive I want to meet you." Her claim is that Jesus Himself appears to her in a dream and gives her directions. She says that from the day of that dream there has been no sickness, no pills. And for the first 40 days she lives a high spiritually satisfying life.

Her life of prayer has continued. There has come over her, not just a peace, but a desire to serve others in greater need than herself. A Seminary has invited her - though she is far past what many would call "college age" - to enroll and prepare for more service to Christ.

As our interview with her proceeded she grew more and more engaged in the process, going to shelves and pulling down volume after volume of notes she has kept through the years of her journeying and her Christian experience. Walking at first through her doorway, one would not imagine that here lives a person whose life has such vast influence and eternal significance.

By her own claim, she is "living in Heaven now." No worries, no cares. Only wants to serve Jesus and the needy until she is called Home.

But then, shouldn't it always be so? Those truly valuable parts of the body are hidden away secretly doing their service. Those surface members shine out to the public but don't necessarily keep the body alive...

Could I ask you to pray for Byung? And could I ask us all to learn from her?

308. we just wanted to help, part 1

Yet another story gained firsthand in Seoul this summer. May the Lord speak to you through these tales as to what your part is to be...

I am a South Korean citizen, but I am from North Korea. I was arrested along with my husband for helping North Korean refugees.

There were eight of them. Seven adults and one child. Among those eight was a woman who had been sent back to North Korea before, was arrested and imprisoned, but who had escaped the camp and come back to China. Now she will be arrested again.

There was a woman in her twenties and yes, that eight-year-old child. A group desperate for hope and freedom, willing to take a chance for a new life. This is a story often told in North Korea, and I tell you my own version of it.

We started our trek westward in the winter of 2009. We passed through major Chinese cities, and came to a bordering country in a couple of weeks. We traveled through this country via train to go to yet another nation.

Meanwhile, my husband, who like myself has a Korean passport, was supposed to come through customs with no problem from the other side of the border. He was to bring my group on to the next destination. I thought we would meet him within an hour.

Two hours later he was still not there. I called by cell phone to try to contact him. But it was dead. I realized something was not in order. We found later that he had been arrested in customs after the names and passports of all the refugees were found in his bag. One nation's police called the other nation's police, and we too were exposed.

I bought ten tickets to the next destination, and told all the travelers, "Something has gone wrong, take these tickets, get on board, scatter, hide yourself. Don't sit in the assigned seats!"

I decided on a train rather than a taxi, where all might be caught at one time. At least, with a train some would have a chance to run. But though I had told them to spread out, they were so shocked by what was happening that they all sat in their assigned seats!

I myself did not get on the train for the sake of the North Koreans' safety. Later, several police found me.

"Where are those people who were with you?"

" I don't know."

But as soon as I said that, they hurried to the train and caught six of them, forcing them to de-board. Because authorities already had checked our seat assignments at the ticket booth, the two refugees not caught were the ones that did not sit in their own seat. They were hiding in the bathroom.

Those two escaped altogether, and went to a South Korea embassy in a neighboring land. But the other six and I were brought by police back to the first country where we had arrived.

Now, I know that even though I was a foreigner in the land in which I was arrested, if I break a country's law I am supposed to pay the penalty. I was ready for that. But I couldn't comprehend why we were now being made subject to another country's law instead of the one where we were caught.

The two nations were working together to bring this about.

We were all lined up, and escorted by the new police, carrying machine guns , and we were then taken by them into prison.

We'll finish this one next time. As always, we ask your prayer for those on either side of the border.

309. we just wanted to help, part 2

Here's the conclusion to the story about some South Korean citizens who were born in North Korea and wanted to help others...

I could not sleep all night. I wasn't just nervous, I was being constantly interrogated. The interrogators acted as though they had caught some international spy group. They made a big deal of it for several nights of questioning.

This is the fate of North Korean people in this land, where we receive worse treatment than animals, just as though we were in North Korea.

During the process of questioning I knelt to my questioners and begged them, "Please do not send these people back to North Korea. It is all my fault."

But they said, "What's that to you or us? We have an agreement with North Korea, we will have to send them back. We have nothing to do with whether they live or die, and we really don't care."

At that time I was four months pregnant. Endangering the life of my child, I did not sleep for several days because of the intense questioning. At one point I even fainted. They thought I was faking it and began to scream at me. When I awakened I was in an office. My lips were dry and chapped, my face was pale.

I heard someone say, "Better be careful, we are going to kill her." They took me into an office to give me some basic medical treatment. My spirit revived and I tried to talk sense to the authorities.

"Look, if North Korea were economically sound and had a measure of freedom like in here or in South Korea, would North Korean refugees come here, leave their own country, and face dangers like this? If these people go back to North Korea they will die! Please don't send them back, even if they have to stay in this prison for several years."

I told you there was an eight-year-old girl among us. The Chinese police gave her candy and delicious food. Carefully they asked her where and how did you meet these people?

She exposed everything.

The police suggested to me the next day, that there was only one way to stay out of prison. "Bring money, and you will be free." These out of court settlements, quite common, were negotiated with me because I am a South Korean citizen. The six North Korean prisoners received no such offers. They were sent back to North Korea and their fate is unknown to this day.

"How much?" I asked.

"100,000 yuan ($19,000) will free you and your husband."

I borrowed a phone and explained to a friend our situation. He got the money and gave it to them. But after it was received, they only released me, and demanded $30,000 more for my husband.

Shortly after my release, I lost my baby. And I didn't know that since I was pregnant I didn't even have to go to prison. They were just using me to get money.

My husband stayed in prison. I was speechless, defenseless. And I was expelled from the country after this.

My husband got no trial. His imprisonment has been the darkest time in my life. All my money is lost. My heart aches constantly, even now, thinking of those six people. I can hardly sleep. I did everything I could to stop refugees from going to North Korea, and to free my husband, but the police took the money and kept my husband. There is no justice in this. There is no humanity in this. There is no conscience in this.

I hope the South Korean government will aggressively take care of this ongoing defector matter. Perhaps quiet diplomacy is not going to solve this problem.

Oh yes, I talked to my husband last week...for ten minutes.

We can believe that the big-hearted gesture of those who allowed this conversation has more to do with continued greed than Christian charity. The struggle with this good woman continues. It is given to us, the Body of Christ, to struggle with and for her. Will you join this struggle?

310. how i left nk, part 1

Here is a bi-lingual story! Though I met and shared fellowship this summer with the brother whose story follows, the writer of this one is another member of the Seoul USA team.

남 선생님 간증문
Mr. Nam's testimony

저에게는 여섯 형제와 두 명의 자매가 있었는데 어렸을 때는 정부에서 배급이 제때 나왔고 저의 어머님도 부업을 하셔서 집에 식량사정이 넉넉했습니다.

I grew up with six brothers and two sisters and the rationed food was enough in my childhood because my diligent mother had a side job just to make sure. I never felt a shortage.

저는 소년대같은 공산주의 자녀라면 밟는 정규과정등을 거쳤습니다. 이것은 제 의지에 의한 것이 아니라 북한에서의 일상적인 삶이었기 때문입니다. 저의 집은 부유한 사람들의 전유물인 라디오가 없었기에 매일 길 거리에서 스피커를 통해서 울리는 공산당 선전 내용 외에는 어떤 네트워크 뉴스도 듣지 못 했습니다.

I traveled the normal route of national training that any children of communist had to go through. Everything was laid out, there were no choices. This was life in North Korea. I never saw any one else's culture. Never watched television. Radios were only for the rich, and I was not in that category. So I never listened to "network news," but I did hear propaganda daily emanating from strategically placed public speakers.

자라면서, 처음 십에서 십오 년 동안 저와 제 친구들은 예수님의 이름에 대하여 들어 본 적이 없습니다. 어렴풋이 기억하건 데, 학교 한글 교과서에 미국인 선교사를 괴물로 묘사하여 실은 것을 본 적이 있습니다. 한 아이가 과수원에서 단지 사과를 따 먹으려고 했는데, 선교사가 잡아서 그 아이를 나무에 묶고 그 아이의 이마에 "도둑놈"이라고 써놓은 그림이었습니다.

As all of my fellows, for the first ten to fifteen years of my life, I never heard the name of Jesus. Well, not exactly. There was this "information" in my Korean language text book. Pictures and text showed an American missionary capturing a poor innocent child who merely wanted to get an apple from the orchard. This monster tied the child on some wood, and placed a label on his forehead reading "thief".

계속 되어진 북한정부의 노예교육 때문에, 제 삶의 목적은 오로지 김일성과 당을 위해 존재했습니다. 군에서 제대한 후 나이 27살에, 요직을 거쳐서 미래에 성공하기 위해서 공산당에 입당하였고 그 후에 일자리를 얻을 수 있었으며 승진도 하면서 좋은 인생을 누리는 것같았습니다.

Because of the constant brainwashing, the goal of my life was somehow to help Kim Il Sung and the Party prosper. After my own service in the military, at age 27, I entered the Party, a prerequisite to any type of career advancement. A company hired me immediately. Then came Party promotions, and life was proceeding according to plan.

1980년대 후반에 북한사회는 쇠퇴하기 시작하면서 배급비율이 적어지고 심지어는 2주 까지도 지연되기도 했습니다. 제 가족 성분이 그리 나쁘지 않아서 저희는 제때 배급을 받을 수는 있었지만 그 양은 이전 같지 않았습니다. 여전히 많은 시간 사상교육 그리고 공산당 선전이 있었지만, 식량배급은 갈수록 나빠졌습니다.

In the late 80's, North Korean society began to decline. Nationwide, rations were down, and/or delayed for up to two weeks. My own family status gave me less delay, but not more rations. There were still lots of talk, lots of propaganda, but less and less food.

1990년대 초에 들어서는 상황이 더욱더 악화되면서 일년 간격을 두고 저의 아버님과 어머님이 돌아 가시게 되었습니다.

By the beginning of the 90's, things were even worse. Soon both of my parents had died, within a year of each other because of starvation.

그 당시 몇 몇 기관이나 직장은 여유분 땅이 있어 초과 곡식을 얻을 수 있었으나 사인에게 개인적으로 농사지을 여유분의 땅은 할당되지 않았습니다. "왜 직장은 되고 개인은 안됩니까? 왜 사람들이 굶어 죽어가는데 이런 제한이 필요합니까? 왜 주민 스스로 독립하여 살기 위해 노력 할 수 없습니까? 이것은 정말 부당합니다."라고 저는 항변하였습니다.

There were few institutes or companies could obtain extra grains, but no space could be allotted for individual farming. Why allow companies but not farmers? Why the need for such control when people are starving and dying? Why can't people be independent and take care of themselves? What terrible injustice, I reasoned.

저는 집권당 권력서열에 있는 분에게 편지를 썼습니다. "왜 저희 개인은 여유분의 땅을 가지고 자유롭게 경작할 수 없습니까?"

I wrote a letter to the ruling Party, the very seat of authority. "Why can't individuals have extra lands for private gardens?" I asked.

당은 서한으로 제게 답변해 주지 않았습니다. 대신에 당원이 찾아와서 제게 왜 이 편지를 썼는지 물어 보았습니다. "동무는 노동당에서도 서열이 낮은 계급인데, 어떻게 감히 김일성 장군님을 괴롭히는 편지를 쓸 수 있네?"

There was no reply. Not by letter. Instead, a Party member visited and asked me why I wrote this letter. "You are a lowly officer in the Labor Party. How dare you write a letter to Kim Jong II to disturb?"

그들은 저를 해고했고, 그런 과감한 조치에도 불구하고 또다시 경고처분을 내렸습니다. 첫 번째 경고는 그냥 넘어 갔지만, 두 번째 경고는 만일 제가 당의 노래를

크고 분명하게 부르지 않으면 무엇인가 대가를 받게 될 것이라는 심각하고도 강도 높은 것 이었습니다.

They cut my job. As a member of the party, I was worthy of a warning, even two, before more drastic measures were taken. They skipped the first letter, and wrote me the serious second warning, a severe statement of what would be coming if I did not sing the Party song loud and clear.

저는 이런 사회에서는 살아 남을 수 없다는 것을 깨달았습니다. 군부의 혜택, 절대적인 충성 그리고 제 자신의 장미 빛 계획들도 모두 사라지면서 더 이상 북한사회에서는 아무것도 할수 없었고 미래가 없었습니다. 그래서 저는 마음에 "북한을 탈출 하겠다"는 큰 결심을 하게 되었습니다.

I thought that I could not survive in this society. The military upbringing, the extreme loyalty, the plans for my own career, all gone. "My future is not here. I cannot develop, improve, progress." That was the moment of decision.

아무런 설명 없이 냉정하게 제 아내와 아들을 부모님이 계신 집으로 보내고 나서, 저는 북한을 탈출 하였습니다. 이 시기는 1990년대 2에서 3백만 명이 아사하는 단군이래 정말 심각한 상황이었고 길거리에서 매일 죽은 시체를 볼정도였습니다.

Sending my wife and son off to my family's house with no explanation, a more merciful action than it appears on the surface, I escaped. It was the mid 90's, that horrific epoch in Korean history when 2-3 million died of starvation. Dead bodies on the streets every day.

북한정부는 항상 이 문제를 감추려 했고 이 당시 굶주림 때문에 아픈 사람을 치료소에 데려가는 것은 불법을 하면 정부에게 비판을 받았습니다. 의사들은 굶주림 때문에 아사한 사람을 특별한 질병으로 죽은 것으로 보고했는데 이것이 북한정부가 사실대로 알려 진 숫자보다 왜곡하고 축소하여 보고하는 방법이었습니다.

The government was in denial. It became illegal to suggest to the visiting medical attendant that the person in question had died of hunger. That would be considered a criticism of the government. Doctors were to report that such and such person died of a particular disease. That is why North Korean figures regarding the starved of those years would be hugely less than the known facts.

저는 원래 동해 근처에 살았었는데 북한을 남에서 북으로 가로질러 압록강을 건넜으며 5일이 걸렸습니다.

I lived by the East Sea, set out across the country, south to north, and crossed at the Yalu River. That part of the trip took five days.

Where that trip leads is the subject of the next and final episode. Please pray for Mr. Nam in the interim...

311. How I left nk, part 2

The conclusion of our two-language story of Mr. "Nam" of North Korea. As always, shared in hopes you will pray for this family and all those in similar situations. "Remember the prisoners, as though bound with them..."

제가 북한 쪽에서 중국으로 넘어가는 국경근처는 풀도 없고 나무들도 없었는데 이는 북한 국경 수비대원이 자기들이 조용하고도 쉽게 감시할 수 있도록 고의로 만들어 놓은 것입니다. 이러한 의도 되어진 철저한 감시는 누구도 쉽게 강을 건널 수 없게 만들었습니다.

When I arrived at the crossing point, I noted that there were no trees or grass on the North Korea side. This was by design. The guards there could see quite well anything that was going on. Constantly spotlights scanned the area making it impossible for anything standing to move undetected.

어쨌던 저는 기어가고 미끄러져 가고 해서 둑을 지나 강 바위들 사이를 가로질렀습니다.

I crossed into China by crawling and slithering across the bank and the river between rocks.

제가 처음 중국측에 닿은 마을은 넓은 들판에 생강 꽃이 만발한 곳이었는데 이곳에서 한달을 일했습니다.

My first stop on the other side (at the first town I encountered) was a place where large fields of ginseng flourished. For the first month I worked in the fields.

제가 일을 마치고 자유시간이면 아는 중국인도 없고 의사소통도 안되었기 때문에 적응하기 무척 힘들었습니다. 몇몇 조선족 일꾼이 있었는데, 이들은 국경 근처는 단지 일하기 위해서 왔습니다.

Though free, it was an awful time of adjustment, with little ability to communicate, not knowing Chinese. There were at least some Korean-Chinese , workers, as there are all up and down that border area.

또 한가지 문제는 계속되는 중국경찰의 검문이었습니다. 북한 탈북자를 잡아서 북송하게 되면 그들에게 포상금이 주어지기 때문에 그들은 탈북자를 잡기 위해서 혈안이었습니다.

The other problem was the constant surveillance of the Chinese police. They tried their best to sniff out refugees, hoping to gain the reward obtained for nabbing one and sending him back. There were frequent raids.

저는 남서쪽에 있는 다른 도시로 옮겼습니다. 그곳에서 3개월 동안 일했었습니다. 그러나 여전히 경찰의 잦은 검문이 저를 두렵게 했습니다.

I had to move to another city in the southwest. There I worked for three months. But still too many raids, too much fear.

저는 중국 각 도시에 있는 한국 대사관과 영사관을 방문하기 시작했습니다. 처음에는 보기 좋게 거절당했고 공관원 들은 심지어 저를 보려고 하지고 하지 않았습니다. 왜냐하면 많은 북한 탈북자들이 찾아 오고 있고 그들 모두를 남한으로 데려가기 위해 받아 들이기는 힘들었기 때문이었습니다.

Next I began visiting Korean embassies & consulates in Chinese cities. I was flatly refused at the first one. They didn't even want to see me. There were just so many North Koreans coming over that there was no way they could process them all..

1997년, 이전 지내던 곳보다 보다 훨씬 남쪽에 있는 중국의 주요 도시 중 한곳에 체류하던 중 그동안 많은 탈북자들의 시도가 성공하지 못했지만 남한 정부의 정책변화로 인해서 이제는 탈북 망명신청이 쉬워 졌다는 소식을 접하게 되었습니다. 저는 망명신청을 하기 위해서 서류를 작성했습니다.

In a major Chinese city further south, 1997, I was able actually to get news. Not so many defectors made it this far. The traffic flow being light, the door was open. I set up an appointment and signed the asylum papers.

감사하게도 저의 신청이 받아 들여 졌습니다. 남한의 김영삼 대통령이 중국에 항구 짓는 토목공사를 하면서 탈북자들이 망명하는 것을 도왔기 때문입니다. 그래서 결국 이 시기에 많은 탈북자가 남한으로 올 수 있었습니다.

And the papers were approved! I was held there. The idea was that the political situation set up by then President of South Korea, Kim Young Sam, involving the building of a harbor in China, would eventually get a lot of defectors sent into South Korea.

꽤 오랜 시간 동안 한국대사관은 저희 탈북자들을 보호하며 거주할 곳까지 지원해 주었습니다. 그러나 재정은 천천히 바닥이 났고 상황은 절망적이 되었습니다. 저는 주중 한국대사관에 우리가 어떻게 되느냐고 물었지만 대답이 없었습니다. 그때는 남한에 김대중 정부가 들어설 때 이었습니다.

So for quite some time, the Embassy tried to protect me and many others by setting aside housing, etc. But slowly the money dried up. Things were looking bleak. I went in to ask, "What can we do?" No good answers. And by the time, I went again, the Kim Dae Jung government had taken over South Korea.

김대중 정부는 탈북자들에게 우호적이지 않았고 남한과 북한이 좋은 관계를 이어 가기를 원했습니다. 이것은 북한에서 어떤 주민도 훔쳐서 남한으로 데려올 수 없다는 것을 의미했습니다

The new government proved to be unfriendly to North Korean defectors. It was the new Kim's idea that the South and the North should have a good relationship with each other. That precluded automatically any "stealing" of citizens from the King of the North.

이 아이디어에 의해서 김대통령은 탈북자들이 남한으로 오는 것을 막았고 중국과 제3국에 있는 대사와 영사들까지도 바꾸었습니다.

By this policy, President Kim blocked the entry of refugees into his land. Further, he changed all the ambassadors and consuls in China and the third countries.

저를 관리하고 있던 공관원이 "어떻게 우리가 너를 보호해 줄 수 있겠냐? 이제 네 살길을 찾아라"라고 말했고 저는 제가 마지막에 살았던 도시로 돌아가서 부두에서 다시 일을 하기 시작했는데 그러면서 남한에서 중국으로 오는 사업가들과 교류하기 시작했습니다.

The persons in charge of me asked, "Hey, how can we take care of you, provide your room and board? You're on your own!" So I went back to the last city where I had lived. Worked in a harbor. Then I began to interact with South Korean vendors coming into China.

그러나 여전히 중국경찰의 검색으로 인하여 제가 북한 탈북자라는 것이 발각되어 그곳에 더 이상 머물 수가 없었습니다.

But still the raids come. They knew I was a North Korean. There would be no peace there.

저는 더 이상 중국에 머무를 수 없었습니다. 더 이상 할 일자리도, 머물 숙소도 없었습니다. 저는 어떤 대가를 치르더라도 남한으로 가겠다고 마음에 결정함으로 탈북자들이 중국을 떠나 제삼국을 통해 남한으로 넘어간 루트를 따라 움직여 마침내 태국에 도착했습니다.

I simply could not stay in China. There were no jobs, no places to live. My decision: I would do whatever it took, even give my life, to attempt to get to South Korea. I headed to far western China, finally leaving that country for Thailand, using a well-traveled route of North Korean defectors.

이 탈북자 루트를 따라 저는 지속적인 위험없이 여행할 수 있었습니다. 단지 매콩강을 건널 때 강한 급류에 거의 익사할 뻔 했습니다.

It was a well-traveled route, but not without constant danger. At the Mekong river, I almost drowned in the severe current.

태국에 이르자 마음에 안심을 하고, 잠시 거울 속을 들여다 보게 되었는데, 거울 속의 제 모습이 마치 해골처럼 보였습니다. 처음엔 거울 속의 제 자신을 알아 보지 못했습니다. 사실, 저는 20일 동안 제 자신의 모습을 본 적이 없었습니다. 탈북 루트를 따라 태국으로 오면서 산속에서 주로 자며 살아 남기 위해서 날 옥수수와 바나나 심지어 아무거나 닥치는 대로 먹으며 여행했었습니다.

As soon as I was in Thailand, my heart was relieved. I saw my face in a mirror, looking like a skeleton. I simply didn't recognize myself. In fact, I hadn't even seen myself for twenty days. There were not many mirrors up in the mountains where I slept night after night, surviving on raw corn, bananas, and whatever else I could find.

어쨌든, 저는 결국 살아서 남한으로 오게 되었습니다. 저는 이 점 정말 주님께 감사를 드립니다.

But, survive I did, and I am here in South Korea, and for that I praise God!

저는 믿는 자가 되었습니다. 저는 제 삶을 통해서 하나님이 그분의 계획하심으로 저를 인도 하셨다는 것을 믿습니다. 이런 하나님의 인도하심은 제가 북한을 넘어 중국에 왔을 때부터 시작했었습니다.

I have become a believer. I am on God's path that leads to life. For me that pathway began when I first crossed over into China.

저는 UU와 함께 할 수 있는 기회가 있어 행복합니다. 제가 처음 UU에 훈련 받을 때, 심지어 제 자신이 복음으로 회심되는 것을 고려하지 않았었습니다. 그러나 이제는 UU훈련을 통해 북한에 복음의 횃불을 밝히는 역할을 하고 싶습니다.

I'm happy to have chance to associate with the Underground University course of study. When I first started that training, I did not consider myself to have been born again. But through those studies, I now want to be a gospel light which will be turned on in North Korea.

I believe his wish shall be granted, don't you? Thank you for supporting him with your intercessions.

312. from somewhere at the nk-china border

The following, another letter carried over by our contact in China, serves as a fitting conclusion to the messages I was able to carry back from my summer mission trip. Here you see a summation of the life of the believer who is in or out of North Korea. Strong in faith in the midst of seriously difficult situation. Uncertain about the future yet rejoicing in it somehow. These men and women not only deserve our prayer, but serve as a beacon to those whose life is less committed. May God help us to see...

I thank God Who died on the cross in order to give us grace, a grace that caused us to repent of our sins. This is a God Who treats us as a precious soul, though we are so sinful.

I thank God that Jesus came into this earth to save earth's people, and I am grateful too for His servants and teachers trying to save more souls, as God's will demands.

I am thankful to know God, and to come to this different country, even though we have a difficult life.

In North Korea we still serve Kim Jong Il and the people are crazy about the Juche ideology. We work every day so hard but eat only two meals. And the meals are worse than pig's food. No clothing. And even if we are sick and dying there is no medicine, no treatment.

This kind of life is hellish. I have so many things to say but my tears are in front of me, and I can only sigh. Still, I am really thanking God and God's servants and teachers, because my family met the Lord and we are living in His grace and we have His love.

My heart is torn because I met my Heavenly Father so late.

Oh these precious servants of God. They provide the money and materials we need with God's love. I am very thankful.

My husband and I promise to God that we will work for Him until the end of our lives, with strong faith, ever learning His Word.

We are praying that God's grace will be on all the people of North Korea. We are asking that all of you pray that way too. Yes, we want reunification of the two Koreas, but we want it to be under the Gospel, not just a political unity. We want the praises of God and true prayer to spread all over the land.

Until that day, which we truly expect to come, I will learn His ways and stand strong in the faith.

Amen and amen.

And now?

So there you have it. Two full years of a man's life.

I came home from Korea in 2009 a very sick man. They called it post-traumatic stress syndrome. Secondary. They say I had lived their lives so much, that I was infected with their fears.

Others suggested stress in other parts of my life.
Some called it a demon.
Old age.
Whatever it was, it slowly passed, after much prayer and praise and fellowship, and some medicine too. Thank God I am healed.

For many months I could not look at these stories. The pain was too great. My life took a different turn altogether, and I realized that, like Romania before it, and other passions from the Scripture that have ripped through my heart, North Korea was not to be a resting place, a destination, but a milestone and now a fond memory.

Nevertheless, I gave so much of my heart in these two years, that it is necessary that I collect all these thoughts and pass them on. ..."that nothing be wasted."

I do hope you can use them.

bob, June 2012

Printed in Great Britain
by Amazon